THE VISUAL DOCUMENTARY

CROSBY, STILLS, NASH &

BY JOHNNY ROGAN

CONTENTS

OMNIBUS PRESS
LONDON · NEW YORK · SYDNEY

For Anne Cesek and Pete Long

Copyright © 1996 Johnny Rogan
This edition copyright © 1996 Omnibus Press
(A Division of Book Sales Limited)

Edited by Chris Charlesworth
Cover & Book designed by Mike Warry, 4i Limited
Picture research by Johnny Rogan and Nikki Russell

ISBN 0.7119.4982.4
Order No.OP 47776

Exclusive Distributors:
Book Sales Limited, 8/9 Frith Street, London W1V 5TZ, UK.

Music Sales Corporation,
257 Park Avenue South New York, NY 10010, USA.

Music Sales Pty Limited,
120 Rothschild Avenue, Rosebery, NSW 2018, Australia.

To the Music Trade only:
Music Sales Limited, 8/9 Frith Street,London W1V 5TZ, UK.

Photo credits: Richie Aaron: 71T,88,115,117,122/3; Glenn A.Baker
Archives/ Redferns: 13,100CL; Jay Blakesberg/Retna:163C; Lou
Cohan: 118; Jim Cummins/Star File: 107main; Dagmar/Star File:
71B,73B,79; Henry Diltz/Retna:13CR&B,148B,149T,151;John
Einarson Collection: 21; David Ellis/Redferns: 62B,110L; Michael
Garland/ Retna: 153; Mick Gold: 70; Harry Goodwin: 4L,19; Bob
Gruen/Star File: 161; Harry Harris: front cover; London Features
International: 5L, 6BL&R,7L,10, 17, 40/1, 44, 45T&B, 46/7,
56main, 58, 67T, 69, 70/1main, 73T, 86, 87, 89, 91, 98B,103T,106T
L&R,106BR,107B, 109inset,111B, 113TR,113CL,118T,133B,145,
146,150,154,158/9; 160T,162T,164T&B,176; Pete Long: 124/5,
126B; Terry Lott:114L; Steve Morley/Redferns: 84/5; Pictorial
Press: 6T,7R,9,16,20, 22, 62/3, 66,72T,76/7,78,93B, 96T&B,
97main,98T,102main,103C&B, 104,105,106BL,119,162/3 main;
Barry Plummer:128,133T; Neal Preston/Retna: 160B,167; Chuck
Pulin/Star File:152; Michael Putland /Retna: 57,72B,76B,
80,82/3,108B; David Redfern: 98CR, 110/1main; Redferns:108T;
Relay Photos: 32/3; Retna: 140; Rex Features:56,39,43,48,52T,54,
55T,56B,64L&R,90T,92,94BR,97CR,99, 107T,121,131T,132,157,
162B,169,170/1; Ebet Roberts/Redferns: 112,142/3,156; Johnny
Rogan Archives: 11B,15,28,51T,52B,55B, 60T,67B,68,81,85T,90B,
93TR,94BL,98CL,100/1,102T,109main, 110T,111T,126T,130,148T,
149B,164inset; David Seelig/Star File: 114inset,136,138/9;
Michael J.Spilotro/Star File: 120; Star File: 165; Irv Steinberg/Star
File: 12; R.E.Teese/Star File: 134,137; Barrie Wentzell/Star File:
back cover,74/5,176inset as b/c; Vinnie Zuffante/Star File: 168.

Every effort has been made to trace the copyright holders of the
photographs in this book but one or two were unreachable. We
would be grateful if the photographers concerned would contact us.

Printed and bound in Singapore.

A catalogue record for this book is available from the British Library.

The right of Johnny Rogan to be identified as the author of this work
has been asserted by him in accordance with the Copyright,
Designs and Patents Act 1988.

BY THE SAME AUTHOR:

Timeless Flight: The Definitive Biography Of The Byrds
Neil Young: Here We Are In The Years
Roxy Music: Style With Substance
Van Morrison: A Portrait Of The Artist
The Kinks: The Sound And The Fury
Wham! (Confidential) The Death Of A Supergroup
Starmakers & Svengalis: The History Of British
 Pop Management
The Football Managers
Timeless Flight Revisited
The Guinness Encyclopaedia Of Popular Music
 (Consultant editor)
Morrissey & Marr: The Severed Alliance
The Smiths: The Visual Documentary
The Complete Guide To The Music Of The Smiths
 & Morrissey/Marr
The Complete Guide To The Music Of Neil Young

During the period spent preparing this book three people proved of
particular importance… I first encountered Pete Long back in the
mid-70s. He'd placed a card on our university notice board asking fo
CSN&Y followers to get in touch. I was amazed to find that he not on
had all the bootleg albums I'd amassed in recent years but a growing
collection of tapes too. At that time there was only a small number o
bootleg concerts available and we traded avidly. Over the years we
became friends, linked by an overwhelming belief in the potency of
CSN&Y at their peak. Pete never seemed to lose his appetite for the
tape game and is now a world authority on Neil Young. He generous
provided a significant number of tapes to supplement my own, whic
has helped the book enormously. He also checked and corrected the
Neil Young portions of the book and assisted with the dating of sever
key incidents. His forthcoming opus on Young's concert performances will be one of the most detailed studies of its kind and, having
seen it grow over the years, I await the finished product with eager
anticipation. More than anybody, Pete has shared my enduring
enthusiasm for the quartet in all their manifestations and also
suffered the attendant disappointments and frustrations along the w
My mainman in America these days is Doug Hinman, another formidal
researcher who used his library skills to help track down a wealth o
information in record time. I now owe him some of the same for his
epic tome on The Kinks' performing history.
Peter Doggett, apart from his role as editor of *Record Collector*, remains
great CSN&Y fan and has done as much as anybody over the past
decade and more to publicise their importance. In common with
Brian Hogg and Colin Larkin (in the *Top 1000 Albums Of All Time*),
courageously insists that David Crosby's *If I Could Only Remember*
Name is the greatest album ever made. Peter was there on the phor
when I needed long discussions, moral support, instant chart
references and critical feedback. Official record company release
dates are often subject to late change and can be notoriously

ACKNOWLEDGEMENTS

unreliable. Where possible we have cross-referenced these with US Top 200 entries to provide a more accurate point of sale release date than those previously published. Peter was unstinting with his time in helping to finalise these and cast a swift critical eye over the final manuscript too.

My own fascination for CSN&Y stretches back to my school days when their initials along with the title BYRDS graced the back of various exercise books and folders. The other day I found a school diary entry from 22 May 1969 which read: "Got *NME* today, Nash-Stills-Crosby are to appear at Albert Hall". It reminded me that it took quite a while before the familiar CS&N monicker became generally known. Some weeks later their début album was issued and the conversion had begun. It was complete by the time Young arrived for *Déjà Vu* .

The contents of this book draw on a lot of memories and experiences, from my LSD-exploratory, courtly love youth through a decade of solitary university study and another spent writing books like these. From the distant past, I'd like to thank a number of people who shared my passion or helped contribute to this book in ways that they have probably forgotten. At Pimlico School, Anne Cesek was the first person I met who had a similar collection of CSN&Y-related albums. I always admired her taste and discrimination. Simon Drew at Recordsville, Wilton Road, boasted all the releases on import and was a marvellous fellow enthusiast. Deborah Novotny escorted me to various concerts, especially during the crucial 1971 period. After leaving school I entered a monastery, but Alan Roberts eventually tempted me back into the secular world by sending news of Manassas' arrival in England. The ticket he despatched for the Rainbow show still lies in its envelope unused, but I could not resist the lure of a second concert so I left the mountain retreat and turned up at the Sundown completely shaven-headed, beatific and content. From the *Dark Star* era of the mid-70s, Preflyte Prockter, Nick Ralph and Colin Larkin kept the faith and Pete Long and Lou Cohan kept on swapping those tapes. Over at *Zig Zag*, Frame and Tobler were older, occasionally wiser and always a help and inspiration.

Since then there have been many interviews and related projects that have contributed to this volume. Obviously, I have drawn on my previous books on The Byrds and Neil Young. Dave Zimmer's authorised biography of CS&N is a fine achievement as is Crosby's hefty autobiography *Long Time Gone*. Also very useful were the books on Young by Scott Young, John Einarson, John Robertson and David Downing. *Broken Arrow*, the Neil Young journal run by the diligent Alan Jenkins, deserves your support, as does *Full Circle*, The Byrds' flavoured fanzine edited by Chrissie Oakes. From the latter, a warm hand to associates Barry Ballard, George Guttler, Eckhard Volker and Peter Curt Holmstedt. Italy's *Wooden Nickel* was a welcome and much missed source of CSN&Y news, but Francesco Lucarelli, Stefan Frollano and Belgium's Herman Verbeke keep the spirit alive. Thanks also to Colin Green for some last minute tape lists that I needed quickly.

CSN&Y's exploits have made good copy over the years and the following newspapers and magazines were invaluable for contemporaneous information, concert datings or choice quotes: *Chicago Tribune, Crawdaddy, Creem, Dark Star, Disc, IM&RW, LA Times, Melody Maker, New Musical Express, People Magazine, Philadelphia Enquirer, Record Collector, Record Mirror, Rolling Stone, San Francisco Chronicle, Song Talk, Sounds,Vox* and *ZigZag*.

On a personal level, past and present thanks to Anne and Karl, Alan Culligan, Alan Russell, Marie Lorigan, Pauline Kelly, Gill Chester, Cathy Shea, George Kenyon, John Etherington, Wally Hammond, George Guttler, Roger Leighton, Teresa Walsh and Hilary Donlon.

Finally, I would like to thank CSN&Y, the original five Byrds, Crazy Horse, Jim Dickson, Terry Melcher, Derek Taylor... and all the other interviewees over the years.

JOHNNY ROGAN

PREFACE

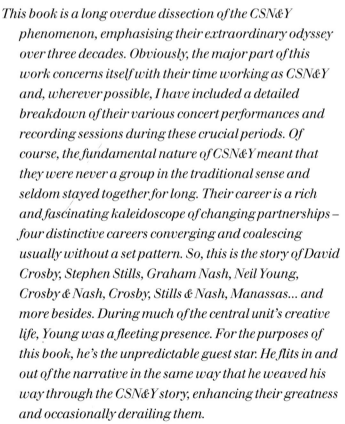

This book is a long overdue dissection of the CSN&Y
  phenomenon, emphasising their extraordinary odyssey
  over three decades. Obviously, the major part of this
  work concerns itself with their time working as CSN&Y
  and, wherever possible, I have included a detailed
  breakdown of their various concert performances and
  recording sessions during these crucial periods. Of
  course, the fundamental nature of CSN&Y meant that
  they were never a group in the traditional sense and
  seldom stayed together for long. Their career is a rich
  and fascinating kaleidoscope of changing partnerships –
  four distinctive careers converging and coalescing
  usually without a set pattern. So, this is the story of David
  Crosby, Stephen Stills, Graham Nash, Neil Young,
  Crosby & Nash, Crosby, Stills & Nash, Manassas... and
  more besides. During much of the central unit's creative
  life, Young was a fleeting presence. For the purposes of
  this book, he's the unpredictable guest star. He flits in and
  out of the narrative in the same way that he weaved his
  way through the CSN&Y story, enhancing their greatness
  and occasionally derailing them.
Throughout their time together, CSN&Y reflected the ideals
  and aspirations of a large proportion of what became
  loosely known as the Woodstock generation. For some,

the very letters of their name symbolised the flowering of
  Sixties' idealism and the pinnacle of artistic achievement in the new age of the supergroup. But what was it
  that made CSN&Y so important and so influential? Was it
  simply that they captured their moment in rock history so
  emphatically? Perhaps. They certainly articulated young
  America's feelings of spiritual unrest and were not afraid
  to name the heroes and villains on the political
  landscape. Bobby Kennedy's assassination inspired
  Crosby's 'Long Time Gone'; Bobby Searle's incarceration
  prompted Nash's 'Chicago' and the Kent State shootings
  inspired Young to savage Richard Nixon in 'Ohio'; Stills
  even featured a catch-all condemnation of political
  corruption and civil unrest in the on-stage favourite,
  'America's Children'. Such cynicism could not disguise
  the underlying Utopian hope which was celebrated in
  songs such as 'Teach Your Children', 'Wooden Ships' and
  'We Are Not Helpless'. True to the hippie dream, CSN&Y
  always preferred a happy ending.
Beyond the peace and love proselytising, CSN&Y embodied
  their audience's quest for emotional enlightenment.
  Listening to their work at the dawn of the Seventies, it is
  immediately noticeable how much personal politics and
  complicated inter-relationships dominated their

NASH& YOUNG

thoughts. Their ability to compose affecting and believable love songs at the beginning of the singer-songwriter boom, ensured that they retained a strong advantage over weaker contemporaries. When they sang, the sentiments transcended the limitations of the standard lovelorn ballad and took on a higher significance. At times, they seemed to be expounding and dramatising a shared personal philosophy of love. On reflection, part of the appeal was the element of soap opera voyeurism in connecting the composition to the woman – Judy Collins ('Suite: Judy Blue Eyes'; 'So Begins The Task'); Joni Mitchell ('Lady Of The Island'; 'Our House'; 'Sweet Joni') and Rita Coolidge ('Cherokee'; 'Sugar Babe'; 'Cowboy Movie'). Real life dramas added to the charm of these songs, although you didn't have to know the names to feel the passion in the best of them. When Crosby sang 'Guinnevere' or Stills 'Helplessly Hoping' it was clear that the subject of the song had already undergone apotheosis.

Often, it seemed that CSN&Y was doomed to self-destruction as a result of the intense romanticism implicit in their work and lives. Nash realised the dichotomy when he pointed out: "We've cancelled a lot of studio time because of women troubles. Women are the most important thing in the world, next to music." The qualification was crucial. Relationships came and went, people died, but the music went on. When CSN&Y, as soloists or in whatever permutation, lost sight of that central principle, then the work suffered, and so did their careers.

History now attempts to limit the nature of CSN&Y's appeal, as if their legendary association with Woodstock and its aftermath are enough to explain them away. But it was never that simple. They were immensely gifted in a way that has seldom been acknowledged or appreciated. Masters of the acoustic ballad, they also had a hard rocking, electric identity, summed up in the fiery Stills/Young partnership. Great romantic love songs and searing political commentaries could be performed side by side in their live shows without any sense of incongruity. At their peak, CSN&Y served as both guitar gods and bed-sit companions. Such strengths made them appear unassailable, deific and multi-dimensional in their talents. They were radically new but also endearingly familiar; they had successfully shed their former skins as pop idols, but retained the sense of history and glamorous pop grandeur associated with The Byrds, The Hollies and The Buffalo Springfield. For a time, they had it all and, at their best, created what some would argue was the finest music written by anyone from their generation.

JOHNNY ROGAN

TOP: THE BYRDS' FIRST PUBLICITY PHOTOGRAPH
LEFT: THE BYRDS, LONDON, 1965
RIGHT: THE HOLLIES

In the age of the supergroup, CSN&Y represented the ultimate combination of complementary talents. As their early career chronologies show, they each experienced feelings of frustration working in the standard group formats of the period. Developing egos resulted in leadership battles within The Byrds, The Hollies and The Buffalo Springfield, which could not be easily resolved. Song publishing seemed a major area of contention in all three units, exacerbated by the fact that individual talents were blossoming. Crosby was fired from The Byrds just as he was reaching new creative peaks as a writer; Stills and Young were in a similar position during the recording of Buffalo Springfield Again; and Nash was locked into a contractual writing partnership with colleagues who failed to appreciate groundbreaking work like 'King Midas In Reverse'. Such tensions often contributed to the quality of the work produced, but too much creativity was suppressed in the pursuit of group democracy. Here were four young singer/songwriters brought up in the era of the beat group who gradually realised they wanted greater scope for their music.

Crosby dreamed of a musical community, wherein he could play with whomever he liked, free from the petty jealousies and political infighting to which he was so prone while in

The Byrds. Domestically, Crosby was already living with different partners, so why not attempt a musical open marriage too?

This was a notion that seemed appealing to Stephen Stills, who had grown weary of trying to save Buffalo Springfield from their self-destructive tendencies. The moment he invited Crosby to play with Buffalo Springfield at Monterey, a link was forged which neither could easily forget. Young had already left the Springfield twice and his mercurial nature ensured that he could later accept and exploit the concept of the "non-group" which so appealed to Crosby

Nash seemed the most stable of the four, having survived in The Hollies for the best part of a decade. But the old world of beat groups seemed increasingly restrictive as 1967 wore on. Nash wanted to progress, perhaps to grow like The Beatles and The Rolling Stones had done, but the public would not easily accept that from the chart-loving Hollies. They seemed trapped in the pop game, unsure about whether they should wear kaftans or white suits, or sing about King Midas or Jennifer Eccles. The lure of America proved irresistible to the self-improving Nash and after he met Crosby he was never the same. Once these musicians took on board the idea of "playing with friends" the concept of CS&N and CSN&Y simply required a leap of the imagination.

1941

14 AUGUST

David Van Cortlandt Crosby, born in Los Angeles to society family, Floyd and Alphi Crosby. His father is a successful Hollywood cinematographer with Academy Awards for *High Noon* and *Tabu*.

1955

Crosby appears in Crane School's production of *HMS Pinafore*, singing the part of the First Lord Of The Admiralty.

1957–58

Crosby performs in Cate School's student production of *Cuttin' Capers,* singing lead vocal on 'Dear Mr Lonelyhearts'. After a run of appalling school reports, he forms an acoustic duo with his elder brother Chip (Ethan), performing at coffee houses in the Santa Barbara area. Already a rebel, with a precocious interest in sex and music, Crosby falls foul of the law and is arrested for burglary along with a couple of local kids. "We did it

and Fred Neil, who help him improve his guitar technique.

After moving to Florida, Crosby forms a folk trio with his brother and Bobby Ingram – later adding another friend, Mike Clough.

1962

The ever restless Crosby leaves his brother's group and travels to Chicago, finally moving to San Francisco in the autumn. There he lives on a boat with madcap folkie Dino Valenti. At the end of the year (27 December), Crosby copyrights his first composition, 'Cross The Plains' (almost certainly the "mystery" song covered by Travis Edmonson).

1963

In an early attempt to kickstart the hippie movement, Crosby, Valenti, Paul Kantner, David Freiberg and some other friends set up their own commune in Venice, Los Angeles. As Crosby recalled: "We never wanted for food, nor smoke nor a guitar to play on… and we spent most of our time doing exactly as we pleased."

> *"We never wanted for food, nor smoke nor a guitar to play on…*
> *and we spent most of our time doing exactly as we pleased."*
>
> DAVID CROSBY

more for the rush than anything else," Crosby confessed to me. "We did it a number of times. I worked out a system which worked pretty well. I did it until once I had to confront a woman whose house we had ransacked. She wanted her wallet back. It had the only existing picture of her old man who had died in the war. She was in tears… and it changed it completely. It was not just taking stuff. All of a sudden it was somebody's precious things. It made quite an impression on me and I would never take anything now. It's just not right."

1960

Crosby unsuccessfully pursues an acting career in Hollywood before dropping out and returning to music. Before long, he is playing at the Unicorn Club on Sunset Boulevard with a set that includes blues standards 'Willie Gene' , 'God Bless The Child', 'Motherless Children' and the George Gershwin evergreen, 'Summertime'.

1961

While performing in Hollywood, Crosby befriends folk musician Travis Edmonson, who introduces him to marijuana and later records David's first composition. The California high life is interrupted by the news that Crosby's girlfriend is pregnant, an announcement that prompts him to flee across the USA. He ends up in New York, plays the Bitter End and Café Rafio, and duets with blues singer Terry Collier. Other important influences include Bob Gibson

The idyllic lifestyle is compromised when Crosby again teams up with his brother's trio, this time in the commercial folk aggregation The Les Baxter Balladeers. Short haired and suited, Crosby feels ill at ease with this sell-out routine but lasts long enough to appear on the rare album *Jack Linkletter Presents A Folk Festival*. After an arduous bus tour, he returns to Hollywood, playing jazz-tinged folk at his old haunt, the Unicorn. There, he is discovered by aspiring producer/manager Jim Dickson, who offers the opportunity to record after hours at World Pacific Studios.

1964

Dickson seeks a record deal for his new charge, armed with demos of such songs as 'Come Back Baby', 'Willie Gene', 'Get Together' (written by Valenti) and Crosby's own composition 'Brotherhood Of The Blues'. The two former will later appear on the Together Records' compilation *Early L.A.* , while the others have never been issued.

Warner Brothers are offered the chance to sign Crosby as a soloist but decline. Dickson continues to record Crosby material, such as 'Everybody's Been Burned' and his adaptations of the traditional 'I Know My Rider' and the Civil War song 'Jack Of Diamonds'. It soon becomes evident that his best chances of success lie in forming a group. At this point, folk musicians Jim McGuinn and Gene Clark have recently arrived in Hollywood intent on playing Beatle-influenced songs and forming a duo similar to

Britain's Peter And Gordon. Their line-up is soon expanded with the spontaneous recruitment of Crosby. Gene Clark recalls the memorable evening when he first saw the angelic-voiced David: "We'd started to write a few songs and then one night we went along to a hootenanny at the Troubadour and there was this guy called Crosby who came on stage and played a few songs. I told McGuinn that I thought he was good and he said that he had worked with him before and that they were friends and had hung out in the Village together. We went into the lobby and started picking on the stairway where the echo was good and David came walking up and just started singing away with us doing the harmony part… We hadn't even approached him."

Crosby immediately introduces his new finds to Jim Dickson, who agrees to provide recording facilities at World Pacific and take on management duties. The newly formed Jet Set undergo torturous nightly rehearsals, gradually honing their raw Everly Brothers/Beatles-inspired material into a form approaching folk rock. Among the songs they rehearse is a beautifully understated Crosby ballad 'The Airport Song', which remains his only recorded lead vocal from this period. Two of the group's songs, 'Please Let Me Love You' b/w 'Don't Be Long', are subsequently issued on a single by Elektra Records, while Dickson considers the next move.

It is clear that fresh blood is required to embellish the trio's sound, particularly as Crosby is proving an inept bass player. Enter mandolin player Chris Hillman from bluegrass group The Hillmen who, despite never having played a bass before, soon masters the instrument. The line-up is completed by Michael Clarke, a Brian Jones lookalike with no drumming experience beyond playing around with a conga. He proves content to learn his trade rehearsing on cardboard boxes. Crosby, meanwhile, usurps Gene Clark as rhythm guitar player and thrusts a tambourine into his hands.

On 10 November 1964, the Jet Set (McGuinn, Clark & Crosby) sign to CBS Records, the company having initially insisted that they will only sign vocalists. Sixteen days later, over a Thanksgiving Day dinner, the group rechristen themselves The Byrds. History is made.

1965

20 JANUARY

'Mr Tambourine Man' is recorded at Columbia Studios in Hollywood, produced by Terry Melcher. Dickson had brought The Byrds the song through his connections with Bob Dylan and his manager Albert Grossman.

FEBRUARY/MARCH

The Byrds start a scene at Ciro's in Hollywood, attracting a sizeable following. Bob Dylan joins them on stage. Ex-Beatles publicist Derek

DAVID CROSBY, 1965

Taylor is completely entranced: "The dance floor was a madhouse. A hard core of Byrd followers – wayward painters, disinherited sons and heirs, bearded sculptors, misty-eyed nymphs and assorted oddballs – suddenly taught Hollywood to dance again." Manager Jim Dickson sums it up succinctly: "It was more fun than anything that any of us or any of the audience had ever experienced. It made people fanatically crazy for The Byrds."

12 APRIL–22 JUNE

'Mr Tambourine Man' is released in the US and secures local radio play. Ten days later (April 22), the group back Jackie DeShannon on a demo of 'Splendor In The Grass', which she later issues as a B-side. With their fame spreading, The Byrds undertake a tour of California, supporting The Rolling Stones. Radio play for 'Mr Tambourine Man' intensifies and, by the third week of June, the single stands at number 1, escalating the group to national fame. During the same week (June 21), The Byrds' *Mr Tambourine Man* album is issued with Crosby prominent in the harmonies but yet to write or sing his own material. Jim Dickson: "David announced that he wasn't going to sing on 'Chimes Of Freedom', he was leaving... I sat on his chest and said, 'The only way you're going to get through that door is over my dead body. You're going to stay in this room until you do that vocal'. And David burst into tears."

28 JUNE

Having just completed an arduous tour across America, accompanied by a busload of beautiful young people from Ciro's , the group

return to Columbia Studios. There, they record Crosby's 'Flower Bomb Song', but it remains in the vaults. The composition contains some of David's earliest free love views with such lines as "I'm going to make the love gun that will blow your mind". As Jim Dickson notes: "Everybody, myself included, felt that 'Flower Bomb' had no business being a song, let alone being part of The Byrds". Although Crosby admits the song is one of his worst, the backing track remains an intriguing lilt.

JULY

A busy month for The Byrds. An appearance at Jane Fonda's Independence Day party in Malibu is followed by a tour of dance halls and an appearance at Columbia Records' Annual Convention.

Meanwhile, 'Mr Tambourine Man' is breaking internationally and reaches number 1 in the UK on 14 July. Against Dickson's better judgement, The Byrds agree to embark on a UK tour, unaware that they are being billed as "America's Answer To The Beatles".

AUGUST

Poorly rehearsed, undernourished, dreadfully ill and consuming far too many drugs, The Byrds are in no state to take on The Beatles as the new pop gods. Nevertheless, John Lennon and George Harrison attend their warm-up show at the club Blaises, after which they smoke dope at Brian Jones' place. Paul McCartney is also on hand at the Flamingo to drive them home after the gig. The summer itinerary is a familiar Sixties' litany of backwater gigs and suburban mediocrity:

Imperial Ballroom, Nelson (August 3), TV *Scene At 6.30*/Central Pier, Morecambe (4), Fairfield Hall, Croydon (5), TV *Ready Steady Go*/Flamingo Club (6), Adelphi, Slough (7), Coventry (8), TV *Gadzooks* (9), East Grinstead (10), *Discs A Go-Go*/Bristol (11), Shrove Theatre & Pavilion, Worthing (11), Gaumont, Ipswich (13), Astoria, Finsbury Park (14), Gaumont, Bournemouth (15), Pavilion, Bath (16), Guildhall, Portsmouth (17). Derek Taylor: "I found the concerts very unnerving. I had tears in my eyes every night. I thought it was so wonderful. But the audiences had gone expecting heaven".

The Byrds leave disappointed, but at least their second single, 'All I Really Want To Do', reaches number 4 in the UK and they receive kind words from both The Beatles and the Stones. Crosby is stoical and takes compensatory pleasure in turning Derek Taylor on to marijuana on the flight home.

26 AUGUST

Derek Taylor thanks England and publicises The Byrds' "homecoming" gig this evening at the Hollywood Palladium. Crosby and McGuinn are still high after a night spent tripping with John Lennon and George Harrison. McGuinn: "We were on acid, playing 12-strings in the shower in this large bathtub which used to belong to the Gabors. We were showing them what we knew about Ravi Shankar and they'd never heard of him."

SEPTEMBER

Back in the studio, The Byrds record Crosby's prototype science fiction/hippie anthem

THE BYRDS ON 'READY STEADY GO', AUGUST 1965

THE BYRDS, 1966

1967

14 JANUARY
At the Golden Gate Park, San Francisco, Crosby attends "The Gathering Of The Tribes: The Human Be In". The event inspires his composition 'Tribal Gathering'.

6 FEBRUARY
The Byrds' celebrated fourth album *Younger Than Yesterday* is released, with Crosby increasingly in the ascendant. 'Renaissance Fair' and 'Everybody's Been Burned' rank alongside the best of his work while the wilfully experimental 'Mind Gardens' displays his love for breaking rules. The album closes with a less impressive re-recording of 'Why' which nevertheless hints at Crosby's continued need to ensure his work is available on album.

22 FEBRUARY
The Byrds appear alongside The Buffalo Springfield and The Doors at the CAFF benefit concert, Valley Music Theatre, Woodland Hills, CA. Reviewer, Tracy Thomas: "The Byrds closed the first half playing mostly songs from their new album. Unfortunately, the quartet will do anything for music but rehearse. One felt like introducing them to each other."

24 FEBRUARY
The Byrds return to London for the first time since the disastrous 1965 tour. On this occasion, they forgo live appearances, but attend a fan club gathering at the Roundhouse (February 25), travel to Stockholm for a Radio Hus special (27) and promote their new single 'So You Want To Be A Rock 'n' Roll Star' on *Top Of The Pops*. Crosby celebrates their first evening back in England by visiting The Beatles at Abbey Road, where he is given a pre-release tape of 'A Day In The Life'.

30 APRIL
The Byrds appear at the Hiram Bithorn Stadium, Puerto Rico, in one of their more exotic excursions of the period.

'Stranger In A Strange Land', plus his reading of Dino Valenti's 'I Don't Ever Want To Spoil Your Party'. Neither version is issued.

Meanwhile, recording the new album is proving problematical. Producer Terry Melcher: "In the middle of one session Mike Clarke left his drum stool, walked over to Crosby, smashed him in the mouth and literally knocked him off his stool."

OVEMBER
The group undertake another US tour as part of Dick Clark's Caravan Of Stars. Crosby makes the trip more palatable by consuming considerable quantities of drugs and blasting his fellow Byrds with the music of John Coltrane and Ravi Shankar.

NOVEMBER/1 DECEMBER
The Byrds' third single, 'Turn! Turn! Turn!' climbs to number 1 in the US charts. The following day the album of the same name is issued including Crosby's minimal collaboration with McGuinn on 'Wait And See'.

DECEMBER
After returning from a trip to Hawaii, the group end the year on a memorable note, recording the Clark/Crosby/McGuinn classic 'Eight Miles High' and Crosby's 'Why' at RCA Studios in Hollywood. These versions will remain unissued until the archive recording *Never Before* in 1987.

1966

NUARY
The Byrds secure a two-week residency at the Trip in Hollywood, after which they appear in concert with The Dillards.

ARCH
Gene Clark leaves The Byrds, the victim of pop star fame coupled with an aversion to flying. His departure ensures Crosby's increased creative role as a writer and vocalist.

MAY
'Eight Miles High' peaks at US number 14 and subsequently UK 28. Although rightly

regarded as a classic, its progress in America is impeded by a radio ban for alleged drug references.

SPRING
The Byrds play the Winterland, San Francisco, CA (March 31) and the Fillmore Auditorium, San Francisco (April 2).

JUNE
The Byrds play at the Camden Music Fair, New Jersey, with The Little Flowers. Later this month, they appear at the Hollywood Bowl as part of The Beach Boys' Summer Spectacular.

18 JULY
The third Byrds' album *Fifth Dimension* is released. Crosby takes an unconvincing lead vocal on 'Hey Joe', co-writes the psychedelic tinged 'I See You' and sings his raga-influenced 'What's Happening?!?!' As Crosby explained: "It was one of the very first of my 'Well, gee, who am I? What's going on here? Where's the instruction booklet? How come nobody knows what's going on?' songs. I've written a great many of those. I'm still writing them too."

28 JULY
The Byrds record 'I Know My Rider' (aka 'I Know You Rider'), which is intended as their next single, but fails to appear. At the same session, they attempt Crosby's 'Psychodrama City', a slightly playful reflection on LA life.

1-11 SEPTEMBER
The Byrds play the Whisky A Go Go, supported by The Daily Flash. It is here that Chris Hillman, irked by Crosby's more dominant role in The Byrds, announces: "Ladies and gentlmen – the David Crosby show."

OCTOBER
The Byrds appear at the Village Gate, New York.

8 DECEMBER
Crosby's 'It Happens Each Day' is recorded but will fail to make the next album.

16-24 MAY
The Byrds appear at the Whisky for a nine-day residency supported by the up-and-coming Doors. Around this same period, Crosby can be heard alongside fellow Columbia artistes Chad And Jeremy talking about his star sign on *The Astrology Album*.

10 JUNE

The Byrds combine with The Doors and The Jefferson Airplane for the Fantasy Faire and Magic Mountain Music Festival at Crosby's favourite spot, Mt. Tamalpais. More than 15,000 people turn up for the musical love-in.

17–18 JUNE

On consecutive days, Crosby appears with The Byrds and The Buffalo Springfield at the Monterey International Pop Festival. On-stage, he dominates The Byrds in a way that would have been unthinkable even one year before. Not only is the set more Crosby-influenced with 'Hey Joe', 'Renaissance Fair', 'Lady Friend' and 'I Know My Rider' all featured, but he also handles all the song introductions. His intriguing and then controversial comments on the Kennedy assassination leave McGuinn unimpressed while the decision to deputise with the Springfield is considered almost treacherous. McGuinn: "At the time of the Monterey Festival we weren't getting along very well. There was a power struggle in The Byrds about who was going to be leader… Crosby wanted to be leader and it wasn't going well for him… Then Stephen Stills was looking at David and wanted him to be in his band, so you had these different forces."

30 JUNE

The Byrds terminate their contract with Tickner/Dickson in favour of the money-minded Larry Spector. Jim Dickson: "People got soured. I had to put up with a lot from David Crosby. He's great when he's up, but when he's down he can ruin your day, your week, your month!"

13 JULY

Crosby finally achieves the ultimate accolade – a Byrds' A-side written solely by himself. 'Lady Friend', with its distinctive rhythm and dramatic use of brass, is classic Crosby, but fails to make any impression as a single. In retaliation, McGuinn and Hillman refuse to include the track on their forthcoming album. "They wouldn't put it on the record because it was mine and not theirs," Crosby insists. "That's why there was a lot of bitterness on my part. It wasn't a joke, it was a very real problem I was up against. Do you understand that?"

18 AUGUST

The Byrds record Crosby's 'Triad', a composition that reflects his promiscuous philosophy. "It was a song I didn't think was in particularly good taste," claims McGuinn who omits the track from the next Byrds album. Crosby: "They felt me getting stronger. I think they either resented it or were worried by it. The resistance to my material was just like the resistance of The Hollies to Nash's material. It was just dumb. They were territorial. They were afraid. And I kept writing better and better songs." Fortunately, Crosby's friends The Jefferson Airplane appreciate 'Triad' and feature the song on their next album, *Crown Of Creation*.

20 OCTOBER

Goffin/King's 'Goin' Back' is the new Byrds single, released against the wishes of Crosby who declines to appear on the recording. "One of our big disagreements was over 'Goin' Back'," McGuinn confirms. "He didn't like that at all. So I thought, well his heart wasn't in it. At this point he was hanging out with The Buffalo Springfield a lot, playing around town with other groups, sort of shopping for a new position. I figured that he wanted to get out of it."

LATE OCTOBER

McGuinn and Hillman sensationally sack Crosby on the grounds that he has become too dictatorial in pursuing his musical preferences. Crosby recalls the fateful day: "They came over and said they wanted to throw me out… They came zooming up my driveway in their Porsches and said that I was impossible to work with, that I wasn't very good anyway and they'd do much better without me. And frankly I've been laughing ever since… But, it hurt like hell. I didn't try to reason with them. I just said, 'It's a shameful waste. Goodbye'."

NOVEMBER/DECEMBER

With the compensation he has received from The Byrds, Crosby buys a boat, *The Mayan*, and sails away to consider his future. While in Florida, he stops off at Coconut Grove, where he discovers an aspiring singer/songwriter, Joni Mitchell. They soon become romantically entwined and Crosby goes on to secure her a record deal and produce her début album. David: "When I first saw her she was in a coffee house in Florida. I walked in and I was expecting, 'Oh, they call the wind Maria', and there was this girl going, 'I had a king in a tenement castle'. My mind just went, 'Pow'. I sat there for a full set and said, 'Oh my God, I'm in love – and, not only that, she's talented. I can't live!'."

DAVID CROSBY, 24 JULY 1967

1945

JANUARY
Stephen Arthur Stills is born in Dallas, Texas.

1953-63

Stills' family moves constantly during his childhood and adolescent years, staying in Houston, Illinois and Florida. Along the way, Stills learns to play drums and piano and, while attending a military academy in St Petersburg, Florida, he takes up blues guitar. In Gainesville, Florida, he plays drums in a local group, The Radars, and briefly joins The Continentals as guitarist, alongside future Eagle Don Felder. At the end of the Fifties, Stills settles in the Republic of Panama and then Costa Rica, where he assimilates the Spanish and Latin American influences in his music.

1963-64

Stills travels to New Orleans, works in a bar, then plays the local coffee houses with folk singer Chris Sarns (aka Farns). "We'd get drunk and make up songs on stage," Stills reminisces. "We had a good time until one fateful New Year's when I got really drunk and the owner threw me out."

Stills moves East to New York and settles in Greenwich Village, where he forms a trio with Peter Torkelson and John Hopkins. During this period, he also hangs out with folksinger idol Fred Neil and again teams up with Chris Sarns. After playing as a duo, Stills and Sarns join the commercial folk aggregation The New Choctawquins, who soon metamorphose into the nine-piece Au Go-Go Singers. The new line-up includes Ohio singer Richie Furay, who appears on record with Stills for the first time on *They Call Us Au Go-Go Singers*, released on Roulette Records.

1965

The Au Go-Go Singers undertake an extensive tour of the USA before splitting up. Stills joins a breakaway folk group called The Company and during a Canadian tour they visit the Fourth Dimension Club in Ontario. It is here that Stills first meets Neil Young, who is playing in The Squires. Their folk-rock influenced sound so impresses Stills that he threatens to leave The Au Go-Go Singers and join The Squires there and then. After a night out on the beer with Young, however, he considers the more sensible option of returning to New York, working out visa problems, arranging accommodation and securing bookings. His main aim is to form a beat group with Furay and Young, but the plan founders as a result of changing addresses and a lack of communication. By the time Stills finally reaches Young in Toronto some months later, the mercurial one has abruptly decided to become a protest folk singer. As Stills succinctly

put it, "Neil wanted to be Bob Dylan and I wanted to be The Beatles. We were, as I said, very young. All of a sudden, he decided he was going to break up his band and go play coffee-houses and so I just threw up my hands in disgust and went to California."

With Los Angeles currently entranced by The Byrds, the most obvious path to instant success seems folk rock. On July 12, Stills registers his first song for copyright: 'Don't You Feel Rained On?' He then finds an ideal songwriting partner in Van Dyke Parks and together they compose several numbers, including the unreleased 'Hello I've Returned'. Forming a group around the writing team proves less easy and the peripatetic Parks soon moves on to other projects – later working with both The Byrds and The Beach Boys.

Meanwhile, Stills falls in with ex-Greenwich Village folkie Ron Long in the significantly named Buffalo Fish. Before long they recruit Peter Torkelson, but after a short series of bookings on the Californian folk circuit the trio disbands.

BUFFALO SPRINGFIELD

1966

JANUARY
Stills is considered as a possible recruit for the studio-created Monkees, but instead the role goes to his friend Peter Torkelson (later Tork), whom he has persuaded to audition for the part. Meanwhile, Stills befriends freelance producer/manager Barry Friedman and persuades Richie Furay to leave Greenwich Village and join "his group" in Hollywood.

FEBRUARY/MARCH
Furay flies out to LA only to discover that Stills has yet to form a group. The two start working together and Stills next cajoles Ken Koblun into joining their venture. After barely a week, Koblun returns to Canada for the greater

security offered by Three's A Crowd.

C. 1 APRIL
One of the most famous meetings in rock history takes place. While stuck in a traffic jam on Sunset Boulevard, Stills and Furay spot Neil Young and his bass player Bruce Palmer driving on the other side of the road in their unmistakable black hearse. After a short car chase, the musicians are at last reunited. It transpires that Young has had another change of heart since his Mynah Birds phase and is now ready to accept Stills' original offer to form a folk rock group. Rehearsals at Friedman's house sound promising, with drummer Billy Mundi completing the line-up. However, he is soon replaced by Dewey Martin, fresh from bluegrass group, The Dillards. Initially, the fledgling group call themselves The Herd but soon alter the name to Buffalo Springfield, in honour of a steamroller whose manufacturing plates they see from their window.

15 APRIL
Buffalo Springfield appear at the Swing Auditorium, National Orange Showgrounds, San Bernardino, opening for The Byrds. At least four further support dates follow on The Byrds' prestigious West Coast tour.

MAY
Byrds' bassist Chris Hillman persuades Elmer Valentine, manager of the Whisky-A-Go Go, to give The Buffalo Springfield a residency. Among the acts they appear alongside are Johnny Rivers (May 11–22), Captain Beefheart (24–27), The Grass Roots and The Doors. Hillman takes Crosby to see his new find and even considers managing the group, but is dissuaded by Byrds' leader Jim McGuinn. Strangely, The Byrds' own management Dickson/Tickner also resist the opportunity to oversee the group, who are still looked after by the inexperienced Dickie Davis. Instead, the Springfield sign to producers Charlie Greene and Brian Stone, who secure a percentage of the publishing income and help finalise a deal with Atlantic subsidiary, Atco.

18 JULY
Buffalo Springfield record Stills' country-tinged 'Go And Say Goodbye', which is scheduled as the group's début single, but will later be replaced by Young's 'Nowadays Clancy Can't Even Sing'.

25 JULY
Continuing their run of memorable support slots, Buffalo Springfield appear at The Rolling Stones' Hollywood Bowl concert. The publicity value is emphasised by their boast of becoming the first hitless group to secure a booking at the 20,000-seater venue.

OCTOBER
While preparing their first album, Buffalo Springfield record three songs that will remain unissued: Stills' 'Neighbour Don't You Worry',

Richie Furay's 'My Kind Of Love' and Young's 'Down Down Down'.

11-13 NOVEMBER
Buffalo Springfield play the Fillmore Auditorium, San Francisco supporting Country Joe And The Fish

21-26 NOVEMBER
Buffalo Springfield appear at the Whisky for the final time. During their week's residency Stills is joined on stage by Monkee Peter Tork and they perform the novelty song 'Alvin The Alligator'.

2/3 DECEMBER
The group return to San Francisco to play a free gig at the Avalon Ballroom with The Daily Flash and Congress Of Wonders.

5 DECEMBER
'For What It's Worth', Stills' protest against the recent LA "riots", is recorded as the group's second single.

1967

JANUARY
Buffalo Springfield release their self-titled début album which features seven songs composed by Stills: 'Baby Don't Scold Me', 'Go And Say Goodbye', 'Sit Down I Think I Love You', 'Hot Dusty Roads', 'Everybody's Wrong', 'Leave' and 'Pay The Price'. Within weeks of the album's release, however, 'For What It's Worth' climbs into the US charts, eventually peaking at number 7. Atco respond by substituting the song for 'Baby Don't Scold Me' on all future copies of the album.

EARLY JANUARY
During the first week of January, the group play a series of gigs at Ondine's in New York on a bill with Otis Redding and Mitch Ryder And The Detroit Wheels. Redding joins the Springfield on-stage during their set. Despite their new-found fame, tempers fray and Palmer trades blows with Stills on stage. "He slapped me across the face," Stephen recalled. "So I went purple with rage and put him through the drums right in the middle of a club in New York. Everyone was very shocked."

9 JANUARY
An eventful day for Buffalo Springfield during which they record Stills' unreleased 'We'll See', Furay's unissued 'My Kind Of Love' plus an attempt at Young's 'Mr Soul'. Back at their hotel, police gather to arrest the erring Bruce Palmer on a drugs charge, which culminates in his imprisonment and "voluntary departure" to Canada.

MID-JANUARY
Manager Dickie Davis deputises for Palmer on the television show *Hollywood Palace*. and the group is also featured on *American Bandstand*. At

short notice, Love bassist Ken Forssi agrees to sit in for several dates at Hollywood club Gazzarri's.

25 JANUARY-10 FEBRUARY
Former Young acolyte Ken Koblun is recruited as a temporary replacement for Palmer, for a series of performances comprising The Tempo, San Francisco (January 25), Hullabaloo (27), Rolling Hills High School, LA (28), TV *Where The Action Is* (February 1), Hullabaloo (2), Earl Warren Showgrounds, Santa Barbara (3), plus a week billed alongside The Seeds in San Bernardino (4), Hollywood Palladium (5), Cinnamon Cinder, Long Beach (6), Albuquerque, New Mexico (8), Santa Fe (9) and Lubbock, Texas (10).

MID-FEBRUARY
Bassist Jim Fielder from The Mothers Of Invention is the latest substitute for Palmer, with a surprisingly long tenure of three months.

22 FEBRUARY
Buffalo Springfield and The Byrds once more share the same bill, this time appearing at the Valley Music Theater in Woodland Hills in a benefit concert for CAFF (Community Action For Fact And Freedom).

26 FEBRUARY
CBS-TV broadcast Buffalo Springfield's appearance on *The Smothers Brothers* television show performing 'For What It's Worth' and 'Go And Say Goodbye'.

> *"He slapped me across the face. So I went purple with rage and put him (Palmer) through the drums right in the middle of a club in New York. Everyone was very shocked."*
> STEPHEN STILL

MARCH
Work is in progress on a new album *Stampede*. Among the rumoured outtakes are Stills' unreleased 'We'll See', 'So You Got A Lover', 'Neighbor Don't You Worry' and 'Come On (Here)'. Although no final track listing is published and the album is ultimately unreleased, sleeve artwork is completed with Palmer's place being taken by Dickie Davis, disguised in a black hat.

13 MARCH
According to Atlantic files, the group record 'No Sun Today' and 'Who's The Next Fool' (composers unknown) at Sound Recorders, L.A.

18 MARCH
Stills finds unexpected fame as a hit songwriter when The Mojo Men enter the US charts with 'Sit Down I Think I Love You'.

APRIL
Buffalo Springfield continue an extensive tour of California including the University Of California, Santa Barbara (April 1), San

Francisco's Rock Garden (11–16), the Fillmore West (28–30) and Hollywood Bowl (29).
On April 8, they are featured on the television show *Hollywood Palace* (originally taped in January) performing 'For What It's Worth' and 'Mr Soul', the latter featuring Neil Young on lead vocal.

MAY
Palmer surreptitiously slips over the border and rejoins the Springfield, just in time for a tour supporting The Turtles. Although Palmer strengthens the group's sound, they are still not free from internal bickering and are about to suffer another major setback.

LATE MAY
Young leaves the group in complete disarray when he quits on the eve of a prestigious appearance on Johnny Carson's *The Tonight Show*. As Stills explained to *Rolling Stone*: "We were supposed to go back to do the *Johnny Carson Show* for a whole bunch of money and that would have led to a spot on Sullivan's show which was at the time the big thing to do... Neil flipped out and wouldn't come and went and hid in the San Fernando Valley at some chick's house so we couldn't do *The Johnny Carson Show*. But by that time everybody was too crazy and that's when Neil had to quit, exactly at the time when it meant the most."

2 JUNE
Buffalo Springfield depart for a poorly received tour of the East Coast, electing to continue as a quartet rather than replacing Young. After two desultory performances in Boston (June 3–4), they are told "Don't come back!" As Richie Furay noted, "We weren't a whole band without Neil".

6 JUNE
Atlantic files indicate that work is being done on Stills' epic 'Bluebird'. It is indicative of relations in the group that he uses drummer Buddy Miles and bassist Bobby West for the session.

8-9 JUNE
Struggling on as a quartet, the group play a couple of dates in Colorado, returning immediately to California to prepare for an appearance at the Monterey Pop Festival in one week's time.

10 JUNE
The group manage to find a replacement for Young in Doug Hastings, recently of San Franciscan group The Daily Flash. David Crosby also offers his assistance: "I rehearsed with them for a few days and said that I'd sit in with them to cover. I was just trying to help."

NEIL YOUNG/STEPHEN STILLS, 1967

18 JUNE

At Monterey, the new-look Buffalo Springfield play their one and only gig as a six-piece with Crosby guesting on rhythm guitar. Furay and Stills sing three song each, Young is represented in spirit by 'Nowadays, Clancy Can't Even Sing' and Crosby provides a Byrds' styled backing harmony for a recently completed composition, 'Rock & Roll Woman'.

SET LIST: A CHILD'S CLAIM TO FAME: PRETTY GIRL WHY: FOR WHAT IT'S WORTH: NOWADAYS. CLANCY CAN'T EVEN SING: ROCK & ROLL WOMAN: BLUEBIRD.

27 JUNE

At a beach house in Malibu, Stills and Jimi Hendrix drop copious amounts of acid and jam for over 12 hours in a superstar line-up that includes Buddy Miles, Hugh Masekela and Bruce Palmer. When the police arrive to investigate the disturbance, they are so impressed that they keep watch while the ensemble plays on.

MID-JULY

Buffalo Springfield are touring at the same time that The Jimi Hendrix Experience are supporting The Monkees. Stills teams up with Hendrix at New York's Waldorf Hotel for another jamming interlude, with Micky Dolenz briefly joining in.

During the same period, Buffalo Springfield play at an Indian reservation in Hayward.

1-6 AUGUST

The Springfield circus returns to California for six consecutive nights at San Francisco's Fillmore.

10 AUGUST

Doug Hastings departs from the group after a three-month stay.

11 AUGUST

Neil Young returns to the fold after an absence of nearly four months for a performance this evening at the Teen And Twenty Club, Huntington Beach. With this morale booster, the group are ready to recommence work on their next album.

30 AUGUST

Buffalo Springfield record Stills' 'Rock & Roll Woman' (inspired by Grace Slick) at Sunset Sound Studios, LA. The distinctive riff is provided gratis by Crosby, who declines a writing credit.

1 SEPTEMBER

Work takes place on Stills' 'Hung Upside Down' at Sunset Sound.

NOVEMBER

After playing their favourite gig at The Earl Warren Showgrounds, Santa Barbara (November 4), Buffalo Springfield undertake a tour supporting The Beach Boys and Strawberry Alarm Clock. Ten dates featuring

19 shows are played, including the Back Bay Theater, Boston (23–24). At two of these dates, in Washington and Connecticut, Palmer falls ill, forcing Stills to deputise on bass.

DECEMBER

The group's celebrated *Buffalo Springfield Again* is released and will later sell in excess of 250,000 copies, although it fails to secure a Top 40 entry. Stills is in spectacular form throughout and establishes himself as a songwriter of distinction, composing 'Hung Upside Down', 'Everydays', 'Rock & Roll Woman' and his most famous Buffalo Springfield song, 'Bluebird'.

17 DECEMBER

Stills enters the studio with The Monkees to add guitar to their song 'Lady's Baby'. The track is later included on *The Birds, The Bees And The Monkees*.

21-31 DECEMBER

Buffalo Springfield close the year with another flurry of gigs, playing the Fillmore Auditorium (December 21–23) and the Cheetah, Venice, California (29–31).

1942

FEBRUARY
Graham William Nash, born Blackpool, England.

1947

Nash first meets Allan Clarke at school. They sing together in school choirs over the next few years.

1955-60

Clarke and Nash form a duo, The Two Teens (later The Guytones and Ricky and Dane), who play at local working men's clubs, specialising in Everly Brothers' influenced material. During 1959, Nash co-writes his first song with Clarke: 'Hey, What's Wrong With Me?'

1960-61

Clarke and Nash play in local groups The Four Tones, The Dominators Of Rhythm and The Deltas (the latter featuring bassist Eric Haydock).

1962

DECEMBER
Nash, Clarke and Haydock form breakaway group The Hollies, adding Tony Hicks (lead guitar) and Don Rathbone (drums). Hicks' previous group, The Dolphins, also features future Hollies Bobby Elliott and Bernie Calvert.

1963

JANUARY
The Hollies play the Cavern in Liverpool, where they are discovered by EMI producer Ron Richards and subsequently signed to Parlophone.

4 APRIL
The Hollies' record their début single, a cover of The Coasters' '(Ain't That) Just Like Me', the flip side of which is Nash/Clarke's first composition, 'Hey What's Wrong With Me'. At the same session, they complete Nash/Clarke's 'Whole World Over', which is held over for the follow-up single, 'Searchin'.

15 MAY
Clarke/Nash's 'Now's The Time' (from the film *It's All Over Town*) is recorded at Abbey Road Studios and will later be used as the B-side of their first Top 10 single, 'Stay'.

7 JUNE
The Hollies play their first BBC radio session, appearing on the Light Programme's *The Talent Spot*.

JULY
Drummer Bobby Elliott replaces Don Rathbone, who briefly becomes the group's manager. "Don wasn't a great drummer," notes Tony Hicks. "He didn't really make it and he realised himself he was struggling so he wasn't that bothered. Bob stood out as a drummer, so I suggested him to the rest of the band."

OCTOBER
The Hollies' second single 'Searchin" reaches number 10 in the *NME* charts.

NOVEMBER
The Hollies release a cover of Maurice Williams And The Zodiacs' 'Stay' which gives them their second UK Top 10 hit.

15 DECEMBER
The Hollies join the Bobby Rydell/Helen Shapiro package tour.

1964

7 FEBRUARY
The Hollies issue their début album *Stay With The Hollies*, which features only one song co-written by Nash, 'Little Lover'. The following week their cover of Doris Troy's 'Just One Look' is released and goes on to reach UK number 2, the group's biggest hit to date.

4 APRIL
Nash attends the sessions for The Rolling Stones' first album, contributing to the unreleased 'Andrew's Blues'.

25 APRIL
The Hollies join the star-studded *NME* Poll Winners' Concert at the Empire Pool, Wembley.

15 MAY
'Here I Go Again' is released and continues the consistent UK Top 10 run, reaching number 4.

30 JUNE
Clarke/Nash/Hicks' 'Come On Back' (B-side of 'We're Through') is recorded, along with 'Set Me Free' and 'Don't Feel Too Bad', both of which are featured on *In The Hollies Style*.

25 AUGUST
At Abbey Road, the group complete their sixth single, 'We're Through', which will peak at UK number 7. This is the first A-side written by Clarke/Nash/Hicks, using their familiar pseudonym "L. Ransford". "We started to realise that these guys were getting well paid for writing the songs," Allan Clarke recalls, "so we started trying to write our own hits. 'We're Through' was very different to everything else around at the time. It wasn't as big a hit as the earlier singles, but we thought we were on the right track."

SEPTEMBER
The Hollies tour with visiting US act, The Dixie Cups.

NOVEMBER
The Hollies issue their second album, *In The Hollies Style*, with Nash credited as co-writer on 'Don't You Know', 'To You My Love', 'Time For Love', 'Please Don't Feel Too Bad', 'Come On Home', 'You'll Be Mine' and 'Set Me Free'.

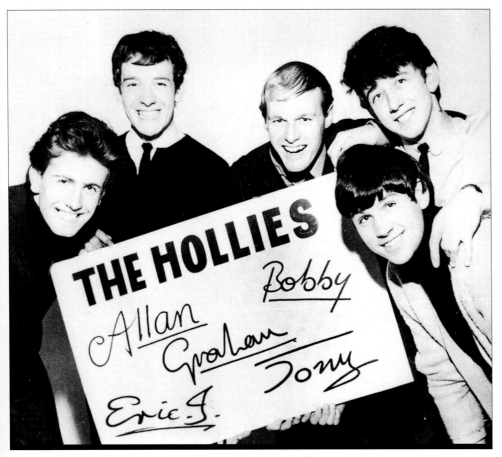

10 NOVEMBER

'Put Yourself In My Place', the first 'Ransford' composition for their next album, is completed at Abbey Road.

1965

22 JANUARY

The Hollies release the Goffin/Titelman cover 'Yes I Will' which peaks at number 10. The flip side 'Nobody' is written by Clarke/Hicks/Nash.

5-18 MARCH

The Hollies support The Rolling Stones on their UK tour.

16 APRIL

On the strength of one minor hit, The Hollies open their first US tour appearing at Brooklyn's Paramount Theater, New York.

21 MAY

The Hollies' 'I'm Alive' is released and soon reaches number 1 in the UK.

25 JUNE

Gralto Music (an acronym of Graham, Allan and Tony) is set up with publisher Dick James.

13 JULY

At Abbey Road, Clarke, Hicks and Nash's 'Too Many People' and 'I've Been Wrong' complete the group compositions for the new album.

14 JULY

'I'm Alive' (backed with the group's 'You Know He Did') is replaced at number 1 by The Byrds' 'Mr Tambourine Man'. Nash recalls first seeing Crosby during this period, when The Byrds toured the UK.

30 JULY

The Hollies film material for the US television programmes *Shindig* and *The Red Skelton Show*.

27 AUGUST

The Graham Gouldman-composed 'Look Through Any Window' is released and peaks at number 4 in the UK. Its B-side, 'So Lonely', is the usual Clarke/Hicks/Nash offering.

10 SEPTEMBER

The Hollies, the group's third album, credits Nash as co-writer on 'Too Many People', 'When I Come Home To You', 'I've Been Wrong' and 'Put Yourself In My Place'.

4-31 DECEMBER

The Hollies embark on a UK tour to coincide with the release of their cover of George Harrison's 'If I Needed Someone'. Harrison complains that their version is "rubbish", adding: "They've spoilt it. The Hollies are all right musically, but the way they do their records they sound like session men who've just got together in the studio without ever

seeing each other before. Technically they're good, but that's all." Two weeks later (December 17), Nash informs the *NME*: "Not only do these comments disappoint and hurt us but we are sick and tired of everything The Beatles say or do being taken as law."

28 DECEMBER

Graham Nash makes his debut as an actor. His appearance in the play *Stage One Contest* is broadcast this evening on Rediffusion Television.

1966

5 JANUARY

'If I Needed Someone' enters the *NME* chart at number 24, its peak position. "Our treatment of it wasn't that clever," Bobby Elliott concedes. "Then George Harrison came out in the press with a lot of criticism and the record stopped selling." The B-side is another Clarke/Nash/Hicks composition, 'I've Got A Way Of My Own'.

18 FEBRUARY

The Hollies release 'I Can't Let Go', co-written by Chip Taylor. The B-side 'Running Through The Night' is another Clarke/Nash/Hicks composition.

7 MARCH

The Hollies undertake a 12-day concert tour of Poland, accompanied by Lulu. This same week, 'I Can't Let Go' reaches number 1 in the *NME* charts.

27 MARCH

The Hollies fly out for a six-week tour of US colleges and also appear at the Trip in Hollywood. However, they are banned from performing on several US television shows due to union difficulties. A scheduled return visit to America in June is postponed when the group fails to secure working permits.

10 MAY

The Hollies collaborate with Peter Sellers on the Bacharach/David film theme *After The Fox*. Jack Bruce is featured on bass.

15 MAY

Klaus Voormann deputises for Hollies' bassist Eric Haydock on *Sunday Night At The London Palladium*. Haydock claims he is suffering from nervous exhaustion. Calvert is retained for the next recording session, 'Bus Stop' (May 18), and joins The Hollies on a three-week tour of Europe, beginning May 21. This same month, the group Mirage release 'Go Away', co-written and co-produced by Nash.

17 JUNE

The Hollies' single 'Bus Stop' is released and subsequently reaches the UK/US Top 5.

JUNE

The Hollies' fourth album *Would You Believe* is

released, with Nash credited as co-writer on 'Hard, Hard Year', 'Oriental Sadness', 'Fifi The Flea' and 'I've Got A Way Of My Own'.

Eight Nash/Clarke/Hicks compositions (including the rare 'Like Every Time Before') appear on The Everly Brothers' *Two Yanks In England* on which The Hollies are prominently featured, along with Jimmy Page and John Paul Jones. During this same month, Nash visits LA and meets Cass Elliott, who introduces him to marijuana and David Crosby.

29 JULY

Eric Haydock's sacking is officially confirmed. The bassist insists: "It's a raw deal... It's true I missed a few dates through illness but, on each occasion, I have produced a doctor's certificate". Nash is unrepentant: "The uncertainty had been getting us down, particularly when we knew that we were as tired and overworked as he was." Upon their return to the UK, the group spends a month playing Sunday concerts in Blackpool.

7 OCTOBER

The Hollies release the inventive 'Stop! Stop! Stop!', which rapidly climbs to number 2 in the UK. The main writer on this single is Tony Hicks.

15 OCTOBER - 6 NOVEMBER

The Hollies commence a 21-date package tour with The Small Faces and Paul Jones. The Nashville Teens and Paul And Barry Ryan are also featured on some dates. The Hollies' set includes 'A Taste Of Honey', 'Times They Are A-Changin'', 'Bus Stop' and 'Stop! Stop! Stop!' Within a week of this tour, the group is scheduled to return to the USA on a Dick Clark package tour.

2 DECEMBER

The Hollies release their fifth album *For Certain Because*, which credits Nash as co-writer on 'What's Wrong With The Way I Live', 'Pay You Back With Interest', 'Tell Me To My Face', 'Clown', 'Suspicious Look In Your Eyes', 'It's You', 'High Classed', 'Peculiar Situation', 'What Went Wrong', 'Crusader', 'Don't Ever Think About Changing' and 'Stop! Stop! Stop!'.

1967

FEBRUARY

'On A Carousel' is released and reaches number 5 (UK) and number 11 (US). According to Gralto Music, the song is credited to Nash/Hicks/Clarke, as is the flip side, 'All The World Is Love'. This same month, The Hollies are scheduled to tour Germany (February 9-11) and Yugoslavia (February 16-19). The tour is interrupted when Bobby Elliott bursts an appendix. Ex-Dakota Tony Mansfield is enlisted as a temporary replacement.

11 MARCH - 2 APRIL

The Hollies appear on a UK package tour

GRAHAM NASH, 1967

accompanied by The Spencer Davis Group, The Tremeloes and Paul Jones. They also form their own production company at this time.

27 MAY

'Carrie Anne' is the new Hollies single. Nash insists: " 'Carrie Anne' is going to be the last of our really commercial singles... It's time for The Hollies to grow up. I want to make records which say something... After five years of screamagers I'm getting a little tired."

JUNE

The Hollies release their sixth album *Evolution*, with Nash credited as co-writer on 'Then The Heartaches Begin', 'Stop Right There', 'Water On The Brain', 'Lullaby To Tim', 'Have You Ever Loved Somebody', 'You Need Love', 'Rain On The Window', 'Heading For A Fall', 'Ye Olde Toffee Shoppe', 'When Your Light's Turned On', 'Leave Me' and 'The Games We Play'.

25 JUNE

Nash attends the live recording session of The Beatles' 'All You Need Is Love'.

29 JUNE

The Hollies return to Yugoslavia, where Nash writes 'Marrakesh Express', a composition that they will never record. During their concerts in Zagreb, the group distribute flowers to audiences, unfurl a banner on stage proclaiming "Hollies Love Peace" and wear black arm bands in sympathy with the recent Jagger/Richard jail sentences.

JULY

Nash's co-written 'Carrie Anne' becomes a transatlantic Top 10 hit, and the group's first US success with Epic. Interestingly, the song was inspired by The Byrds. Tony Hicks recalls, "I started writing 'Carrie Anne' in a hotel in Stavanger, Norway, around the time of The Byrds' 'Mr Tambourine Man'. I had the tune and was singing 'Hey, Mr Man'. We wrote the verses up at Elstree Studios while we were doing a television show and Allan chipped in with the middle eight. Carrie Anne was the nearest girl's name we could find to 'Mr Man'." The flip side is another Nash/Clarke/Hicks number, 'Signs That Will Never Change'.

15 JULY

John Walker's 'Annabella' peaks at number 25 in the *NME* chart. The song is Nash's sole hit collaboration with writers Nicky James and Kirk Duncan. The same songwriting team will later contribute material to solo albums by John Walker and Nicky James, plus the single 'Coming From The Ground' by Lee Kings.

3 AUGUST

At Abbey Road Studios, The Hollies are busily working on Nash's 'King Midas In Reverse' and 'Everything Is Sunshine'. As usual, the composing credits are split three ways with Clarke and Hicks.

10 AUGUST

Following two days in Majorca, The Hollies undertake a short tour of Sweden.

SEPTEMBER

John Walker's album *If You Go Away* features two compositions co-written by Nash, Nicky James and Kirk Duncan: 'Good Day' and 'Reaching For The Sun'.

12 SEPTEMBER

The Hollies record the unreleased 'Ashes To Ashes' at Abbey Road.

22 SEPTEMBER

The startling 'King Midas In Reverse' is released but it barely scrapes into the UK Top 20. "It was too early," Nash reflects. "We wanted to break away from the usual pop records that we had been doing, but people wouldn't have it".

NOVEMBER

The Hollies release their seventh album, *Butterfly* with Nash credited as co-writer on 'Dear Eloise, 'Away Away Away', 'Maker', 'Pegasus', 'Would You Believe', 'Wishyouawish', 'Postcard', 'Charlie And Fred', 'Try It', 'Elevated Obsessions', 'Step Inside' and 'Butterfly'. Composing credits from memoranda at their publishing company arguably give a clearer indication of the true writers, solely crediting Clarke for 'Would You Believe', Hicks for 'Pegasus' and Nash for 'Postcard', 'Away Away Away', 'Maker' and 'Butterfly'. Two other songs, 'Go Away' and 'Without You', are registered to Clarke/Hicks/Nash at Gralto Music, but are not attempted in the studio.

Although *Butterfly* proves the group's most ambitious work to date, it is poorly received by the public and fails to register a chart entry. Nash is now feeling the pressure imposed by chart demands, a situation made almost untenable by the relative failure of 'King Midas In Reverse', his finest composition to date.

13 NOVEMBER – 10 DECEMBER

Having just completed a lightning tour of Japan, The Hollies embark on a three-week, 12-city tour of the USA, including appearances on *The Joey Bishop Show* and *The Mike Douglas Show*.

Meanwhile, Nash remains in contact with David Crosby, fresh from being fired from The Byrds. It is now only a matter of time before friendship leads to musical collaboration.

1945

12 NOVEMBER

Neil Young is born at Toronto's General Hospital.

1949

AUGUST

Young's family move to Omemee, Ontario, where they will live for the next eight years before returning to Toronto.

1951

AUGUST

Young contracts polio during the epidemics of the 50s and is hospitalised. Although he is not seriously incapacitated, the disease leaves him stiff-jointed, with a noticeable limp.

1960

Scott Young leaves his wife Rassy Ragland and later remarries. Ragland takes her sons to Winnipeg, an odyssey later captured in song on 'Don't Be Denied'.

1961

JANUARY-JUNE

Young makes his performing début, playing rhythm guitar with school group The Jades at Earl Grey Community Center (January 6 or 7). The group soon split up and Young briefly joins The Esquires.

1961-62

Young enrols at Kelvin High School, continuing to play alongside friend Ken Koblun in minor

groups, The Stardusters, The Twilighters and The Classics. During this period, Young claims to have written one of his first songs, 'Image In Blue'.

1963

JANUARY-JUNE

Young launches The Squires, who play regularly at community clubs and high schools in their area.

23 JULY

The Squires record two instrumentals written by Young: 'Aurora' and 'The Sultan'.

SEPTEMBER

'Aurora'/'The Sultan' is released as a single on the small Winnipeg label, V Records, after which the group continue their run of parochial gigs.

1964

3 JANUARY

Young débuts as a singer, covering The Beatles' 'It Won't Be Long' and the Berry Gordy-composed 'Money' in The Squires' otherwise instrumental set. Further Beatles' covers soon follow.

25 JANUARY

The Squires secure a gig at the Fourth Dimension, a folk club in Winnipeg.

2 APRIL

For their second recording session, The Squires play the instrumental 'Mustang' and two Young compositions: 'I Wonder' and 'Ain't It The Truth'. Although neither is issued at this time, Young will later revive 'Ain't It The Truth' in concert with the Blue Notes over 20 years later.

AUTUMN

The Squires' set includes a cover 'Farmer John' which Young will finally release on *Ragged Glory*. Two other songs from this period, Young's 'Hello Lonely Woman' and 'Find Another Shoulder', remain unissued but are subsequently featured in the Blue Notes' repertoire.

12 NOVEMBER

Young celebrates his 19th birthday by composing the twee 'Sugar Mountain' just before The Squires' evening set at the Flamingo Club in Fort William.

23 NOVEMBER

The Squires record the unreleased 'Together Alone' and 'I'll Love You Forever', the latter dedicated to Young's girlfriend of the time, Pam Smith.

DECEMBER

The group privately record the uncredited composition, 'I'm A Man (And I Can't Cry)'.

1965

18 APRIL

Young meets Stephen Stills for the first time at the Fourth Dimension coffee house in Fort William. Indefinite plans are hatched to form a group.

MAY

The Squires briefly change their name to The High Flying Birds, which sounds like an advertisement for David Crosby's colleagues, but is actually a folk song which Stills sang in The Company.

12 JUNE

The High Flying Birds (*nee* The Squires) perform their final gig – an evening session at Smitty's Pancake House, Fort William.

16 JUNE

On the way to Sunbury, Ontario, Young's hearse breaks down in Blind River, an incident that inspires the song 'Long May You Run'.

SUMMER

Young and his sidekick Ken Koblun settle in Yorkville, Toronto, rehearsing under the names Four To Go and The Castaways. Young composes 'Girl In The Mirror' and 'Casting Me Away From You', the arrangement of which will later inspire 'The Emperor Of Wyoming'.

SEPTEMBER/OCTOBER

Still in Yorkville, Young reinvents himself as a Dylan-inspired protest singer. He plays several local gigs but is not well received. During a visit to Greenwich Village he attempts to contact Stills, but instead meets up with Stephen's buddy Richie Furay, whom he teaches 'Nowadays, Clancy Can't Even Sing'.

NOVEMBER

Young returns to New York to record seven

THE SQUIRES

NEIL YOUNG, 1967

songs for Elektra Records: 'Nowadays, Clancy Can't Even Sing', 'Sugar Mountain', 'The Rent Is Always Due', 'Runaround Babe', 'Don't Pity Me Babe', 'Ain't Got The Blues' and 'Extra Extra' (aka 'When It Falls, It Falls On You'). Although the songs have a period charm, they are clearly insubstantial, falling below the standard of contemporaneous singer songwriters. Elektra, not surprisingly, pass up the chance to sign Young.

1966

JANUARY

Young copyright registers 'Baby Go', which he has co-written with Craig Allen of Canadian group, The Allen Ward Trio. Allen later receives a namecheck on the rear sleeve of *Buffalo Springfield Again*.

JANUARY-FEBRUARY

Within the space of a month, Young again reinvents himself, this time as a potential R&B exponent. A friendship with bassist Bruce Palmer leads him into The Mynah Birds, featuring soul singer Ricky James Matthews. Soon, the group head for Detroit with vain hopes of establishing themselves as Tamla Motown stars. They succeed in recording between eight and sixteen songs for the label, including the Young/ Matthews collaborations 'I'll Wait Forever' and 'It's My Time'. Alas, the results remain unreleased.

MARCH

The Mynah Birds' career comes to an abrupt end when it is discovered that Matthews is AWOL from the US Navy. He is arrested and imprisoned for draft evasion, leaving Young to return to Toronto. Determined to break away, Young persuades Palmer that they should head for Hollywood in search of the elusive Stills.

1 APRIL

The famous meeting between Stills/Furay and Young/Palmer takes place on Sunset Strip. The foursome recruit drummer Billy Mundi who is soon replaced by Dewey Martin, via Byrds' manager Jim Dickson. The new group launch themselves as The Buffalo Springfield.

JULY

Buffalo Springfield record Young's 'Nowadays Clancy Can't Even Sing', which will subsequently be issued as a single with Furay on lead vocal.

OCTOBER

The group record Young's 'Down Down Down', which he later incorporates as the centrepiece of 'Country Girl'.

1967

JANUARY

Buffalo Springfield's eponymous début album is issued with Young taking writing credits on 'Nowadays, Clancy Can't Even Sing' 'Flying On

The Ground Is Wrong', 'Do I Have To Come Right Out And Say It?', 'Burned' and 'Out Of My Mind'. Furay, a more accomplished and confident vocalist than Young, provides mannered readings of the first three songs which reflect the Beatles-influenced pop sound of the time. However, it is Young's expressive vocal on the harrowing 'Out Of My Mind' that looks forward to his later solo work.

9 JANUARY

According to Atlantic archives, the Springfield record Young's 'Mr Soul', which owes a considerable debt to The Rolling Stones' '(I Can't Get No) Satisfaction'.

13 MARCH

The group are listed as recording 'No Sun Today' and 'Who's The Next Fool?', neither of which is issued. Copyright searches fail to identify these tracks as Young compositions.

8 APRIL

A second version of Young's 'Mr Soul' is cut to be released as a single.

6 MAY

Young records some solo tracks, including the instrumental 'Whiskey Boot Hill' and 'Slowly Burning', the latter remaining unreleased.

LATE MAY

Young, at his most unprofessional, abandons the Springfield on the eve of their intended television appearance on Johnny Carson's *The Tonight Show*. "I sort of dropped out of the group, "Young vaguely observed. "I couldn't handle it. I don't know why but something inside of me felt I wasn't on track".

Stills: "He decided that it wasn't worth it, probably he knew the same thing that Bruce wasn't gonna be able to handle it, and he probably thought I was just as crazy as he was".

JUNE

The Cascades release the single 'Flying On The Ground Is Wrong', which producer Jack Nitzsche claims features Young on guitar.

30 JUNE

Atlantic files indicate that some studio work or masters are delivered for Young's 'Down Down Down' and the uncertain composition, 'Nobody's Fool'.

10 AUGUST

Reconsidering his future, Young returns to the Springfield for a show the following evening in Huntington Beach and agrees to work on a new

album. He later criticises his cavalier approach to the group, admitting: "I was going crazy, joining and quitting and joining again. I began to feel that I didn't have to answer or obey anyone. I just wasn't mature enough to deal with it. I was very young."

14 AUGUST

Young copyrights 'Whiskey Boot Hill' and 'Expecting To Fly'. The latter is completed in New York 10 days' later with stupendous string arrangements by producer Jack Nitzsche, ensuring the song's status as Young's most ambitious work to date.

18 AUGUST

Young belatedly copyrights 'Extra! Extra!', 'High School Graduation', 'One More Sign' (all unreleased and recorded the previous year), plus 'The Old Laughing Lady' and 'Round And Round'. It is intriguing to note that the latter has been composed this early as it will not appear on record until as late as Young's second solo album.

9 OCTOBER

Buffalo Springfield work on a number of songs for their second album, including Young's epic 'Broken Arrow', a surrealistic collage that betrays his love of experimentation.

30 OCTOBER

Young copyright registers the unreleased 'Sell Out'.

14 NOVEMBER

Atlantic's files indicate that Buffalo Springfield are recording Young's 'On The Way Home', which will later appear on *Last Time Around*.

20 NOVEMBER

Young copyrights 'Down To The Wire', which will remain unissued until the release of the retrospective compilation *Decade* in 1977. A version with Stills on lead vocal is also recorded but remains officially unreleased, appearing only on the *Stampede* bootleg.

9 DECEMBER

Buffalo Springfield Again includes Young's 'Mr Soul', 'Expecting To Fly' and 'Broken Arrow'. The distinctive arrangements ensure that the album sounds noticeably eclectic with Stills and Young each displaying their songwriting talents to considerable effect.

This same day, Love's influential *Forever Changes* is released. According to singer Arthur Lee, Young is involved in the production of 'The Daily Planet'.

> *"I was going crazy, joining and quitting and joining again. I began to feel that I didn't have to answer or obey anyone. I just wasn't mature enough to deal with it. I was very young."*
>
> **NEIL YOUNG**

PART II
SO BEGINS THE TASK
1968-1972

Crosby and Stills could easily have launched themselves as solo artistes during 1968/69, just as Young had done after the demise of Buffalo Springfield. Astonishingly, Crosby had already written most of the songs which would be scattered across the various CSN&Y, C&N and solo ventures covering the next five years. There is a school of thought which suggests that, had they chosen the solo route at this point, they might have been in a stronger position later down the line, both in establishing separate careers and understanding and respecting the crucial importance of their partnership. Once they played together though, they fell in love with the music they were making and the need for solo gratification seemed unimportant. Initially, CS&N was the perfect musical union. This was no mere jamming session among musical friends but a fusion of talent that was greater than anyone could have imagined. The vocal combination was unique, the songwriting articulate, the arrangements exceptional and the playing impressive.

By the time their début was released, CS&N had recruited Neil Young, a decision that was to have serious implications for the remainder of their career. Once the public heard the four together, it would always be difficult to feel entirely satisfied with lesser permutations. The superlative quality of the début album coupled with the decision to play their second gig at Woodstock, captured the public imagination at a crucial time. Seemingly overnight, CSN&Y became the ultimate metaphor of late Sixties' idealism and artistic ambition, the living embodiment of what was loosely termed the Woodstock nation.

Déjà Vu was a definitive moment in terms of commercial success and artistic ambition. Adjectives such as "brilliant" were commonplace among reviewers. Even the detractors at Rolling Stone were forced to criticise the album through superlatives, calling it "too perfect and too good to be true." It seemed inconceivable that the foursome could ever walk away from the godhead that CSN&Y represented, but they did so – wilfully and with consummate ease. Songwriters supreme, acclaimed practitioners of both acoustic and electric material –how could this all be contained in a four way set-up? They each had a surplus of songs and a need to make their mark through related solo activities. Usually such projects are severely anti-climactic but the wonder of CSN&Y was the unerring quality of their music during this intensely productive period. From 1969–72, they released a series of albums which were consistently excellent and propagated the myth among their more intense following that they really were infallible.

The prolific Young was the first to take advantage of the CSN&Y legacy with After The Goldrush, a work that garnered several "album of the year" awards. Stills, no doubt realising the importance of fashioning a strong début, completed probably the finest work of his career; an amazingly eclectic collection that played up all his strengths while revealing none of his weaknesses. Twenty-five years on, it still sounds a remarkable record, with a freshness and majesty beyond all expectation. It was matched by Crosby whose If I Could Only Remember My Name was a staggering achievement, years ahead of its time and virtually unmatched in its era. Even Nash, who carried the least weight of expectation, came up with what seemed a career best of well-crafted tunes. There was an astonishing confidence and self-belief in these releases, as if the participants knew that they could singlehandedly produce the greatest music of the early Seventies.

Ironically, it was Young who first threatened to oversweeten the pill with Harvest and then realised the long term career consequences of becoming known as "the man who sang 'Heart Of Gold'". Meanwhile, Crosby & Nash forged a partnership which was perfect for the time and brought the acoustic intimacy of CSN&Y to its proper place in small halls. Conversely, the seemingly boundless ambition of Stills resulted in the formation of Manassas, whose superb double album and attendant world tour won lavish critical praise. For long periods, it seemed as if all four members of CSN&Y would continue to develop at this astonishing rate, pummelling all potential rivals to oblivion with each successive album. But these early years of fame were to be the true watershed for the partnership. Hereafter, it would be different, not simply because they were increasingly divorced from their times, but due to the familiarity of their music. They had already reinvented themselves creatively in the most dramatic fashion imaginable after The Byrds, The Hollies and the Springfield but, in order to transcend their time, they were required to do it all again.

1968

JANUARY

The Hollies record 'Wings' (co-written by Nash), which is featured on the charity album, *No One's Gonna Change Our World*. According to Clarke, the song is inspired by Neil Young's 'Expecting To Fly'.

2 JANUARY

Atlantic archives suggest that several Buffalo Springfield master recordings are belatedly logged with the company, including two group compositions, 'Raga No. 1' and 'Raga No. 2', plus Young's unreleased composition 'Whatever Happened To Saturday Night', and 'Theme Jazz' and 'Ball Park' (both of which were probably incorporated into 'Broken Arrow').

3 JANUARY

The Notorious Byrds Brothers is released, containing the last of Crosby's work with the group. He plays bass on 'Old John Robertson', sings on 'Change Is Now' and composes 'Tribal Gathering' and 'Dolphin's Smile'. The backing track of his song 'Draft Morning' is used, with McGuinn and Hillman adding some new lyrics. "It was one of the sleaziest things they ever did," Crosby complained to me. "I had an entire song finished. They just casually rewrote it and decided to take half the credit. How's that? Without even asking me!... How would you feel? You'd be pissed off, wouldn't you? Well, I was pissed off!... I'm all over that album, they just didn't give me credit. I played, I sang, I wrote, I even played bass on one track and they tried to make out that I wasn't even on it, that they could be that good without me. And that was bullshit because I was there."

5 JANUARY

Buffalo Springfield are entering their last phase, punctuated by the final departure of the ever-troubled Palmer, who is replaced by producer Jim Messina in February. Across the Atlantic, The Hollies embark on a short tour of Ireland (January 5–7).

6 JANUARY

The Springfield appear once more at the Earl Warren Showgrounds, Santa Barbara. Meanwhile, The Hollies are touring the Midwest and East Coast, promoting their album, *Butterfly*.

13 JANUARY

The Byrds (minus the departed Crosby) appear on the same bill as The Buffalo Springfield at the Sports Arena, San Diego.

FEBRUARY/MARCH

The Hollies tour the USA, appearing on *Hollywood Palace*, *The Dating Game*, *The Johnny Carson Show*, *The Smothers Brothers' Show* and *The Ed Sullivan Show*.

10 FEBRUARY

Crosby sees The Jimi Hendrix Experience at the Shrine Auditorium, Los Angeles. Prior to the show, he jams with Hendrix, Buddy Miles and Harvey Brooks. He later accompanies Hendrix to a party at Peter Tork's house.

14 FEBRUARY

The Hollies play a Valentine's Night show at the Whisky A Go-Go attended by various luminaries including Crosby, Stills, John Sebastian and several members of The Mamas And The Papas. Nash is increasingly drawn towards his new American friends as his relationship with The Hollies continues to worsen.

20 MARCH

Having just announced his intention to leave The Buffalo Springfield again, Young is arrested on a marijuana charge, along with Richie Furay, Eric Clapton and Jim Messina. After a night in custody, the musicians are released on bail.

This same evening, The Hollies complete their US tour and fly off for appearances in the Philippines, Japan and Singapore.

27 MARCH

The Hollies return to the charts with the banal Clarke/Nash composition 'Jennifer Eccles', as Graham temporarily buckles down to commercial dictates in the hope of being allowed to record a solo album later in the year. "It really brought home to me how much I'd prostituted myself as an artist," he says of the offending disc, for which he also received a minor credit on the B-side, 'Open Up Your Eyes'.

28 MARCH

Crosby enters Hollywood Recorders and with Paul Rothchild at the controls records demos of 'Song With No Words', 'Tamalpais High (At About 3)', 'Games', 'Laughing' and instrumental snatches of 'The Wall Song' and 'Wooden Ships'. This session testifies to Crosby's incredible creativity during this period. Here he is fresh out of The Byrds with a scintillating song catalogue that will be spread over three different albums.

2 APRIL

While Crosby is touching gold, his new friend is unsuccessfully attempting to record another album with The Hollies. They remain resistant to his singer/songwriter style arrangements but initially agree to record the upbeat 'Marrakesh Express'. A backing track is completed at Abbey Road Studios, but remains unissued and instead will be carried over for work with Crosby and Stills.

EARLY APRIL

Buffalo Springfield undertake a second major tour with The Beach Boys, which is curtailed after a handful of dates. Later in the spring, Stills goes on to work with Judy Collins, jams

with Al Kooper and Mike Bloomfield and is offered the chance to join Blood, Sweat & Tears.

10 APRIL

Crosby copyright registers two of his "post-Byrds" compositions: 'Triad' and 'Games'. The former was originally recorded at CBS during his final Byrds sessions in late 1967. However, since his agreement with Tickson Music had run out in June of that year, the song now comes under the aegis of "David Crosby".

This same day, *McGough And McGear*'s eponymous album is released, with Nash featured on guest vocals.

5 MAY

Buffalo Springfield perform their final gig at the Long Beach Arena in California. Soon after this, the charges brought against Young and his fellow musicians earlier in the year are reduced to the anodyne "disturbing the peace". Young receives a small fine for his sins. Meanwhile, his new manager Elliot Roberts sets about securing a solo deal with Reprise Records. Stills remains committed to Atlantic as label president Ahmet Ertegun has made it clear that he considers him to be the premier talent among the Springfield.

6 MAY

Joni Mitchell releases her first album, *Songs To A Seagull*, produced by David Crosby. Stills is also involved, playing guitar on 'Night In The City'. As well as occasional session work, Stills teams up with drummer Dallas Taylor before reaching the eminently logical conclusion: "A drummer and a guitarist do not a band make".

10 MAY

The Stills/Young composition 'Kahuna Desert' is belatedly registered for copyright.

17 MAY – 29 MAY

The Hollies head a UK package tour with The Scaffold and Paul Jones. Their appearance at London's Lewisham Odeon (May 25) is recorded for a live album, which is ultimately unreleased. The tour's opening date coincides with the *NME* headline, "Graham Nash May Split Hollies". The singer frankly admits: "I believe in a completely different musical direction to that in which The Hollies are going and right now I feel as if I'm letting myself down not doing as I want... I want to do everything. I want to write songs and sing them and produce them and mix them and have a say in the cover. This is because I think I'm right. Songwriting is now one of the biggest things in my life. I could be consumed completely in the fire of writing songs."

6 JUNE

Bobby Kennedy's assassination prompts Crosby to write one of his best compositions of the period: 'Long Time Gone'.

"We're not a group, just one aggregate of friends."

DAVID CROSBY

8 JUNE

In an attempt to play down the rumours of Nash's impending departure, a "spokesman for The Hollies" announces that both Graham Nash and Bernie Calvert will be recording albums in the future, adding "these solo ventures do not indicate a split in the group".

10 JUNE

Crosby's 'Laughing' is registered for copyright, along with the unreleased anti-war song, 'You Sit There'. At this point, Crosby has yet to sign to a new publishing company so songs are still registered under his own name.

13 JUNE

Less than one week after Bobby Kennedy's assassination, Crosby records his first demo version of 'Long Time Gone' at Western Recorders, LA, with Stills in attendance. It's salutary to consider that, within a few months of *The Notorious Byrds Brothers*, Crosby has already written all his contributions to the first CS&N album and beyond.

17 JUNE

At Wally Heider's studio, Crosby produces 'Hello' b/w 'Good Day' as a single for his manager Larry Spector's "pet" group, Things To Come, which features Russ Kunkel on drums. On the same day, Nash is at Abbey Road recording 'Do The Best You Can', his final B-side composition with The Hollies.

24-26 JUNE

Crosby produces and records a demo of 'Guinnevere' employing the services of The Grateful Dead's Jack Casady (bass) and The Modern Folk Quartet's Cyrus Faryar (bouzouki).

By this point, Crosby and Stills are intent on working together and their new material is revealed in a three-song demo of distinction: 'Guinnevere', 'Long Time Gone' (with additional lyrics) and '49 Reasons'. Even without the harmonies of Nash, the songs are impressive enough to warrant superlatives and indicate a brilliant partnership in the offing.

JULY

Nash records his final composition with The Hollies, 'Like Every Time Before', which will be issued as a single in Germany. He also composes 'Yellow Ribbon' which is released this month by the group Piccadilly Line. During the same period, he visits Los Angeles and hangs out with Cass Elliott, John Sebastian, Joni Mitchell and Crosby/Stills. Impromptu singing sessions take place at their various houses in Laurel Canyon, where Nash witnesses the startling vocal blend and songwriting power of the Crosby/Stills partnership. They proudly play Stephen's 'Helplessly Hoping' and 'You Don't Have To Cry' while Nash looks on attentively. He asks them to play the latter twice more, then joins in with a high harmony that astonishes the assembled onlookers. "Crosby and me just looked at one another," Stills enthused. "It was one of those moments." Driving home that evening, the two musicians rave about the unique vocal combination, but are sceptical of Nash ever leaving The Hollies. "We didn't think it could ever happen," Stills concluded. "David and I were talking about it and he was saying, 'No, he'd never do it... those guys have been together for ever... but, boy, what a sound!' We were really full of it, but we didn't dare approach him."

Instead, they persuade Cass Elliott to act as a go-between and sound out Nash about the possibility of working with them in the future. He is more than enthusiastic about the idea and leaves the USA knowing that his days in The Hollies will soon be at an end.

22 JULY

The album *Super Session* is released, with Stills and Al Kooper jamming on Bob Dylan's 'It Takes A Lot To Laugh, It Takes A Train To Cry', Donovan's 'Season Of The Witch', Willie Cobb's 'You Don't Love Me' and Harvey Brooks' 'Harvey's Tune'.

AUGUST

Rumours of Nash's unrest in The Hollies continue and are evidently not alleviated by a season in cabaret crooning 'Puff The Magic Dragon', 'Dang Me' and 'A Taste Of Honey'.

5 AUGUST

Buffalo Springfield release *Last Time Around,* a collection compiled from various sessions. As Young explained: "*Last Time Around* was pieced together by Jim Messina because neither Steve nor I gave a shit... We just didn't want to know." For all that, it's a surprisingly good album, even though Young receives only two full writing credits – 'I Am A Child' and 'On The Way Home'. Freed from the political battles, Furay is given a generous hand in the song selection and emerges with his dignity intact, even providing a surprise highlight with the eerie 'In The Hour Of Not Quite Rain', a poem composed by Michaela Callen. Palmer insists that the latter is the finest song the group has ever recorded.

Finally, Stills dominates proceedings with a varied selection of rock, country and Latin-American tunes. 'Questions' points the way forward to 'Carry On' while 'Four Days Gone' proves one of his best compositions. Indeed, you suspect that he would probably have preferred to retain this song for a higher profile release.

12 AUGUST

The Hollies record two songs co-written by Nash, 'Survival Of The Fittest' and 'Man Of No Expression'. Both remain unissued. During the same period, at a hotel in Leeds, Nash recalls composing first drafts of 'Lady Of The Island' and 'Sleep Song'. With 'Right Between The Eyes' also completed, he has a strong selection of material ready for any work with Crosby/Stills.

23/24 AUGUST

Young records the instrumental 'The Emperor Of Wyoming' and 'The Loner', which will be the opening two tracks on his début solo album. During this same month, he moves into a redwood house in Topanga Canyon with girlfriend Susan Acevedo, who runs a café in the area.

5 SEPTEMBER

Crosby's latest composition 'Is It Really Monday?' is registered for copyright, along with 'Guinnevere' and 'Long Time Gone', each under his own name. The former remains unreleased to this day and no tape of the session is readily available.

9 SEPTEMBER

Jefferson Airplane's *Crown Of Creation* is released, featuring Crosby's 'Triad'.

27 SEPTEMBER

The Hollies fly to Sweden to promote "British Week". At the Konserthuset, Stockholm, their set includes 'Stop! Stop! Stop!', 'Times They Are A-Changin'', 'The Very Next Day', 'Do The Best You Can', 'On A Carousel' and 'Butterfly'. Further concerts follow in Gothenburg (29) and Helsinki (30), after which they travel to Amsterdam and Brussels.

28 SEPTEMBER

Young records the striking 'What Did You Do To My Life?', a song that captures his child-like naïveté far more effectively than the more famous 'I Am A Child'.

30 SEPTEMBER

Young attempts 'Birds' (which will ultimately be saved for his third album) and an early version of 'Everybody Knows This Is Nowhere'.

OCTOBER

Nash's composition 'Burn Your Hatred' appears on Mama Cass' album *Dream A Little Dream,* which also features Stills on guitar. This same month, Nash announces his intention to leave The Hollies at the end of the year. Their decision to record a tribute album to Bob Dylan is cited as the final breaking point in a long and troubled relationship. "I'm sure that was the reason he wanted to leave," Allan Clarke concurs. "But in his mind he'd started to leave before that, when he met Crosby and Stills. The alternative was a Dylan album.... His frustration wasn't really with the material. He thought the group was being misguided. But he didn't just leave The Hollies: he left England, he left his wife, everything."

1/2 OCTOBER

Young's surrealistic travelogue 'The Last Trip To Tulsa' and the often overlooked but exceptional 'Here We Are In The Years' are recorded over two days.

4-16 OCTOBER

The Hollies undertake a tour of North America and the USA. Meanwhile, 'Listen To Me' enters the UK charts.

7/9 OCTOBER

Work is in progress on Young's songs of unrequited love, 'If I Could Have Her Tonight' and 'I've Been Waiting For You'. The latter, with Jim Messina on bass, is pieced together over several sessions. "In the beginning we put down acoustic guitar and bass and drums," Young recalled. "That's the smallest track I ever did, one guitar, bass and drums."

17 OCTOBER

Studio work on 'The Old Laughing Lady', 'I've Loved Her So Long' and 'String Quartet From Whiskey Boot Hill' completes the sessions for Young's forthcoming solo album.

18 OCTOBER

The Monkees' latest single 'As We Go Along' features Neil Young on guitar. The track was originally cut at Wally Heider's on May 30, less than a month after The Buffalo Springfield's final gig.

This same day, Scaffold's 'Lily The Pink' is issued and will soon dominate the number 1 spot over Christmas. Nash appears as guest vocalist.

NOVEMBER

Crosby, Stills and Nash are living in London's Moscow Road, rehearsing material, staying up late, getting stoned and eagerly awaiting Graham's imminent departure from The Hollies. At this point, they have not yet announced their title and are referred to as Nash, Crosby, Stills. Crosby lays down their philosophy emphatically: "We're not a group, just one aggregate of friends." Nash describes them as "three people who get together to express their individuality". They love to play for the privileged few that visit, and one obscure composition is mentioned in their songlist, 'Black Wing'.

16 NOVEMBER

"Hollies Split Shock" scream the *NME* headlines. Although currently at number 1 in the album charts with *Hollies Greatest Hits* and still in the Top 20 with 'Listen To Me', Nash confirms his departure which will follow the Save Rave concert in December. The breaking point in his relationship with the group comes with their decision to record an album of Bob Dylan covers. Publishing niggles are

also evident. Nash: "Another bone of contention was our music company Gralto. If I wrote a song the three of us got the credit... That was OK as long as we were all writing but I found I was writing most of the songs and the other two were getting equal credit". Interestingly, Nash makes no mention of Crosby or Stills, stating cryptically, "I go my way as a solo singer and songwriter". On this same night The Hollies appear at the London University Ball, attended by the Queen Mother.

23-28 NOVEMBER

Young secures a week's residency, supporting Joni Mitchell at New York's Bitter End.

DECEMBER

The Monkees' film soundtrack album *Head* features Stephen Stills on additional guitar on 'Do I Have To Do This All Over Again'. The session took place the previous January during the final phase of Buffalo Springfield's career.

1 DECEMBER

Young marries Susan Acevedo in Topanga Canyon. The newly-weds set up home in their hilltop house along with Acevedo's seven-year-old daughter, Tia. Young: "I moved out there, got married and settled down and everything and I just started really digging on being home. I have another life that doesn't have anything to do with rock 'n' roll."

8 DECEMBER

Nash's farewell gig with The Hollies takes place before Her Royal Highness Princess Margaret at the London Palladium. The occasion is The Save Rave!, a charity show for the Invalid Children's Aid Association. "That was a bit strained," Tony Hicks explains. "I remember David Crosby coming into the dressing room which made it more strained. But we weren't too bothered. Graham wasn't happy and he was going. Simple as that. All we had to do was get back in the charts." After the show, Graham removes his white suit for the

In the presence of
Her Royal Highness The Princess Margaret, Countess of Snowdon
and the Earl of Snowdon

THE SAVE RAVE!

LONDON PALLADIUM
Sunday, 8th December 1968
for the funds of the
INVALID CHILDREN'S AID ASSOCIATION

last time, then disappears into the night with the attendant Crosby and Stills.

9 DECEMBER

Stills' guitar work is in evidence on two new releases this week: The Monkees' *Head* ('Do I Have To Do This All Over Again'), and Judy Collins' *Who Knows Where The Time Goes* .

10 DECEMBER

Nash flies out to America with his colleagues and temporarily moves into Crosby's LA home. Within the next fortnight, the first Crosby, Stills & Nash collaborations, 'Helplessly Hoping' and 'You Don't Have To Cry', are recorded at the Record Plant, New York. The latter, supervised by Doors' producer Paul A. Rothchild, will later be unearthed for the CS&N boxed set in 1991. The trio insist that they will be playing live, with a stage act consisting of an acoustic set, three solo spots and a hard-driving finale featuring a pianist and drummer.

28-30 DECEMBER

An eventful year ends with Nash and Joni Mitchell attending the Miami Music Festival in Gulf Stream Park, where they back Richie Havens on 'Get Together'.

1969

JANUARY

CS&N relocate to Sag Harbour, Long Island, where they complete rehearsals for their forthcoming album. During the same month, Nash visits Johnny Cash's house and plays 'Marrakesh Express' before a star-studded list of guests including Bob Dylan, Joni Mitchell, Kris Kristofferson and Shel Silverstein. Meanwhile, Stills can be heard playing bass on Richie Havens' new album, *Richard P. Havens 1983*.

JANUARY-FEBRUARY

Young undertakes a low-key solo acoustic tour, performing at New York's Bitter End, followed by Le Hibou, Ottawa and The Riverboat, Yorkville, Toronto. He also sits in with The Rockets at the Whisky around this time, a collaboration that soon results in the formation of Crazy Horse.

7 JANUARY

Stills records a demo of '49 Bye Byes' (erroneously labelled 'No One Left To Please' on the tape box).

13 JANUARY

Joan Baez's *Any Day Now* is issued with Stills guesting on guitar.

22 JANUARY

The release of *Neil Young* confirms the emergence of the Canadian as a major singer/songwriter, but only to a select *cognoscenti*. Commercially, the album is a disappointment – the only work in his canon to fail to reach the US Top 200. Although he later

CROSBY IN THE STUDIO, 1969

STEPHEN STILLS, 1969

complains about the production and enforces a subtle remix, the original album remains one of his most engaging and impressive pieces.

EBRUARY

Nash is freed from EMI (UK) and Epic (USA) and signed to Atlantic in a trade-off involving Richie Furay's Pogo (later Poco), who sign to Epic. It is revealed that CS&N's forthcoming début album will be a double featuring two sides of acoustic music and two sides of electric. The latter will feature Harvey Brooks and Phil Harris (both ex-Electric Flag) and drummer Dallas Taylor (ex-Clear Light). This proposal is soon supplanted by news that the work will be a largely acoustic single album, minus Brooks and Harris.

FEBRUARY

The Monkees' *Instant Replay* features the Davy Jones/Bill Chadwick composition 'You And I' on which Young guests on lead guitar. The track was originally cut on 10 May 1968, five days after the break-up of Buffalo Springfield.

FEBRUARY

According to *Rolling Stone*, sessions for CS&N's album commence on this day at Wally Heider's Studio.

FEBRUARY

Studio work is undertaken on 'Marrakesh Express' (with Jim Gordon on drums) and 'Wooden Ships', the latter written on a boat in Fort Lauderdale with Stills and Paul Kantner.

-17 FEBRUARY

Neil Young and Crazy Horse play their first known gigs together in New York.

FEBRUARY

A Valentine's evening spent with Graham Nash prompts Joni Mitchell to write him a love song, 'Willy'.

FEBRUARY

While Young and Crazy Horse are playing on the East Coast, CS&N commence studio work on 'Guinnevere', 'Helplessly Hoping' and 'Pre-Road Downs' (featuring an uncredited Cass Elliott). CS&N also record Lennon/McCartney's 'Blackbird', a song they first heard when they were rehearsing in London the previous year. Although the track proves perfect for their harmonic blend and is subsequently featured frequently in concert, they decline to issue the recording until their retrospective boxed set in 1991.

FEBRUARY

'Wooden Ships' is recorded at Wally Heider's Studio. When it is released three months later, Crosby and Stills receive writing credits, but Paul Kantner, who has contributed two of the verses, requests that his name be omitted to avoid contractual problems with his manager/publisher Matthew Katz.

MARCH

Young continues gigging with Crazy Horse and commences work on a new album, completing 'Cinnamon Girl' (March 20); 'Cowgirl In The Sand' (21); 'Running Dry (Requiem For The Rockets)', 'Everybody Knows This Is Nowhere', 'Round And Round' (all 24); 'The Losing End' (26) and 'Down By The River' (29). The latter, later commandeered by CSN&Y, is a violent tale of passion, but Young insists, "There's no murder in it. It's about blowing your thing with a chick."

3 MARCH

CS&N work on '49 Bye Byes' (combining two Stills' songs: '49 Reasons' and 'Bye Bye Baby'), plus 'Lady Of The Island' and 'Long Time Gone'. The latter causes Crosby to exclaim: "I found my voice! Five years I've been singing and I finally found a voice of my own. Every time I sang a lead part with The Byrds I choked up because I was so scared. But these two loved me enough to let me find my own voice."

18 MARCH

Stills plays with Jack Bruce, Buddy Miles, Buddy Guy, Eric Clapton and Jimmy Page in a jamming session at a disused lino factory in Staines, Middlesex. The results are later captured in the film *Supershow*. Among the material covered is Stills' 'Black Queen'.

21 APRIL

The Flying Burrito Brothers' *The Gilded Palace Of Sin* is released, with Crosby adding harmony to 'Do Right Woman'.

25 APRIL

At Atlantic Studios, Stills attempts to record 'Ivory Tower' for the first time. This is, most likely, a working title for 'Sugar Babe', with the coy reference to Rita Coolidge tagged on at a later recording.

SPRING

With the CS&N album readied for release, the trio lay plans for a summer tour. Although they are quite capable of undertaking a full acoustic tour, Stills is eager to play more electric. "David and Graham were in favour of us going out as a sort of augmented Simon and Garfunkel," he recalled, "but I didn't want to. I wanted a band."

Crosby & Nash's reluctance is understandable. They have already proven themselves performing in front of friends and are aware that the ineffable magic conjured in the studio might be compromised by adding another voice and a longer than anticipated electric set. After some discussion they agree to work out a half acoustic, half electric set,

leaving Stills to find an organ player to fill out the sound. Initially, he seeks the assistance of Steve Winwood and Mark Naftalin, but neither is available to tour. Atlantic president Ahmet Ertegun is the first person to suggest the possibility of recruiting Young. At first Stills is sceptical, quite rightly pointing out that the Canadian had left Buffalo Springfield on two occasions and might let him down again. But the idea of working with Young, perhaps even re-igniting the original spirit of the Springfield, is ultimately irresistible. "So I flew back to California," Stills explains, "went over to Neil's house and asked him what he thought. He'd been to one of our rehearsals and really dug the group sound... so he came along with us and we became Crosby, Stills, Nash & Young which I thought contained just enough of the family element but still retained the individual names so we could all go off in our own directions if and when it folded."

According to Young, his agreement depends upon receiving equal billing, a controversial request considering that he has yet to record with the trio, while they are on the brink of releasing a best-selling album. After some discussion, Stills diplomatically accepts Young's wishes, while a sceptical Nash is won over by the general air of enthusiasm. Crosby, for his part, still insists that he was unaware that the subject of Young's billing had ever been an issue. Any underlying objections are apparently over by the time they visit Young to listen to his latest work and convey the good news. As Crosby recounts: "We thought of him as an equal and intended to bill him as an equal from the very first afternoon we went to his house. And that's the truth. I respected him very much and I never thought of it any other way, and I don't think the other guys ever thought of doing it any other way either... We already knew how good he was. All three of us thought of him as a songwriter of equal value to us. We all knew that we were tremendously successful and he hadn't been yet, but we also knew what he was... He'd already established himself as an equal with Stills in the Springfield, and thereby as an equal with us. He was our contemporary and a friend."

With Young recruited as an additional vocalist, guitarist and keyboard player, the quartet still require a rhythm section. Drummer Dallas Taylor is already in, having played on several tracks on the album, but the bassist is a less obvious choice. Eventually, they settle on Stills and Young's ex-Springfield partner Bruce Palmer. Although the line-up is a formidable one, it is immediately noticeable that Stills has effectively reunited three fifths of the Springfield under the CS&N banner. The possibility of

importing old conflicts and eroding the special
relationship between the CS&N fellowship is
now inextricably part of the package.

14 MAY

Young releases his first collaboration with
Crazy Horse, *Everybody Knows This Is
Nowhere*. Several of the songs featured on the
album will later be adapted for concert
performances with CSN&Y.

20 MAY

At the Record Plant, Stills guests with Jimi
Hendrix and Buddy Miles on Timothy Leary's
You Can Be Anyone This Time Around, which is
finally released in April 1970.

11 JUNE

CSN&Y warm up in the studio playing the old
favourites 'Horses In A Rainstorm',
'Guinnevere' and 'Helplessly Hoping', plus
some jamming with drummer Buddy Miles. On
this same day, a bundle of Stephen Stills'
tapes/lyrics are copyright registered by Gold
Hill Music with apparent haste and ensuing
confusion. They include such titles as 'The
Sparrow', 'Judy', 'Bye Bye Baby' and 'You Make
It Hard' (all of which, the astute will note, are
fragments from poems that were fused
together for 'Suite: Judy Blue Eyes'). Other
working titles include 'No Tomorrow' ('Do For
The Others'), 'Only Part Somehow' ('So Begins
The Task') and 'Ivory Tower' ('Sugar Babe'),
plus the belatedly released 'My Love Is A
Gentle Thing'. Five other Stills' compositions
from the list are unissued: 'All I Know Is What
You Tell Me', 'Dreaming Of Snakes', 'The Need
Of The Giving', 'Visiting Hours' and 'Rocky
Mountain Rhyming'.

15 JUNE

CS&N, plus Neil Young, Bruce Palmer and
Dallas Taylor record an electric version of
'Helplessly Hoping' which remains
unissued until the CS&N boxed set in 1991.
At the same session, they record a playful
version of The Four Tops' 'It's The Same
Old Song'.

16 JUNE

Crosby, Stills & Nash (officially scheduled for
May 29) is released to critical and public acclaim.
Then and now, the definitive example of their
vocal and songwriting power, the album
perfectly encapsulates its time. The exquisite
harmonies, outstanding arrangements, highly
accomplished playing and confident songwriting each contribute to a sound that is
remarkably fresh and hugely influential.
Despite the supergroup tag, there is nothing
artificial, remote or impersonal about this music.
What emerges is a distinctive style, highlighted
by some of the strongest songs of the era,
embracing both the political and the personal.
Doomed lovers and restless radicals, the trio
articulate the pathos and positivity of late 60s
youth, more poignantly than any of their rivals.

CROSBY, STILLS, NASH & YOUNG, JULY 1969

> *"While the others warm to the festival vibes, Young remains strangely detached, and slightly disorientated..."*
>
> **JOHNNY ROGAN**

17 JUNE

While listening to World Pacific tapes for The Byrds' archival *Preflyte* album, Jim Dickson unearths the rare 'Tomorrow Is A Long Ways Away'. Crosby is registered as co-writer for the electric version of the song.

Meanwhile, Atlantic files reveal that CSN&Y are busy recording Stills' 'Bluebird Revisited' (which he will later re-cut for his second solo album) and 'So Begins The Task' (which he saves for Manassas). The foursome also enjoy themselves playing a couple of Four Tops' hits, 'It's The Same Old Song' and 'Reach Out I'll Be There', and two further songs of unknown origin referred to on the tape boxes as 'Boat Song' and 'Far On'. Neither of these titles is copyright registered to any of the group members during this period.

26 JUNE

According to Atlantic's files, some work is completed on a CSN&Y session featuring 'Go Back Home', 'Change Partners', 'Ivory Tower' and The Beatles' 'Blackbird'.

16 JULY

Stills records '4+20' for his first solo album but the song is so entrancing that Crosby & Nash persuade him to use it on *Déjà Vu*. It emerges as one of Stills' most effective and moving performances. One might have assumed that it was an autobiographical work written around late 1968 (Stills' 24th birthday) but, according to Stephen, the song concerns an 84-year-old man who started and ended his life with nothing. How Stills manages to make 4 plus 20 equal 84 is a mathematical mystery.

19 JULY

Atlantic's song files indicate that CSN&Y are working on a song, tentatively titled 'Everyday We Live'. No composer credit is given. It may be a mislabelling of Stills' 'We Are Not Helpless', which featured the phrase "Everyday we *learn*" and on which both Crosby & Nash appeared. On this day, work is also undertaken on the inexplicably mistitled 'You Can Dance Real Good'.

25 JULY

CSN&Y are advertised to play their début live show at the Fillmore East, but the date is postponed due to Graham Nash's throat problems.

2 AUGUST

On the day that Young records 'Oh Lonesome Me', bassist Bruce Palmer is fired from CSN&Y. "Bruce never managed to make it into the band," Crosby tells me. "Stephen liked the way he played and wanted to help him out. Stephen's a very generous man and he likes to make that sort of gesture to people. He got us

into trouble a lot of times that way. Palmer was unstable."

Palmer's replacement is Greg Reeves, a former Tamla Motown bassist, who is recommended by Young's ex-partner Ricky James.

3-10 AUGUST

Young's latest sessions with Crazy Horse continue with 'Wondering' (August 3), 'I Believe In You' (4), 'Birds' (7), and the unreleased composition 'Everybody's Alone' (10).

11-15 AUGUST

CSN&Y undertake rehearsals at Peter Tork's home in Studio City.

16 AUGUST

CSN&Y perform their first gig at the Chicago Auditorium Theater, supported by Joni Mitchell. Their acoustic set reflects their folk community background as the three guitarists huddle close to each other, while Nash stands above them to add the high harmony. With solo cameos to show off their individual songwriting talents, the audience is effectively seeing four performances for the price of one. Such variety is heightened by their second half electric set in which Young frequently switches to organ, leaving Stills to play most of the lead work. The ability to display their talents as both folk troubadours and rock 'n' rollers gives the group a unique edge, which will soon make them one of the biggest draws in rock music. At this concert, they receive three standing ovations and show their solidarity with Joni Mitchell by duetting with her on the closing number – a cover of Dino Valenti's 'Get Together'.

18 AUGUST

In the early hours of the morning, CSN&Y appear at the Woodstock Music And Arts Fair: An Aquarian Exposition in White Lake, New York. It proves the ultimate baptism of fire for the quartet who are sandwiched between the revered Butterfield Blues Band and the bombastic Blood, Sweat & Tears, then in their zenith as a commercial act. On the same bill that day are Joe Cocker, Country Joe And The Fish, Ten Years After, The Band, Johnny Winter and Jimi Hendrix. The intimidating presence of the cream of their contemporaries is exacerbated by the scarcely believable size of the crowd. Original estimates speak optimistically of 200,000 people turning out, but by the day of the festival the numbers exceed half a million, with almost as many being turned away. As the hours pass, CSN&Y

creep further up the bill, unsure of when they will finally go on. Stills recalled: "It was cold and it had rained like hell and we'd been waiting for hours because the equipment hadn't arrived. We were going to use The Band's PA and then we decided to let everyone do their thing first." By the early morning there are still over 30,000 stragglers on site, eagerly awaiting Hendrix and unsure about the still untested CSN&Y. It would be an understatement to describe the group as nervous as Stills realised when he told the audience: "This is the second time we've ever played in front of people, man. We're scared shitless!"

At least Young is spared some of this tension, joining his colleagues after they have completed a handful of acoustic songs. While the others warm to the festival vibes, Young remains strangely detached, and slightly disorientated by the scale of the event. "I went there but I wasn't really into it," he recalled. "It was so big and everything. I didn't know what we were doing, and I saw all these people. It wasn't like it seems now. It was great for the people and for a lot of the musicians... but, for me, I didn't even know what I was doing there."

After performing a full acoustic and electric set comprising 16 songs, CS&N and the reluctant Young establish themselves as the undisputed stars of the festival. Influential *Rolling Stone* critic Greil Marcus praises their performance as "a scary, brilliant proof of the magnificence of music". Ultimately, it proves much more than that. Their achievement rests not so much on the music as the personal empathy they displayed towards the audience, articulating and reflecting its ideals in everything from dress to political pronouncements, stoned asides and an endearing belief in the power of a community united by music. The mythos that Woodstock enshrined was ultimately embodied in the foursome and hereafter their name would become synonymous with the event.

19 AUGUST

Still high from their exploits the previous morning, Crosby and Stills make a surprise appearance alongside Joni Mitchell and members of The Jefferson Airplane on *The Dick Cavett Show*, which is broadcast on ABC this evening. Stephen performs an impressive version of '4 + 20', gamely recovering after missing a line in the second verse. It's a strange show, with Cavett representing the youthful voice of the establishment while Crosby & Stills relate the gospel according to Woodstock.

26-31 AUGUST

CSN&Y play six nights at the Greek Theater, Griffith Park, LA. The set list below provides a

> *"We're actually doing it for free. So, as you didn't pay, shut up, 'cos we're not civilised."*
>
> **DAVID CROSB**

good insight into Young's standing during these early shows. He premières 'Birds' from the forthcoming *After The Goldrush*, returns to his first album for 'I've Loved Her So Long', introduces the organ-based 'Sea Of Madness' and is allowed to close the show with a lengthy rearrangement of 'Down By The River'. Stills, meanwhile, contributes impressive versions of 'So Begins The Task' and 'Bluebird Revisited', both of which will ultimately be held over for post-CSN&Y releases.

SET LIST (AUGUST 26): SUITE: JUDY BLUE EYES: BLACKBIRD: HELPLESSLY HOPING: GUINNEVERE: LADY OF THE ISLAND: BLACK QUEEN: BIRDS: I'VE LOVED HER SO LONG: YOU DON'T HAVE TO CRY: SO BEGINS THE TASK: PRE-ROAD DOWNS: LONG TIME GONE: BLUEBIRD REVISITED: SEA OF MADNESS: WOODEN SHIPS: DOWN BY THE RIVER.

EPTEMBER

CSN&Y record the frantic 'Down By The River' for inclusion in the television programme, *The Music Scene.* As Crosby tells me: "I prefer our version of that song. I didn't like Crazy Horse's."

SEPTEMBER

Donovan's *Barabajagal* is released, with Nash appearing as guest vocalist on 'Happiness Runs'.

SEPTEMBER

Atlantic's archives reveal the usual warm-up versions of 'Horses Through A Rainstorm' and 'Guinnevere', plus Young's 'Sea Of Madness' and 'Birds'.

SEPTEMBER

Atlantic's files log work at Wally Heider's, on Young's 'Sea Of Madness' and Nash's 'Our House' and, confusingly, 'Pre-Road Downs' and 'Suite: Judy Blue Eyes', which have already been released.

SEPTEMBER

A proposed CSN&Y gig at London's Hyde Park, in imitation of the Stones' recent tribute to Brian Jones, is cancelled.

/14 SEPTEMBER

CSN&Y decline the opportunity to appear on the television show *Hollywood Palace*. Instead they turn up at the free Big Sur Folk Festival, along with such contemporaries as Joan Baez, John Sebastian, Joni Mitchell and the UK's Incredible String Band.

The CS&N segment begins with a very impressive rendition of 'Helplessly Hoping', more reminiscent of The Everly Brothers than later in-concert versions. Proceedings are then interrupted by a disillusioned heckler who berates the trio for their superstar accoutrements, ostentatious fox fur coats and financial motivation in playing the festival. Crosby retorts: "We're actually doing it for free. So, as you didn't pay, shut up, 'cos we're not civilised." As if to prove this point, Stills leaves the stage and allows himself to become enmeshed in a heated altercation. "The human comedy rolls on," sighs Crosby in exasperation,

while Stills is on the brink of dumping his cavilling opponent in a nearby pool. "If you push him in the pool Stephen I'll never forgive you..." cries Nash, while Crosby urges, "Peace and love, people – kick his ass!"

The audience then becomes involved in the fracas, prompting Crosby to defend the recalcitrant heckler: "He's just as much a part of this thing as we are, unfortunately, man."

After the fuss is resolved, Crosby is heightened enough to sing a shimmering 'Guinnevere', with those resplendent harmonies perfected over months of informal get-togethers at friends' houses. Nash's 'Lady Of The Island' is also well performed with an intimacy surprising amid such a large gathering. He is followed on-stage by Young who is evidently amused by Stills' shenanigans and exhorts his fellow musicians to be "positive, positive, positive". His version of 'Birds' has the added bonus of strong CS&N harmonies, which gives the song a resonance missing from later solo efforts. He follows up with 'I've Loved Her So Long' which is interrupted by the sighting of a whale, prompting Nash's pun "Home rule for Whales."

Stills returns for '4+20' and feels obliged to explain away his ideological disagreement with the heckler by providing a lecture on

hippie ethics. His summation of the CSN&Y good vibes is amusingly captured in the film *Celebration At Big Sur*, where he explains: "We think about – like the guy was saying. We look at these fur coats, fancy guitars, fancy cars and say, 'Wow, man! What am I doing?' So when somebody gets up and freaks out like that, it kind of strikes a nerve and you end up right back in that old trap. And where that guy is at is in that same trap – and that's getting mad about something. And that ain't nothing, you know, and I had some guys to love me out of it, and I was lucky. We've got to just let it be, because it all will be, however it's gonna."

After closing the "wooden music" segment with 'You Don't Have To Cry', Stills introduces Dave Mason, whom they back on 'World Of Changes' and 'Only You Know And I Know'. An acoustic encore of 'Suite: Judy Blue Eyes' follows, before Young, Reeves and Taylor re-emerge for the electric set. Young's ragged and obviously hurried 'Sea Of Madness' is succeeded by a powerful version of 'Long Time Gone', with heavy organ backing. Nash then reintroduces Stills who is about to sing "a song on our new album, when it comes out". Proof that the final selection for *Déjà Vu* came from any number of songs is emphasised by what follows: 'Bluebird Revisited'.

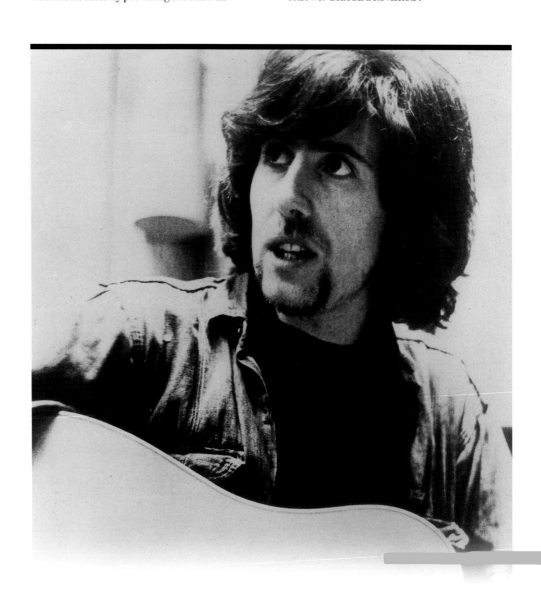

The final segment of the show features solid electric workouts of 'Pre-Road Downs', 'Wooden Ships' and an elongated 'Down By The River', complete with troubled tuning. Part of the set is later captured for posterity on *Wooden Nickel*, one of the earliest rock bootleg releases.

Commenting on the weekend, seasoned critic Ralph J. Gleason compliments Stills as "one of the best lyric songwriters in all of contemporary music" and congratulates CSN&Y "who provided not only the excitement but the most musically rewarding moments. They have a superlative repertoire of songs, they are all excellent musicians and each of them can sing beautifully. David Crosby's 'Long Time Comin'' has already joined the roster of themes of the new generation. It is a fine song and they do it superbly."

SET LIST (SEPTEMBER 13): HELPLESSLY HOPING; GUINNEVERE; LADY OF THE ISLAND; BIRDS; 4+20; YOU DON'T HAVE TO CRY; SEA OF MADNESS; WOODEN SHIPS; DOWN THE RIVER.
(SEPTEMBER 14): SUITE: JUDY BLUE EYES; PRE-ROAD DOWNS; LONG TIME GONE; BLUEBIRD REVISITED; SEA OF MADNESS; DOWN BY THE RIVER; GET TOGETHER (WITH JONI MITCHELL).

19–20 SEPTEMBER

CSN&Y complete four shows in two nights at the Fillmore East, New York. *The Village Voice* is quick to trumpet the first night as a personal triumph for Captain Manyhands: "Clearly, the dominant instrumental voice was Stephen Stills'. He is one of the most remarkably versatile musicians I've ever heard – in any context – but more than that, he is an artist, a performer who understands that silences, too, are part of music."

Backstage, there is anything but silence. Stills carelessly overruns his acoustic solo segment, prompting a fierce argument during the intermission. Fired up by the conflict, the foursome effectively settle their differences during a fierce, cathartic electric set. *The New York Times* picks up on the mood and reports: "During their first set on Friday the best moment was when Mr Stills and Mr Young traded guitar lines back and forth during an extended instrumental in the country song, 'Down By The River'."

Overseeing all four concerts is *NME*'s New York correspondent June Harris, who is completely astonished by the proceedings. After recovering from the shows, she enthuses: "Opening night was fantastic! Rarely have I seen an act with so much magnetism, so much individual strength and talent! As each of the four shows unfolded, yet another member of the group began to take a special aura. For most Americans, David Crosby is the figurehead – maybe because he's the most articulate and poetic... The group, still new, still without the benefit of months and months of rehearsal, is incredible. It's love and warmth and audience communication. It's not far out, sound blasting rock, but taste and simplicity and incredible material."

SET LIST (SEPTEMBER 20): SUITE: JUDY BLUE EYES; BLACKBIRD; HELPLESSLY HOPING; GUINNEVERE; LADY OF THE ISLAND; GO BACK HOME; 4+20; ON THE WAY HOME; BROKEN ARROW; I'VE LOVED HER SO LONG; YOU DON'T HAVE TO CRY; PRE-ROAD DOWNS; LONG TIME GONE; BLUEBIRD REVISITED; SEA OF MADNESS; WOODEN SHIPS; DOWN BY THE RIVER.

20 SEPTEMBER
Crosby's girlfriend, Christine Gail Hinton, is killed in a car accident north of San Francisco. The tragedy leaves David traumatised and gigs scheduled for early the following month are cancelled. As Nash acutely observed: "David went to identify the body and he's never been the same since."

WINTER
Nash's relationship with Joni Mitchell reaches its denouement after the highs recorded on 'Our House' and 'Willy'. Throughout the romance, Crosby has shown no signs of jealousy, living up to his free love philosophy with remarkable candour. Recalling his untainted friendship with Nash, he explains: "I credit it to us all really caring about each other. We all loved each other very much and these were not very possessive relationships. When I went with Joan I loved her and all of it was a wonderful time but I didn't expect to stay there, and neither did she. When she went to Graham, my feeling was 'how could I feel unhappy about two people I really loved being together?' I couldn't see anything wrong with that. I didn't feel I owned her in the first place and we avoided most of the pitfalls there."

OCTOBER
Young switches tack and records a version of 'Helpless' with Crazy Horse, plus the obscure 'All The Things I Gotta Do Girl'. The latter may well be Danny Whitten's 'Look At All The Things', which subsequently appeared on the first Crazy Horse album. Both these Young/Crazy Horse collaborations remain locked in the tape vaults.

OCTOBER
Atlantic's session files reveal that some work is done on Crosby's 'Song With No Words (Tree With No Leaves)', Stills' 'Bluebird Revisited', 'Questions' and probable warm-ups of 'Helplessly Hoping' and 'Blackbird', plus Nash's 'Right Between The Eyes' and 'When You Were Asleep' ['Sleep Song'], Young's 'Round And Round' and the cover of Joni Mitchell's 'Woodstock'. Two further titles are mentioned: Nash's unreleased 'Cologne' ['Why Baby Why'] and 'He Died For Mary'.

OCTOBER
CSN&Y work on another unreleased song, tentatively titled '30 Dollar Fine'.

OCTOBER
Atlantic files indicate that further studio work is undertaken on Nash's 'Teach Your Children'

and Young's 'Helpless'. Crosby is particularly impressed by the emotional power of 'Helpless', stressing: "I liked the harmonies and the overall power of the thing. However, I thought it was unfortunate that he did his songs so much by himself. He wouldn't let us have much to do with them. He would cut the tracks by himself, then we would arrange them vocally and sing them."

24 OCTOBER
Nash's 'Teach Your Children' (*Déjà Vu*) and Crosby's 'Laughing' (*If I Could Only Remember My Name*) are worked on at Wally Heider's Studio C, San Francisco. Atlantic tape files also indicate studio work on Stills' 'Ivory Tower' ('Sugar Babe'), 'Beginning' (probably 'So Begins The Task'), Crosby's 'Almost Cut My Hair' and Young's unreleased 'Everybody's Alone'.

25 OCTOBER
CSN&Y appear on *The Tom Jones Show* performing 'You Don't Have To Cry' and 'Long Time Gone'. Jones joins Crosby for the latter which proves one of the most memorable and amusing vocal showcases of the period. Although the memory of Jones The Voice singing along with CS&N later causes them no small embarrassment, Stills is quick to add: "I really dig Tom Jones... he's got incredible chops".

27 OCTOBER
Atlantic files indicate that further studio work is undertaken on '30 Dollar Fine', 'Woodstock' and 'Our House'.

30 OCTOBER
Studio work is logged for CSN&Y's version of Stills' 'Questions' (later 'Carry On'), Crosby's 'Déjà Vu' and 'Almost Cut My Hair' and the uncredited and possibly mislabelled composition, 'You're Wrong Baby'.

1 NOVEMBER
More session work is done on Nash's 'Teach Your Children'. The track had begun as a folk tune until Stills decided to "make it swing" with a more upbeat arrangement. With Jerry Garcia brought in on steel guitar, the song will finally emerge as a rare country outing from the trio.

3 NOVEMBER
Studio time is logged at Wally Heider's for Crosby's 'Déjà Vu' and 'Almost Cut My Hair'. The latter proves one of his most passionate

songs to date but the unembarrassed proselytising lyrics later make him an easy target for conservative critics. "I've been criticised for it a lot," Crosby admits. "A lot of people think it's my most juvenile piece of work, but I like it because it feels good. It expressed a feeling of a time and of an awful lot of people."

5 NOVEMBER
CSN&Y record 'Woodstock', written by Joni Mitchell who, of course, did not attend the festival. An alternate take of the song is used for the closing credits of the film. This may be the version which Young commented upon when

> *"It was a very tough time for me. It was right after Christine got killed and I was not at my best as a functioning person. I would sometimes come into the studio and end up crying, being unable to deal with it all".*
>
> **DAVID CROSBY**

he criticised Stills for needlessly re-recording an excellent vocal take. A third alternate mix of the song appears on the CSN boxed set. This same day work is logged for Young's 'Country Girl' and Nash's 'Our House'.

6 NOVEMBER
The interminable studio logging details work on 'Blackbird', 'Ivory Tower' ('Sugar Babe'), 'Questions', 'Almost Cut My Hair', 'Our House', 'Black Queen', 'Country Girl', 'Helpless' and the unissued '30 Dollar Fine'.

7 NOVEMBER
CSN&Y record Young's 'Helpless' for the forthcoming *Déjà Vu*. Studio time is also invested in Stills' 'Change Partners' and 'Sugar Babe', 'Woodstock' and the unissued '30 Dollar Fine'. There is also some early work noted for the Stills/Young amalgam 'Everybody I Love You'. Finally, the Atlantic files log this date for a warm-up version of The Beatles' 'You've Got To Hide Your Love Away' plus the unissued and largely unknown 'Master My Fear', 'She Can't Handle It' and 'Whole People'.

9 NOVEMBER
CSN&Y return to Crosby's former home town for a performance at the University of California, Santa Barbara.

12 NOVEMBER
Further studio time is allotted to work on The Beatles' 'Blackbird' and the erroneously titled 'Sea Song' (probably Crosby's 'The Lee Shore').
   "It was a very tough time for me," Crosby explains, in mitigation of the seemingly endless studio sessions. "It was right after Christine got killed and I was not at my best as a functioning person. I would sometimes come into the studio and end up crying, being unable to deal with it all".

13–16 NOVEMBER

An eventful four-night stint at the Winterland Ballroom sees CSN&Y at their most engaging. There is drama on the second night when Crosby loses his voice, having sacrificed his vocal cords during a Vietnam Moratorium earlier in the week. It says much for the confidence of the group that they can disguise such shortcomings so effectively. Part of their charm comes from an intense engagement with the audience mixed with liberal helpings of subtle comedy and undisguised camaraderie. Nash is particularly effective at this, introducing his fellow musician as "my brother Stephen Stills" and making The Hollies the butt of his hippie humour. "Anyone see The Hollies on television tonight?" he asks the audience. "The shit they gave me. Ever worked for four years with four *straight* people?"

As for the music, it is exemplary. In addition to the material from the current album, they reach back to The Buffalo Springfield and Stills adds a surprise version of John Sebastian's 'How Have You Been'. For those generous or misguided enough to describe CSN&Y as the new Beatles, Nash deadpans "Rock on George for Ringo one time," quoting the catchphrase in 'Honey Don't' from *Beatles For Sale*.

The sense of event at Winterland is noted by Ralph Gleason, arguably America's leading rock music critic of the period, who observes: "If there is such a thing as a supergroup, they qualify. They are certainly the most lyrical expression of contemporary music of any group save The Beatles. Everything they do, they do flawlessly. Almost too good to be true… Although they do almost all of the songs from their hit album, they resist the temptation to do them exactly as on the LP. They play with the voicings, getting an unusually sophisticated and delightful blend, as well as engaging in expert contrapuntal vocal effects, lines playing against each other in perfect arrangement."

SET LIST (13 NOVEMBER): SUITE: JUDY BLUE EYES; BLACKBIRD; ON THE WAY HOME; GUINNEVERE; LADY OF THE ISLAND; HOW HAVE YOU BEEN; BLACK QUEEN; HELPLESS; I'VE LOVED HER SO LONG; YOU DON'T HAVE TO CRY; LONG TIME GONE; DOWN BY THE RIVER; FIND THE COST OF FREEDOM.

17 NOVEMBER

Crosby & Nash record David's 'Song With No Words (Tree With No Leaves)', a track which will later feature regularly in their performances as a duo in 1971. This version was belatedly issued on the CSN boxed set, while a superior arrangement can be heard on Crosby's solo album, *If I Could Only Remember My Name*. Atlantic files suggest that the final version of Crosby's 'Déjà Vu' was completed this same evening.

22 NOVEMBER

CSN&Y fly to Hawaii for a performance at the Honolulu International Center Arena on the anniversary of JFK's assassination.

26 NOVEMBER

Copyright records reveal a previously unknown writing collaboration between Crosby and Terrance O. Callier (Terry Collier) on the unreleased composition 'Naiomi'.

Meanwhile, CSN&Y appear at the Denver Coliseum in Colorado, near to where Stills purchases a log cabin as a winter retreat.

SET LIST: SUITE: JUDY BLUE EYES; BLACKBIRD; HELPLESSLY HOPING; GUINNEVERE; TEACH YOUR CHILDREN; LADY OF THE ISLAND; BLACK QUEEN; 49 BYE BYES/AMERICA'S CHILDREN; I'VE LOVED HER SO LONG; HELPLESS; ON THE WAY HOME; YOU DON'T HAVE TO CRY; PRE-ROAD DOWNS; SO BEGINS THE TASK; LONG TIME GONE; WOODSTOCK; WOODEN SHIPS; DOWN BY THE RIVER; ALMOST CUT MY HAIR.

29 NOVEMBER

CSN&Y's tour continues with a visit to the Veterans' Memorial Coliseum, Phoenix, Arizona.

2 DECEMBER

Further studio work takes place on Stills' '4 + 20' and the oddly titled 'Everyday We Live'.

5 DECEMBER

CSN&Y return to the Golden State for an appearance at the State Fairgrounds, Sacramento.

6 DECEMBER

CSN&Y appear at the Altamont Speedway, near Livermore in Northern California, for a free festival to appease critics of the "bread head" Rolling Stones, who have recently been attacked in print by Stephen Stills' champion, Ralph Gleason. The other acts on the bill read like a litany of Crosby's friends: Jefferson Airplane, Santana and The Flying Burrito Brothers. What is intended to serve as another mini-Woodstock ends up as the dark mirror for all the optimism of the age. The fateful decision to employ Hell's Angels to police the event creates a cauldron of smouldering intimidation and undisguised violence, which will eventually cost the life of Meredith Hunter, whose grisly slaying is brutally captured in the film of the event, *Gimme Shelter*.

The presence of CSN&Y at such a negatively epochal event is so antithetical to everything they represent that for years it is effectively written out of rock history. Their non-appearance in the film induces widespread amnesia among the rock press, while they seldom talk of the disaster, preferring to accentuate the stoned bliss of Woodstock. But CSN&Y were participants at Altamont, which is akin to reminding us of Crosby's heroin use amid the non-addictive splendour of LSD.

By the time they take the stage, CSN&Y are painfully aware of the violence preceding their arrival. The Jefferson Airplane had found themselves in conflict with the Angels' heavy-handed stewarding to such an extent that Marty Balin had been bludgeoned unconscious. Although The Flying Burrito Brothers' set calms matters somewhat, sporadic assaults ensue as CSN&Y look on aghast.

Music is a secondary consideration by this stage, but they rally as best they can. Stills introduces a funky, electric 'Black Queen', with a noticeable Motown R&B feel. Meanwhile, men and women are subject to random attacks from Hell's Angels wielding billiard cues. From the stage, a muffled Crosby implores: "Hey, crazy people, stop hurting each other, man. You don't have to. Please, man. You can always talk, man." The words prove as ineffectual as Jagger's pathetic pleas later in the night. After a jagged 'Pre-Road Downs', Crosby sings an intense 'Long Time Gone', urging the bloodied audience to "speak your mind, that is if you still have the guts." Both the sentiments and execution of the song are deadly appropriate. A lengthy 'Down By The River' allows the foursome to lose themselves in a jamming session, after which they make a hasty exit, scrambling into a waiting helicopter, and escaping from the ugly carnage.

> "If there is such a thing as a supergroup, they qualify. They are certainly the most lyrical expression of contemporary music of any group since The Beatles."
>
> RALPH GLEASON

Later that evening, they squeeze in a two-hour show at the Pauley Pavilion, UCLA, supported by Taj Mahal. There, at least, they can expect a civilised reception and are duly granted the anticipated accolades from the *Los Angeles Times*, whose discerning critic Robert Hilburn confirms them as "an unqualified success", adding "each is an immensely talented writer, singer and musician". Not for the first time, Stephen is singled out for special commendation with Hilburn proclaiming: "Still in his mid-20s, Stills is one of the most impressive talents in rock. His blues vocals are more daring and his lyrics more universal than almost anyone else on the contemporary scene. He is also an exceptionally fine guitarist who does not employ the artificial flashiness that many mistake for artistry in some guitarists."

SET LIST: (ALTAMONT EXTRACT): BLACK QUEEN; PRE-ROAD DOWNS; LONG TIME GONE; DOWN BY THE RIVER.

13 DECEMBER

After playing in Pittsburgh (December 11) and Cleveland, Ohio (12), CSN&Y return to the scene of their first gig at the Chicago Auditorium. Young includes 'Country Girl' and 'Helpless' from the forthcoming *Déjà Vu*, while Stills extends his "America's Children" poem to discuss the merits of the current Democratic Convention at the Hilton.

Meanwhile, *Rolling Stone* report Crosby's plan to transform 'Wooden Ships' into a movie, with a script by science fiction writer Theodore Sturgeon. Although there will be continued talk of a film project over the next year, nothing emerges.

14–18 DECEMBER

The CSN&Y tour stretches further across America with appearances at the Masonic Temple Theater, Detroit, Michigan (December 14), Tingley Coliseum, Albuquerque, New Mexico (17) and the Hofheinz Pavilion, Houston, Texas (18).

21 DECEMBER

One of the more amusing and delightfully shambolic appearances by CSN&Y takes place at an outdoor football stadium in Balboa, San Diego. The opening 'Suite: Judy Blue Eyes' is plagued with sound problems and the musicians find it difficult to hear themselves. "It's feeding back," they cry impatiently. Recovering their poise midway through the song, they are about to hit the crucial crescendo 'chestnut brown canary', when a plane swoops overhead, completely drowning out their harmonies for several seconds.

After struggling through 'Suite: Judy Blue Eyes', Nash jokes: "I don't know which one of you was conducting the aeroplane, but you made a fantastic job!"

Stills is determined to push on, but fails to get beyond the opening line of 'Blackbird' before Crosby interjects, "Let's wait until we can get it right. There's a continuing feedback problem here that we're having... It appears to have something to do with the guitar mike and the monitors."

Following further technical adjustments, a very tentative 'Blackbird' is completed, by which time they are more than pleased to introduce Neil Young. That, in itself, proves a mixed blessing for the Canadian is known to have tuning problems when placed under duress... and so it proves.

After an agonising wait, Young performs a pleasing 'On The Way Home' which is notable for some attractive acoustic strumming. The quartet then debate what to play, given the various sound problems, and eventually decide upon the old acoustic faithful, 'Helplessly Hoping'. Unfortunately, it is terminated before the end of the first verse as a result of an even louder plane which sounds as though the pilot is using the stadium as a landing base. Looking skyward, Stills wryly observes: "Boy, there sure is a lot going on today."

As if feedback, technical problems and intrusive aeroplanes weren't enough, there next follows an outburst in the audience. A crazed young man, clearly unable to take all the excitement, starts pushing his way to the front, crying: "I'm sorry. I don't care." Observing from high, Nash proclaims: "He must be a drunk! Grass people don't act like that." Stills is surprisingly sympathetic to the troubled interloper and simply adds: "If ever a man needed a friend!"

At last, the interruptions temporarily cease, as the musicians desperately attempt to refocus on 'Helplessly Hoping', but they betray a detectable uncertainty, as if they're already wondering what will happen next. Young calms matters with 'Helpless', which features a slightly shaky piano accompaniment, after which Stills is ready for his solo spot.

"It's really hard to concentrate in a football

STEPHEN STILLS AT WOODSTOCK

stadium," he points out. "We played kind of quiet for a while to get everyone a bit mellow." Clearly, it's time to raise the pace and Stills responds with the wailing, acoustic 'Black Queen', followed by the now familiar '49 Bye Byes/For What It's Worth/America's Children' medley in which he tells us that we should let the "pigs" fight among themselves rather than allowing them to attack the "children".

The audience is now ready for the electric set, commencing with the frantic 'Pre-Road Downs' which, Nash correctly observes, "warms the cockles of your heart." Stills selects the country 'n' western-tinged 'So Begins The Task', but is again outdone by a pesky plane during the final verse. Crosby responds to the aeronautical onslaught with a brutish 'Long Time Gone' with Young providing the organ backing. The audience is now ready to rock, but David insists that it is "Twilight Zone time". Rather than racing into the next song, he encourages the crowd to sit back and listen to a "science fiction story." Once they're sitting comfortably, he begins: "It's about these guys who survive something – an accidental war... one of our modern wonders... Anyway, they survive and they run into each other in the woods and instead of knocking each other off – which, of course, is what people are supposed to do – accidentally, one of them smiles at the other. So they decide to be friends and they band together and survive... They work out a language and music and decide that they dig each other and after a while they love each other and start to get it on and they ride off into the sunset. But, mind you, it couldn't happen here. It's only a fantasy... it's called 'Wooden Ships'."

Stills then produces the new guitar that his comrades have just bought him for Christmas and tunes the instrument in preparation for a final assault. Eventually, they click into 'Wooden Ships' which builds into a powerful jam, successfully wrestling with the continued feedback from the monitors. With passions high, they close with the epic 'Down By The River', its tortuous, jagged rhythms uninterrupted by stage announcements, stoned hecklers or noise polluting planes.

SET LIST: SUITE: JUDY BLUE EYES; BLACKBIRD; ON THE WAY HOME; HELPLESSLY HOPING; HELPLESS; BLACK QUEEN; 49 BYE-BYES/AMERICA'S CHILDREN; PRE-ROAD DOWNS; SO BEGINS THE TASK; LONG TIME GONE; WOODEN SHIPS; DOWN BY THE RIVER; FIND THE COST OF FREEDOM.

22 DECEMBER

Atlantic's files suggest that further studio work is executed on CSN&Y's version of Stills' stoical song of rejection 'So Begins The Task'. Reflecting on his turbulent love life during this period, Stills, paraphrasing Lawrence Durrell, observes: "There are three things men can do with women: love them, suffer for them or turn them into literature. I've had my share of success and failure on all three."

28 DECEMBER

CSN&Y record the Graham Nash/Terry Reid composition 'Horses Through A Rainstorm' at Stills' house in Laurel Canyon and work it up at Wally Heider's. Despite featuring all four members, the song is not deemed strong enough for inclusion on *Déjà Vu*, and remains unheard by the general public until the 1991 CSN boxed set. According to Atlantic's files, Stills' remarkable 'Carry On' is also cut this same evening in what its composer claims was "a grand total of eight hours from conception to finished master". It is accompanied by a backing track for Crosby's 'The Lee Shore'. The latter, a full CSN&Y recording, features Young on acoustic guitar and harmonica and Stills on lead. Although Crosby's solo reading of the song in concert is later featured on the live *4 Way Street*, this exemplary recording remains in the vaults until the CSN boxed set in 1991.

1970

6 JANUARY

CSN&Y appear at London's Royal Albert Hall, playing before a star-studded audience that includes Paul McCartney, Donovan, Marsha Hunt and Julie Felix. "That was the first time we've ever really been affected by nerves," Stills tells *Melody Maker*, forgetting for a moment how scared shitless he was at Woodstock. "At the Albert Hall we felt somehow as if we were on trial, as if they'd come to judge us rather than our music... We got criticised for spending a long time tuning up, which is partly justified because I like to tune up while I'm playing a little bit of music, so that it doesn't sound unpleasant. But when Neil gets nervous he plays very hard and puts his guitar out of tune and then has to tune it back again."

Revealingly, critic and columnist Miles Kington claims that Crosby offers the strongest acoustic set and Young the weakest. At least the Canadian receives some positive comments for the *tour de force* 'Down By The River' as UK reporters adjust their critical spectacles to ponder CS&N's unusual decision in adding another songwriter to their ranks.

SET LIST: SUITE: JUDY BLUE EYES; BLACKBIRD; ON THE WAY HOME; TEACH YOUR CHILDREN; TRIAD; GUINNEVERE; LADY OF THE ISLAND; OUR HOUSE; COUNTRY GIRL; HELPLESS; BLACK QUEEN; 49 BYE BYES/AMERICA'S CHILDREN; PRE-ROAD DOWNS; SO BEGINS THE TASK; LONG TIME GONE; THE LONER; WOODEN SHIPS; DOWN BY THE RIVER; FIND THE COST OF FREEDOM.

/11 JANUARY

CSN&Y undertake a brief visit to Scandinavia, appearing at the Konserthuset, Stockholm (January 9) and the Falkoner Centret (11).

Meanwhile, back in the USA, studio work or tape delivery of some description is logged at Atlantic for the unreleased Stills' composition 'Right On Rock And Roll', the unissued CSN&Y version of 'So Begins The Task' and 'Almost Cut My Hair'. Contrary to claims on the CSN boxed set, the latter is clearly not recorded on January 9 (when the quartet was still in Stockholm), but had been completed the previous November.

SET LIST: SUITE: JUDY BLUE EYES; BLACKBIRD; YOU DON'T HAVE TO CRY; ON THE WAY HOME; TEACH YOUR CHILDREN; TRIAD; GUINNEVERE; OUR HOUSE; HELPLESS; COUNTRY GIRL; BLACK QUEEN; 49 BYE BYES/AMERICA'S CHILDREN; HELPLESSLY HOPING; PRE-ROAD DOWNS; SO BEGINS THE TASK; LONG TIME GONE; THE LONER; WOODEN SHIPS; DOWN BY THE RIVER; FIND THE COST OF FREEDOM.

FEBRUARY

Stills settles in England, first renting, and subsequently buying, Ringo Starr's 15th

century manor, Brookfield House, in Elstead, Surrey. There he surrounds himself with the luxuries of an English gentlemen: a sauna, fine wines, antiques, and a couple of thoroughbred horses named Major Change and Crazy Horse. Amid the splendour, Stills eagerly prepares material for his all important first solo album.

11 FEBRUARY

Nash belatedly copyright registers 'Wings', 'Teach Your Children' and 'Our House', along with 'Right Between The Eyes' (inadequately titled 'A Man's A Man'), plus several more songs, which remain unissued: 'Be Patient', 'Can Any Man', 'Song For My Father' and 'Why, Baby, Why'.

19 FEBRUARY

The final masters of *Déjà Vu* are registered at Atlantic Records.

20 FEBRUARY

Stills begins studio work on 'Old Times, Good Times', 'Go Back Home', Sit Yourself Down' and 'To A Flame' at Island Studios in London.

24 FEBRUARY

Stills' 'Carry On' and '4+ 20' are registered for copyright purposes.

24 FEBRUARY – 28 MARCH

Young undertakes a tour with Crazy Horse, taking in Cincinnati, Philadelphia, Boston, New York and Santa Monica. The shows are most notable for his acoustic readings of several Buffalo Springfield classics, including 'Broken Arrow', 'Flying On The Ground Is Wrong' and 'Expecting To Fly'. The set list below, from the Electric Factory, Philadelphia (February 28), features the only known live version of Young's cover of 'Oh Lonesome Me'.

SET LIST: ON THE WAY HOME; I AM A CHILD; BROKEN ARROW; FLYING ON THE GROUND IS WRONG; DANCE. DANCE. DANCE; EXPECTING TO FLY; THE LONER; WINTERLONG; EVERYBODY KNOWS THIS IS NOWHERE; WONDERING; OH LONESOME ME; CINNAMON GIRL; COME ON BABY LET'S GO DOWNTOWN; DOWN BY THE RIVER.

8 MARCH

Stills makes a guest appearance on Ringo Starr's 'It Don't Come Easy'. He also works with Apple recording artiste Doris Troy, who helps him improve his vocal technique.

EARLY MARCH

At Island Studios, Stills and Eric Clapton deign to guest on each other's solo albums. Stills plays bass on, and provides backing harmonies to, 'Let It Rain' and Clapton engages in a guitar duel on the astonishing 'Go Back Home'. There is also a drinking contest, which culminates in Stills writing and performing the bluesy 'Black Queen'. "I just walked in the studio and did it," he told Allan MacDougall. "Before that Eric and I had played 'Tequila' for about an hour and a half and then all of a sudden he was gone. He disappeared. He realised that if he didn't go he

CROSBY, STILLS, NASH & YOUNG

was going to pass out in the studio, so he got someone to drive him home while he was still able to reach the car... I stumbled right into the studio and that's what came out. I'd been out to Eric's house the night before listening to Blind Willie Johnson records, and so the vocal quality is *arrrgh*. It sounds like a saw. It hurts physically, it hurt my throat to sing like that, but it sure does sound neat." The rough demo will subsequently feature on Stills' début solo album, accompanied by a dedication to Jose Cuervo Tequila.

15 MARCH
Stills records 'Old Times Good Times' at Island Studios with Jimi Hendrix on lead guitar. They also record several jams which remain unissued.

16 MARCH
John B. Sebastian is released with Crosby and Stills playing guitars on 'She's A Lady', Nash singing high harmony on 'What She Thinks About' and Stills playing lead guitar on 'Baby Don't Ya Go Crazy'.

18 MARCH
Confusingly, one week before the release of *Déjà Vu*, two Stills/Young collaborations are registered for copyright, 'Everybody I Love You' and 'Everybody We Love You'. The former we know about, but was the latter possibly considered under that title in tribute to The Rolling Stones?

This same day, Stills and Jimi Hendrix entertain Germaine Greer and others with an after-hours jamming session at The Speakeasy in London.

21 MARCH
Reprise tape archives indicate that Young has delivered tapes of the following: 'Only Love Can Break Your Heart', 'Winterlong', 'Come On Baby Let's Go Downtown', 'After The

Goldrush', 'Till The Morning Comes', 'Tell Me Why', 'Don't Let It Bring You Down' and 'Southern Man'.

23 MARCH
Déjà Vu (officially scheduled for March 11) is released and soon climbs to number 1 in the US charts. One of the most important albums of its era, it captured the full creative weight of CSN&Y and confirmed their standing in the popular imagination as the only group likely to fill the musical gap left by the break-up of The Beatles. Despite CSN&Y's insistence that they will not follow the standard group game plan, few believed that they could walk away from music this powerful. Their critics would have been amazed to learn that the foursome would not complete another studio album for an astonishing 18 years.

13 APRIL
Nash's recent writing spree continues with the unreleased 'Isle Of Dew'.

14 APRIL
Stills flies into LA from London and then proceeds to enact the lyrics of Crosby's 'Almost Cut My Hair' by spotting a cop in the mirror of his rear view mirror, driving off quickly and crashing into a parked car near his Laurel Canyon home. He fractures his wrist, thereby delaying CSN&Y's forthcoming tour. Stills retires to Hawaii to recover amid pleasant surroundings.

3 MAY
Reprise archives indicate that Young has recorded the fragmentary 'Cripple Creek Ferry' which will be featured on his third album.

4 MAY
Four students are killed at Kent State University, Ohio by National Guardsmen, an event that will soon prompt retaliatory action by CSN&Y.

10 MAY
Stills' problems continue when he is thrown from a horse and tears a knee ligament. Doctors insist that he can still play CSN&Y's Denver concert in two days' time but will be confined to a cast for the next couple of weeks.

11 MAY
Bassist Greg Reeves falls victim to delusion and disillusionment, maintaining that he should be allowed to perform his own material in concert, a concession already made to Young. With their drummer also threatening to emerge as a songwriter, the quartet decide that Reeves must be fired. He is immediately replaced by Calvin Samuels, fresh from working on Stills' solo album.

As an incredulous Nash explains, "Dallas was writing songs and Greg was writing songs and Greg, actually more than Dallas, was constantly wanting to do their songs on stage. And they weren't ready... It's taken me 10 or 15 years to get where I am now. Greg couldn't handle the refusal of not wanting to do his material on stage. It wouldn't have worked because it was a little naïve."

12 MAY
A disastrous gig in Denver ends in an explosion of sensitive egos. Crosby & Nash complain of hoarseness from over strenuous rehearsals; Samuels has problems playing the group's material at such short notice; and Stills has taken to wielding his walking stick like a baton as though he were an orchestra leader. To top it all, Young is in bitter conflict with drummer Dallas Taylor over his playing and afterwards offers the ultimatum: "Either he goes, or I go". Dallas goes.

14 MAY
CSN&Y are scheduled to play the Chicago Auditorium, but split up prior to the gig, amid acrimony and squabbling. The combination of Stills' coked-up dominance and the recent problems with the rhythm section all take their toll on the music, which is reason enough to

NEIL YOUNG, ROYAL ALBERT HALL, JANUARY 1970

call a halt. "The music was rubbish and we knew it," Nash concluded. "We had to cool ourselves out before we could get back again."

Crosby eloquently summed up the group dynamics that precipitated the split. "Graham and I had a natural competitive problem with Stills because he's a lead player and he was always a dominant force. The idea was that we were equals in this band and that no-one was the leader. That's one of the reasons we used our own names... I think Stephen always felt that Nash and I were resentful or trying to obstruct him, and I felt that Stephen was overbearing. I felt that he didn't really give us credit where it was due. In a thoughtless moment he'd say things like, 'They're just my back-up singers' to people. That would naturally piss us off."

Stills admits being affected by fame and occasionally hogging the limelight on-stage, but even he felt undone by the sudden disintegration of the group. Reflecting on all that had been lost, he later told biographer Dave Zimmer: "If a voice of reason could have cleared that fog, we would have realised our full potential and CSN&Y would be mentioned in the same breath with The Beatles and the Stones... We all lost right there, that day, to indulgence. We lost it all".

18 MAY

Nobody is entirely certain when the four will reconvene, but common sense and simple economics dictate that they must fulfil some of their outstanding dates or lose a fortune in litigation. Accepting the inevitable, they agree to continue the tour later in the month, knowing that they will be free to pursue other ventures thereafter.

Interestingly, Stills reveals to Penny Valentine that CS&N may have been influenced by Young's career strategy: "Subconsciously, I think we all figured when Neil came into the band that he'd done things the right way by having been out on the road alone in the first

place. And when the heat got too bad and we started falling apart, when we were hurting each other and doing really nasty things to each other and starting to work out our frustrations on each other like it was a marriage, we realised we'd have to hold up and go do a record by ourselves or something and come back together later – keep the balance."

20 MAY

During the same week that the film *Woodstock* is premièred in London, the triple album of the same name is released. Stills recalls his embarrassment after witnessing their rough version of 'Suite: Judy Blue Eyes': "There's a wonderful moment in the film when we're doing the 'Suite' and I'm sitting there and between each line I've got this horrible grimace on my face and I keep reaching and fiddling with my guitar. By the time we got two thirds through it I finally had the guitar in tune. It's all there in real life living colour – Stephen Stills trying to tune his guitar, keep it together and make an impression at Woodstock."

The album also purports to feature Young's composition 'Sea Of Madness' but in a classic piece of jiggery pokery this turns out to be a version of the song taken from another date on the tour. It makes you wonder how many more songs purporting to be Woodstock performances may have been borrowed from elsewhere... or is Young the peculiar exception?

21 MAY

CSN&Y record 'Ohio' and 'Find The Cost Of Freedom' at the Record Plant in LA with new drummer Johnny Barbata. Crosby recalls the dramatic circumstances that precipitate the recording:

"It was done in one day. Neil and I were sitting in Butano Canyon up North. I handed him *Life* magazine with a report of the Kent State killings. He read the article, picked up the guitar, and started writing the song. I watched

him write it. He and I then got on the plane, went to Los Angeles, went into the studio with Stills and Nash, made the record and put 'Find The Cost Of Freedom' on the back of it. We gave it to Ahmet Ertegun that evening; he took it to Atlantic on the plane that night, and it was out a week later."

Arguably their greatest moment together in the studio, 'Ohio' displays a strength in unity that they would seldom match in later collaborations. Crosby's anguished screams of 'why' at the close of the song brilliantly capture the sense of anger and disbelief that they all felt. It's no surprise to learn that he openly wept at the end of the session.

29/30 MAY

With Calvin Samuels and Johnny Barbata, CSN&Y resume their interrupted tour with performances at the Boston Garden (May 29) and the Civic Center, Baltimore (30). *The Washington Post* provides a glowing review, suggesting that "Like The Band, CSN&Y are four marvellously talented individuals who lose nothing to collectivity. Their harmony is perfect, and each one is vocally strong as an individual. The toughest part of watching them is trying to figure out who's best..."

SET LIST (MAY 29): SUITE: JUDY BLUE EYES; ON THE WAY HOME; TEACH YOUR CHILDREN; TELL ME WHY; TRIAD; GUINNEVERE; SIMPLE MAN; MAN IN THE MIRROR; DON'T LET IT BRING YOU DOWN; ONLY LOVE CAN BREAK YOUR HEART; BLACK QUEEN; 49 BYE BYES/AMERICA'S CHILDREN; LOVE THE ONE YOU'RE WITH; PRE-ROAD DOWNS; LONG TIME GONE; HELPLESSLY HOPING; OHIO; AS I COME OF AGE; SOUTHERN MAN; CARRY ON; FIND THE COST OF FREEDOM.

2 JUNE

CSN&Y begin a week's residency at New York's Fillmore East. With Bob Dylan in attendance, Stills cannot resist his competitive streak and upstages his comrades, causing no small consternation during the interval. As Nash explained: "On the first night of the Fillmore, Steve was drinking a bit, and instead of doing his solo number or saying he felt like doing a second one, he did four. He was actually right because the audience wanted it and he was getting off on it, but when he came off for the 15-minute break I got mad at him and we had a huge shout-up. But by the time the break was over and we got back on-stage and into the electric part, it was cool and then some of the music he was putting down just blew my mind. That's the way it is."

SET LIST: SUITE: JUDY BLUE EYES; ON THE WAY HOME; TEACH YOUR CHILDREN; TELL ME WHY; TRIAD; GUINNEVERE; SIMPLE MAN; MAN IN THE MIRROR; BIRDS; ONLY LOVE CAN BREAK YOUR HEART; BLACK QUEEN; 49 BYE BYES/AMERICA'S CHILDREN; LOVE THE ONE YOU'RE WITH; PRE-ROAD DOWNS; LONG TIME GONE; HELPLESSLY HOPING; OHIO; AS I COME OF AGE; SOUTHERN MAN; CARRY ON; FIND THE COST OF FREEDOM; WOODSTOCK.

3 JUNE

Despite their recent problems, good vibes are back in abundance at the Fillmore East.

Following a spirited 'Suite: Judy Blue Eyes', Nash jokes: "As you can see we broke up a week ago!"

Warming to the banter, Crosby retorts: "Here we are in pieces!"

They then announce, in deference to Young: "We'd like to do a tune called tuning up!"

While the audience waits, a jokey snatch of 'Rock Island Line' is thrown in for amusement until Young is finally ready to perform 'On The Way Home'. He moves a little more swiftly into the much appreciated new song 'Tell My Why', which is initially announced as 'Star Spangled Bummer'.

Crosby maintains the stoned humour during his solo set. "I've got to decide who I'll be tonight," he ponders. "Don't laugh. It's hard enough to remember what I'm doing." His memory is sufficiently intact to conjure an exceptional acoustic reading of 'Triad', after which Nash emerges from the wings for a duet.

"What do you want to do?" Nash enquires. Feigning stage fright, Crosby exclaims, "I'd like to leave now!"

Huddled together, the duo threaten to perform 'A Song With No Words' but Crosby loses his nerve so they stick to the more familiar 'Guinnevere'... "where Nixon and Spiro can't go". Their performance anticipates the concentrated intimacy of later shows as a duo.

"If we're lucky we'll squeeze a new song out of Willy," Crosby says hopefully. We do, but not before Nash provides an apologetic preamble: "As a performer and writer, it's almost usual to always want to improve on what you're doing. That's the goal. You've always got to improve and got to be better. I went totally in the opposite direction with this song. This is one of the simplest songs I ever wrote. It's so simple I was frightened of playing it to the lads. But they sang on it."

'Simple Man' follows, by which time Nash is in full conversational flow and eager to tell us the origins of several new tunes in his repertoire. "This is a song I wrote off Cuba..." he enthuses. "David and I sailed around America just for something to do. We went all the way from Fort Lauderdale on the East Coast all the way through the Caribbean and through Panama and all the way up the other side. This is called 'Tight Rope Song'." It is, in fact, the as-yet untitled 'Man In The Mirror'.

Nash's stories and Crosby's hippie humour obviously appeal to Young who is less reticent than usual and even seems in the mood for some audience communication himself. Pausing briefly, he announces: "I'm going to do this tune for you... I've never done it this way before." An acoustic version of 'Down By The River' follows, which sounds impressive, even without the now familiar Crosby/Nash harmonies.

Unsurprisingly, Stills is not about to be outdone by this plethora of newly arranged material and duly revives 'Bluebird' for his solo spot. It's intriguing to hear the song played acoustically, even though Stills makes no attempt to duplicate the pyrotechnic guitar work that characterised the Springfield's electric version. "I just figured that I'd do that. I haven't done it ever that way in front of people," he concludes.

He then announces a "country blues" ('Black Queen'), before quietening the mood with the plaintive '4+20' and concluding with the raucous '49 Bye Byes/America's Children' medley and an uncertain 'Love The One You're With'. Students of set lists will note that his solo spot is actually longer than that of the previous night which makes you wonder whether Nash's memory is at fault in suggesting that he overran at the first show.

Returning for their electric set, the foursome commence with 'Pre-Road Downs', building up gradually to the lengthy guitar workouts on 'Southern Man' and 'Carry On'. Along the way, Stills features 'As I Come Of Age', a song intended for CSN&Y but destined to appear on a solo album. The evening ends with 'Woodstock', an anthem still relevant in 1970 but soon to be dropped from their set.

SET LIST: SUITE: JUDY BLUE EYES; ON THE WAY HOME; TEACH YOUR CHILDREN; TELL ME WHY; TRIAD; GUINNEVERE; SIMPLE MAN; MAN IN THE MIRROR; DOWN BY THE RIVER; ONLY LOVE CAN BREAK YOUR HEART; BLUEBIRD; BLACK QUEEN; 4+20; 49 BYE BYES/AMERICA'S CHILDREN; LOVE THE ONE YOU'RE WITH; PRE-ROAD DOWNS; LONG TIME GONE; HELPLESSLY HOPING; OHIO; AS I COME OF AGE; SOUTHERN MAN; CARRY ON; FIND THE COST OF FREEDOM; WOODSTOCK.

4 JUNE

CSN&Y are now settling into their Fillmore residency, with Young extending his acoustic 'Down By The River' by featuring the song in a medley with 'Cinnamon Girl'. This same day, 'Ohio' is released and will soon be competing with 'Teach Your Children' in the US Top 20.

SET LIST: SUITE: JUDY BLUE EYES; ON THE WAY HOME; TEACH YOUR CHILDREN; TELL ME WHY; TRIAD; GUINNEVERE; SIMPLE MAN; MAN IN THE MIRROR; CINNAMON GIRL/DOWN BY THE RIVER; ONLY LOVE CAN BREAK YOUR HEART; BLACK QUEEN; 49 BYE BYES/AMERICA'S CHILDREN; LOVE THE ONE YOU'RE WITH; PRE-ROAD DOWNS; LONG TIME GONE; HELPLESSLY HOPING; OHIO; AS I COME OF AGE; SOUTHERN MAN; CARRY ON; FIND THE COST OF FREEDOM.

5 JUNE

For the fifth night at the Fillmore, Crosby rings the changes by featuring 'Laughing' and 'The Lee Shore' in his solo spot. It is clear each member is determined to try a new combination of songs on specific nights.

SET LIST: SUITE: JUDY BLUE EYES; BLACKBIRD; ON THE WAY HOME; TEACH YOUR CHILDREN; TELL ME WHY; LAUGHING; THE LEE SHORE; SIMPLE MAN; MAN IN THE MIRROR; CINNAMON GIRL/DOWN BY THE RIVER; ONLY LOVE CAN BREAK YOUR HEART; BLACK QUEEN; 49 BYE BYES/AMERICA'S CHILDREN; LOVE THE ONE YOU'RE WITH; PRE-ROAD DOWNS; LONG TIME GONE; HELPLESSLY HOPING; OHIO; AS I COME OF AGE; SOUTHERN MAN; CARRY ON; WOODSTOCK; FIND THE COST OF FREEDOM.

6 JUNE

Nash pulls the biggest surprise of all by playing an acoustic 'King Midas In Reverse', the only time that CSN&Y and its various combinations ever attempted a Hollies' song. This piece of history will later be captured for posterity on the CD version of *4 Way Street*. Young, meanwhile, is determined to extend his acoustic medley by adding 'The Loner' to 'Cinnamon Girl' and 'Down By The River'.

SET LIST: SUITE: JUDY BLUE EYES; BLACKBIRD; ON THE WAY HOME; TEACH YOUR CHILDREN; TELL ME WHY; TRIAD; GUINNEVERE; SIMPLE MAN; KING MIDAS IN REVERSE; THE LONER/CINNAMON GIRL/DOWN BY THE RIVER; BLACK QUEEN; 4+20; 49 BYE BYES/AMERICA'S CHILDREN; LOVE THE ONE YOU'RE WITH; PRE-ROAD DOWNS; LONG TIME GONE; HELPLESSLY HOPING; OHIO; AS I COME OF AGE; SOUTHERN MAN; CARRY ON; WOODSTOCK; FIND THE COST OF FREEDOM.

7 JUNE

For the final night at the Fillmore, Nash and Young are responsible for providing some variety by introducing 'Sleep Song' and 'Don't

Let It Bring You Down'. Two other songs, 'Man In The Mirror' and 'Black Queen', will later be featured on the CS&N boxed set.

SET LIST : SUITE: JUDY BLUE EYES; BLACKBIRD; ON THE WAY HOME; TEACH YOUR CHILDREN; TELL ME WHY; TRIAD; GUINNEVERE; SLEEP SONG; MAN IN THE MIRROR; DON'T LET IT BRING YOU DOWN; THE LONER/CINNAMON GIRL/DOWN BY THE RIVER; BLACK QUEEN; 49 BYE BYES/AMERICA'S CHILDREN; LOVE THE ONE YOU'RE WITH; PRE-ROAD DOWNS; LONG TIME GONE; HELPLESSLY HOPING; SOUTHERN MAN; AS I COME OF AGE; OHIO; CARRY ON; WOODSTOCK; FIND THE COST OF FREEDOM.

MID – LATE JUNE

Following their week at the Fillmore, CSN&Y continue their rescheduled tour with appearances at Rhode Island Auditorium, Providence, RI (June 9), the Spectrum, Philadelphia, PA (10), the Olympia Stadium, Detroit, MI (12), the Memorial Coliseum, Portland, OR (16), the Oakland Coliseum, CA (19) and the LA Forum, CA (26/28). "These dates and several other concert commitments finally were made only under the gun of threatened lawsuits that involve money amounting to a couple of fortunes," claims the *Philadelphia Inquirer*.

A review of their Oakland concert at least provides a pleasing pointer for the future by audaciously suggesting that their solo sets eclipse their group efforts. Certainly, the acoustic section allows them to ingratiate themselves to devoted audiences, even though the in-jokes are sometimes a little too self-satisfied. In introducing 'Guinnevere', Crosby announces, "This is a place where Tricia Nixon doesn't get to go."

"She might be groovy," Nash interjects.

"The kind of girl who'd give bad head," Crosby retorts, without a flicker of sexist distaste from the audience.

Stills continues the Nixon-baiting, not merely in 'America's Children' but, weirdly, in introducing Young's 'Only Love Can Break Your Heart' when he says: '*I'd* like to sing a song about President Johnson, Spiro D. Agnew, Richard Nixon, Ronald Reagan, the Vietnam War, Cambodia... and refuse."

Revealingly, it is the man who wrote 'Ohio' who refrains from making any political statement at all. Nor is this simply Young allowing his music to do the talking. His political songs are a natural outgrowth of his time with CSN&Y and once free from their influence he will once more become an apolitical creature, a stance culminating in the apologetic 'Campaigner'.

While the audience still laps up the group's comments on the political state of America, there are signs that reviewers are growing weary. As a reporter at Oakland remarks, "Each member of the group deserves a review of his own. Actually, Crosby should have two. One for his music, which was almost up to Stills and Young; another for his mouth. Crosby has been playing the verbal buffoon since Monterey. It's past the point of tedium."

At least nobody seems to be complaining

too much about the quality of the music. Stills is unquestionably on form at Oakland, bravely tackling a pensive '4 +20' and exciting the audience with an enticing electric version of 'Helplessly Hoping'. He even has the cheek to remind his compatriots of recent squabbles: "The last time I did an extra song they threw me out of the group," he reveals.

"Thanks for telling them!" Nash concludes.

SET LIST: SUITE: JUDY BLUE EYES; ON THE WAY HOME; TEACH YOUR CHILDREN; TELL ME WHY; TRIAD; GUINNEVERE; SIMPLE MAN; THE LONER/CINNAMON GIRL/DOWN BY THE RIVER; ONLY LOVE CAN BREAK YOUR HEART; 4+20; BLACK QUEEN; 49 BYE BYES/AMERICA'S CHILDREN; LOVE THE ONE YOU'RE WITH; PRE-ROAD DOWNS; LONG TIME GONE; HELPLESSLY HOPING; SOUTHERN MAN; AS I COME OF AGE; OHIO; CARRY ON; WOODSTOCK; FIND THE COST OF FREEDOM.

1 JULY

By the time the quartet play the Kiel Auditorium, St Louis, even local newspapers are aware that the end is nigh: "The word is that CSN&Y have come to the end of the road as a team. They say that the pressures have turned what started out as a beautiful alliance into a sour arrangement of necessity".

4 JULY

Nash records 'Simple Man', his bemused response to the loss of lover Joni Mitchell. Written during the afternoon prior to the group's opening Fillmore gig, it was performed live by Nash that very evening with Mitchell sitting in the audience.

In introducing 'Guinnevere', Crosby announces, "This is a place where Tricia Nixon doesn't get to go."

"She might be groovy," Nash interjects.

"The kind of girl who'd give bad head," Crosby retorts, without a flicker of sexist distaste from the audience.

Stills continues the Nixon-baiting, not merely in 'America's Children' but, weirdly, in introducing Young's 'Only Love Can Break Your Heart' when he says: "I'd like to sing a song about President Johnson, Spiro D. Agnew, Richard Nixon, Ronald Reagan, the Vietnam War, Cambodia... and refuse."

5-6 JULY

Two nights at the Chicago Auditorium are recorded for possible inclusion on the forthcoming live album *4 Way Street*.

9 JULY

The last CSN&Y show for four years takes place at the Met Center Arena, Minneapolis. In deciding to pursue solo ventures, the foursome are walking away from a financial windfall. At this point they are on £50,000 a night, making them one of the highest paid groups in the world. Whatever criticisms they have attracted, their decision to stick to their principles and spiral off into other projects, despite many financial temptations, is admirable.

GRAHAM NASH, 1970

JULY

Some poignancy is added to the recent CSN&Y split as a result of a romantic subplot. Stills has become entranced by singer Rita Coolidge, who is invited to appear with her sister Priscilla on his solo album. Enter Nash, who whisks Rita away, thereby sundering his already frayed relationship with Stills. It will be some time before the two recover from the love triangle, which results in a complete breakdown of communication. Interestingly, Coolidge serves as something of a catalyst, inspiring songs from Nash, Stills, and Crosby. David's 'Cowboy Movie', once seen as simply a musical western, turns out to be an allegory of the group's destruction. As Crosby told me: "That was the story of CSN&Y. You have to know who's who. The Indian Girl? That's Rita Coolidge. Stephen is Eli, our fastest gunner, kind of mean and young from the South. The Duke, the dynamiter, that's Nash. Young Billy, that's Neil. And old, weird Harold with the 12 gauge – that's me. I smeared my face up with blood from my thumb, lay down on the floor and played real good possum. I'm crazy but I ain't real dumb. That Indian she wasn't an Indian, she was the law – the law of how things naturally happen, the law of human nature, the law of averages. At the time that was a factor. It wasn't the only one, but it was a factor. Listen to it now that you know the story."

13 JULY

Nash copyright registers 'Man In The Mirror' (mistitled 'Mirror Man') and 'Simple Man'.

14 JULY

Crosby appears on-stage with The Grateful Dead at Euphoria, San Raphael.

6 AUGUST

Work continues on Crosby's first solo album, with Graham Nash and Neil Young contributing to that alluring opening track, 'Music Is Love'.

14 AUGUST

While Crosby celebrates his 29th birthday, the exiled Stills is arrested for illegal possession of cocaine and barbiturates at a hotel in La Jolla. Although three other people are there, only he and companion Joanna Babb are arrested. They are taken to San Diego County Jail and then released on $2,500 bond. The following year, Stills takes the rap and is fined $1,000 for the misdemeanour. "It was just dumb," he tells reporter Michael Watts. "I took some pills, got blown away, blew my cool and it ended up like I was OD-ing on pills and so they had to call an ambulance. We were all drugged up and somebody crashed on the door and I got up and staggered over to it... and the couple across the

hall were standing there and went '*aarrrgh*'. They called the manager and everybody. I don remember anything else until the lights went on in the room and it was full of policemen. Ar that ended that trip".

7 SEPTEMBER

Young's *After The Goldrush* (officially scheduled for August 29) is released and effectively establishes his reputation world-wide, reaching the Top 10 in both the US and UK. The Canadian admits that his work with CSN&Y has been crucial in securing commercial success, but adds that this album represents "the spirit of Topanga Canyon".

11 SEPTEMBER

Doris Troy's eponymous album on Apple features Stills guesting on his old Buffalo Springfield composition 'Special Care'. He als co-writes two songs on the album with Troy, George Harrison and Richard Starkey: 'Gonna Get My Baby Back' and 'You Give Me Joy Joy'.

16 SEPTEMBER

The cover photo for Stills' solo album is shot a his cabin in the Colorado mountains with 18 inches of snow on the ground. Meanwhile, a poem is to be included on the sleeve, 'A Child Grew Up On Strings' by Charles John Quarto.

The poet subsequently releases an album, produced by Nash.

8 SEPTEMBER

Jimi Hendrix is found dead. The tragedy shakes Stills who was still hoping to record with the guitarist at some future date. In mourning, he climbs a mountain and weeps for two hours. Instructions are immediately sent to Atlantic to add "Dedicated To James Marshall Hendrix" to the artwork of his forthcoming album.

8 SEPTEMBER

Atlantic archives log session work on Nash's 'Man In The Mirror'.

OCTOBER

Stills promises that CSN&Y will get back together again but, in the meantime, he announces his plan to form a 14-strong big band and tour America next summer. Presently, he is enjoying working with his horses and intends to concentrate on writing poetry and producing a book of original song manuscripts, paintings, photos, poems and sketches to be published in 1971.

Nash, meanwhile, is preparing his first solo album and plotting a possible tour with Crosby. He is currently renting a £200-a-week flat in Chelsea and entertaining reporters from *NME*, *Disc*, *Sounds* and *Melody Maker*. Not to be outdone by Stills, he also insists that he is producing a book, which will feature a portfolio of his photos. To those enquiring about the fate of CSN&Y, he offers the home-spun philosophy: "All we wanted to do from the start was to play with each other and sing with each other when it was groovy and then, when it wasn't, not to. That's all we ever set out to do and that's what we're still doing".

OCTOBER

Lois Griffiths' arrangement and lyrics for the song 'Just For This One Moment' have music added by Stills, which is officially copyrighted on this afternoon in the USA. In the evening, Stills appears playing piano with The Rolling Stones at Rai-Halle, Amsterdam.

OCTOBER

Crosby and various members of The Grateful Dead record an early version of 'The Wall Song' (completed on December 13), which is over twice the length of the one that later appears on the first Crosby/Nash album.

NOVEMBER

The Hollies' album *Confessions Of The Mind* features the final song co-credited to Nash, 'Survival Of The Fittest'.

Meanwhile, Crosby is at Wally Heider's Studio C where, over the next month, he records various outtakes including 'Kids And Dogs', 'Dancer', 'The Lee Shore', 'Triad', 'Motherless Children' and 'Gothic Blues' (later adapted for 'Where Will I Be?'). He also jams with Nash and zither player Laura Allen on the unreleased 'Coast Road'.

9 NOVEMBER

The BBC broadcast Crosby & Nash *In Concert*, one of the most impressive documents of their live performance ever captured on film. Originally intended as a Crosby solo show, Nash's appearance kick-starts the performing partnership between the two which will continue on and off for the next two-and-a-half decades. The eight-song set list features 'Simple Man', 'Marrakesh Express', 'Guinnevere', 'Song With No Words (Tree With No Leaves)', 'Teach Your Children', 'Right Between The Eyes', 'The Lee Shore' and an astonishing 'Traction In The Rain'.

12 NOVEMBER

Stephen Stills is released and outflanks Young's recent effort in the US charts, peaking at number 3. Several critics speculate whether the closing track 'We Are Not Helpless' is some kind of riposte to Young's 'Helpless' but Stills insists it is not, pointing out that the opening line is borrowed from the novel *Failsafe*. Among the various solo albums released over the years, this is unquestionably one of the most accomplished and enduring, and probably Stills' finest hour. Incredibly eclectic, it displays Stills' eagerness and ambition to reveal the full extent of his musical powers in a series of songs that are all top notch. While the album features musical heavyweights Jimi Hendrix, Eric Clapton and Ringo Starr, their presence is subservient to the power of Stills' songwriting. In the wake of his contributions to *Crosby, Stills & Nash* and *Déjà Vu*, this album set a songwriting standard that proved impossible to sustain, but who would have guessed that in 1970?

17 NOVEMBER

Reprise tape archives reveal that Young has delivered 'Soldier', which will later be featured on the soundtrack to his film, *Journey Through The Past*.

30 NOVEMBER – 2 DECEMBER

Young plays a residency at Washington's Cellar Door, a gig he will later make reference to in 'The Needle And The Damage Done'. During this same period, his marriage ends and he becomes romantically involved with Carrie Snodgress, star of the film *Diary Of An American Housewife*.

4–5 DECEMBER

Young enjoys two prestigious solo appearances at Carnegie Hall, which are recorded for part inclusion on an intended live album that is later scrapped. In interviews, Young stresses that he would gladly play for nothing just for the opportunity to appear at this celebrated venue. The seriousness with which he takes the date is indicated by some stern words to a fan who has the audacity to shout out a request. "Listen, let me tell you one thing," Young insists. "As a performer, when you play Carnegie Hall, you look forward to it for a number of years. I don't

take playing here lightly at all and I think that you should have enough faith in me to know that I would plan ahead and include all of the songs that I thought you'd want to hear. That's OK at the Maple Leaf Gardens... but I'm not Grand Funk Railroad."

The set features effective acoustic readings of well known electric songs, plus a preview of 'Old Man' and the still unreleased 'Bad Fog Of Loneliness' (aka 'Singlemindedness').

SET LIST: DOWN BY THE RIVER; CINNAMON GIRL; I AM A CHILD; EXPECTING TO FLY; THE LONER; WONDERING; HELPLESS; SOUTHERN MAN; NOWADAYS, CLANCY CAN'T EVEN SING; ON THE WAY HOME; TELL ME WHY; ONLY LOVE CAN BREAK YOUR HEART; OLD MAN; AFTER THE GOLDRUSH; FLYING ON THE GROUND IS WRONG; DON'T LET IT BRING YOU DOWN; COWGIRL IN THE SAND; BIRDS; BAD FOG OF LONELINESS (SINGLEMINDEDNESS); OHIO; SEE THE SKY ABOUT TO RAIN; SOUTHERN MAN.

5 DECEMBER

Atlantic archives reveal that work is conducted on Nash's 'I Used To Be A King' and 'Wounded Bird'.

7 DECEMBER

Crosby and Nash are heavily involved in Paul Kantner & Jefferson Starship's newly released *Blows Against The Empire*. Crosby co-writes, plays guitar and sings on 'A Child Is Coming'; Nash co-writes 'Home' and plays conga on 'Hijack'; Crosby co-writes, plays guitar and sings on 'Have You Seen The Stars Tonite'; and both Crosby & Nash add vocals to 'Starship'. Although uncredited, Nash is reputed to have mixed the entire second side of the album.

17 DECEMBER

Crosby and assorted members of The Grateful Dead undertake rehearsals for their forthcoming gig, playing 'Alabama Bound', 'Eight Miles High', 'Cowboy Movie', 'The Wall Song', 'Bertha' and 'Bird Song'.

20 DECEMBER

Crosby teams up with The Grateful Dead's Jerry Garcia, Phil Lesh and Mickey Hart at the Matrix, San Francisco, performing 'Drop Down Mama', 'Cowboy Movie', 'Triad', 'The Wall Song', 'Bertha', 'Deep Elem Blues', 'Motherless Children', 'Laughing', 'Eight Miles High' and 'China Cat Sunflower'.

28 DECEMBER

The ten songs from Stills' first solo album are registered for copyright over a month after the album's release in what seems a surprising oversight. On this same day, Atlantic files reveal that Crosby attempts 'The Lee Shore' at Wally Heider's.

31 DECEMBER

Nash sees in the New Year at his San Francisco home, tinkering on a Wurlitzer piano and composing 'Girl To Be On My Mind'.

1971

2-3 JANUARY

Crosby teams up with Jerry Garcia, Paul Kantner, Grace Slick, Jack Casady, Jorma Kaukonen, David Freiberg and Bill Kreutzmann in the grandly named Planet Earth Rock And Roll Orchestra. Among the songs completed are Crosby's 'Is It Really Monday?' and 'You Sit There', plus the traditional 'Wayward Stranger' and Garcia's 'The Mountain Song' (with additional lyrics later added by Kantner).

6 JANUARY – 1 FEBRUARY

Young undertakes a tour of Canada and the USA, appearing in Vancouver (January 6), Portland (7), Seattle (9), Eugene (10), Edmonton (12), Winnipeg (13), Minneapolis (14), Chicago (16), Detroit (17), Toronto (19), Boston (21), Connecticut (22), St Louis (24), Boulder (27), Pasadena (29), Los Angeles, Royce Hall, UCLA (30), Berkeley, SF (31) and LA Music Center (February 1). The version of 'The Needle And The Damage Done' performed at the Royce Hall will later be featured on *Harvest*. Crosby makes a cameo appearance at the Community Centre, Berkeley show, singing on 'Dance, Dance, Dance'.

SAMPLE SET LIST (BERKELEY COMMUNITY CENTER, JANUARY 31): ON THE WAY HOME: TELL ME WHY: OLD MAN; JOURNEY THROUGH THE PAST; COWGIRL IN THE SAND; HEART OF GOLD: A MAN NEEDS A MAID: SUGAR MOUNTAIN; DON'T LET IT BRING YOU DOWN: LOVE IN MIND; THE NEEDLE AND THE DAMAGE DONE: OHIO; SEE THE SKY ABOUT TO RAIN; DOWN BY THE RIVER; DANCE, DANCE, DANCE: I AM A CHILD.

9 JANUARY

Nash records 'I Used To Be A King' for his first solo album, *Songs For Beginners*. The track boasts a formidable line-up of Crosby, and Young, with Jerry Garcia (pedal steel), Phil Lesh (bass) and Johnny Barbata (drums).

12 JANUARY

Crosby's first solo album is mixed at Wally Heider's Studios.

14 JANUARY

Crosby's experimental collaborations with Planet Earth Rock And Roll Orchestra continue with 'Leather Winged Bat' and 'Electric Bat'.

30 JANUARY

Crosby & Nash play a benefit for the Winter Soldier Investigation at the University of Detroit Memorial Building. Their performance encourages them to start arranging a tour which will see them on the road by September.

This same day, Reprise archives indicate that Young has delivered 'The Needle And The Damage Done'.

FEBRUARY

Stills is busy recording his second solo album in Miami. Intent on pursuing a brass-based work, he recruits the Memphis Horns to embellish the tracks. "I really was trying to come to grips with becoming an arranger – a real one," Stills tells reporter Penny Valentine. "I was writing charts for strings and horns and that really is the whole trip with the big band... I dig it and it's groovy and there's some of this that's overdone a bit too. It doesn't really matter, I'm happy".

This same month, Jimi Hendrix's *The Cry Of Love* is released, with Stills reputedly playing additional guitar on 'My Friend'.

6-8 FEBRUARY

Reprise tape archives reveal session work is taking place on Young's 'Old Man', 'Heart Of Gold' and the unissued 'Bad Fog Of Loneliness' and 'Dance, Dance, Dance'.

9 FEBRUARY

In Maui, Crosby and a number of friends, including former Byrds manager Jim Dickson, gorge themselves on acid and descend into the Haleakala Center, the world's largest volcanic crater. They emerge safely from their eventful trip, leaving Crosby refreshed and ready to complete a fantasy film *Family* (subtitled *A Day In The Life*). David is intending to produce and star in the film, as well as providing a soundtrack. Predictably, the venture proves a little too far out for sponsors United Artists and is abandoned.

12 FEBRUARY

Graham Nash records the autobiographical 'Military Madness', one of his most popular live songs, with Dave Mason on lead guitar and backing vocals courtesy of Rita Coolidge and P. P. Arnold.

23 FEBRUARY

Young records an all acoustic set for BBC's *In Concert* series, introducing several of the songs that will appear on *Harvest*. In what is the

apotheosis of his hippie phase, he regales the studio audience with 'Out On The Weekend', 'Journey Through The Past', 'Heart Of Gold', 'Don't Let It Bring You Down', 'A Man Needs A Maid', 'Love In Mind' and 'Dance, Dance, Dance'.

24 FEBRUARY

Young copyrights a batch of recent songs including 'See The Sky About To Rain', 'Journey Through The Past', 'Love In Mind', 'A Man Needs A Maid', 'The Needle And The Damage Done' and two still unreleased items: 'In The Wild' (aka 'In The Wind') and 'Singlemindedness' (aka 'Bad Fog Of Loneliness').

27 FEBRUARY

Young performs his first solo concert in the UK, appearing at London's Royal Festival Hall. Before a rapt audience, he courageously bypasses recently released material and premières a series of new compositions. During

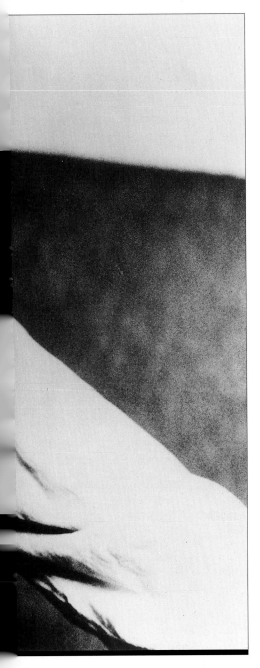

an 80-minute performance, he plays 21 songs, featuring 11 that have yet to appear on record.

SET LIST: ON THE WAY HOME; TELL ME WHY; OLD MAN; JOURNEY THROUGH THE PAST; COWGIRL IN THE SAND; THE BRIDGE; THE LONER; DON'T LET IT BRING YOU DOWN; SEE THE SKY ABOUT TO RAIN; OUT ON THE WEEKEND; I AM A CHILD; OHIO; LOVE IN MIND; ONLY LOVE CAN BREAK YOUR HEART; HEART OF GOLD; A MAN NEEDS A MAID; HARVEST; THE NEEDLE AND THE DAMAGE DONE; NOWADAYS, CLANCY CAN'T EVEN SING; DANCE, DANCE, DANCE; EXPECTING TO FLY.

28 FEBRUARY

Nash records 'Chicago'/'We Can Change The World', which he wrote partly as a plea to Stills and Young to play a benefit gig for the Chicago Seven. They declined. The song originally featured in several CSN&Y concerts as a stark but powerful acoustic number and was captured as such on the live album *4 Way Street*. This electric version provided the climax to Nash's forthcoming *Songs For Beginners* with a battalion of backing singers including Vanetta Fields, Shirley Matthews, Clydie King and Dorothy Morrison.

1–3 MARCH

Young's 'A Man Needs A Maid' and 'There's A World' are recorded at Barking Town Hall with the London World Symphony. A special bed has to be brought to accommodate his slipped disc.

3 MARCH

Guerrilla Music register copyright for the following Crosby songs: 'Cowboy Movie', 'Laughing' (previously registered to David Crosby in 1968), 'Music Is Love', 'Traction In The Rain' and 'What Are Their Names?'

8 MARCH

Crosby releases his first solo album, *If I Could Only Remember My Name* (officially scheduled for February 22), which follows the recent strong run of CSN&Y-related works by climbing to number 12 in the US charts and achieving gold record status. This extraordinary album transcends its time like few others from the period. What emerges is a striking and experimental mood piece, laced with exquisite harmonies, unusual time signatures and dazzling choral arrangements. Young, Mitchell and various members of the Jefferson Airplane and Grateful Dead transform the proceedings into a musical love-in, but Crosby's underlying melancholy cuts through the stoned beatitude. The work closes with the disturbing 'I'd Swear There Was Somebody Here', a Gregorian-

styled requiem to Crosby's girlfriend Christine Hinton, whose presence he senses even now. Engineer Stephen Barncard recalls: "It was like a bolt of lightning. I've rarely seen anything that intense... It just happened. I witnessed the creation of the song in real time and recorded it as we went along. It was probably the most remarkable event in my entire life."

22 MARCH

Rita Coolidge's eponymous début album features Stills playing guitar on 'Second Story Window' and 'Crazy Love', with Nash adding vocals to the latter.

29 MARCH

Buffy Saint-Marie's *She Used To Wanna Be A Ballerina* features Young on his own composition, 'Helpless'.

On this same day, *Woodstock II* is released, crediting CSN&Y on 'Guinnevere', '4+20' and 'Marrakesh Express'.

APRIL

Young continues recording material intended for the forthcoming *Harvest*, including 'Alabama' (April 2), 'Harvest' (4), 'See The Sky About To Rain' (6) and the unreleased 'Dance, Dance, Dance' (23).

1 APRIL

According to A&M files, work is completed on a version of Gene Clark's 'One In A Hundred', featuring the original Byrds. This, together with an earlier recording of 'She's The Kind Of Girl', supposedly cut in 1970, will eventually be featured on Clark's solo album, *Roadmaster*, released in Holland during 1973.

2 APRIL

Nash copyright registers the songs included on his forthcoming solo album.

7 APRIL

CSN&Y release *4 Way Street*, a double album tour memento that follows *Déjà Vu* to number 1 in the US charts. It's a striking live album which, despite critical efforts to glorify Young, actually underlines the contributions of Crosby & Nash who are the only members to feature new material on the set. Stills' attempts to take control of proceedings by encouraging the others to overdub vocals in the studio are resisted, particularly by Crosby who insists: "It's got to be pure, man."

Not surprisingly, Stills is less than charitable about the finished product. "I hated *4 Way Street*," he tells *Rolling Stone*. "I was embarrassed to put my name on that record... I mean you've got to be good to get a live album and not have to overdub and do some cheating... I ain't heard a rock 'n' roll band yet that was good enough." Ironically, *Rolling Stone* not only disagree with Stills, but greet the work as CSN&Y's best yet, marvelling with pained condescension that they "all sing and play in the same key on almost every cut".

STEPHEN STILLS

MELODY MAKER, 24 APRIL

19 APRIL

Guerrila Music tardily register copyright for Crosby's 'Orleans', 'Tamalpais High (At About 3)', 'Song With No Words (Tree With No Leaves)' and 'I'd Swear There Was Somebody Here'.

24 APRIL

"David's A Solo Star" trumpets the front page of *Melody Maker*, following the UK release of Crosby's album, which has just gone gold in America. Its sales in the UK are also highly promising, with *MM* noting: "Only a few days after its release, Crosby's album was selling in this country at the rate of 2,000 a day."

Meanwhile, the paper is bombarded with letters and phone calls complaining about Richard Williams' scathing review of *If I Could Only Remember My Name*. Reader M.T. Hutton of Leigh-on-Sea explodes: "Even a ten-year old would realise that it is the most beautiful LP of all time."

Amazingly, all this is front page news with *MM* promising: "A further selection of letters will be printed next week!"

Richard Williams later told me that his negative review of Crosby prompted the biggest mailbag backlash that he had ever known in all his years working on the paper.

12 MAY

Stills plays alongside various members of The Rolling Stones at the wedding reception of Mick and Bianca Jagger at the Cafe Des Arts, San Tropez.

17 MAY

Young's unreleased 'Dance, Dance, Dance' is registered for copyright purposes.

28 MAY

Nash is the last member of CSN&Y to issue a solo album. *Songs For Beginners* is less ambitious than the recent illustrious work of his compatriots, but ably displays his songwriting skill to considerable effect. There is no flab on the record and enough strong material to launch a career as a solo performer had he

chosen to at this point. Despite following an exceptionally strong run of related solo albums, Nash's work climbs to number 15 in the US charts, while his singalong 'Chicago' also charts. Among the credits there lurks a certain Joe Yankee on 'Better Days' and 'Man In The Mirror'. The mystery man is later revealed as Neil Young. Nash also receives the approbation of Young's manager Elliot Roberts who claims that *Song For Beginners* is the best album that any of the four released during this time.

JUNE

Seemon and Marijke's *Son Of America* is part produced by Nash, who also appears on 'I Saw You', 'Everybody's Dancing', 'Vegetable Stew' and 'It Is All There'. This duo are an offshoot from The Fool, whose 1969 album was also produced by Nash.

11 JUNE

The songs for Stills' second solo album issued later this month are registered for copyright purposes.

14 JUNE

Bill Withers' album *Just As I Am* is released with Stills contributing guitar to 'Ain't No Sunshine'.

Around this time, he also guests on Delaney and Bonnie's *Motel Shot*.

21 JUNE

Joni Mitchell's *Blue* is released, with Stills playing bass and guitar on 'Carey'.

22 JUNE

Crosby & Nash part record 'Urge For Going', a Joni Mitchell composition, which unexpectedly surfaces on the CSN boxed set in 1991.

30 JUNE

Hot on the heels of *Songs For Beginners* comes *Stephen Stills 2*, which races to number 8 in the US charts. Inevitably less accomplished and consistent than the groundbreaking début album, it is otherwise a pretty strong set that displays Stills' songwriting still in the ascendant. The brass is sometimes bombastic, most notably when aligned to Stills' most grandiose statements on 'Bluebird Revisited' and 'Open Secret', the latter featuring the immortal line, "Someone tell me have I been gifted or robbed?" set against a melodramatic, show-stopping crescendo. Otherwise, the horns bring additional power to the arrangements and suitably offset Stills' acoustic outings on the album, which are all impressive.

20 JULY

Chris Hillman attends the Stills/Memphis Horns show at the Public Hall, Cleveland and socialises with the singer. As Hillman told me: "Two weeks later, he called me and asked whether Byron Berline, Al Perkins, Rick Roberts and I might come down and do some country stuff on his new album. We went down there and, as it turned out, he wanted to start a band... so, he asked Al and I to join. Having given notice to The Flying Burrito Brothers, I thought, 'Great!' At that point, we hadn't really got a title for the band."

As the set list below reveals, Stills incorporates material from all his recent recordings except *Déjà Vu* and looks forward to the Manassas period with 'Jesus Gave Love Away For Free'.

SET LIST: ROCK & ROLL WOMAN; QUESTIONS; HELPLESSLY HOPING; FISHES AND SCORPIONS: GO BACK HOME; LOVE THE ONE YOU'RE WITH; BLACK QUEEN; KNOW YOU GOT TO RUN; CHANGE PARTNERS; DO FOR THE OTHERS; JESUS GAVE LOVE AWAY FOR FREE; YOU DON'T HAVE TO CRY; 49 BYE BYES/AMERICA'S CHILDREN; ECOLOGY SONG; OPEN SECRET; BLUEBIRD REVISITED.

10-11 AUGUST

Atlantic files log Crosby recording 'Games' at Wally Heider's.

"I've always been a cheap drunk. I've spent a lot of time drinking Scotch on-stage... It was seriously interfering with my ability to perform and stay in tune. It made me braver, but I just wasn't pulling it off."

STEPHEN STILLS

JULY - AUGUST

Stephen Stills And The Memphis Horns embark on a 52-date tour across America, taking in Seattle, Portland, Houston, San Antonio, Dallas, Kansas, Chicago, St Louis, Cleveland, Detroit, Cincinnati, Pittsburgh, Boston, Philadelphia, New York, Washington, Louisville, Oklahoma, Minneapolis, Denver, Salt Lake City, Oakland, Phoenix, Inglewood, Berkeley, San Diego and Hollywood. (See July 20 for sample set list.)

Still recovering from the loss of Rita Coolidge, Stephen takes to drinking heavily on-stage. "I was singing sharp and playing flat," he laments. "You gotta be good, man. People, in the long run, won't put up with a lot of shit."

Adopting the role of the tortured R&B singer adds a frisson to the performances at times but the singing is poor when the drink takes control. While Young will later get away with much worse and turn recklessness to his advantage, Stills becomes his own greatest critic. He later admitted: "I've always been a cheap drunk. I've spent a lot of time drinking Scotch on-stage... It was seriously interfering with my ability to perform and stay in tune. It made me braver, but I just wasn't pulling it off."

16 AUGUST

Bob Gibson's eponymous album on Capitol is released, featuring Crosby as guest vocalist.

10 SEPTEMBER - 17 OCTOBER

Crosby & Nash undertake a two-month acoustic tour of the USA and Canada. Their itinerary takes in Vancouver, Seattle, Kansas, St Louis, Milwaukee, Chicago, Minneapolis, Cincinnati, Columbus, Detroit, Cleveland, Montreal, Toronto, New York, Hartford, Boston, Philadelphia, Dallas, Los Angeles, Berkeley and San Jose. These early performances as a duo are arguably the most memorable that they have ever given, highlighted by an intimacy and humour that will never be forgotten by those who were there and believed.

The opening September show in Vancouver has particular relevance for Nash, as the last time he travelled there, he was temporarily barred entry back into the USA by immigration officials. That incident inspired one of his most notable compositions, which he plays in Vancouver this evening. Recalling the song's origin, he explains: "Coming back across the border, Neil got in, David got in, Stephen got in, but I didn't because I was on an H-1 visa at the time from England. I was not an

American citizen and they weren't going to let me in. In the meantime, there were people asking me for my autograph, you know? I showed that I had money and credit cards, that I'd only come across to work and was going back. And he wouldn't let me in. It pissed me off very badly. I got off the plane in San Francisco, I took a cab to my house, and sat down immediately to the piano. And I wrote 'Immigration Man' on the back of a book called *The Silver Locust* by Ray Bradbury. It was the first thing that I could find."

23-24, 26-27 SEPTEMBER

Studio files indicate that some work takes place on Young's 'Are You Ready For The Country?' and 'Alabama' (featuring Crosby & Nash), and 'Words' (featuring Stills & Nash). "It was in my barn," Young explained. "We recorded there with a truck and it sounded good... So that's where we did those three songs. We cut for two or three days there and we were making the movie, *Journey Through The Past*."

30 SEPTEMBER

Stephen Stills joins Crosby/Nash on-stage during their memorable first appearance at New York's Carnegie Hall. Nash's 'Blacknotes', featured on the duo's second album, is recorded here while Graham is sitting alone on stage nervously awaiting the overdue arrival of his comrades for 'Wooden Ships'. Stills' segment includes plaintive readings of 'Blackbird', 'So Begins The Task' and 'Helplessly Hoping' and an under-rehearsed 'Suite: Judy Blue Eyes'. As Stills recalls: "I was in Florida and I came up, and I came on to the stage. We did a few tunes and there's a marvellous tape of it – and of us completely breaking down in the middle of 'Suite: Judy Blue Eyes'. When we started singing, we really sang it well – and then we would forget the words; but we stumbled our way through it. The crowd goes nuts and then Neil comes on, and the crowd goes nuts again – it was really neat."

In his enthusiasm, Stills wrongly notes Young's presence, but he will appear at the next Carnegie gig in October when the musicians pointedly do not attempt 'Suite: Judy Blue Eyes'.

SET LIST: DÉJÀ VU; MAN IN THE MIRROR; ORLEANS; GUINNEVERE; I USED TO BE A KING; THE LEE SHORE; SOUTHBOUND TRAIN; TRACTION IN THE RAIN; LAUGHING; TRIAD; GAMES; STRANGER'S ROOM; IMMIGRATION MAN; BLACKNOTES; WOODEN SHIPS; BLACKBIRD; SO BEGINS THE TASK; HELPLESSLY HOPING; SUITE: JUDY BLUE EYES; TEACH YOUR CHILDREN; OHIO; MILITARY MADNESS; FIND THE COST OF FREEDOM.

30 SEPTEMBER/1 OCTOBER

Young records the instrumentals 'Gator Rag', 'Gator Rag 2' and 'Gator Stomp' with The Stray Gators.

OCTOBER

Nicky James' self-titled début album features two compositions written by himself, Kirk Duncan and Graham Nash: 'Coming From The

Ground' and 'Good Day'. The songwriting trio also compose six other tracks which remain unissued: 'Agree With Me', 'If You'd Only Come Back', 'I'll Follow You', 'Jake The Fake', 'Miss You' and 'Yellow Rainbow'.

The only other outstanding unreleased composition from Nash while under contract to Dick James' Gralto Music is a collaboration with Scott English: 'Who Can Teach A Songbird How To Sing?' Nash recently told me that the song should have been registered in Gralto's files as 'Who Can Teach A Songbird How To Fly?'

3 OCTOBER

Both Stills and Young make a guest appearance at Crosby & Nash's concert at the Boston Music Hall. As Stills tells *Disc*: "They asked me to come and play. They suggested it was a good idea to let everyone know things were groovy between the three of us. I went and did it and it came off really well... Neil came to the Boston concert of David and Graham's. And they wanted me to come along so all four of us would do it, and it ended up like that."

"We're supposed to be confident tonight," Nash muses, providing Crosby the opportunity to reveal that he is suffering from Lebanese Flu. "I don't know how you can applaud a disease like that," Crosby chides knowingly.

A VERY STONY EVENING WITH CROSBY & NASH

4 OCTOBER

CSN&Y are again reunited, this time for Crosby & Nash's return performance at Carnegie Hall. The highlight of the evening is a sterling version of 'Ohio', which Crosby & Nash have been playing throughout the tour. Hearing all four performing the anthem is a wonderful reminder of the great days of CSN&Y and fuels rumours of an imminent recorded reunion. Indeed, Atlantic is so impressed by these impromptu get-togethers that a souvenir record of this date is suggested. Stills baulks at the proposed title "Crosby & Nash And Friends" and insists that the idea should be shelved until they are ready to record a proper album.

SET LIST: DÉJÀ VU; WOODEN SHIPS; MAN IN THE MIRROR; ORLEANS; I USED TO BE A KING; THE LEE SHORE; SOUTHBOUND TRAIN; TRACTION IN THE RAIN; LAUGHING; WHERE WILL I BE?; TRIAD; STRANGER'S ROOM; IMMIGRATION MAN; HELPLESSLY HOPING; AS I COME OF AGE; YOU DON'T HAVE TO CRY; SO BEGINS THE TASK; HELPLESS; ALABAMA; TEACH YOUR CHILDREN; OHIO; CHICAGO; FIND THE COST OF FREEDOM.

10 OCTOBER

Crosby & Nash appear at the Dorothy Chandler Pavilion, Los Angeles Music Center in a famous show captured for posterity on the engaging bootleg, *A Very Stony Evening*. Although Crosby is feverish and under medication, the drugs he is prescribed merely accentuate his stoned persona, resulting in one of the most entertaining concerts of the era.

"We're supposed to be confident tonight," Nash muses, providing Crosby the opportunity to reveal that he is suffering from Lebanese Flu. His ailment will later provide a title for at least one bootleg record and his audience is amused enough to offer a round of applause.

"I don't know how you can applaud a disease like that," Crosby chides knowingly.

The stoned humour continues throughout the show as the duo transform themselves into a more believable Cheech and Chong. The phrase "Our memory is usually one of the first things to go" is not merely a reference to dope, but accurately describes the loss of temporal distinction that follows a rush of LSD. Judging from the audience's applause, many are familiar with the feeling.

Although few considered this at the time, Crosby actually shows a quiet talent as a comedian at these shows, mimicking voices and making great play out of bizarre lines like

"I'm drinking straight adrenaline." He's quick with the quips too, responding to a request for 'Almost Cut My Hair' with the razor sharp, "I will not cut your hair!" There are also in-jokes for those who have followed his career, like The Byrds allusion in his riposte to Nash's feigned impatience: "You can fire me. It's been done before, folks."

What makes this particular concert so memorable is the strange combination of laughter and seriousness between the inter-song rapping and the actual performance. A bathetic comedy routine suddenly and unexpectedly segues into something sublime like their rendition of 'Orleans' or 'Guinnevere'. The range of emotional expression is absolutely extraordinary at times as songs previously appreciated, but perhaps never fully understood, are revealed in starker shades with their subtleties explored incisively. The opening 'Déjà Vu', minus its elaborate production and tireless studio work, emerges as an even stranger song, with interweaving vocal and rhythm parts displaying Crosby's immense talent at constructing a composition. We hear it again in songs like 'The Lee Shore' and 'Traction In The Rain', where he is obliged to fill in parts with extended hums, delicate rhythmic additions and scat vocals.

As the concert reaches its climax, Nash's more upbeat work provides some high moments. 'Teach Your Children' is a signal to start a singalong, which continues right through the irresistible 'Military Madness', which provokes Crosby to try and chant Nixon out of office and right the wrongs of the world. 'Chicago' is a breathless finale, literally thumped out on the piano, leaving Nash breathless and Crosby hoarse and in need of further medication.

SET LIST: DÉJÀ VU; WOODEN SHIPS; MAN IN THE MIRROR; ORLEANS; I USED TO BE A KING; THE LEE SHORE; SOUTHBOUND TRAIN; TRACTION IN THE RAIN; LAUGHING; GAMES; TRIAD; STRANGER'S ROOM; IMMIGRATION MAN; BLACKNOTES; GUINNEVERE; TEACH YOUR CHILDREN; OHIO; MILITARY MADNESS; CHICAGO.

14 OCTOBER

Young guests at Crosby & Nash's performance at the Community Theater, Berkeley adding 'Helpless' and 'Alabama' to their familiar set. The duo play the same venue the following evening without Young.

SET LIST: DÉJÀ VU; WOODEN SHIPS; MAN IN THE MIRROR; ORLEANS; I USED TO BE A KING; THE LEE SHORE; SOUTHBOUND TRAIN; TRACTION IN THE RAIN; LAUGHING; GAMES; TRIAD; STRANGER'S ROOM; IMMIGRATION MAN; HELPLESS; ALABAMA; TEACH YOUR CHILDREN; OHIO; MILITARY MADNESS; CHICAGO.

17 OCTOBER

Crosby & Nash close their season of acoustic shows with an appearance in San Jose, California.

NOVEMBER

Stills completes the formation of Manassas with Chris Hillman, Dallas Taylor, Paul Harris,

Calvin Samuels, Al Perkins and Joe Lala. Their brief is a fascinating fusion of blues, country, folk, Latin and rock. Stills promises that the experiment will prove his most ambitious and possibly rewarding excursion to date.

2 NOVEMBER

Crosby completes the brilliant 'Where Will I Be?', one of the key tracks on the first Crosby & Nash album. Dana Africa guests on flute.

7 NOVEMBER

Young records 'Words', which also features David Crosby and Graham Nash.

DECEMBER

Doctors inform Stills that unless he has a leg operation soon, he will most likely be crippled with arthritis by the time he reaches 40. He enters hospital this month for treatment.

–6 DECEMBER

Crosby & Nash play their first UK gigs as a duo at the Manchester Odeon (December 2), followed by two nights at London's Royal Festival Hall (4/6). The RFH provides the perfect setting for their understated yet adventurous approach, which demands excellent acoustics and a feeling of intimacy for which the venue is crucial. At their best, as they undoubtedly are at these shows, the duo reinvent themselves as a creative force to be respected and reckoned with. Songs are reinterpreted, not in the radical way we associate with Dylan or sometimes Young, but in an equally effective breaking down of musical components in an attempt to capture the essence of the composition.

The second set at the RFH opens with a splendid 'Déjà Vu' in which the jazz elements and changing time signatures are newly highlighted through Crosby's subtle guitar picking. Cut to its bare bones, the song is not merely engaging or even fascinating, but transcendent in its raw intimacy. It is the peculiar achievement of Crosby & Nash to strip away the brilliant veneer of their music to reveal something more basic, minimal and genuinely human at its source.

'Wooden Ships' is rawer yet also purer in its acoustic setting, with Nash taking the vocal parts usually sung and spoken by Stills. The effect is both disturbing and alluring, as we spot the different accents and listen to the fresh and engaging way in which the vocals interweave.

Again, bathetic humour and banal conversation provide an attractive counterpoint to the deep seriousness of the compositions. The duo tell the audience about their plane trip over, stopping off at Shannon, becoming involved in an altercation with another passenger who objects to their in flight hi-jinx... and other desultory tales. Nash gets into a long explanation about how 'Southbound Train' began as a harmonica solo and why he won't play the instrument live. It's all of quaint interest to fans and fills in the space between tuning, but also throws the listener quite magnificently. One minute you're laughing at some stoned anecdote, then you're suddenly in the midst of 'Traction In The Rain' and 'Laughing' with Crosby at his most hauntingly melancholic. For 'Page 43' he strums an entirely different tune at the beginning *à la* Dylan, then moves into the song that above all others signals his slow retreat from the nightmare of Christine Hinton's death. Even his tuning-up is impressive, reminding you of Paul Kantner's admission that he once constructed entire songs from Crosby's casual castaway doodlings.

'Triad' ("I was told this song was obscene by a group who shall remain nameless") completes Crosby's solo portion in thrilling fashion, leaving the floor to his partner. Confident and happy at his homecoming, Nash is in fine form. After rightly berating me from the stage, he reveals that his mother and grandmother have come down for the show and plays 'Simple Man' for the first time in a while, before moving on to the instructive 'Blacknotes' and faster paced 'Immigration Man'. With Crosby returning, they reach back to 'Guinnevere' and 'Teach Your Children' which set the tone for CSNY's greatest moment, 'Ohio'. The song is perfect for the duo's didactic finale and appropriate in other ways too. More than once, Crosby has said he helped Young write the song, an ambiguous comment but proof enough of his emotional involvement in its composition. What he brings to the song is an intensity of passion, most notably in its remarkable coda, here translated into an expression of exasperation and solidarity. It leads powerfully into the anthemic 'Military Madness' and 'Chicago' during which Crosby cajoles, pleads and ultimately orchestrates the audience.

It is this emotional power that is at the heart of these concerts and makes them unique in the annals of CSN&Y history. Nothing Crosby & Nash will achieve later will ever quite equal the combination of vulnerability and empathy they convey through these remarkable acoustic performances. They will play bigger and more spectacular gigs as part of CSN&Y and will certainly display the power and genius of that combination to greater and enduring effect – but here, amid these acoustic dates, lies the true heart of the unit, playing some of the most emotionally moving music that I, for one, have ever heard.

SET LIST (DECEMBER 6): DÉJÀ VU: WOODEN SHIPS: MAN IN THE MIRROR: TRACTION IN THE RAIN: SOUTHBOUND TRAIN: THE LEE SHORE: LAUGHING: PAGE 43: TRIAD: SIMPLE MAN: BLACKNOTES: IMMIGRATION MAN: GUINNEVERE: TEACH YOUR CHILDREN: OHIO: MILITARY MADNESS: CHICAGO.

6 DECEMBER

Rita Coolidge's second album *Nice Feelin'* features a guest appearance by her current beau Graham Nash. Meanwhile, Paul Kantner/Grace Slick's *Sunfighter* is released, with Crosby/Nash appearing on 'Look At The Wood', 'When I Was A Boy I Watched The Wolves' and 'Diana 2'.

13 DECEMBER

'Page 43', the answer song to 'Where Will I Be?' is completed at Wally Heider's. Already familiar to those who attended C&N's acoustic concerts, this version features the twin guitars of Crosby and Danny Kortchmar. 'The Wall Song', now long overdue on record and in concert, is completed at the same session.

ROYAL FESTIVAL HALL
DIRECTOR: JOHN DENISON, C.B.E.
AN EVENING WITH
CROSBY AND NASH
WITH JUDEE SILLS
SAT., 4 DECEMBER, 1971
8.30 p.m.
Management: Peter Bowyer

GREEN SIDE
Please enter the auditorium by
DOOR 4
LEVEL 4

STALLS £2.00
GANGWAY 2
ROW N   SEAT 4

1972

JANUARY – MARCH

Intense rehearsals for the Manassas album take place in Surrey as the insomniac Stills records countless takes amid painstaking and exhaustive sessions. As Chris Hillman recalls: "We came over after Christmas to Elstead. Stills had undergone an operation on his knee in December and was recuperating at Ringo's house which he later owned. It had a great rehearsal room." Among the visitors is Bill Wyman, who stays around long enough to help Stills compose 'The Love Gangster'.

6 JANUARY

Atlantic files indicate that Crosby & Nash have completed recording 'Southbound Train' for inclusion on their first album as a duo.

7 JANUARY

Manassas record the Stills/Hillman composition 'It Doesn't Matter', which will be the opening track on their double album. A separate set of lyrics composed with Rick Roberts precedes this version and will emerge later on Firefall's first album.

8 JANUARY

Stills completes 'Johnny's Garden', a tribute to the gardener who tends his grounds at Brookfield House, Elstead.

9 JANUARY

Manassas complete 'So Begins The Task', with Fred Neil guesting on backing vocals. Originally written soon after 'Helplessly Hoping', the song was previously recorded and played by CSN&Y but never issued by the foursome.

13 JANUARY

Nash's 'Another Sleep Song' and Crosby's 'Dancer' are recorded at Wally Heider's. 'Dancer' will not appear until the third Crosby/Nash album in 1976.

17 JANUARY

BBC 2 broadcast *Sounding Out* featuring film of rehearsals at Stills' home. Among the songs featured in the programme are '4+20', Bo Diddley's 'Who Do You Love?', Jimmy Reed's 'Take Out Some Insurance On The Baby', Chuck Berry's 'You Can't Catch Me', plus 'Know You Got To Run', 'Hot Dusty Roads', 'For What It's Worth' and 'Word Game'.

24 JANUARY

Grin's *1+1* features Nash on vocals and Young playing alongside Nils Lofgren on 'See What A Love Can Do', 'Outlaw' and 'Pioneer Mary'.

FEBRUARY

CSN&Y's managers David Geffen and Elliot Roberts launch Asylum Records in the UK. Among its first releases is the startling début *Judee Sill*, which features the Nash-produced 'Jesus Was A Crossmaker'.

2 FEBRUARY

Nash celebrates his 30th birthday by downing tabs of acid with Dave Mason at the Italian restaurant Vanessi's and then unsuccessfully attempting to mix Crosby's eerie 'Where Will I Be?'

8 FEBRUARY

The eagerly-awaited Manassas album is mixed at Artisan Studios, LA. Stills, meanwhile, announces his intention to work on recordings with his Memphis Horns' colleague Sidney George and vocalist Linda Stephens. During this same month, he drops into Olympia Studios to write and sing a harmony for a track on Humble Pie's forthcoming album, *Smokin'*. This is the first time any member of the group had even met him.

9 FEBRUARY

The Crosby/Nash sessions continue with 'Immigration Man', one of their more popular songs of the period. Mixing on the album will take place the following week at Artisan Studios, LA.

20 FEBRUARY

Neil Young's much delayed *Harvest* is issued, with Crosby & Stills guesting on 'Alabama', Stills & Nash on 'Words' and Crosby & Nash on 'Are You Ready For The Country?' The record confirms Young's ultimate ascent into the mainstream, providing his sole number 1 album. Despite its commercial success, *Harvest* bothers some critics who rightly point out that it lacks the adventurous edge of his earlier work. Those who fear that Young is in danger of "blanding out" will have a rude awakening over the next two years when he purposely upsets the gravy train.

MARCH

While recuperating from his leg operation, Stills entertains the press at his Surrey home. Speaking of the forthcoming Manassas album, he boasts: "It's better than *Crosby, Stills & Nash Déjà Vu* and my two solo albums. I'm really proud of it. On my two albums I tried to explore the different facets of music that I'm into, but I would constantly be cut short. It seemed to be a very erratic schizophrenic thing."

The major difference with Manassas is that it is clearly not a democracy, but a group project with a definite leader. As Stills rightly notes, "It's not totally a partnership but it's enough of partnership that everyone is satisfied".

6 MARCH

Jackson Browne is released, with Crosby contributing harmonies throughout the record and appearing on the attendant single, 'Doctor My Eyes'. Crosby also provides harmony to 'Highway Song' on Hot Tuna's *Burgers*, issued this same day.

Meanwhile, Stills copyright registers the 2 songs he has written for the forthcoming Manassas double album.

18 MARCH

Young achieves the distinction of topping the US singles and albums charts with 'Heart Of Gold' and *Harvest*, respectively.

22 MARCH

Manassas play their first concert at the Concertgebouw, Amsterdam, Holland. Media interest in the show is considerable, despite the fact that there is a competing European Cup football fixture that evening involving Ajax and Arsenal. Press and photographers assigned to cover the musical event make their presence known as soon as Stills walks on-stage. Locked in the mêlée is *NME* photographer Robert Ellis who observes: "The initial frantic rush of photographers produced ludicrous scenes, the like of which I've not experienced since Dylan at the Isle of Wight. The television crew were completely swamped."

What the privileged onlookers witness is a startling rock début from an extremely well drilled set of musicians whose performances will light up Europe over the succeeding months. Watching Manassas initially is akin to taking a trip into a parallel world of rock history in which Hillman joins Buffalo Springfield and Stills becomes an auxiliary member of The Byrds. The opening 'Rock & Roll Woman' beautifully sets the scene – a Springfield song,

Hendrix, Al Wilson and Duane Allman. The blues theme continues with 'Word Game', the Dylanesque rant that Stills wrote after watching a programme on South Africa.

After dowsing his invective, Stills invites Hillman on-stage, crediting him as the man "responsible for Buffalo Springfield getting its first job". They perform a commendable 'Do For The Others', with Chris providing the harmony. Stills then relaxes and takes the opportunity to plug the soon-to-be released Manassas album, telling the audience: "I like it

pulls one of the major surprises of the evening by returning to one of his finest and rarely heard Springfield songs, 'Four Days Gone'.

Still on piano, he concludes the set with the classic CSN&Y showstopper '49 Bye Byes/For What It's Worth'. By now, the 'America's Children' poem has been dropped in favour of a rap about the freedom offered in European cities, the merits of "far out groups" like The Coasters and The Drifters and how they and everyone else apparently learned everything from "hanging out on the street". With that, the

MANASSAS

co-written by an uncredited Crosby, and now featuring backing vocals from Hillman. Chris maintains this sense of temporal disorientation by taking us back to *The Gilded Palace Of Sin* for 'Hot Burrito # 2'. He can't adequately compensate for Gram Parsons' rich vocal delivery, but we get the message anyway. Manassas are a cornucopia of Californian rock history... and infinitely more besides.

Even while we're coming to terms with such definitions, Stills takes control and provides his own explanation: "It ain't Crosby, Stills, Bangers & Mash and it ain't the Burritos. We call it Manassas. God knows what we'll call it next week... This is one of the first records we played together. It's called 'It Doesn't Matter'."

The opening song from the forthcoming album demonstrates the potential of the Stills/Hillman collaboration most forcibly and while the audience is considering its implications, Stephen embarks on an excursion through his solo years. 'Go Back Home' sees the full Manassas band substituting for Eric Clapton's eventful solo, after which Stephen whisks us through 'Change Partners', 'Know You Got To Run' and a slightly jaunty '4+20'.

A potted history of Stills' involvement with blues music follows before he plays 'Bluesman', respectfully dedicated to Jimi

just about better than anything I've ever done. And these fellows are a joy to work with. I've been through quite a few bands trying to find people who'll play the music just for the sake of the music, being professional enough to go out and entertain. Here's a little song about it – it's called 'Move Around'."

Thereafter, we're back to the classic Stills/Hillman vocal interchange on 'Both Of Us (Bound To Lose)', perhaps Manassas' greatest acoustic song. Hillman also adds a new flavour to the perennial 'Love The One You're With', while Stills returns the compliment by masquerading as McGuinn on 'He Was A Friend Of Mine'. Moving on from the 1965 Byrds' version, Stills adds some lyrics about the death of Bobby Kennedy, turning the song into a double elegy.

Switching genres again, Hillman shows his country roots with 'Fallen Eagle', a swirling mandolin-based song with a caustic ecological message. Country music again holds sway for a retake of 'You're Still On My Mind', popularised on The Byrds' *Sweetheart Of The Rodeo*. Again, it's amusing to hear a new voice interpreting this honky tonk lament.

After another couple of Manassas tunes, Stills looks back to 'Sugar Babe', minus any revealing reference to Rita Coolidge. He then

group alight from the stage after one of the most memorable sets heard since the heyday of CSN&Y.

They return for a brilliant electric foray which virtually duplicates the opening side of their album, moving uninterrupted through 'Song Of Love', 'Rock & Roll Crazies', 'Cuban Bluegrass' and 'Jet Set (Sigh)'. The high quality musicianship reaches its apogee with the penultimate 'Anyway' and searing *tour de force*, 'The Treasure'.

When the crowd is finally calmed, Stills sits alone to sing 'Find The Cost Of Freedom' and is later joined by the entire troupe for a refrain which fills the auditorium. So ends one of the most inspired début concerts of the era, with Stills giving notice that he has found an outfit worthy of succeeding the great CSN&Y.

SET LIST: ROCK & ROLL WOMAN; BOUND TO FALL; HOT BURRITO # 2; IT DOESN'T MATTER; GO BACK HOME; CHANGE PARTNERS; KNOW YOU GOT TO RUN; 4+20; BLUESMAN; WORD GAME; DO FOR THE OTHERS; MOVE AROUND; BOTH OF US (BOUND TO LOSE); LOVE THE ONE YOU'RE WITH; HE WAS A FRIEND OF MINE; FALLEN EAGLE; YOU'RE STILL ON MY MIND; JOHNNY'S GARDEN; DON'T LOOK AT MY SHADOW; SUGAR BABE; FOUR DAYS GONE; 49 BYE BYES/FOR WHAT IT'S WORTH/HANGING OUT ON THE STREET; SONG OF LOVE; ROCK & ROLL CRAZIES; JET SET (SIGH); ANYWAY; THE TREASURE; FIND THE COST OF FREEDOM.

6 MARCH

Crosby & Nash play a concert at San Francisco's Winterland for the Prison Inmates' Welfare Fund. Young makes a surprise guest appearance, contributing 'Harvest', 'Only Love Can Break Your Heart', 'Heart Of Gold' and 'The Needle And The Damage Done'. The last choice is significant, as Young emphasises in his introduction: "I'd like to sing a song that a lot of people in prison will be able to relate to pretty heavily. A lot of people out here will be able to relate to it too. I hope not too many, but I'm sure there's a few."

Crosby & Nash are also sensitive about the songs they perform, with David preferring the positive 'Page 43' to his bleaker work. He also responds to a challenge to play 'Almost Cut My Hair' which works reasonably well in its new acoustic version.

The show obviously has special significance for Nash, whose father had been imprisoned in the Fifties for receiving stolen goods and died shortly after his release. The memory encourages Nash to cut through the usual on-stage *bonhomie* and make a special appeal for funds. He also makes some sensible points about prison reform, telling the audience and radio listeners: "The prisoners – they don't want luxury in there. They just want to be able to live like decent human beings... They should be able also to improve themselves while they're in there, that's the thing. A man shouldn't spend four years in there and be exactly the same when he comes out, maybe even less of a human being. He should be able to improve himself with books and musical instruments in the recreation room. Come on, man, this is the world."

With Young returning to the stage, the trio play out with the rousing crowd pleasers, 'Teach Your Children', 'Military Madness' and 'Chicago'.

SET LIST: WOODEN SHIPS; I USED TO BE A KING; THE LEE SHORE; HARVEST; ONLY LOVE CAN BREAK YOUR HEART; SOUTHBOUND TRAIN; ALMOST CUT MY HAIR; PAGE 43; AND SO IT GOES; IMMIGRATION MAN; HEART OF GOLD; THE NEEDLE AND THE DAMAGE DONE; TEACH YOUR CHILDREN; MILITARY MADNESS; CHICAGO.

?RIL

Stills reveals that he and his roadies have been collating a series of studio outtakes which he intends to release as *Stolen Stills*. Although the project continues to be discussed over the next year, it ultimately remains unreleased.

APRIL

Crosby & Nash's *Graham Nash/David Crosby* is released and reaches an impressive number 4 in the US charts, underlying their present popularity. The set features many of the songs included in their recent acoustic concerts, with electric accompaniment from members of The Section and Grateful Dead. The set is almost evenly divided, with Nash's slight 58-second 'Blacknotes' providing the extra song credit. Strong songs dominate, none more so than

Crosby's remarkable question and answer sequence 'Where Will I Be?'/'Page 43' which rank with his finest work.

12 APRIL

Hot on the heels of his colleagues comes Stills' *Manassas*, which duplicates the chart success of the Crosby/Nash album by peaking at number 4. An extraordinarily eclectic collection, even by Stills' standards, it splits neatly into four sides titled "The Raven", "The Wilderness", "Consider" and "Rock & Roll Is

> *"I like the whole album. A lot of people have said it should have been a single album but I think it's a great double. And it's very rare for me to come from a project and say, 'That's wonderful'. Manassas had really good players in it. It had the capacity to do anything from bluegrass to Latin. It was rewarding. I learned a lot, and it was very stimulating for the period it lasted."*
>
> CHRIS HILLMAN

Here To Stay". For the man nicknamed Captain Manyhands it is the ultimate musical excursion and book-ends a staggering run of consecutive releases going back to *Buffalo Springfield Again*. Listeners outside Holland can only wait in over-eager anticipation for the much touted live extravaganza.

Looking back at the record, Chris Hillman is full of praise. "I like the whole album," he told me. "A lot of people have said it should have been a single album but I think it's a great double. And it's very rare for me to come from a project and say, 'That's wonderful'. Manassas had really good players in it. It had the capacity to do anything from bluegrass to Latin. It was rewarding. I learned a lot, and it was very stimulating for the period it lasted."

MAY

The Everly Brothers' *Stories We Could Tell* is released with Crosby & Nash guesting on vocals.

19 JUNE

Young issues the single 'War Song', inspired by the shooting and incapacitation of George Wallace. With its distinctive steel guitar backing and plea for peace the song emerges as a mellow counterpart to the finger pointing 'Ohio'. The track is billed as "Neil Young with Graham Nash", the sole recording credited to that unique combination. Despite the song's unavailability on album, it fails to dent the US Top 40.

JULY

Manassas begin a summer tour of the USA, which includes an eventful three nights at the Berkeley Community Theater (July 21–23). On the second night, they are briefly joined by former associates Graham Nash and Neil Young, plus Hillman's ex-partner Roger McGuinn. Among the highlights is McGuinn

joining in on The Byrds' classics 'The Bells Of Rhymney', 'He Was A Friend Of Mine' and 'So You Want To Be A Rock 'n' Roll Star'. Over almost three hours, Stills plays most of the Manassas double, buoyed by material from his two solo albums and the obligatory 'For What It's Worth'.

It is interesting to see some of the changes to the set list since the opening concert in Holland, which featured 29 songs. The summer tour streamlines the set to 25 songs, dropping 'Hot Burrito # 2', 'It Doesn't Matter', '4+20',

'Bluesman', 'Do For The Others', 'Move Around', 'Don't Look At My Shadow' and 'Four Days Gone'. The most significant additions are 'Hide It So Deep', 'Pensamiento' and the sublime 'Daylight Again', a lengthy preamble to 'Find The Cost Of Freedom' that Stills improvises over several verses. Although later recorded by CS&N, this original version is considerably longer and superior.

SET LIST: ROCK & ROLL WOMAN; BOUND TO FALL; JOHNNY'S GARDEN; SO YOU WANT TO BE A ROCK 'N' ROLL STAR; GO BACK HOME; CHANGE PARTNERS; KNOW YOU GOT TO RUN; CROSSROADS; WORD GAME; BOTH OF US (BOUND TO LOSE); LOVE THE ONE YOU'RE WITH; HE WAS A FRIEND OF MINE; FALLEN EAGLE; HIDE IT SO DEEP; YOU'RE STILL ON MY MIND; SUGAR BABE; PENSAMIENTO; 49 BYE BYES/FOR WHAT IT'S WORTH; SONG OF LOVE; ROCK & ROLL CRAZIES; JET SET (SIGH); ANYWAY; RIGHT NOW; FIND THE COST OF FREEDOM.

16 JULY

Young makes a brief guest appearance at the Mariposa Folk Festival in Toronto. During Bruce Cockburn's set, he takes the stage to sing 'Sugar Mountain' and 'Helpless'.

9 AUGUST

Stills' copyright documents indicate a collaboration with Merryweather (aka Robert N. Lillie), providing music for the song 'City Boy'. Confusingly, there was also a blues/rock aggregation named Merryweather (featuring Neil Merryweather) that featured Young's ex-colleague Bobby Notkoff on violin. Whether this has any connection with the aforementioned Robert Lillie is debatable.

SEPTEMBER

Manassas undertake a tour of Europe, including appearances in London, Manchester, Paris and Frankfurt. Following the show at the Paris Olympia, Stills first meets Veronique Sanson, whom he will later marry.

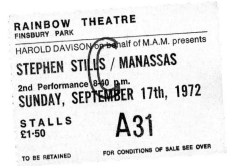

RAINBOW THEATRE
FINSBURY PARK
HAROLD DAVISON on behalf of M.A.M. presents
STEPHEN STILLS / MANASSAS
2nd Performance 8·40 p.m.
SUNDAY, SEPTEMBER 17th, 1972
STALLS
£1·50   A31
TO BE RETAINED   FOR CONDITIONS OF SALE SEE OVER

10 SEPTEMBER

The Grateful Dead play the Hollywood Palladium, with Crosby joining them for the second half of their second set, appearing on 'Dark Star', 'Jack Straw', 'Sing Me Back Home' and 'Sugar Magnolia'.

2 OCTOBER

The title track of the next Stephen Stills/ Manassas album 'Down The Road' is copyright registered along with 'So Many Times'.

9 OCTOBER

Mickey Hart's *Rolling Thunder* is released with Stills playing bass on 'The Main Ten'. Exactly three weeks later, Stills can be heard as guest vocalist on Loggins & Messina's *Loggins &Messina*.

NOVEMBER

Rick Roberts' first solo album *Windmills* is released, with Crosby adding vocals to 'In A Dream'.

This same month, Crosby reunites with the original Byrds to record an album for Asylum Records. Plans are also afoot for a possible collaboration between McGuinn and Crosby but this public exorcism of their old conflict never takes place. Instead Crosby will make a crucial guest appearance on McGuinn's début solo album.

7 NOVEMBER

Young begins sabotaging his promising career as a sentimental singer/songwriter by confounding his audience with the release of *Journey Through The Past*. Although technically a film soundtrack, it is widely regarded as the official follow-up to *Harvest*. Those in search of another 'Heart Of Gold' are no doubt perplexed to discover barely audible Buffalo Springfield footage extracts, some tedious rehearsals from *Harvest* (including an excruciatingly long 'Words' which meanders into oblivion), and an entire side on which Young isn't even featured. One new track emerges from the set, the less than distinguished 'Soldier', which is also poorly recorded. As a knife in the stomach career-stopper, this is a peach. Despite following a number 1 single and album, the double set fails to register a Top 40 entry. The *Rolling Stone* review sums up the prevailing sense of puzzled disillusionment felt by critics, retailers and potential purchasers: "It is outrageous that this album was ever released... It is the nadir of Neil Young's recording activity."

16 NOVEMBER

BBC Television presents Stephen Stills/Manassas *In Concert*. In common with the previous programmes on Neil Young and Crosby & Nash, this is an impressive performance that deserves to be seen more widely.

The set begins with 'Fallen Eagle', featuring Hillman on mandolin, conjuring up memories of the best of the Burritos. Chris remains in the spotlight for his rendition of The Byrds' 'You're Still On My Mind', complete with honky tonk piano backing. With a sense of group democracy established, Stills emerges for 'Sugar Babe', which includes an attractive steel solo from Al Perkins. Stills teases us by omitting the line "Come on sweet Rita" and instead makes an oblique reference to a Gemini lady, mischievously adding, "and you know who I mean".

Next up is one of the highlights of the entire set, as Stills introduces a new song he has written with Nelson Escoto: 'Pensamiento'. Arguably the best of Stills' Spanish/Latin influenced songs, it bodes deceptively well for the group's next album which is presently being recorded.

Stills reverts to a solo routine for three songs from his second album: 'Change Partners', 'Know You Got To Run' and 'Word Game'. The latter is spoilt only by a certain

coyness which prompts Stills to alter the acerbic last line from "they might throw up on you" to "they might hear about you".

Hillman re-emerges for the sprightly vocal trade-off, 'Both Of Us (Bound To Lose)' which, instead of closing with its effervescent samba rhythm, neatly shuffles into 'Love The One You're With'.

Manassas then show their full strength as a rock ensemble with the raucous 'Right Now', with Stills relating a tale of betrayal in love by "one of my best friends", a probable allusion to his rift with Graham Nash. The group close with what initially seems a pedestrian version of 'Anyway' until it suddenly shifts gear and reverts to the infectious samba coda of 'Both Of Us (Bound To Lose)'. It's a grand finale, but Stills has one major card still to play.

Reverting to acoustic guitar, he solemnly intones: "This is a song most of you have only heard a verse to. I wrote kind of a preamble to it..." What follows is a full length version of the exceptional 'Daylight Again'. Stills' narrative style has never been better as he imagines scenes from the American Civil War, singing "They didn't know what else to do, except to fight the men in blue/So they came and so the blood was spilt in the morning dew". Other verses pass in a blur as Stills speaks of "Musket sword and cannon, I'm afraid that was all that could be of use to put forward their point of view/Simple farmers that they were..." And on it goes, speculating on modern warfare and mass communication before reaching an unbelievable crescendo with 'Find The Cost Of Freedom', which Stills screams out like a blues shouter, extending words to breaking point in his passion. Just as the song climaxes, the full Manassas ensemble reconvene for the final refrain and chorus – a brilliant conclusion and possibly Stills' greatest moment on television.

SET LIST: FALLEN EAGLE: YOU'RE STILL ON MY MIND: SUGAR BABE: PENSAMIENTO: CHANGE PARTNERS: KNOW YOU GOT TO RUN: WORD GAME: BOTH OF US (BOUND TO LOSE)/LOVE THE ONE YOU'RE WITH: RIGHT NOW: ANYWAY: DAYLIGHT AGAIN/FIND THE COST OF FREEDOM.

18 NOVEMBER

A crucial and derailing moment in Young's career occurs when his former guitarist Danny Whitten overdoses from heroin. As Young told writer Cameron Crowe: "We were rehearsing with him and he just couldn't cut it. He couldn't remember anything. He was too out of it. Too far gone. I had to tell him to go back to LA... He just said, "I've got nowhere else to go, man. How am I going to tell my friends?' He split. That night the coroner called me from LA and told me he'd O'Ded. That blew my mind... I loved Danny."

Whitten's sordid death propels Young into a downward spiral which will greatly affect his attitude towards his music and career. For the next two years, he will wrest with his demons on-stage and in the studio, in one of the most intriguing and cathartic self-journeys of his life.

20 NOVEMBER

Joni Mitchell's *For The Roses* is released, with Nash playing harmonica on 'You Turn Me On I'm A Radio' and Stills playing guitar on 'Blonde In The Bleachers'.

18 DECEMBER

While their concert schedule continues with dates in California, eight Stills/Manassas songs are copyright registered: 'Do You Remember The Americans?', 'Isn't It About Time', 'Pensamiento' (with Nelson Escoto), plus 'Music Song' (possibly mistitled), 'White Nigger' (originally recorded with Jimi Hendrix), 'Witching Hour' (later recorded by Chris Hillman on his first solo album), 'High And Dry' and 'Thoroughfare Gap'. The last five songs were unissued at the time, although 'Thoroughfare Gap' was revived six years later to become the title track of Stills' 1978 solo album.

31 DECEMBER

Crosby sees out the year with another surprise appearance with The Grateful Dead at San Francisco's Winterland.

NEIL YOUNG, LATE 1972

PART III
PUSHED IT OVER THE END
1973-1976

By 1973, even CSN&Y no longer seemed infallible. A combination of changing times, complacency and personal problems gradually eroded their original power. Crosby no longer had the wealth of new songs with which he could impress the world and his collaboration with Nash had produced no second album. Stills' Manassas project had proven too unwieldy to sustain itself and ended on an anti-climactic note with Down The Road. Young followed the same downward spiral, abandoning the slick accessibility of Harvest for the overblown and much maligned film soundtrack Journey Through The Past. Doom and death seemed to surround the quartet for much of the year. Crosby, still affected by the memory of Christine Hinton's tragic demise, now watched his mother suffering a slow and painful death from cancer; Nash's girlfriend Amy Gossage was murdered by her brother; and Young's Crazy Horse colleague Danny Whitten died from a heroin overdose, paid for by the Canadian's money. The Time Fades Away tour proved a painful exorcism, with Crosby & Nash on mournful harmonies. When CSN&Y roadie Bruce Berry became another drug casualty, Young again used his live shows as a form of cathartic release. When he released a live album of new songs, critics steeped in old myths sensed a spent force, prompting such memorable headlines as "NEIL YOUNG FADES AWAY".

With everyone's career in commercial decline, the lure of CSN&Y as a rallying point seemed irresistible. The foursome did manage to reunite in Hawaii and seemed poised to record a major album, but the sessions foundered. Despite the pleas of their management and record company, they again walked away from a potential multi-million selling album.

Another year passed before the foursome again tried to connect. This time they decided to tour rather than record and, against the odds, fulfilled the public's expectations. Their stadium extravaganza was the stuff of legend – an all outdoor affair destined to become one of the most famous rock tours of all time. With the mid-Seventies approaching, CSN&Y already seemed of another age, lost King Arthurs in search of a Camelot. In different circumstances, the tour might simply have been a gratifying exercise in nostalgia, a chance for concert-goers to experience their own mini-Woodstocks without the mud. Fortunately, CSN&Y were still extremely productive at this point and history was again on their side. During that eventful summer, it seemed as though the ghosts of Sixties' idealism had returned alongside CSN&Y to exact retribution on this new age. Mid-way through the tour, the counter culture's arch nemesis Richard Nixon was dramatically impeached, as if fulfilling the prophecy of 'Ohio'. Against all historical logic, CSN&Y had once again found their time and re-established themselves as the biggest group in the world.

Perversely, they again declined the opportunity to complete that elusive studio follow-up to Déjà Vu and instead wandered off into separate ventures. Careers were temporarily revitalised: Stills released an album that showed his songwriting powers intact; Crosby & Nash relaunched their duo career with the favourably received Wind On The Water; and Young was now in a powerful enough position to win some support for the passionately uncommercial Tonight's The Night.

By 1976, the Holy Grail search for the next CSN&Y album had taken another fateful turn. For several weeks it seemed that the project was definitely underway, but it soon reverted into a Stills/Young collaboration. Bitterness and acrimony followed, with Crosby & Nash accusing their partners of sabotaging the CSN&Y dream for their own selfish ends. In the end, nobody benefited. The much touted Stills/Young tour fizzled out after a month and the attendant album was woefully anti-climactic and sold poorly. Worst of all, the residual resentment seemed likely to close the book on future get-togethers. Even the ever tolerant Nash was now telling reporters categorically that he would never work with Stills or Young again.

At this point, Young removed himself from the narrative, as if determined to distance himself from the suffocating myth that CSN&Y now represented to him. Stills, swamped by personal problems and clearly at a creative low point, swallowed his pride and attempted to make his peace with Crosby & Nash. A remarkable year ended with the trio seemingly back where they started eight years before.

1973

4 JANUARY

Young begins the notorious "Time Fades Away" tour at the Dane County Coliseum, Madison. His backing group, The Stray Gators, features bassist Tim Drummond, steel guitarist Ben Keith, pianist Jack Nitzsche and drummer Kenny Buttrey (later replaced by Johnny Barbata). Over the next three months, they will play often ramshackle shows across the USA, collating enough unreleased material for a raw, yet riveting live album.

SAMPLE SET LIST (TARRANT COUNTY CONVENTION CENTER, FORT WORTH, TX, FEBRUARY 23): ON THE WAY HOME; COWGIRL IN THE SAND; TELL ME WHY; OUT ON THE WEEKEND; HARVEST; OLD MAN; HEART OF GOLD; THE LONER; LAST TRIP TO TULSA; TIME FADES AWAY; NEW MAMA; ALABAMA; LOOK OUT JOE; DON'T BE DENIED; DOWN BY THE RIVER; CINNAMON GIRL; SOUTHERN MAN; ARE YOU READY FOR THE COUNTRY?; LAST DANCE.

19 FEBRUARY

Manassas' show at the Academy Of Music is recorded by Atlantic for a possible live album that fails to materialise.

MARCH

Stills marries Veronique Sanson in Surrey, England. Those in attendance include Graham Nash, Nilsson, Marc Bolan, Marianne Faithfull and several members of The Doors. The festivities continue in New York where Atlantic's Ahmet Ertegun throws a dinner party for the couple at the Carlyle Hotel. Stills tells the guests that Manassas will be splitting into various offshoots and forming their own groups, *à la* CSN&Y.

STILLS MARRIES VERONIQUE SANSON

10 MARCH

Crosby & Nash are added to Neil Young's tour as the singer suffers vocal problems, desultory performances and bad reviews. "Neil didn't really need our help," Crosby told me, "but he did call us and asked us to come, very specifically. He said it wasn't going very well, and that he needed our help. There was another reason I was out there. At the time my mother was in the hospital dying of cancer. I needed the music. It's my major magic. It's the one thing to hang on to when things get crazy. It was the only thing to hang on to when Christine died and it was the only thing to hang on to when my mother died. That's why I wanted to be there."

Nash is also in mourning following the shock news that his girlfriend Amy Gossage has been murdered by her brother. Amid such grief, it is no wonder that the tour is such a dark affair.

12 MARCH

The Byrds reunion album, produced by Crosby, is released and soon enters the US Top 20, eventually achieving gold status. Crosby contributes a reworking of 'Laughing', a cover of Joni Mitchell's 'For Free' and the rarely performed 'Long Live The King'. Despite its merits, the album receives bad reviews and beneath the surface friendliness, some old wounds lay unhealed. "My real feelings are that Crosby was trying to get back at me for firing him," McGuinn told me. "Because he had David Geffen, Elliot Roberts and the financial power of Asylum, he had more say in the matter than he used to, and that's why Gene Clark did more vocals than he normally would have. It was Crosby's *coup d'état*. He was being leader of the group... and with The Byrds' reunion album, it backfired on him. Especially when it came down to the mixing. That's when he panicked."

Crosby counters: "There was no panic and I didn't knife him hardly at all. Maybe I did a couple of times, but compared to what it could have been, it was enormously restrained... I didn't have a vendetta with McGuinn then, and I don't now. It would be foolish to, because I did enormously better than he did, and both he and I know it. And he's got to live with the fact that he said he'd do better without me."

In the wake of the album, McGuinn and Crosby intend to continue their often competitive friendship by recording an album for CBS but the project remains unrealised.

16 MARCH

Manassas appear at the Bananafish Gardens, New York City, for a televised concert broadcast by ABC. 'Carry On' is revived from the CSN&Y days in a less effective version, while other highlights include a sinewy 'Go Back Home', an enthusiastic cover of 'So You Want To Be A Rock 'n' Roll Star' and the old stand-by '49 Bye

Byes/For What It's Worth' with an amazing conga solo from Joe Lala.

SET LIST: CARRY ON; KNOW YOU GOT TO RUN; WORD GAME; DO YOU REMEMBER THE AMERICANS?; SO YOU WANT TO BE A ROCK 'N' ROLL STAR; GO BACK HOME; PENSAMIENTO; 49 BYE BYES/FOR WHAT IT'S WORTH; FIND THE COST OF FREEDOM.

18 MARCH

Crosby is jeered at on stage at the Coliseum Vancouver during the *Time Fades Away* tour for humming 'The Star Spangled Banner'.

31 MARCH

Young's tour ends on a sour note at the Oakland, California, where he sees a member of the audience manhandled by a police officer during 'Southern Man'. The incident persuades him to drop the song from his set for several months.

2 APRIL

The remaining tracks recorded for the new Manassas album ('Guaguanco De Vero', 'Business On The Street', 'City Junkies' and 'Rollin' My Stone') are copyright registered.

7 APRIL

The music press is rife with rumours about a forthcoming CSN&Y reunion album and tour. The *NME* tracks down drummer Dallas Taylor, who seems hopeful about the project, but wary of a certain Canadian. "We all want to do it," he

enthuses. "It's just a matter of getting together and working things out. If Neil Young's in the band I'll have to negotiate. If it's Crosby, Stills & Nash then I'm definitely in. Neil and I don't get along – that's part of the reason I left the group. I like him as a person and I'm sure he likes me as a person, but musically we just don't seem to be compatible and there's a bit of friction in it... I was only 19 when I worked on their first album and I was very confused about the whole thing – but I did feel like just the drummer, and I did feel insulted because I didn't feel I had any respect... that was my childish thing, however valid it is."

8 APRIL

Journey Through The Past is premièred at a film festival in Dallas. The reception is less than encouraging, but Young enjoys himself conducting a question and answer session.

0 APRIL

Manassas' impeccable reputation is compromised by the release of the anti-climactic *Down The Road*. Despite a handful of good songs, including the excellent 'Pensamiento' and 'Guaguanco De Vero', the overall presentation falls far below the standard of their illustrious début. Stills goes further than most negative reviewers and damns the record as "a bit of a turkey," adding "some of the vocals and things should have been done over, but I was lazy".

Chris Hillman elaborates: "That second album is a story in itself. It originally had all this material that was subsequently deleted. There was even a song that Fuzzy, Dallas, Al and Joe wrote called 'Mama Told Me So'. Then Ahmet Ertegun came down and wanted to put more of Steven's songs on it. Thus, there are those tunes such as 'City Junkies' which I don't really care for. That second album wasn't good. It was like the second Souther, Hillman, Furay album where we were breaking up and it wasn't really our greatest effort... Later, it got to the point where Stephen went with CSN&Y to do a tour and I got an offer for SHF and that was the end of Manassas."

AY/JUNE

In the wake of Crosby & Nash's recent appearances with Neil Young, a projected CSN&Y album is now underway at Lahaina on the island of Maui in Hawaii. CSN&Y record several songs including Young's 'Human Highway' and 'Pardon My Heart' and Nash's 'And So It Goes' and 'Prison Song' (the latter two surfacing in different form on *Wild Tales*). Alas, the album is lost, supposedly amid bickering and indecision.

"We tried to do an album and it fell apart," Stills told Cameron Crowe. "Caused everybody a lot of grief... I showed up to play and one day we stopped playing. I just don't know. I don't want to talk about how incredibly famous we are or how we could set the world on fire if we got back together. I want to play. I want to sing. I want to make good records."

This latest setback subsequently causes them to reflect on all that has been lost. "It would have been the best album we ever made," David Crosby told me. "It was going to be called *Human Highway*. 'Time After Time' was saved for it, as was 'Homeward Through The Haze' and 'Wind On The Water'. The cover of the album was to be a Hawaiian sunset. It was the last picture on a roll of film. A stunner. Nash took it; he set the timer. It was the best picture anyone ever took of us. It would have been the best CSN&Y album."

Although the quartet later resume briefly at Young's ranch, the project remains unrealised. A version of 'Through My Sails' (aka 'Sailboat Song') will later be salvaged from the sessions and used on Young's 1975 album *Zuma*. The

fab picture which Crosby mentions is reproduced on the front cover of this book.

11 JUNE

Paul Kantner, Grace Slick & David Freiberg's *Baron Von Tolbooth And The Chrome Nun* is released with Crosby on additional vocals. This same month, the Nash produced *Nice Baby & The Angel* is released by David Blue.

28 JUNE

CSN&Y record 'See The Changes' at Young's Broken Arrow ranch, but the ill-fated venture means that this version will remain unissued until the CSN boxed set in 1991. CS&N later re-record the song for inclusion on their 1977 album.

2 JULY

Roger McGuinn's eponymous first album is released, with Crosby providing startling harmonic work to 'My New Woman' (featuring all five original Byrds) and also appearing on 'Bag Full Of Money' and 'The Water Is Wide'.

20 JULY

Stills copyright registers an intriguing bunch of compositions: 'Love Story' and 'As I Come Of Age' (held over until his next solo album in 1975), 'Right On Rock And Roll' (previously attempted with CSN&Y in January 1970, but still unissued in any form), 'Willy's Tune' (unissued tune dedicated to Nash), 'Gentle Thing' (revised version of 'My Love Is A Gentle Thing'), 'Open Up' (unreleased by Stills, but later covered by REO Speedwagon on *Riding The Storm Out*) and the confusing 'Little Miss Bright Eyes'. The latter would appear to be 'Sugar Babe' (which includes

those words) although that song had already been released on *Stephen Stills 2*. To complicate matters further, 'Sugar Babe' appears to have been previously registered as 'Ivory Tower' (another line from the song). It may be that 'Little Miss Bright Eyes' is an extension of, or a completely different song from, 'Sugar Babe', but the echoing title seems too much of a coincidence.

24 JULY

Crosby provides the music for Dan Peterson's lyric 'Dirt Poor'.

11–12 AUGUST

Young reunites with Crazy Horse for four shows at the Corral Club in Topanga Canyon. For the remainder of the month, he will work on several songs that will later feature on *Tonight's The Night*.

18 AUGUST

Nash records 'Another Sleep Song' which, he claims, was composed in Barbra Streisand's living room. The song proves most notable for Joni Mitchell's enchanting backing vocals, making the performance one of the highlights of Graham's second solo album.

20–25 AUGUST

Reprise Records' files reveal studio recordings are completed on 'Lookout Joe', 'Borrowed Tune', 'Tonight's The Night', 'Tonight's The Night – Part II', 'Albuquerque', 'Roll Another Number (For The Road)', 'Tired Eyes' and 'Mellow My Mind', all of which will appear on Young's *Tonight's The Night* in 1975. The session listing also indicates another attempt at the still unreleased 'Everybody's Alone'.

LATE AUGUST

Manassas embark on a three-date tour playing Maryland, Saratoga Springs, NY, and Edwardville, IL. Drummer Dallas Taylor, still weak from heroin withdrawal, is expected to be replaced. Stills flies in Johnny Barbata for the New York gig, but he is unfamiliar with the set and only plays one song on-stage before Taylor returns. After the show, Stills admits, "I know I've blown my music and offended my friends because I was crazy behind coke, but I'm not like that any more." Having sold his £90,000 Surrey home for double its value, his next plan is to write a book.

STEPHEN STILLS

FRAGILE

MANASSAS

4 SEPTEMBER

Nash copyright registers four songs for his next solo album: 'And So It Goes', 'Hey You (Looking At The Moon)', 'I Miss You' and 'You'll Never Be The Same'. During this same period, he also sings on the track 'On And On' from the album, *Ned Doheny*.

5 SEPTEMBER

Crosby & Nash appear at Cornell University, Ithaca, New York State, for an intriguing acoustic set. Among the highlights are Crosby's still unreleased 'Your Life Is What You Fill Your Day With,' and a reading of Joni Mitchell's 'For Free' fresh from the recent Byrds' reunion album. Nash premières several songs from his next album, including 'And So It Goes', 'Oh! Camil (The Winter Soldier)' and 'Prison Song'. The latter's sentiments are clearly still in his mind when he interrupts Crosby's 'Page 43' to add "please don't get caught" to the words "pass it round one more time". The concert concludes with a rarely heard a cappella medley of 'What Are Their Names?'/'Chicago'. The song list below can be heard on the bootleg album *High Above Cayuga's Waters*.

SET LIST: WOODEN SHIPS; YOUR LIFE IS WHAT YOU FILL YOUR DAY WITH; FOR FREE; GUINNEVERE; IMMIGRATION MAN; OH! CAMIL (THE WINTER SOLDIER); PRISON SONG; PAGE 43; AND SO IT GOES; LONG TIME GONE; WHAT ARE THEIR NAMES?/CHICAGO.

9-12 SEPTEMBER

Young completes work on what will become *Tonight's The Night* adding 'Speaking Out' and 'New Mama'. He also records 'Walk On' – the opening song from *On The Beach*.

13 SEPTEMBER

Crosby & Nash briefly resume their duo outings with a show at Berkeley, California.

20-23 SEPTEMBER

Young plays four nights at LA's Roxy Theater, with Graham Nash as support act. It is a particularly incongruous bill, for Young is premièring his rough and ready "Tonight's The Night" wake, while Nash is playing more straightforward melodic material. At the first show Young plays nine new songs consecutively, with 'Cowgirl In The Sand' as an encore. While the drink flows, Young promises a silver boot to any woman who dares to appear on stage topless. The challenge is accepted by his lover Carrie Snodgress.

21 SEPTEMBER

While Young and Nash are in LA, Crosby is playing solo in Hartford, Connecticut.

27-29 SEPTEMBER

Young's *Tonight's The Night* tour begins with three warm-up university dates in Canada at McMaster, Waterloo and Guelph.

3 OCTOBER

Nash undertakes a short East Coast tour, including an appearance on this date at the Franklin & Marshall College, Lancaster, near Philadelphia. Performing solo serves as a confidence booster, but is never likely to be long term. "I'm a harmony singer, man," Nash says. "That's what I do best, so that's what I'm going to concentrate on. I've proved that I can get people off without help from anybody else so I don't have to keep on doing that."

SET LIST: SOUTHBOUND TRAIN; RIGHT BETWEEN THE EYES; MAN IN THE MIRROR; WILD TALES; YOU'LL NEVER BE THE SAME; AND SO IT GOES; PRISON SONG; IMMIGRATION MAN; OH! CAMIL (THE WINTER SOLDIER); MILITARY MADNESS; TEACH YOUR CHILDREN.

4 OCTOBER

CSN&Y appear together on-stage at Manassas' show at the Winterland, San Francisco. After the show, they talk to the press and express a desire to undertake an acoustic tour. The possibility of CSN&Y performing a UK date is mentioned, but Stills is sceptical, adding, "The cost would be prohibitive unless we could get a show at Wembley and I can't see that happening." How wrong he was.

Manassas' arduous touring schedule continues throughout this month, with immediate commitments at the Memorial Auditorium, Sacramento (October 5); Long Beach Arena (6) with Crosby guesting; plus a return to the Winterland, San Francisco, with Crosby & Nash (7).

15 OCTOBER

Young's *Time Fades Away* is released and peaks at number 22 in the US charts. Flawed yet fascinating, it captures the intensity of the recent troubled concerts, in which Young's ragged performances and vocal shortcomings were much criticised. Here, the weaker moments in the set are mitigated by the power of 'Don't Be Denied' and 'Last Dance'. Perhaps the album's greatest merit is that it features all new material in stark contrast to Young's later live packages.

29 OCTOBER

Jackson Browne's *For Everyman* is released with Crosby providing harmony on the title track, which serves as a riposte to his élitist fantasy of escaping the nuclear war in 'Wooden Ships'. On this same day, Dave Mason's *It's Like You Never Left* is issued with Nash guesting as vocalist on 'Baby Please', 'Every Woman' and 'Headkeeper'.

3-10 NOVEMBER

The *Tonight's The Night* tour hits the UK, with Young confounding audience's expectations in Manchester, Bristol, London, Liverpool and Glasgow.

His performance at London's Rainbow (November 5) sets the tone for the tour, with critics complaining that they are witnessing a complete shambles. "It was Guy Fawkes Night on Monday, but at London's Rainbow Neil Young's performance was a damp squib," claims *Melody Maker*. "There were moments, but most of the act was frankly tedious. He talked too much about nothing and went on too long – over two hours. He made an ominous comment: 'I play more than I talk, so the more I talk the more I play'. Some walked out complaining he was boring. The show was all but stolen by The Eagles who played a professional, relaxed set in support."

By the time, Young returns to London for a prestigious show at the Royal Festival Hall (10), news of the bad reviews and strange performances are rife. "We hadn't anticipated the attentiveness of the English audiences and their almost reverence towards Neil," Nils Lofgren notes apologetically.

Spectators at the RFH concert, scene of his first solo performance in London in 1971, can hardly fathom what they are witnessing. He starts with 'Tonight's The Night', then three-quarters of an hour passes in which he performs rough, unpolished songs, none of which are familiar. Finally, he announces: "I'm going to do an old tune for you now, one that you've never heard before." The sense of relief is palpable... until the words emerge. "Tonight's The Night," sings Young, repeating the new opening number of the set. Some people laugh, others look at each other in astonishment – and, before they know it, Young leaves the stage. Amazingly, he has played an entire set of unfamiliar songs in a slurred drawl and curtailed the performance long before closing time.

And then, a new Neil Young emerges, playing a handful of favourites like 'I Am A Child', 'Cinnamon Girl', 'Helpless' and 'Southern Man' and a surprise 'Flying On The Ground Is Wrong'. Finally, the evening closes with a third attempt at 'Tonight's The Night' after which the audience leaves the hall, bemused by one of the strangest performances they have seen or will ever see.

SET LIST (NOVEMBER 10): TONIGHT'S THE NIGHT; MELLOW MY MIND; WORLD ON A STRING; SPEAKING OUT; ALBUQUERQUE; NEW MAMA; ROLL ANOTHER NUMBER; TIRED EYES; TONIGHT'S THE NIGHT; I AM A CHILD; FLYING ON THE GROUND IS WRONG; HUMAN HIGHWAY; HELPLESS; CINNAMON GIRL; SOUTHERN MAN; TONIGHT'S THE NIGHT.

NOVEMBER
Crosby & Nash, currently on a short tour, appear at the Capitol Theater, Passaic, New Jersey, with guests Dave Mason and Don Henley.

GRAHAM NASH, 1973

12 NOVEMBER
Stills registers another unreleased recording: 'Black Sheep'.

15–23 NOVEMBER
Young takes his show across to Queen's College, New York (November 15), Music Hall, Boston (16), Columbus/Cleveland, Ohio (18–19), the Auditorium, Chicago (20) and the Berkeley Community Center (23).

28 NOVEMBER
Nash completes the copyright registration for his forthcoming album, adding 'Grave Concern', 'Oh! Camil (The Winter Soldier)', 'On The Line', 'Prison Song' and 'Wild Tales'.

DECEMBER
The double album *Buffalo Springfield* features an elongated version of Stills' 'Bluebird'.

7 DECEMBER
Young turns up at the Civic Auditorium, San Francisco to join Crosby & Nash on-stage. An intriguing electric set includes 'Only Love Can Break Your Heart', 'New Mama', 'Prison Song',

'Almost Cut My Hair', 'Pre-Road Downs', 'Military Madness', 'Immigration Man', 'Ohio' and 'Teach Your Children'. The continued interaction between the various parties gives the lie to those sceptics who insist that the participants are constantly in turmoil with each other. On the contrary, the frequency of these get-togethers throughout 1973 underlines the mutual respect they retain for each other's work. More importantly, it emphasises that, despite everything, they still cling to the initial premise of CS&N/CSN&Y as a set of individuals freely uniting without the traditional commitments associated with a group structure.

17 DECEMBER
Stills' 'First Things First' is registered with additional credits to Joseph Shermetzler and Dallas Taylor. When the song was finally issued in 1975, Taylor's credit had been replaced by that of a certain "J Smith", which may have been a pseudonym used by the drummer.

22 DECEMBER
Stills loses a paternity suit instigated by Mill Valley resident Harriet Tunis.

1974

14 JANUARY

Nash's second solo album *Wild Tales* is released, eventually peaking at number 34 in the US charts. Among the album's guest credits are David Crosby, Dave Mason and Joe Yankee (Neil Young). Those that criticise Nash's sentimentality are given a revealing glimpse into his darker side on several tracks, while the social/political commentaries are impressive in

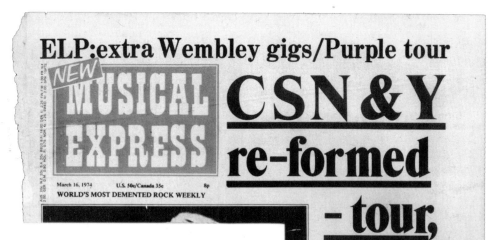

ELP:extra Wembley gigs/Purple tour

NEW MUSICAL EXPRESS

March 16, 1974   U.S. 50c/Canada 35c   8p

WORLD'S MOST DEMENTED ROCK WEEKLY

CSN&Y re-formed – tour, album

Barbara Charone: CHICAGO
Derek Johnson: LONDON

CROSBY, STILLS, Nash & Young are together again. And that's official. One of the hottest-selling properties in international rock when first launched — they have not played together as a foursome for almost four years — CSN&Y are re-uniting for a major U.S. concert tour this summer.

They open in Tampa, Florida, on July 4 and play a string of ten dates in leading football stadiums throughout the country. Our U.S. correspondent Barbara Charone says there is every indication that the tour will arouse as much interest as — if not more than — the recent Bob Dylan tour.

CSN&Y will also be recording together in the near future, although it is unlikely an album will emerge in time for the tour. However, several of the concerts will be recorded, with a live album a strong possible outcome.

There are no plans yet for CSN&Y dates outside the U.S. But, says our correspondent, the possibility of subsequent tours overseas (including Britain) cannot be ruled out — depending upon the band's own reactions to their U.S. dates.
● Stephen Stills talks exclusively with NME, Page 5.

Steve Stills talks to NME Exclusive

Beefheart due/ Stardust tour

their restraint. Indeed, some of Nash's best work is featured on the album which concludes with a beautifully realised collaboration with Joni Mitchell on 'Another Sleep Song'.

This same day, Stills copyrights 'My Angel', co-written with drummer Dallas Taylor.

28 JANUARY

Joni Mitchell's *Court And Spark* is released with Crosby singing on 'Down To You' and Crosby & Nash providing backing vocals on 'Free Man In Paris'. On this same day, Grace Slick's *Manhole* is issued with Crosby singing on 'Theme From The Movie "Manhole"'.

FEBRUARY

With Manassas drifting apart, Stills embarks on a three-month solo tour with a backing group comprising Kenny Passarelli (bass), Donnie Dacus (guitar), Joe Lala (percussion), Jerry Aiello (keyboards) and Russ Kunkel (drums).

2 FEBRUARY

Nash celebrates his 32nd birthday by taking acid at Winchester Cathedral. "I lost who I was and where I was in that experience," he recalled. "It ended 24 hours later lying on my back in the middle of Stonehenge."

9 FEBRUARY

Stills plays Carnegie Hall, a performance that he looks back on later with a characteristically critical eye. "It was right at the beginning of my solo acoustic tour," he told Chris Hillman's songwriting partner Peter Knobler. "I was just a little too drunk to do the crowd justice. I really got furious with myself and so I quit drinking on-stage. Three scotches isn't too bad spread

over two hours but I was fairly well lit by the end of the show. I'd been a little nervous about Carnegie Hall and overdid it. The basic element there being fear."

Stills' self-image is not reflected in the reviews of the concert. *Melody Maker's* US Editor Chris Charlesworth does not detect any obvious drunkenness and the only "fear" he observes emanates from Stills' fellow players. Summing up the show, the exuberant Charlesworth points out: "It's not until Stills

actually performs on his own like this that you understand how really talented he is. He's casual in the extreme, lighting cigarettes during numbers and just tapping his foot to keep the time signature, and he creates an aura of respectful silence all along. He is undoubtedly one of the best guitar players rock has produced, equally at home on either the

acoustic or electric instrument...The new group were tight and musical and all that Stills could hope for in a backing band, even though there were times when they looked a little frightened of their leader."

SET LIST: LOVE THE ONE YOU'RE WITH; WOODEN SHIPS; EVERYBODY'S TALKIN' (AT ME); MY FAVORITE CHANGES; JET SET (SIGH)/ROCKY MOUNTAIN WAY; SPECIAL CARE; CHANGE PARTNERS; BLUESMAN; CROSSROADS/YOU CAN'T CATCH ME; BLACKBIRD; 4+20; WORD GAME; FOUR DAYS GONE; WE ARE NOT HELPLESS; NEW MAMA; BLUEBIRD; 49 BYE BYES/FOR WHAT IT'S WORTH; FIND THE COST OF FREEDOM.

MARCH

Stills continues his solo tour, with support act Maria Muldaur often seen dancing in the wings. For a recorded appearance in Chicago (March 8/9), Stills dons a black fuzzy wig and informs the audience that the jape has won him $200 from the stage crew. He later learns that he has forfeited the bet by not wearing the wig for the entire song.

15 MARCH

"CSN&Y re-formed – tour, album" trumpets the front page of the *NME*. Initial plans are modest with Stills mentioning a mere 10-day tour, supposedly beginning in Tampa on Independence Day. Sceptics are no doubt drawn to the alarming proviso: "If it's not good in rehearsals, I'm not going! Everyone feels the same way... The hardest part is going to be for everyone to remember how to sit and take orders. And me too!"

Stills also appears less than pleased with his present work rate, revealing: "I'm a little slower these days with words... You sit and diddle at the piano and wait for something that sets it off and it takes hours and hours. Finally you get bored and go skiing."

16 MARCH

Crosby appears solo at the Fairleigh Dickenson University, Rutherford, New Jersey. The set is the usual intimate acoustic affair, with Crosby telling some amusing anecdotes and performing a pleasing selection of past classics He also features the still unreleased anti-star tale, 'King Of The Mountain'.

SET LIST: DÉJÀ VU; THE LEE SHORE; TRIAD; LAUGHING; KING OF THE MOUNTAIN; ALMOST CUT MY HAIR; FOR FREE; PAGE 43; GUINNEVERE; LONG TIME GONE; WOODEN SHIPS; WHAT ARE THEIR NAMES?

26 MARCH

Young, currently completing his next album, jams with The Eagles during a benefit show for the Red Wind Indians at Luesta College.

10 APRIL

Nash is interviewed on BBC's *The Old Grey Whistle Test* and explains the rationale behind the CSN&Y reunion and why they are touring without an album. "Instead of going into the studio," he begins, then hesitates. "We tried that once and it didn't work because we discovered that we hadn't really been together enough to get down to the music. So we figured

NEIL YOUNG, 1974

we'd go on the road first and get into the live music and then, when we'd been together two to three months – then we'd go into the studio."

0/27 APRIL

Nash continues publicising CSN&Y in the UK music press. He says he would like the concerts to open with Young's 'When You Dance I Can Really Love', a song that will ultimately not be played at any of the shows. Promising that the tour will not be an exercise in nostalgia, he insists: "We can't really go out and do 'Southern Man' for 18 minutes – or 'Our House' again. We've got to go out and say something we mean now. Not what we meant then. It's going to be difficult, but I think we can pull it off because I've heard the new music and I've heard where we are now."

The current music scene holds no fascination for Nash who laments, "I see a giant hole everywhere. I find very little of that special magic in the music, that indefinable something that was around about 1969/70, the Woodstock period. We're going to bring it back. There's good music around, but I haven't, for a long time, seen people get off like the way they do when CSN&Y really hit".

Apparently, it is not merely the spirit of the times that is out of joint but himself. Despite embarking on a new relationship, he sounds terribly uncertain about his life and hints at his darker side. "I don't know what it is that's lacking," he ponders. "I have almost everything you could wish for, and yet I'm not happy in the least... Here I am, I'm physically and mentally sound, I've invested my money wisely, but I'm still crazy. I'm still not happy. I'm an idealist for sure and that hurts because your ideals get raped. They do. I get disappointed and then I get disappointed that I'm disappointed. And then I get really disappointed."

APRIL

Stills registers copyright in 'My Favorite Changes'.

APRIL

The music press claim that the original Byrds, The Buffalo Springfield and CSN&Y are all reforming for a once in a lifetime appearance at the LA Coliseum on July 6. Alas, despite the provisional booking, it proves too fantastic to ever come about.

MAY

BBC's *The Old Grey Whistle Test* broadcasts a solo performance by Nash who plays 'On The Line' and 'Another Sleep Song'.

MAY

Stills registers copyright in 'Start Over Again', 'In The Way', 'Shuffle Just As Bad' and 'Circlin'. The latter will not appear until as late as *Illegal Stills* in 1976, while 'Start Over Again' remains unreleased.

MAY

Young performs what may be his greatest solo show at New York's Bottom Line, showcasing

several songs from the forthcoming *On The Beach*, plus a riveting 'Pushed It Over The End' (which he announces as 'Citizen Kane Junior Blues') and a surprise reworking of Henry VIII's 'Greensleeves'. The set provides a unique glimpse into Young's psyche at a transitional stage of his career, caught between the craziness of the "Tonight's The Night" tour and the forthcoming CSN&Y stadium extravaganza. Here, at this remarkable one-off show, he displays his ultimate power as a narrative songwriter, previewing the extraordinary 'Ambulance Blues' among a mouth-watering selection of songs.

SET LIST: PUSHED IT OVER THE END: LONG MAY YOU RUN: GREENSLEEVES: AMBULANCE BLUES: ON THE BEACH: ROLL ANOTHER NUMBER: MOTION PICTURES: PARDON MY HEART: DANCE, DANCE, DANCE.

JUNE

Michael D'Abo's *Broken Rainbows* is released, with Nash playing harmonica on 'Fuel To Burn' and contributing rhythm guitar and harmonica to 'Handbags And Gladrags'.

MID-JUNE

CSN&Y rehearse for their summer tour at Young's ranch in Santa Cruz, playing on an open-air stage for several hours a day. They are joined by their new rhythm section: Tim Drummond (bass), Russ Kunkel (drums) and Joe Lala (percussion). During this same period, they record Nash's 'Prison Song', Stills' five-year-old 'Dreaming Of Snakes', and the blues based 'Little Blind Fish' (a strange, almost nursery rhyme lyric and the only known song composed by all four members). The latter two compositions remain unreleased.

29 JUNE

Stills appears on the Democratic Telethon, playing three songs: 'Open Up America', 'We Are Not Helpless' and 'Know You Got To Run'. The first of these is a still unreleased composition, with a positive lyric that proclaims, "Open Up America, time has come for changing". Stills reveals that he wrote the song on a plane that very evening.

JONI MITCHELL JOINS CSN&Y ON STAGE AT WEMBLEY STADIUM

9 JULY

CSN&Y's first show of the tour is at the Coliseum, Seattle, Washington. Riotous clapping greets the foursome as they launch into a newly arranged 'Love The One You're With', which will be used as the opening number at every show. Young pulls the first surprise of the night, adapting an electric 'Cowgirl In The Sand' to the set, just as he had done back in 1969 with Crazy Horse's other epic 'Down By The River'. Nash, who is on particularly fine form this evening, plays a stirring version of 'Grave Concern', which is preceded by a satirical sketch of Richard Nixon attempting to explain away Watergate. The political theme is continued with Crosby's fierce 'Almost Cut My Hair', which features some strikingly jagged guitar work. The electric set concludes with a showstopping 'Ohio', which is greeted by deafening applause.

Throughout this segment, the rhythm section of Tim Drummond, Joe Lala and Russ Kunkel has been exemplary, providing a rock solid backing that works extremely well in the arena setting. It is also noticeable that the songs flow smoothly and quickly, with few delays for tuning and a minimum of on-stage raps.

Almost inevitably, the acoustic set commences with the opening track of CS&N's first album, 'Suite: Judy Blue Eyes'. Stills' voice is noticeably high and after 'Helplessly Hoping' he informs the over-enthusiastic audience: "I can't hear my guitar, and if I can't hear my guitar I sing out of tune and it's horrible". He then wins enough silence for a pleasing rendition of 'Blackbird'.

Nash continues to excel during this performance, with powerful readings of 'Prison Song', 'Southbound Train' and 'Another Sleep Song'. One feature of these gigs is that you're

never sure which of the four will peak at which show. Here, Nash is the key figure, particularly during the mid-section of the evening.

Crosby cameos 'For Free' and 'Guinnevere', while Stills' set is most notable for a version of '4+20' featuring three-part harmony rather than the familiar solo, plus a faster than usual 'Word Game'.

Stills enjoys the lion's share of the songs with a total of 13, plus the co-composed 'Wooden Ships' and Lennon/McCartney's 'Blackbird'. Young manages 10, while Nash logs eight, and Crosby six. During the evening the quartet include an impressive nine as yet unissued compositions: 'Carry Me', 'First Things First', 'My Angel', 'My Favorite Changes', 'As I Come Of Age', 'Human Highway', 'Love Art Blues', 'Long May You Run', 'Traces' and 'Pushed It Over The End'. The last proves the most thrilling, leaving you to consider that On The Beach might have

been an even greater album if room had been made for this minor classic.

A breathless 'Carry On' underlines how difficult it has always been to do this song full justice when played live. By this stage, CSN&Y have been on-stage for close to four-and-a-half hours, but rally for a closing a cappella version of Crosby's 'What Are Their Names?' which segues into the hand-clapping finale 'Chicago'. It is just past 1.30 am before the audience empties through the turnstiles, leaving CSN&Y to consider whether they can maintain this punishing pace for the next seven weeks. After the show, they agree to try and stick to three hours at successive concerts for fear of destroying their voices.

Overall, they could hardly have envisaged a better start to the tour. Those in attendance were fortunate enough to have witnessed a new age in quality stadium rock, played with a

precision and confidence seldom matched since. For the record, this was also the longest set that CSN&Y ever played and featured a staggering 40 songs.

SET LIST: LOVE THE ONE YOU'RE WITH; WOODEN SHIPS; IMMIGRATION MAN; COWGIRL IN THE SAND; CHANGE PARTNERS; TRACES; GRAVE CONCERN; BLACK QUEEN; ALMOST CUT MY HAIR; OHIO; SUITE: JUDY BLUE EYES; HELPLESSLY HOPING; BLACKBIRD; HUMAN HIGHWAY; PRISON SONG; AS I COME OF AGE; CARRY ME; FOR FREE; GUINNEVERE; SOUTHBOUND TRAIN; ANOTHER SLEEP SONG; OUR HOUSE; 4+20; KNOW YOU GOT TO RUN; WORD GAME; LOVE ART BLUES; LONG MAY YOU RUN; A MAN NEEDS A MAID; DON'T BE DENIED; FIRST THINGS FIRST; DÉJÀ VU; MY ANGEL; PRE-ROAD DOWNS; MY FAVORITE CHANGES; LONG TIME GONE; REVOLUTION BLUES; PUSHED IT OVER THE END; CARRY ME; WHAT ARE THEIR NAMES?/CHICAGO.

10 JULY
CSN&Y play at the Pacific National Exhibition Coliseum, Vancouver, where Crosby is still

recovering from vocal exhaustion resulting from the previous night's over-enthusiastic offering. On 'Almost Cut My Hair' his voice is reduced to a hoarse croak and by the close of the electric set he leaves the stage like a boxer relieved to hear the end-of-round bell. During the intermission, he is inconsolable and complains: "I blew my voice. And when I blow my voice, I blow the harmonies". The acoustic set is a painful struggle made worse by noisy members of the audience whom Crosby is forced to quieten. After the show he fails to appear for the post-gig celebrations, and retires to his hotel bedroom. Stills prefers to continue the festivities and plays an impromptu version of The Everly Brothers' 'Wake Up Little Susie' for an amused Joni Mitchell.

Throughout the tour Young will travel separately from his colleagues. While Crosby, Stills and Nash fly from show to show, Young drives from city to city in his elaborate camper/coach with only his wife, a roadie and his dog for company. Observers note that this mode of transport keeps him more relaxed than if he were permanently in the company of his three colleagues.

13 JULY

CSN&Y appear at Alameda County Coliseum, Oakland, before 75,000 people. The electric set is well received with Crosby and Young enjoying themselves performing the "I can't recall..." Nixon satire prior to Nash's 'Grave Concern'. After a riveting 'Ohio', they take a short break while the microphones are adjusted for the acoustic set. Young needs a lengthy tuning interlude prior to 'Human Highway', but the audience remains patient. Both Crosby and Nash provide a pleasing trilogy of songs, with Graham attempting to play 'Another Sleep Song' then changing his mind and singing a new composition, 'It's All Right'. This will remain unissued until as late as *Earth And Sky* in 1980.

Young dominates the closing part of the show with selections from *On The Beach*, including the brilliant 'Ambulance Blues'. Perhaps feeling that he is expressing his darker side too much, Young abruptly decides to throw in a lighter number for the masses. "Here's a song you can all sing on to make this thing vibrate," he remarks, sounding like a stoned hippie from a Crosby/Nash concert. "You'd

better sing on it," he adds, "because the song is pretty lame without you. It's good to know where it's at."

'Sugar Mountain' follows, after which Young leaves the stage to Stills for a romp through 'Know You Got To Run' and the inspired pairing of 'You Can't Catch Me' and 'Word Game'. Young then returns for two compelling readings of 'Don't Be Denied' and 'Pushed It Over The End' confirming his huge presence at this exceptional gig.

SET LIST: LOVE THE ONE YOU'RE WITH; WOODEN SHIPS; IMMIGRATION MAN; TRACES; COWGIRL IN THE SAND; GRAVE CONCERN; BLACK QUEEN; OHIO; SUITE: JUDY BLUE EYES; BLACKBIRD; HUMAN HIGHWAY; CARRY ME; FOR FREE; THE LEE SHORE; PRISON SONG; IT'S ALL RIGHT; OUR HOUSE; LONG MAY YOU RUN; ONLY LOVE CAN BREAK YOUR HEART; AMBULANCE BLUES; SUGAR MOUNTAIN; KNOW YOU GOT TO RUN; YOU CAN'T CATCH ME/WORD GAME; DON'T BE DENIED; DÉJÀ VU; PRE-ROAD DOWNS; FIRST THINGS FIRST; LONG TIME GONE; REVOLUTION BLUES; PUSHED IT OVER THE END; CARRY ME; CHICAGO.

14 JULY

For their second gig at the Oakland, CSN&Y modify the set slightly during the acoustic section and introduce a crowd-pleasing 'Only Love Can Break Your Heart' and a pensive version of 'The Lee Shore'. The show begins and ends with Stills' 'Love The One You're With'. Afterwards, promoter Bill Graham describes the evening as "One of the most significant musical events of the decade".

SET LIST: LOVE THE ONE YOU'RE WITH; WOODEN SHIPS; IMMIGRATION MAN; TRACES; COWGIRL IN THE SAND; GRAVE CONCERN; BLACK QUEEN; OHIO; SUITE: JUDY BLUE EYES; ONLY LOVE CAN BREAK YOUR HEART; THE LEE SHORE; FOR FREE; PRISON SONG; ANOTHER SLEEP SONG; LONG MAY YOU RUN; AMBULANCE BLUES; CHANGE PARTNERS; KNOW YOU GOT TO RUN; YOU CAN'T CATCH ME/WORD GAME; DON'T BE DENIED; FIRST THINGS FIRST; DÉJÀ VU; MY ANGEL; PRE-ROAD DOWNS; LONG TIME GONE; REVOLUTION BLUES; PUSHED IT OVER THE END; CARRY ME; CHICAGO; LOVE THE ONE YOU'RE WITH.

16/19 JULY

The tour continues with performances at the Tempe Stadium, Arizona (July 16) and the Royals Stadium, Harry S. Truman Sports Complex, Kansas, Missouri (19). As Crosby reminds us: "We can only get this group together for a little while ever; once in a while. It's a very fragile, explosive mixture and that's why it works. There's not a chance in hell of getting this band to work solid for a year and that's what we'd have to do if we didn't play such big gigs. It's simple math."

SET LIST (JULY 19): LOVE THE ONE YOU'RE WITH; WOODEN SHIPS; IMMIGRATION MAN; TRACES; COWGIRL IN THE SAND; ALMOST CUT MY HAIR; BLACK QUEEN; OHIO; ON THE WAY HOME; SUITE: JUDY BLUE EYES; HELPLESSLY HOPING; ONLY LOVE CAN BREAK YOUR HEART; THE LEE SHORE; FOR FREE; PRISON SONG; SIMPLE MAN; LONG MAY YOU RUN; AMBULANCE BLUES; SUGAR MOUNTAIN; CHANGE PARTNERS; KNOW YOU GOT TO RUN; YOU CAN'T CATCH ME/WORD GAME; PRE-ROAD DOWNS; FIRST THINGS FIRST; DÉJÀ VU; MY ANGEL; LONG TIME GONE; REVOLUTION BLUES; PUSHED IT OVER THE END; CARRY ON.

1 JULY

The balance of power in the set list shifts towards Young, who sings a dozen of the 32 songs at the County Stadium, Milwaukee, WI. Among the songs included is the first known public performance of the still unreleased 'Homefires'.

SET LIST: LOVE THE ONE YOU'RE WITH; WOODEN SHIPS; IMMIGRATION MAN; TRACES; COWGIRL IN THE SAND; BLACK QUEEN; OHIO; ON THE WAY HOME; SUITE: JUDY BLUE EYES; HELPLESSLY HOPING; ONLY LOVE CAN BREAK YOUR HEART; THE LEE SHORE; GUINNEVERE; SIMPLE MAN; PRISON SONG; LONG MAY YOU RUN; HOMEFIRES; THE NEEDLE AND THE DAMAGE DONE; CHANGE PARTNERS; YOU CAN'T CATCH ME/WORD GAME; DON'T BE DENIED; FIRST THINGS FIRST; DÉJÀ VU; MY ANGEL; PRE-ROAD DOWNS; LONG TIME GONE; MILITARY MADNESS; REVOLUTION BLUES; PUSHED IT OVER THE END; CARRY ON; CHICAGO; WALK ON.

2 JULY

CSN&Y appear at the Civic Center Arena, St Paul, Minnesota. Bob Dylan is hanging out backstage and Stills pointedly dedicates 'Word Game' to him. After the show, Dylan impresses Stills by playing him some songs from the forthcoming *Blood On The Tracks*, which will soon be acclaimed as one of his greatest albums.

In the midst of all the reunion celebrations taking place on the tour, Crosby is surprisingly quick to remind the media that this is merely another phase in the kaleidoscopic career of the four members. "My guess is that we won't stay together," he predicts. "We'll make an album and not stay together. I think the soonest you would see us come together after we made the album would be the next summer."

In the event, Crosby's prediction proves sadly over-optimistic.

JULY

Young's *On The Beach* (officially scheduled for July 10) is issued with Crosby guesting on 'Revolution Blues' and appearing on the title track. The album is no mere return to form, but a groundbreaking work and arguably Young's greatest achievement to date. With the exposure provided by the current CSN&Y tour, it allows him greater autonomy than perhaps even he could have imagined.

JULY

Backstage at the Mile High Stadium, Denver, Colorado, Nash is collared by *Melody Maker's* US correspondent Chris Charlesworth, who wants to know about money as well as music. "I get totally pissed when people insinuate that we're only in it for the money," Nash tells him. "Man, we could have made millions over the last four years, believe me. But we didn't because we didn't feel like it. We didn't feel like playing together and, if we're in it for the money, you tell me why we didn't go out and play over the last five years anyway."

Charlesworth concedes the point, leaving Nash to wax sentimental on the CSN&Y philosophy: "Can you imagine what it's like to be a part of a really hot band and then not play for four years because we didn't feel that

musical honesty. Now we feel it on stage. This is a band... a real band. Did you see any bad vibes? Do you think we could fake it that good? I'm not into this vibe trip, but I know that we're more considerate of each other's feelings, we give each other a little more space, we'll take suggestions and not close them off immediately like used to happen, and that's because everyone's really secure in who they are individually... I think before we didn't feel solid enough inside ourselves to be totally comfortable all the time. Now that we've grown up a little, now that we've proven that we can all move people individually, we know we want to be a band. You heard it for yourself."

SET LIST: LOVE THE ONE YOU'RE WITH; WOODEN SHIPS; IMMIGRATION MAN; TRACES; ALMOST CUT MY HAIR; COWGIRL IN THE SAND; PRE-ROAD DOWNS; ONLY LOVE CAN BREAK YOUR HEART; OLD MAN; FOR FREE; SIMPLE MAN; PRISON SONG; SUGAR MOUNTAIN; AMBULANCE BLUES; CHANGE PARTNERS; BLACK QUEEN; YOU CAN'T CATCH ME/WORD GAME; SUITE: JUDY BLUE EYES; LONG TIME GONE; DON'T BE DENIED; FIRST THINGS FIRST; DÉJÀ VU; REVOLUTION BLUES; PUSHED IT OVER THE END; MILITARY MADNESS; OHIO; CARRY ON.

28/31 JULY

While Nash tucks into a traditional breakfast of bacon and eggs, Crosby psyches himself up for the next gig by walking up a nearby mountain. In the evening they appear at the Jeppesan Stadium, Houston, Texas, after which they have a few days' break before playing the Texas Stadium, Dallas, Fort Worth (July 31).

5/6 AUGUST

For CSN&Y's opening night at the Boston Garden, Young is in an unusually talkative mood, chatting to the audience frequently, as if it's a homecoming gig. He again pulls a surprise by inserting 'The Losing End' into the set, once more using an old Crazy Horse number in a new way. "We're just winging it tonight," he tells the crowd. "We didn't have a plan when we came here." He then returns to CSN&Y's first golden era by featuring the epic 'Down By The River', the ultimate example of a Crazy Horse song reinvented for the million dollar quartet. By the time we hear the rich harmonies on 'Only Love Can Break Your Heart', the unstinting generosity of the others towards Young is evident.

Crosby is characteristically exuberant throughout the evening, extravagantly telling the audience that he and his comrades will play every song in their respective repertoires. As if that isn't enough, he adds: "I feel like singing the 'Star Spangled Banner' in honour of how well the Constitution's working," Instead, he plays 'For Free', informing the umpteenth audience on the tour that his favourite songwriter is Joni Mitchell.

Nash dedicates the new song 'It's All Right' to his girl friend Callie, who is accompanying him on the tour. Young then returns for three acoustic songs, beginning with his number 1 hit 'Heart Of Gold'. He is forced to stop before reaching the end of the first verse due to the effusive reception. "Sorry about that folks," he says. "I just can't play in two keys at the same time."

Stills has far greater problems beginning '4+20' when the noise levels reach an unacceptable level. "Hey, hush up back there!" implores Crosby, while his partner attempts to put his guitar in tune. When the audience fails to respond, Crosby loses his patience and shouts: "Hey, you dorks at the back there – shut up!"

By this point, Stills is wondering whether he will ever begin the song. "I can't hear myself think," he mutters. "Not that there's much thinking going on, you understand!"

Eventually, he plays '4+20', only to abandon the song after the second verse in frustration at the continuing din. While Nash takes up the protest, Stills decides to change tack and launches into a fast 'Word Game', which mollifies the noise-makers. Relieved to complete the acoustics, the players leave the stage to prepare for their electric set.

Thereafter, things improve and the final segment of the show passes in a flurry of excellently performed songs, most notably Crosby's 'Déjà Vu' and Young's 'Revolution Blues' and 'Pushed It Over The End'.

SET LIST: LOVE THE ONE YOU'RE WITH; WOODEN SHIPS; THE LOSING END; PRISON SONG; ALMOST CUT MY HAIR; IMMIGRATION MAN; DOWN BY THE RIVER; TEACH YOUR CHILDREN; ONLY LOVE CAN BREAK YOUR HEART; BLACKBIRD; HELPLESSLY HOPING; GUINNEVERE; FOR FREE; IT'S ALL RIGHT; LOVE ART BLUES; OUT ON THE WEEKEND; HEART OF GOLD; CHANGE PARTNERS; 4+20; YOU CAN'T CATCH ME/WORD GAME; PRE-ROAD DOWNS; FIRST THINGS FIRST; DÉJÀ VU; MY ANGEL; BLACK QUEEN; REVOLUTION BLUES; PUSHED IT OVER THE END; MILITARY MADNESS; OHIO; CARRY ON.

6 AUGUST

For their second night in Boston, CSN&Y modify the set slightly, with Nash adding 'Simple Man' and 'Grave Concern' and Young importing 'Old Man' and 'On The Beach'. The previous night's 30-song set is reduced to 25, with Crosby dropping his solo spot and singing lead on a mere three songs during the evening.

SET LIST: LOVE THE ONE YOU'RE WITH; WOODEN SHIPS; IMMIGRATION MAN; TRACES; GRAVE CONCERN; BLACK QUEEN; THE LOSING END; ALMOST CUT MY HAIR; OLD MAN; TEACH YOUR CHILDREN; ONLY LOVE CAN BREAK YOUR HEART; BLACKBIRD; THE LEE SHORE; SIMPLE MAN; OUR HOUSE; SUGAR MOUNTAIN; CHANGE PARTNERS; WORD GAME; DÉJÀ VU; FIRST THINGS FIRST; ON THE BEACH; MY ANGEL; MILITARY MADNESS; OHIO; CARRY ON.

> "Man, we could have made millions over the last four years, believe me. But we didn't because we didn't feel like it... If we're in it for the money, you tell me why we didn't go out and play over the last five years."
>
> **STEPHEN STILLS**

8 AUGUST

An eventful evening at the Roosevelt Stadium, Jersey City, New York. With Richard Nixon's resignation hot news, CSN&Y feel at their most potent. Stills makes his feelings known during the altered first line of the opening song: "When you're Gerry Ford..." After completing 'Love The One You're With' he announces, "That was dedicated to Mr Gerald Ford, the next President of the United States."

"President Nixon resigned!" Nash hollers, as if the news has not yet sunk in. Judging from the audience response, the Roosevelt Stadium is populated by excited Democrats. The pushing at the front of the stage is disconcerting enough to encourage a call for calm.

Crosby is obviously relishing the announcement of Nixon's resignation and sings an impassioned 'Long Time Gone', ad-libbing lyrics such as "Speak about the madness – in defence of this country I gotta say, it's still a free place and you still can damn well speak your mind..." He continues in this mood during the satirical introduction to 'Grave Concern'.

All is well at this point but, by the time the quartet move into their acoustic sets, the audience is becoming unruly. Young manages to get through 'Old Man', amid complaints about the noise. Nash attempts an uptempo 'Teach Your Children' in the hope of rising above the distracting chatter, but it proves largely ineffectual. Young quickly strums the opening chords of 'Only Love Can Break Your Heart', and is then forced to stop. Glancing ahead, he exclaims: "I don't know what it is because I can't really see. But if there's something... if everybody's standing up or something, why don't you sit down?"

The audience cheers, prompting Nash to adopt a schoolmaster tone and demand: "Come on now! Please for everybody's sake, try and sit down. We know it's a very important night."

By now, it is so loud that the musicians can barely hear their own instruments, while Nash laments: "We really want to do some acoustic music."

That plan is abandoned, resulting in a curtailed set of 21 songs, the lowest number played on the entire tour. Crosby launches into the electric 'Déjà Vu' as shouts of "Sit down!" can be heard in the background. Seven songs later, the foursome leave the stage, closing with a blistering 'Ohio'. When they return for an encore, Nash announces: "On the day that President Nixon resigned everyone has to carry on". A lengthy 'Carry On' follows, after which Young finally manages to complete the previously abandoned 'Only Love Can Break Your Heart', before Nash ends the show on a suitably political note with 'Chicago'.

SET LIST: LOVE THE ONE YOU'RE WITH; WOODEN SHIPS; IMMIGRATION MAN; LONG TIME GONE; TRACES; GRAVE CONCERN; BLACK QUEEN; PRE-ROAD DOWNS; OLD MAN; TEACH YOUR CHILDREN; DÉJÀ VU; FIRST THINGS FIRST; DON'T BE DENIED; COWGIRL IN THE SAND; PRISON SONG; ALMOST CUT MY HAIR; MILITARY MADNESS; OHIO; CARRY ON; ONLY LOVE CAN BREAK YOUR HEART; CHICAGO.

9 AUGUST

CSN&Y are forced to play through a rainstorm during their appearance at the Atlantic City Racecourse, New Jersey. Nash, meanwhile, is reminding journalists of the immemorial CSN&Y ethic: "All those people who say that we broke up are just a bunch of stupid assholes. All that actually happened was we didn't record together as a unit... though we all appeared on each other's solo projects and also showed up at each other's concerts to help out. Anyway, we've all grown up a lot since those days, we're more aware of what's going on in each other's heads."

11 AUGUST

At the Rich Stadium, Orchard Park, Buffalo, NY, CSN&Y throw in an unidentified instrumental directly after Crosby's 'Almost Cut My Hair'. Later, Stills adds a new composition to the set titled 'Myth Of Sisyphus', which proves one of the most memorable songs heard during the tour.

SET LIST: LOVE THE ONE YOU'RE WITH; WOODEN SHIPS; IMMIGRATION MAN; HELPLESS; GRAVE CONCERN; BLACK QUEEN; LOVE ART BLUES; ALMOST CUT MY HAIR; INSTRUMENTAL; TEACH YOUR CHILDREN; ONLY LOVE CAN BREAK YOUR HEART; THE LEE SHORE; FOR FREE; OUR HOUSE; LONG MAY YOU RUN; CHANGE PARTNERS; MYTH OF SISYPHUS; YOU CAN'T CATCH ME/WORD GAME; DON'T BE DENIED; FIRST THINGS FIRST; DÉJÀ VU; MY ANGEL; MILITARY MADNESS; LONG TIME GONE; PUSHED IT OVER THE END; PRE-ROAD DOWNS; OHIO; CARRY ON.

14 AUGUST

Two nights at the Nassau Veterans' Memorial Coliseum, Uniondale, Long Island are previewed by the *NME*'s Roy Carr, who is eager to report a traffic jam: "On the way to Nassau Coliseum, our motorcade came to an abrupt halt right in the middle of the 59th Street Bridge when Neil Young's GMC Camper – which he is using as both home and transportation for the entire tour – suddenly ran out of fuel. This mishap held up the nose to bumper rush hour traffic in a humid temperature not far short of 90 degrees."

The set is a revelation, with Stills introducing 'Johnny's Garden' from the Manassas days and Crosby performing the yet to be released 'Time After Time'. Young's ever expanding song list continues with revivals of 'Birds' and 'Mellow My Mind', plus the unreleased message to a departing president, 'Goodbye Dick'.

SET LIST: LOVE THE ONE YOU'RE WITH; WOODEN SHIPS; IMMIGRATION MAN; HELPLESS; JOHNNY'S GARDEN; TRACES; ALMOST CUT MY HAIR; TEACH YOUR CHILDREN; ONLY LOVE CAN BREAK YOUR HEART; THE LEE SHORE; TIME AFTER TIME; IT'S ALL RIGHT; OUR HOUSE; BIRDS; GOODBYE DICK; MELLOW MY MIND; AMBULANCE BLUES; CHANGE PARTNERS; MYTH OF SISYPHUS; WORD GAME; DÉJÀ VU; FIRST THINGS FIRST; DON'T BE DENIED; CARRY ME; PRE-ROAD DOWNS; BLACK QUEEN; PUSHED IT OVER THE END; MILITARY MADNESS; OHIO; CARRY ON.

"Hey, Neil, don't play any dark shit numbers. You've got so many good numbers to choose from. Just play those things you really want to play and don't waste your energies on other things".

DAVID CROSBY

CSN&Y ON STAGE IN NEW YORK, AUGUST 1974

AUGUST

Prior to the second Nassau gig, journalists note how solicitous and protective CS&N are towards Young. This is perceived, somewhat bizarrely, as a reaction to the poor sales of Young's post-*Harvest* work. Whether Young needs such reassurance is doubtful, but Crosby is always there with an amusing quip. When the Canadian stresses his uncertainty about which numbers to perform, Crosby cheekily advises: "Hey, Neil, don't play any dark shit numbers. You've got so many good numbers to choose from. Just play those things you really want to play and don't waste your energies on other things".

"OK," Young laughs, no doubt impressed by such sagacity. But he still throws in the awkward 'Roll Another Number'.

SET LIST: LOVE THE ONE YOU'RE WITH; WOODEN SHIPS; IMMIGRATION MAN; DOWN BY THE RIVER; GRAVE CONCERN; JOHNNY'S GARDEN; ALMOST CUT MY HAIR; TEACH YOUR CHILDREN; ONLY LOVE CAN BREAK YOUR HEART; THE LEE SHORE; TIME AFTER TIME; SIMPLE MAN; IT'S ALL RIGHT; LOVE ART BLUES; HAWAIIAN SUNRISE; PARDON MY HEART/THE OLD HOMESTEAD; BLACKBIRD; MYTH OF SISYPHUS; SUITE: JUDY BLUE EYES; DÉJÀ VU; FIRST THINGS FIRST; ON THE BEACH; CARRY ME; PRE-ROAD DOWNS; WALK ON; BLACK QUEEN; ROLL ANOTHER NUMBER; LONG TIME GONE; OHIO; CARRY ON.

AUGUST

NME take the unusual step of re-reviewing Young's *On The Beach*, which had previously been slated. Ian MacDonald provides a fresh, incisive reading, arguing: "That an album as bleak and miserable sounding as *On The Beach* has been preceded by no less than six albums almost all equally bleak and miserable-sounding, can easily obscure the fact that the record represents a departure… And that could be the main reason why the majority of Neil Young fans won't get into *On The Beach*. The pill is no longer sugared – either by Sweet Melody or by garlands of posies… Young has, quite simply, welched on the deal. Which, in turn, suggests he's Woken Up… *On The Beach* isn't, as previously interpreted, the fag-end of Neil Young's romance with rejection, but actually quite a positive piece of work in the Merciless Realism bracket of Lennon's primal period."

On this same day, CSN&Y appear at Foreman Field Stadium, Norfolk, Virginia. They then have a day off as a result of the cancellation of their show at Philadelphia's JFK Stadium.

SET LIST (TAPE EXTRACT): CHANGE PARTNERS; MYTH OF SISYPHUS; DON'T BE DENIED; LONG TIME GONE; BLACK QUEEN; REVOLUTION BLUES; PRE-ROAD DOWNS; PUSHED IT OVER THE END; MILITARY MADNESS; OHIO; CARRY ON.

19 AUGUST

CSN&Y begin a three-day residency at the Capitol Center, Landover, Maryland. Six weeks into the tour, they seem revitalised and in good spirits. Young's dog Art is the subject of much discussion as he wanders on and off the stage between songs. As Nash quips: "One of the only reasons we know if we're playing good is when he comes on stage and just hangs out. If he doesn't come on stage, then we know we're playing real bad."

This evening's set is well received with Crosby in particularly fine form, blasting out a powerful 'Almost Cut My Hair', then extolling the pleasures of sex and drugs in 'The Lee Shore' while imagining "a place warm enough to grow it and your lady's lying there and she doesn't have anything on…" There's also his new song 'Time After Time', which is refreshing to hear mid-way through the tour. In between songs, it is Crosby who enjoys the smart asides, remarking: "Neil just frustrates the fuck out of me. I can't stand it. He writes a lot. I write about one song every three months and he writes about three every week. I hate him. It just drives me nuts!"

Ironically, this is one show where Young's new songs are at a premium and instead he prefers to revisit 'Old Man' and 'Heart Of Gold'. Towards the end of the evening, Young announces that they are going to play "a couple of new ones" but after Crosby's recently written 'Carry Me' the remaining three are the old favourites, 'Military Madness', 'Ohio' and 'Carry On'. Who'd have thought it? A CSN&Y gig in which Crosby plays more new material than Young, Stills and Nash.

SET LIST: LOVE THE ONE YOU'RE WITH; WOODEN SHIPS; IMMIGRATION MAN; TRACES; GRAVE CONCERN; JOHNNY'S GARDEN; HELPLESS; ALMOST CUT MY HAIR; TEACH YOUR CHILDREN; ONLY LOVE CAN BREAK YOUR HEART; THE LEE SHORE; TIME

AFTER TIME; SOUTHBOUND TRAIN; IT'S ALL RIGHT ; OLD MAN; HEART OF GOLD; CHANGE PARTNERS; SUITE: JUDY BLUE EYES; DÉJÀ VU; FIRST THINGS FIRST; ON THE BEACH; BLACK QUEEN; PRE-ROAD DOWNS; CARRY ME; MILITARY MADNESS; OHIO; CARRY ON.

20/21 AUGUST

For their final two nights in Maryland, CSN&Y vary the set with Nash introducing 'Fieldworker' and Young replacing 'On The Beach' with 'Revolution Blues' and 'Ambulance Blues'. The following night, Young features the unreleased 'Homefires', while Nash revives 'Lady Of The Island'.

SET LIST (AUGUST 20): LOVE THE ONE YOU'RE WITH; WOODEN SHIPS; IMMIGRATION MAN; HELPLESS; GRAVE CONCERN; JOHNNY'S GARDEN; ALMOST CUT MY HAIR; TEACH YOUR CHILDREN; ONLY LOVE CAN BREAK YOUR HEART; THE LEE SHORE; TIME AFTER TIME; FIELDWORKER; OUR HOUSE; LONG MAY YOU RUN; AMBULANCE BLUES; OLD MAN; WORD GAME; SUITE: JUDY BLUES EYES; FIRST THINGS FIRST; DÉJÀ VU; CARRY ME; REVOLUTION BLUES; PRE-ROAD DOWNS; BLACK QUEEN; OHIO; CARRY ON.

23 AUGUST

An unhappy homecoming for Stills is the only way to describe CSN&Y's show at the Tampa Stadium, Florida. They attempt to provide some varied music, with Young offering 'Walk On' and the unreleased 'Homefires', but overall the evening is blighted by the unruly crowd. The acoustic set is reduced to a struggle of wills, which reaches a head after Crosby's 'Guinnevere'. "Listen, cool it for a second," he implores. "We've got a few more stories to tell, then we can get back to the dance party."

Stills is clearly growing impatient and calls upon his former residency in the area as a means of restoring order. "I went to high school in this town," he points out. "We're trying to do some beautiful songs for you. We're trying to keep our shit together, so we suggest you do the same."

He is largely ignored and Nash's 'Simple Man' passes without enticing the crowd from their noisy chatter. "You gotta stop yelling," Crosby insists angrily. "All you guys gotta shut up. I mean it. Stop! If you want to hear any more music at all, everybody be quiet."

Like an ineffectual teacher, Crosby simply startles the hordes for a minute or two which enables Young to complete 'Human Highway' relatively uninterrupted, but it doesn't last. Stills finally tells it as he feels, denouncing the crowd as a disgrace in a few sarcastic words. "I'm gonna tell you something," he coyly begins. "We've played upwards to 60,000 people. You're the rudest crowd we've ever seen." His anger is then turned to spectacular advantage as he remembers other negative aspects of Tampa, recalling, "There's a man used to come here and play every once in a while – Lightnin' Hopkins. I used to have a car and when I used to go back home over the other side of town I got bricks thrown at me and I got called Nigger Lover." Enflamed by this memory, Stills launches into a passionate 'Word Game', spitting the words out with utter contempt for the rude crowd, the small time racism and parochial narrow-mindedness that even now threaten to spoil this gig. By the end of the song he has reached a froth of

indignation, summed up in the words, "they might throw up on you". His performance is the highlight of the evening, closing the acoustic set on a suitably vengeful note.

SET LIST: LOVE THE ONE YOU'RE WITH; WOODEN SHIPS; IMMIGRATION MAN; HELPLESS; GRAVE CONCERN; JOHNNY'S GARDEN; WALK ON; ALMOST CUT MY HAIR; TEACH YOUR CHILDREN; ONLY LOVE CAN BREAK YOUR HEART; THE LEE SHORE; GUINNEVERE; SIMPLE MAN; OUR HOUSE; HUMAN HIGHWAY; HOMEFIRES; OLD MAN; MYTH OF SISYPHUS; WORD GAME; DÉJÀ VU; FIRST THINGS FIRST; DOWN BY THE RIVER; BLACK QUEEN; PRE-ROAD DOWNS; REVOLUTION BLUES; CARRY ON; OHIO.

25 AUGUST

The CSN&Y tour rolls on to the Memorial Stadium, Memphis, Tennessee. Memories of the acoustic débâcle at Tampa linger, convincing Crosby & Nash that playing stadiums is akin to a game of Russian roulette. As Crosby admitted: "The doom tour pissed me off... It was a rip-off by us of the audiences. If a person can't see your face they can't tell how you're feeling about what you're doing. And if they can't tell how you feel about what you're singing, they're not getting it. And to charge somebody 10 bucks to sit on a piece of mud, 30 yards away literally – it doesn't matter if you've got a PA system bigger than God – it's not fair."

Crosby's objections, understandable in view of their performances in Tampa and Jersey City, will sound less convincing when applied to most of the other dates in which eve the acoustic sets sound mightily impressive and extremely clear. In fact this tour compares favourably with those later undertaken by CS&N which sound lacklustre and anonymous by comparison.

SET LIST (EXTRACT): LOVE THE ONE YOU'RE WITH; WOODEN SHIPS; IMMIGRATION MAN; HELPLESS; MILITARY MADNESS; JOHNNY'S GARDEN; REVOLUTION BLUES; ONLY LOVE CAN BREAK YOUR HEART.

5 AUGUST

With no new CSN&Y product to promote, Atlantic issues the presumptuous *So Far*, largely against the wishes of the quartet who rightly argue that a career resumé from a mere two albums is both unnecessary and absurd. Nevertheless, Atlantic prove their point in sales terms when the album reaches number 1. The chart position merely underlines what they could have sold with a new studio or live album.

?-29 AUGUST

CSN&Y enjoy three nights at the Chicago Stadium, playing in the city that hosted their first ever show back in 1969 and provided much of the material for the live *4 Way Street*. On the opening night they perform 35 songs, including Young's 'Pushed It Over The End', which is recorded here and subsequently released in Italy eight years later. Young also

> "*I think Stills, in particular, liked playing the enormous places, because he liked being big. And, in 1974, we were probably the biggest group in the world. Stephen liked that. It was enormously satisfying for him to have The Beach Boys, Santana, The Band and Joni Mitchell open for us. That was quite something.*"
>
> **DAVID CROSBY**

débuts 'Star Of Bethlehem' which will later appear on *American Stars 'n Bars*.

Reviews of the Chicago sojourn are very favourable, with *Sounds* enthusing: "Each tune of the second electric set picks up on the momentum gained during 'Suite: Judy Blue Eyes'. The electricity in the hall keeps buzzing, the music reaching incredible pinnacles. Stills and Young play like madmen possessed by some guitar playing demon all the way through 'Déjà Vu', 'Black Queen' and 'Revolution Blues', while Nash and Crosby sing like angels who've been to heaven and back. Both performers and audience are totally blown away..."

AUGUST

CSN&Y reach the closing stages of their tour, this time playing the Municipal Stadium, Cleveland, Ohio. The set is as well balanced as ever, bringing to mind Crosby's analysis of the group's appeal. "There's a reason for CSN&Y being as good as it is," he insists. "The main one that comes to mind is the fact of having each other's material to juxtapose our tunes with. It makes everything much stronger. A Neil Young song sounds better after a David Crosby song than it does after another Neil Young song. Technically, it works, emotionally it works, and

in terms of balancing each other it's a hugely more workable thing."

SET LIST: LOVE THE ONE YOU'RE WITH; WOODEN SHIPS; IMMIGRATION MAN; HELPLESS; MILITARY MADNESS; JOHNNY'S GARDEN; TRACES; ALMOST CUT MY HAIR; TEACH YOUR CHILDREN; ONLY LOVE CAN BREAK YOUR HEART; THE LEE SHORE; TRIAD; OUR HOUSE; HAWAIIAN SUNRISE; HARVEST; OLD MAN; MYTH OF SISYPHUS; YOU CAN'T CATCH ME/WORD GAME; SUITE: JUDY BLUE EYES; DÉJÀ VU; MY ANGEL; WALK ON; BLACK QUEEN; PRE-ROAD DOWNS; CARRY ON; ON THE BEACH; OHIO.

2 SEPTEMBER

CSN&Y return to Canada for an appearance at the Varsity Stadium, Toronto, Ontario. Young receives a good reception but chooses not to play any unreleased material apart from 'Traces'. However, he does feature 'Helpless' and 'Ambulance Blues' which feature Ontario and Toronto in the lyrics. Towards the end of the set it rains heavily, but the crowd remains enthusiastic. The Toronto press describe CSN&Y's performance as "a memorably historic occasion".

SET LIST: LOVE THE ONE YOU'RE WITH; WOODEN SHIPS; IMMIGRATION MAN; HELPLESS; MILITARY MADNESS; JOHNNY'S GARDEN; TRACES; ALMOST CUT MY HAIR; TEACH YOUR CHILDREN; ONLY LOVE CAN BREAK YOUR HEART; THE LEE SHORE; FOR FREE; IT'S ALL RIGHT ; OUR HOUSE; SUGAR MOUNTAIN; AMBULANCE BLUES; OLD MAN; CHANGE PARTNERS; YOU CAN'T CATCH ME/WORD GAME; DÉJÀ VU; DON'T BE DENIED; PRE-ROAD DOWNS; BLACK QUEEN; CARRY ON; OHIO.

8 SEPTEMBER

The US leg of the tour ends with a gig at the Roosevelt Raceway, Westbury, Long Island, New York. Reflecting on the tour as a whole, Crosby recalls that Stills & Young were very positive about these stadium gigs. "I think Stills in particular liked playing the enormous places because he liked being big. And in 1974, we probably were the biggest group in the world. At that moment, it was either us or the Stones. Stephen liked that. It was enormously satisfying for him to have The Beach Boys, Santana, The Band and Joni Mitchell open for us. That was quite something. I don't know how much Neil dug it. I think he dug playing and I think he dug what it would do... I think he wanted to play the big places. It was my memory of it that he did."

Typically, Stills is the usual mixture of praise and comic humility: "David Crosby is an incredible musician. He's to the point now where he never makes mistakes. Sometimes he'll play a little too much of something but he doesn't play out of tune... I've done all of it. I've been the most obnoxious superstar... I'm still

arrogant. I can be an absolute bastard. I have a bad habit of stating things pretty bluntly. I'm not known for my tact. I've done all of it. I've gotten all carried away with myself, being a rich man at 25. Sometimes it's difficult to deal with, and you make mistakes."

SET LIST: LOVE THE ONE YOU'RE WITH; WOODEN SHIPS; IMMIGRATION MAN; HELPLESS; MILITARY MADNESS; JOHNNY'S GARDEN; WALK ON; ALMOST CUT MY HAIR; TEACH YOUR CHILDREN; ONLY LOVE CAN BREAK YOUR HEART; THE LEE SHORE; TIME AFTER TIME; SOUTHBOUND TRAIN; ANOTHER SLEEP SONG; OUR HOUSE; HAWAIIAN SUNRISE; LONG MAY YOU RUN; AMBULANCE BLUES; OLD MAN; CHANGE PARTNERS; MYTH OF SISYPHUS; YOU CAN'T CATCH ME/WORD GAME; SUITE: JUDY BLUE EYES; DÉJÀ VU; FIRST THINGS FIRST; DON'T BE DENIED; BLACK QUEEN; REVOLUTION BLUES; PUSHED IT OVER THE END; PRE-ROAD DOWNS; CARRY ON; SUGAR MOUNTAIN; OHIO.

11 SEPTEMBER

Stills copyrights 'Myth Of Sisyphus', co-written with Kenny Passarelli.

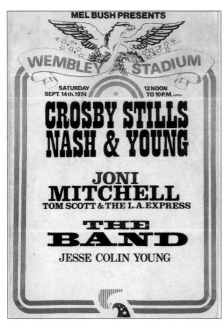

14 SEPTEMBER

The music press call it "the concert of the century". CSN&Y at Wembley Stadium becomes a landmark of its era, the ultimate outdoor gig with a scarcely believable line-up, featuring Jesse Colin Young, The Band and Joni Mitchell as support. The hallowed Wembley turf is protected by coconut matting at a cost of £5,000 and the football ground's stewards marvel at the consistently good behaviour of the 72,000 patrons. By the time CSN&Y appear at around 6.30pm, the audience can already look back on a brilliant day blessed by sunny weather.

Nash emerges from backstage first, greeting the masses with a casual "How you doing?" before the incessant rhythms of 'Love The One You're With' envelop the stadium. The first surprise of the evening occurs during 'Helpless' when Joni Mitchell steps from the wings to contribute to the harmonic blend. Nash keeps the catchy songs coming with 'Military Madness' and 'Immigration Man'

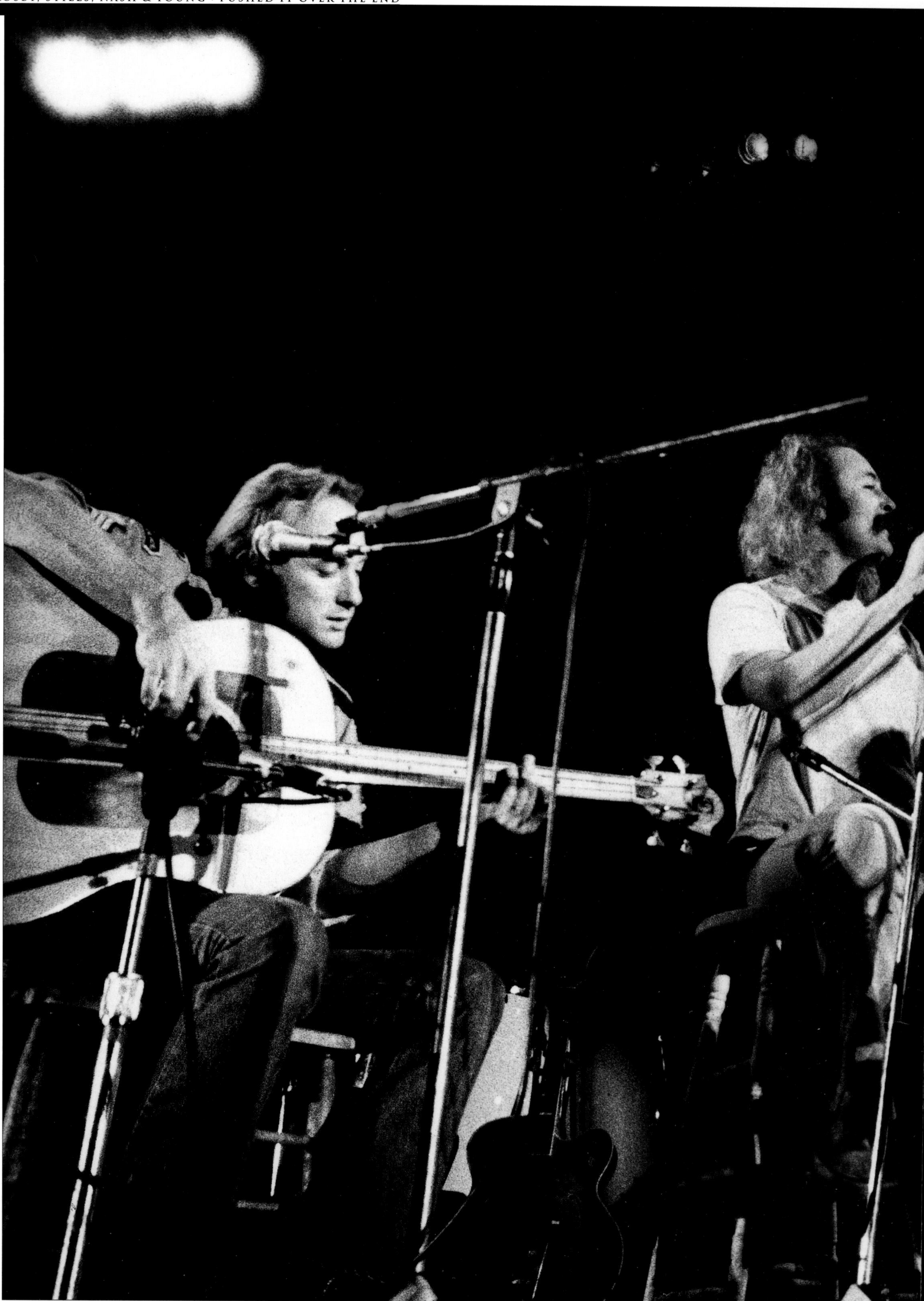

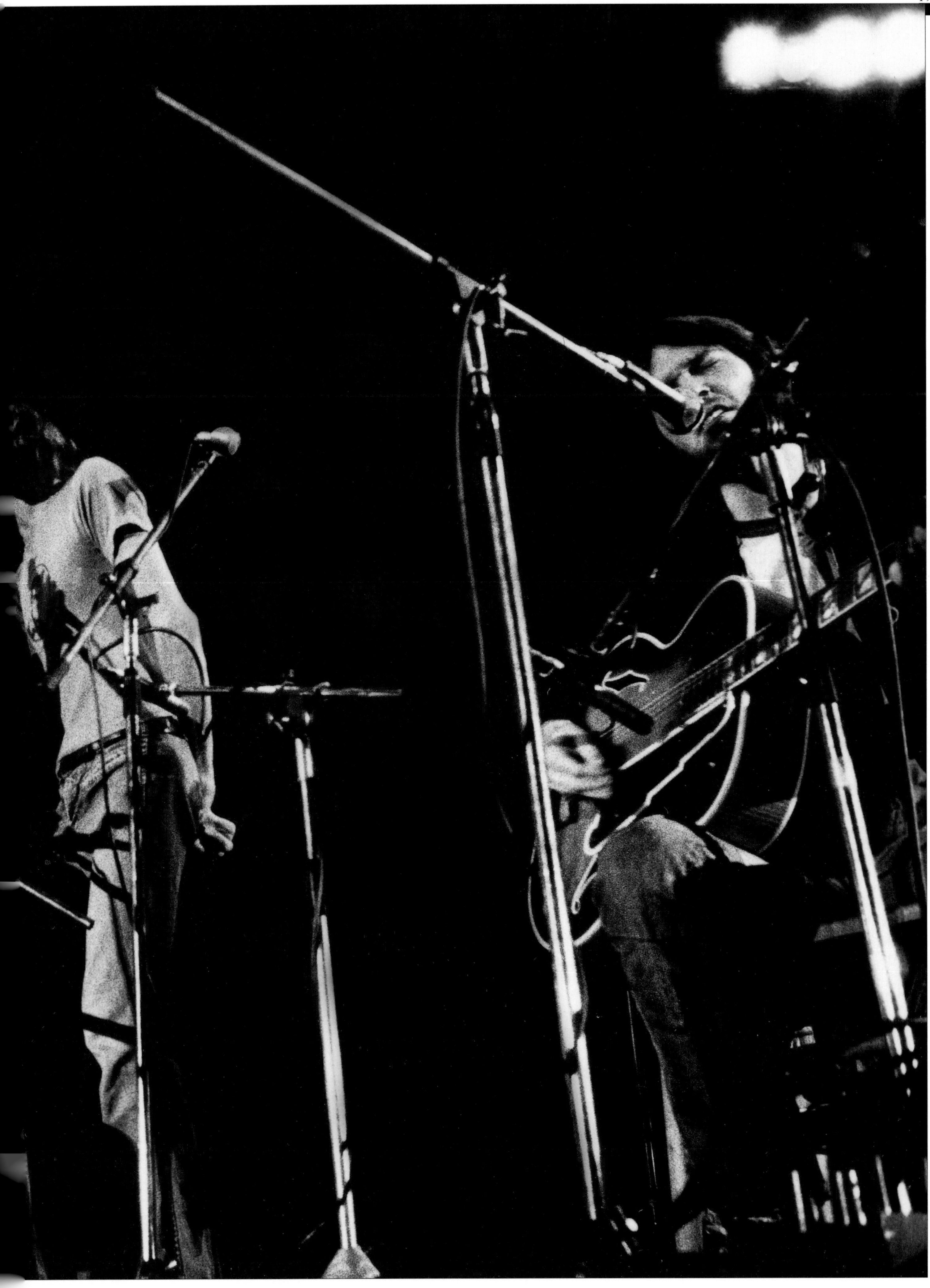

while Stills pays tribute to his former Elstead home in 'Johnny's Garden'. Young then introduces the first new song of the day – an exuberant 'Traces' – after which Crosby closes the electric set with an arresting 'Almost Cut My Hair'.

The lengthy acoustic segment features a wealth of new material, with Crosby tackling 'Time After Time' and Nash singing his love song to Callie: 'It's All Right'. Young elects to keep the mood sunny and features three new songs in a row: 'Hawaiian Sunrise', 'Star Of Bethlehem' and 'Love Art Blues'. Their lightness contrasts markedly with the recent material from *On The Beach*, which is conspicuously absent from the set's running order. It's left to Stills to provide the best new song of the evening so far, impressing his followers with a thrilling 'Myth Of Sisyphus'. What makes the acoustic section so memorable is the presence of Joni Mitchell

who transforms the music at times, contributing to 'Another Sleep Song', 'Only Love Can Break Your Heart', 'Old Man' and the closing 'Suite: Judy Blue Eyes'.

The foursome return for an eight-song electric set, beginning with a spacy version of 'Déjà Vu', an impressive 'Don't Be Denied' and insistent 'Black Queen'. The highlight though is Young's extraordinary 'Pushed It Over The End', one of the greatest songs never to appear on a CSN&Y album. Along with 'Myth Of Sisyphus' it provides an enduring memory of the power of the quartet at the height of their influence and popularity. After a lengthy 'Carry On', it's all over and the stadium erupts in seemingly incessant screams for an encore. Around me I hear a loud cry for 'Southern Man' while praying and screaming for 'Ohio'. CSN&Y answer the prayer and close what will be their last live concert of the decade with the song that most effectively summed

up their era. So ends perhaps the most memorable one-day rock concert ever seen in Britain up until the momentous Live Aid at the same venue.

For the liggers, there is a chance to see Stills & Young in action later that evening when they play 'Vampire Blues' and 'On The Beach' with several members of Led Zeppelin and The Band at a party at Quaglino's, Piccadilly.

SET LIST: LOVE THE ONE YOU'RE WITH: WOODEN SHIPS: IMMIGRATION MAN: HELPLESS: MILITARY MADNESS: JOHNNY'S GARDEN: TRACES: ALMOST CUT MY HAIR: TEACH YOUR CHILDREN: ONLY LOVE CAN BREAK YOUR HEART: THE LEE SHORE: TIME AFTER TIME: IT'S ALL RIGHT: ANOTHER SLEEP SONG OUR HOUSE: HAWAIIAN SUNRISE: STAR OF BETHLEHEM: LOVE ART BLUES: OLD MAN: CHANGE PARTNERS: BLACKBIRD: MYTH OF SISYPHUS: YOU CAN'T CATCH ME/WORD GAME: SUITE: JUDY BLUE EYES: DÉJÀ VU: FIRST THINGS FIRST: DON'T BE DENIED: BLACK QUEEN: PUSHED IT OVER THE END: PRE-ROAD DOWNS: CARRY ON: OHIO.

21 SEPTEMBER

Reviews of the Wembley show make interesting reading. *NME* ponder on the historical implications of CSN&Y achieving godhead and argue: "The thought of CSN&Y as being on the same acceptance level as Dylan or the Stones is a profoundly disquieting one. In no way are they a part of any musical or social revolution." Then, recalling the close of the concert when 'Ohio' erupted, they admit: "It was the finest possible ending, giving full play to CSN&Y's strengths and completely eliminating their weaknesses. They finished as they had begun – powerful, unified and genuinely impressive... Everybody got what they paid for; nobody got burned."

Sounds offers a less ambiguous viewpoint, simply stating: "Like a dream come true, three masters of the California sound and one transplanted Englishman, flawlessly revealed how after all these years and all those changes, they remain unchallenged title holders as the definitive American band... It was rock 'n' roll at its most potent."

4 OCTOBER

Young copyright registers three still unreleased songs: 'Hawaiian Sunrise', 'Love Art Blues' and 'Four Walls', plus 'Homestead' ('The Old Homestead').

8 OCTOBER

Crosby registers copyright for his songs 'Carry Me' and 'Time After Time'. They will appear on the next two Crosby/Nash albums in 1975 and 1976, respectively.

18 OCTOBER

Reprise Records log recording details for 'World On A String', the last song to be completed for *Tonight's The Night*.

25 NOVEMBER

Dan Fogelberg's *Souvenirs* is released, with Nash singing harmony on 'Part Of The Plan' and 'The Long Way'.

2–16 DECEMBER

Young records 'Separate Ways', 'White Line', 'Star Of Bethlehem', 'Try', 'Daughters', 'Deep Forbidden Lake', 'Homegrown', Love Is A Rose', 'We Don't Smoke It No More', 'Vacancy' and 'Give Me Strength'. Several of these songs are intended for the album *Homegrown* which will be completed but never released.

16 DECEMBER

CSN&Y regroup at the Record Plant, Sausalito, but only manage to complete 'Wind On The Water' and 'Homeward Through The Haze', which Crosby & Nash will later re-record for their second album. Crosby also offers them the thrilling 'Critical Mass' but it meets with a muted response. "At that point, it just said 'Vocal Piece' on the box and he played it for Neil," Nash recalls. "And Neil wanted to know where the words were! Then he played it for

Stephen and – nothing. Stephen just didn't hear it. Finally, he played it for me and I just thought it was an incredible piece of music, and couldn't figure out how the hell it came out of Crosby's head."

With one of Crosby's better compositions greeted so coolly, it comes as no surprise to learn that the sessions are again ultimately unproductive. Cutting a new album should have been a cinch but, it seems, the times are now against them. Former negative traits reassert themselves, most notably, Stills' truculence and Young's selfishness. As Crosby recalls: "Neil went out of the room and never came back!"

Young later counters the negative press reports about the inconclusive sessions, arguing, "Everybody always concentrates on this whole thing that we fight all the time among each other. That's a load of shit. They don't know what they're talking about. It's all rumours... We went down to the Record Plant in Sausalito, rented some studio time and left with two things in the can – a song of David's and a song of Graham's that were great. We were really into something nice. But a lot of things were happening at the time. Crosby's baby was born. Some of us wanted to rest for a while. We'd been working very hard. Everybody has a different viewpoint and it just takes a while to get them all together. It's a great group for that, though... We really did accomplish some things at those sessions. And just because the sessions only lasted three days people start building up bullshit stories... Looking back, we might have been wiser to do the album before the tour, while we were still building up the energy. But there's other times to record."

Of course, if they had attempted the album beforehand, they probably wouldn't have completed the tour. Having played together for several months, they were in the perfect position to round off the year by delivering a masterwork. Instead, they let the moment slip by.

Young's absence robbed them of momentum and, finally, Stills and Nash fell out over a petty argument about a minor chord placing in 'Guardian Angel'. The grand reunion ends with Graham throwing Stephen out of his house in a musical equivalent of the Rita Coolidge wars.

D-SEPTEMBER

CSN&Y scatter. Young and Nash take a break in Holland, while Crosby returns to California to witness girlfriend Debbie Donovan giving birth to his daughter, Donovan Ann. Meanwhile, Paris beckons for Stills who can be seen at the Olympia, guesting at his wife Veronique Sanson's first show there in two years. He also appears on her new album *Le Maudit*, playing bass on 'On M'Attend La Bas'. Inevitably, this prompts rumours of a joint album, but Stills laughs off the notion, claiming: "The only time I sing with Vero is when we sing duets to our son and that's about as close as I'm going to come to getting involved with her career."

On the question of a CSN&Y recording, Stills promises that they will return to the studio in December, but adds that he also wants to complete a new solo album, titled *As I Come Of Age*.

1975

JANUARY

While at the Caribou Ranch, Nederland, Colorado, Stills attends the sessions for Souther, Hillman, Furay's second album. He is invited to add some guitar work, but is clearly hampered by his own excesses. "He peaked too soon," recalls Hillman's occasional co-writer Peter Knobler. "Recording didn't begin until nine and by that time Stephen was loaded. He tried to put down a few lines but nothing was doing. His fingers stuck and the music wasn't there. He blamed the guitar, the new strings, the set-up. As if in restitution, he tried to teach the drummer a new beat that would liven up the take. Sitting behind the drum set at four in the morning, all flopsweat and hard talk, Stills was a sorry sight. When he left at nine there were no intoxicants of any kind on the ranch. He had made a raid and downed them all. Nobody seemed surprised."

"Self-destruction is a very common ailment," Stills observes sage-like.

3–7 JANUARY

Reprise Records' archives indicate work in progress on Young's 'Love Art Blues', 'Home Fires', 'The Old Homestead', 'Long May You Run' and 'The Tie Plate Yodel no. 3'.

27 JANUARY

Crosby registers 'Homeward Through The Haze' for copyright purposes. Nash adds 'Fieldworker' and 'Wind On The Water'.

> "Sitting behind the drum set at four in the morning, all flopsweat and hard talk, Stills was a sorry sight. When he left at nine there were no intoxicants of any kind on the ranch. He had made a raid and downed them all. Nobody seemed surprised."
>
> **PETER KNOBLER**

2 FEBRUARY

Nash celebrates his 33rd birthday by taking some acid during a visit to Winchester Cathedral. "It was probably my favourite acid trip," Nash recalls nostalgically. The eerie results are later captured on CS&N's next album.

25 FEBRUARY

Young copyright registers a number of unreleased songs which appear to be taken from the sessions for the unissued *Homegrown*: 'Vacancy', 'Homefires', 'Separate Ways', 'Florida', 'Kansas', 'White Line', 'Mexico' and 'Try'. Four other songs from the listing will eventually be released: 'Homegrown', 'Love Is A Rose', 'Star Of Bethlehem' and 'Little Wing'.

10 MARCH

Crosby's 'Low Down Payment' is registered for copyright. Meanwhile, 'Carry Me', one of his most effective autobiographical songs, is completed at Sound Labs, LA. According to

David, Nash's 'Mama Lion' and 'Marguerita' (held back for *Whistling Down The Wire*) are recorded at the same session.

17–18 MARCH

Crosby jams with The Grateful Dead at Bob Weir's home studio. Among the songs attempted are 'Homeward Through The Haze' and 'Low Down Payment'.

23 MARCH

Young appears with Bob Dylan and The Band at the SNACK benefit, Kezar Stadium, Golden Gate Park, San Francisco. Among the songs featured is the humorous Dylan/Young collaboration 'Knockin' On The Dragon's Door'.

18 APRIL

Stills completes 'My Love Is A Gentle Thing' at Wally Heider's, but the song will remain unissued until the CSN boxed set in 1991.

28 APRIL

Elvin Bishop's album *Juke Joint Jump* features Stills guesting on guitar on 'Rolling Home'.

11 MAY

Crosby & Nash record 'To The Last Whale', the striking finale to *Wind On The Water* and their most successful ecological song.

18 MAY

The wrath of Dewey Martin descends on Stills and Young who are sued by the drummer for $150,000. Martin insists that he signed away his interests in the Springfield under duress and is seeking retroactive royalties from Atlantic and his fellow members for earnings since 1968.

19 MAY

James Taylor's *Gorilla* is released, with Crosby & Nash singing on 'Mexico' and 'Lighthouse'.

JUNE – AUGUST

The Stephen Stills Band set forth on an extensive US tour. The line-up comprises Donnie Dacus (guitar), Rick Roberts (vocals/guitar), George Perry (bass), Tubby Ziegler (drums) and Joe Lala (percussion).

2 JUNE

Stills registers copyright for 'Cold Cold World', 'Turn Back The Pages' and 'To Mama, From Christopher And The Old Man'.

5 JUNE

Crosby appears with Phil Lesh and Ned Lagin at the Dominican College, San Rafael, where they preview the album *Seastones*, released later this month. "The concert we did took you outwards to Mars – edge city," Crosby recalls. "Listen to *Seastones*. That's me singing some experimental stuff – very advanced cuckoo music. A lot of what I do is sub-speech, proto-speech, talk that makes you feel as if you're hearing something you understand, but you can't quite catch the words. In the middle is Phil Lesh playing a synthesiser by his bass, and Jerry Garcia playing his guitar through every tone modifier in existence. It made for an astounding thing."

In addition to Crosby, the album features such luminaries as Jerry Garcia, Grace Slick, David Freiberg and Spencer Dryden. "Lagin's fascinating," Crosby enthuses. "Mostly I'm working with him to learn how to create a vocal synthesiser and how to work up a set of chops with it. Work up the instrument and then bring it back into our arena to stretch what we're doing."

8 JUNE

Crosby's 'Bittersweet' is written and recorded this same day for the forthcoming *Wind On The Water*.

18 JUNE

Nash records 'Cowboy Of Dreams' for inclusion on *Wind On The Water*. The song was written about Neil Young in reply to 'Only Love Can Break Your Heart'.

20 JUNE

After a two-year delay, Young's *Tonight's The Night* is finally released. It receives a mixed reaction from critics, but Young's more perceptive observers acknowledge that it is one of his greatest achievements. As an act of public exorcism it has few equals in rock history, while its unflinching treatment of drug-related death is both harrowing and fascinating. Although generally perceived as commercially unsuccessful, the album does in fact climb to a respectable number 25 in the US charts, a clear indication of Young's post-CSN&Y marketing appeal.

23 JUNE

Stephen Stills' new album *Stills* is a spectacular return to form, and the last of his solo ventures to reach the US Top 20. It features an exceptionally strong selection of songs, which he will struggle to equal on later recordings. "I sat on that album for a while," Stills explained, shortly after switching from Atlantic to CBS Records. "It takes the whole onus of CSN&Y off me."

11–12 JULY

Reprise Records' archives indicate work in progress on Young's 'Cortez The Killer', 'Barstool Blues', 'Ride My Llama', 'Danger Bird' and 'Drive Back'.

26 JULY

Stills appears on the televised Democratic Telethon performing 'Myth Of Sisyphus'.

27 JULY

Young appears with The Stephen Stills Band at the Greek Theater, Berkeley, as guest guitarist. Prior to his arrival on stage, Stills performs both 'The Loner' and 'Human Highway', then tells the audience: "That was the new policy. I've got one Neil Young song every album." The flattery is characteristic of Stills' generosity towards his erstwhile partner and bodes well for a future collaboration.

The extra work involved in learning several Young songs distracts Stills sufficiently to forget the closing section of 'Word Game'. He abandons the song and suddenly shifts into a sterling version of 'Buyin' Time', after which he valiantly returns to 'Word Game' which is then completed in emphatic fashion. As a reward for his labours Stills leaves the band to play some of their own material and cameo Rick Roberts performing 'Colorado', his finest moment from his stay in The Flying Burrito Brothers.

The arrival of Young towards the end of the evening is greeted with loud applause and, as he promised earlier, Stills plays 'The Loner' for a second time, plus another song of Young's that he has covered, 'New Mama'. It is bizarre to see Young reduced to passing notes on stage as a result of his recent throat operation. He doesn't exactly make Stills' life easy by

encouraging him to tackle 'On The Beach', a lengthy number from his recent album rather than a familiar CSN&Y singalong. Stills performs the song adequately, adding a small footnote to Young's live career in the process. Young stays around to back his partner on 'Black Queen', after which Stills tells the audience: "He's gonna do one more... it's really kind of frustrating for him not to be able to sing on the gig." This time, Stills tackles 'Suite: Judy Blue Eyes', then closes the show with 'Find The Cost Of Freedom'.

SET LIST: LOVE THE ONE YOU'RE WITH: JOHNNY'S GARDEN; CLOSER TO YOU; THE LONER; WOODEN SHIPS; CHANGE PARTNERS; TREETOP FLYER; EVERYBODY'S TALKIN' (AT ME); KNOW YOU GOT TO RUN; HUMAN HIGHWAY; CROSSROADS; YOU CAN'T CATCH ME/WORD GAME; BUYIN' TIME; WORD GAME (REPRISE): INSTRUMENTAL INTERLUDE; GOING TO THE COUNTRY: COLORADO; IN THE WAY: TURN BACK THE PAGES; THE LONER; NEW MAMA: ON THE BEACH: BLACK QUEEN; SUITE: JUDY BLUE EYES; FIND THE COST OF FREEDOM.

28 AUGUST

Staysail Music are registered as copyright holders for the latest batch of Crosby compositions: 'Critical Mass', 'Bittersweet', 'Naked In The Rain' (lyrics by Nash) and 'Winning'. The latter is later retitled 'King Of The Mountain' and, although played in concert and available on bootleg, remains otherwise unreleased. On this same day, Nash's Thin Ice Music register 'Cowboy Of Dreams', 'Mama Lion', 'Take The Money And Run', 'Marguerita', 'Love Work Out' and 'J.B.'s Blues'; all of these will appear on the next two Crosby/Nash albums.

SEPTEMBER – DECEMBER

While The Stephen Stills Band reconvene for the autumn leg of their itinerary, Crosby & Nash embark on a US tour with an electric backing band featuring Danny Kortchmar (lead guitar), Tim Drummond (bass), David Lindley (slide guitar) and Russ Kunkel (drums). As Crosby informs *Sounds*: "People who don't go out and play live all the time wind up having very abstracted positions about their material. I think it's very groovy to look at ourselves as creators and writers and stuff, but we're also communicators, and if we

don't think about the audience hearing it and don't actually go out and try it, one to one, we're doing everyone a disservice."

5 SEPTEMBER

Reprise Records' tape archives log this date for the recording of 'Pocahontas' and 'Lookin' For A Love', with 'Human Highway' added the following evening.

15 SEPTEMBER

Crosby & Nash release *Wind On The Water*, a highly impressive album, featuring the cream of their current repertoire. At this point, they are both writing strong material and establishing themselves as a highly viable combination. The album climbs to number 6, easily outselling the recent solo efforts from Stills and Young and vindicating the decision to switch labels from Atlantic to ABC Records. As Nash explains: "Having spent many thousands of dollars on tape with CSN&Y we did an about-turn and decided to concentrate on me and David, and not worry about it. Let the past go... CSN&Y is a very magical thing to me – something very precious – and the tendency to want it to materialise can stop you in your forward motion a lot of times. Frankly, we were getting sick of that happening and decided to forget it."

6 OCTOBER

Dave Mason's *Split Coconut* is released with Crosby & Nash appearing on 'You Can Lose It', 'She's My Friend', 'Give Me A Reason Why' and 'Two Guitar Lovers'.

8 OCTOBER

Crosby and Nash's 'Broken Bird' is registered for copyright in preparation for their next album.

13 OCTOBER

Young undergoes an operation on his vocal cords, resulting in the postponement of an acoustic tour in November.

On this same day, Art Garfunkel's *Breakaway* is released, with Crosby & Nash providing harmonies to the title track.

22 OCTOBER

The Crosby & Nash tour rolls on through Springfield, Massachusetts, prompting surprisingly effusive reviews. In England, *Melody Maker* report on the duo's progress, with US correspondent Steve Lake remarking: "If anybody had told me five years ago that 'Déjà Vu', David Crosby's nicely off-the-wall reincarnation ditty from the album of the same name, was going to wind up as some *avant garde* live *tour de force* I'd probably have laughed in their face... The point is that Crosby and Nash, apparently written off by Atlantic... are taking chances nobody expected of them, putting behind them much of the gratuitous self-congratulation that grated on live CSN&Y gigs, and generally coming on as mature musicians. It's very encouraging."

NOVEMBER

In *Melody Maker*, Crosby names his favourite record of all time as *The Music Of Bulgaria* by the Bulgarian National Folk Ensemble. "It's really the most incredible vocal music that's ever been recorded – there's just no other words. These Bulgarian housewives make the best of us look like children." Nash concurs, also mentioning the album as a favourite in later interviews.

0 NOVEMBER

Young releases his second album this year, *Zuma*. Highly acclaimed, with 'Cortez The Killer' universally cited as the outstanding track, the album surprisingly fails to chart higher than *Tonight's The Night*, despite its FM appeal.

9 NOVEMBER

Reprise Records indicate that Young's 'Homegrown' is delivered on this day.

2/23 NOVEMBER

Young again joins Stills in concert, this time at the Roscoe Maples Pavilion, Stanford University, Palo Alto (22) and UCLA Westwood, LA (23). During the latter, Stills presumptuously announces "The spirit of The Buffalo Springfield is back".

4 NOVEMBER

Joni Mitchell's *The Hissing Of Summer Lawns* is released, with Crosby & Nash providing backing vocals on 'Free Man In Paris'. On this same day, Carole King appears with the duo at the Zelerbach Hall, Berkeley, San Francisco.

5 NOVEMBER

Carole King again joins Crosby & Nash on stage, this time at the Anaheim Convention Center, California. She appears for 'Carry Me' and sings two songs: 'High Out Of Time' and 'I'll See You In The Spring', the latter provisionally slated for inclusion on the next C&N album. Nash suggests these get-togethers are good therapy: "Carole King being a solo performer, is much more afraid to go out on the road than we are together... She's been overcoming her fear of audiences, she's been having a good time, she knows now that people aren't down on her, and she feels much easier about her forthcoming tour now. So, as well as writing good songs and turning David and me on with good singing, she's been overcoming some of her own fears."

-28 NOVEMBER

Reprise Records' tape archives indicate work in progress on Young's 'Like A Hurricane', 'Lotta Love', 'Sedan Delivery' and 'White Line'.

ECEMBER

Young plays a number of bar dates with Crazy Horse in Northern California, including the Inn At The Beginning, Cotati, the Marshall Tavern, Point Reyes and the Catalyst.

1/2 & 12 DECEMBER

Crosby & Nash embark on a brief visit to Japan, accompanied by Craig Doerge and David Lindley. They appear in Budokan (December 1/2) and the Osaka Festival Hall (12). The set list alternates Crosby/Nash songs with cameo solo sets in between. During the first half, 'Southbound Train' gets a great reception. Other highlights include a compelling version of 'Naked In The Rain' (with Joel Bernstein on guitar) and Nash's 'Lady Of The Island' with its harmonica accompaniment. The language barrier does not prevent some humour from emerging in the big hall, with Crosby and Lindley playing around on a mock version of 'Born Free'. Lindley plays a short interlude between the solo sets, impressing the crowd with a French fiddle song that he dedicates to bluegrass supremo Bill Monroe. Crosby's solo set features 'King Of The Mountain' which, despite its promotion during the tour, will fail to make the next album. There is also an intriguing version of 'Triad' with pianist Craig Doerge adding a New Orleans jazz feel to the song. The usual highlight of these shows is the 'Wind On The Water' segment, but here Crosby's 'Critical Mass' introduction is omitted, robbing the song of much of its drama. The closing songs are well received with Crosby threatening to "turn up the volume, and make your fillings itch" while a mass singalong accompanies 'Teach Your Children' and 'Chicago'.

SET LIST: IMMIGRATION MAN; THE LEE SHORE; SOUTHBOUND TRAIN; PAGE 43; MAMA LION; HOMEWARD THROUGH THE HAZE; COWBOY OF DREAMS; NAKED IN THE RAIN; FIELDWORKER; LONG TIME GONE; LADY OF THE ISLAND; SIMPLE MAN; FIDDLE SONG; OUR HOUSE; GUINNEVERE; KING OF THE MOUNTAIN; TRIAD; CARRY ME; WIND ON THE WATER; MILITARY MADNESS; WOODEN SHIPS; TEACH YOUR CHILDREN; CHICAGO.

8 DECEMBER

Atlantic issue *Stephen Stills Live,* taken from his shows at the Chicago Auditorium, on 8–9 March 1974. It's an unnecessary release that merely reminds us how much more we would prefer a CSN&Y live album from the same year.

31 DECEMBER

At Alex's, Woodside, California, Stills & Young see in the New Year with an unannounced acoustic set. They are booked into Miami for recording work throughout the following month.

1976

JANUARY

Sessions for the forthcoming Stills/Young album are progressing surprisingly smoothly. "We cut about 12 tunes in 15 days," Stills notes. Reprise tape archives list the following: 'Midnight On The Bay', 'Make Love To You', 'Long May You Run', 'Black Coral', 'Ocean Girl', '12/8 Blues (All The Same)', 'Fontainebleau', 'Let It Shine' and 'Guardian Angel'.

One reason for the sterling work is the presence of producer Tom Dowd, who takes on the role of musical director. "Ostensibly, he was the producer and got things moving along more efficiently than even we could have done," Stills explains. "He was a great help."

Reflecting on these initial sessions, Stills notes: "For Neil it was a departure from some of his darker moments, mainly because we had a great time and looked forward so much to going in the studio. I think it was very educational for me and him both because we picked up on what was right about the way we each recorded and also corrected some of the things we had been doing wrong. Neil had me going for the guitar parts at the same time as we recorded the backing track... the way we used to have to do it... live in the studio with very little overdubbing at all."

As for the possibility of conflict, Stills is confident that old battles will not be re-enacted: "Neil and I have been together for so long. We've got to the point where we've grown up enough. Neil and I would never have a scream out. We don't raise our voices to each other."

26 JANUARY

Carole King's *Thoroughbred* is released with Crosby & Nash singing on 'High Out Of Time' and 'I'd Like To Know You Better'.

3 MARCH – 2 APRIL

Young completes a world tour with Crazy Horse, appearing in Japan, Norway, Denmark, West Germany, France, Holland, Belgium, England and Scotland. For most onlookers, the highlight of these concerts is the astonishing 'Like A Hurricane' which Young performs in the eye of a giant electric fan situated on the side of the stage. The sample set list below from Jaap Eden Hal, Amsterdam, Holland (March 26) features two unreleased songs, 'Sad Movies' and 'No-one Seems To Know'.

SET LIST: TELL MY WHY; MELLOW MY MIND; AFTER THE GOLDRUSH; SAD MOVIES; THE NEEDLE AND THE DAMAGE DONE; A MAN NEEDS A MAID; NO-ONE SEEMS TO KNOW; HEART OF GOLD; COUNTRY HOME; DON'T CRY NO TEARS; DOWN BY THE RIVER; THE LOSING END; LIKE A HURRICANE; LET IT SHINE; DRIVE BACK; SOUTHERN MAN; CORTEZ THE KILLER; CINNAMON GIRL.

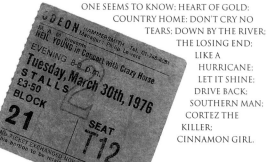

12 MARCH

Following the Japanese leg of his world tour, Young takes a few days' break in California, where he contacts Crosby & Nash and invites them to attend the Criteria sessions in Miami with a view to transforming the album into a CSN&Y project.

"Neil suggested that all four of us make an album together," Stills recalls, "but that wasn't right because by that time we'd got all the tracks and half the singing done already." Nevertheless, the idea is pursued, with alarming consequences.

MARCH/MAY

Atlantic's tape log provides a confusing catch-all list of songs supposedly recorded at Criteria in March by CSN&Y. The list reads: 'Little Blind Fish', 'Can't Handle This', Separate Ways', 'Taken At All', 'No-one Seems To Know', 'Traces', 'Beaucoup Gumbo', 'Western Witches', 'Will To Love', 'Talk Too Much' and 'Fontainebleau'. The unreliability of the listing is confirmed by the non-inclusion of 'Human Highway', which *was* cut by CSN&Y. Moreover, witnesses at the studio, reporting at the time, confirm that the foursome definitely worked out harmonies on 'Midnight On The Bay', 'Mutiny', 'Black Coral' and 'Ocean Girl'.

To confuse matters further, Atlantic's tape log also includes an exhaustive list of titles credited solely to Stills & Young, among which are several songs of Crosby/Nash origin, such as 'Taken At All' (erroneously titled 'Lost It On The Highway'), 'Time After Time', 'Mutiny', and the unissued 'Last 100 Years Of Freedom'.

Breaking down both song lists at least confirms that work of some sort was done at Miami on the following compositions by Neil

Young: 'Long May You Run', 'Human Highway', 'Fontainebleau', 'Ocean Girl', 'Let It Shine', 'Will To Love', 'Midnight On The Bay' and his unreleased 'Traces', 'Separate Ways' and 'No-one Seems To Know'.

Stills songs worked on include 'Make Love To You', 'Guardian Angel', 'Black Coral', 'Beaucoup Gumbo', 'Treetop Flyer', the unreleased junkie-inspired song 'One Way Ride (One Way Ticket)' and 'Walk Before You Run' (co-written with Barry Gibb).

In addition, several songs of unknown authorship, some probably mistitled, are listed including: 'Western Witches', 'Talk Too Much', 'After Hours' (possibly Stills' unissued 'Visiting Hours'), '10 90', 'Let Me Down', 'Can't Handle This' and 'Sleep'.

When both Crosby & Nash and Young leave the studio mid-way through the sessions Stills, wearing a T-shirt emblazoned with the words 'I'm An Exhibitionist', vents his frustration by jamming ferociously with his band (featuring George 'Chocolate' Perry, Joe Vitale, Jerry Aiello and Joe Lala) until 6 am. The Atlantic listing details these jams which include the titles 'Secrets', 'My Girl' (most likely the Otis Redding classic), and the self-explanatory 'Steven – Joe Chocolate Jamming'.

26 APRIL

John David Souther's *Black Rose* is released, with Crosby adding vocals to 'Banging My Head Against The Moon' and 'Baby Come Home'.

MAY

The CSN&Y dream ends in Miami amid accusations of treachery. Events reach a head when Crosby & Nash are forced to return to California to remix their album for ABC. They take with them a tape of the CSN&Y songs with the intention of returning as soon as possible. Meanwhile, Stills and Young make the fateful decision to revert to the original idea of recording the album as a duet and wipe Crosby & Nash's vocals from the master tape. Stills rationalises the decision and attempts to play down the seriousness of its implications. "David and Graham came down to Miami but they had an album of their own to do, so they had to go back to California," he points out. "I thought, 'Wait a minute, if we're going to do this, if we're going to do a CSN&Y album again, then let's do it properly. You guys go finish your own album and Neil and me will do this and when all this is finished, then we'll get together again'. If we were going to do one together, we'd start together at the beginning and not half-way through... Hell, there was all that talk about Graham and me fighting but that's no big deal. Neil went off into seclusion but that's no big deal either. He just gets that way."

sounds corny but that's the way I feel. CSN&Y is, to me, an incredibly special thing that we should not fuck around with. We have no right as individuals... I see Stephen's career going downhill and I see Neil's career going downhill... They're panicking, man. I say, 'If you're scared shitless and you think your career's going downhill then to get it back you should make a great CSN&Y album'... Then what happened? You tell me, because David and I have got no axes to grind."

3 MAY

Stills issues another solo album *Illegal Stills*, which is a considerable step down in quality from his recent work. Pleasant, but decidedly average, it contains nothing astonishing and sells only moderately well, peaking at number 31 in the US. Stephen admits that he played less guitar than usual because of the competing Stills/Young collaboration. "Guitar just wasn't

registered: 'Taken At All' and the still unreleased 'Last 100 Years Of Freedom'.

29 MAY

NME reveals that Stills' European tour, tentatively scheduled for next month, has been cancelled. It had been hoped that he would head the West Coast Rock Show planned for Cardiff's Ninian Park on June 5, but the ongoing Stills/Young project puts paid to that. "It is a great disappointment that the public should suffer on the whim of one artiste," cry the promoters.

22 JUNE

James Taylor's *In The Pocket* is released, with Crosby & Nash singing on 'Nothing Like A Hundred Miles'. Around this same period, Nash also features on Waylon Jennings' *Are You Ready For The Country*, contributing vocals to 'Mac Arthur Park Revisited'.

JUNE – JULY

The Stills/Young tour takes in the Pine Knob Theater, Clarkston, MI (June 23), Cobo Hall, Detroit, MI (24), Boston Garden, MA (26), Civic Center, Springfield, MA (27), Spectrum Sports Arena, Philadelphia, PA (29), Nassau Veterans' Memorial Coliseum, Hampstead, Long Island, NY (July 1/2), International Convention Center, Niagara Falls, NY (4), Rochester Community War Memorial Auditorium, NY (5), Civic Center, Providence, RI (7), Capitol Center Largo, MD (9/10), Civic Center Arena, Hartford, CT (11), Richfield Coliseum, Cleveland, OH (13), Coliseum, Charlotte, Virginia, NC (18), University of Columbia, SC (20).

The shows offer occasional surprises such as Young's unissued 'Evening Coconut', the first airing of 'Stringman', an acoustic 'Like A Hurricane' and Stills' revival of the Manassas guitar opus 'The Treasure', but generally the performances are erratic in quality. Reviewing the show in Nassau (July 1), *The New York Times*' John Rockwell speculates on "an ill-conceived evening", concluding, "The sound was rough and overloud. The lack of any sweet high voices made material most often heard from the complete CSN&Y sound bottom-heavy. Mr Young, even with that wonderful quavering, utterly distinctive sound he makes, wasn't shaping his phrases with the introspective care of which he is capable. And most disappointing of all, there was nothing from his most recent solo albums."

The later performances reveal a marked improvement, with Stills throwing in a rousing finale of 'Star Spangled Banner' for Independence Day and both artistes extending their respective repertoires to include old favourites. Too often, however, inspiration lapses into indulgence. Even the reviewers present wildly differing perspectives. *The Washington Post* proclaims, "It's a combination that makes for a splendid show... Each seems to bring out the best qualities in the other. Young, usually a brooding figure, is performing with

Crosby, clearly disappointed by the decision, emphasises his continued commitment to the CSN&Y ideal. "I'm not here to trade guitar licks with some mother and pretend that I'm the fastest gun in the West," he snorts. "Crosby, Stills, Nash & Young when it was hot was a mutual chemistry, an immensely supportive thing. We gave to each other very, very strongly. When it works I'd be the last to deny it and I have never claimed that we could equal its power. I wish I didn't love them. It would make the whole damn thing a lot easier, but that's how it is. I do, you know."

The usually diplomatic Nash is so disgusted by the Miami fiasco that he pours out his feelings in angry frustration. "They're in it for the wrong reasons," he complains. "They're in it for the bucks, the manipulation and the career moves and I'm in it for great music. It

needed on some of those songs," he explained. "I didn't have anything to inspire me to the scale. It's the last time, except on the rarest of occasions, that I'll try to overdub a lead guitar solo. I learned on-stage that I play so much better and with so much more fire live."

10 MAY

Terry Reid's *Seed Of Memory* is released, with Nash providing vocal accompaniment as well as producing the record.

14 MAY

Crosby's 'Foolish Man' is registered for copyright, along with Nash's 'Cathedral', 'Mutiny' and 'Skychild'. The latter will not be released until as late as 1980 when it appears on *Earth And Sky*. On this same day, two Crosby/Nash collaborations are copyright more inspiration and vitality than he has in years, and Stills, who has a reputation for self-indulgence when working on his own, is playing his taut guitar lines with an admirable sense of discipline..."

Cameron Crowe, who attends the same show, notes: "Stills had difficulty singing on mike and sometimes even remembering words. The harmonies sounded ragged. Young, in the process of keeping the vocals faithful, became too tense to cut loose on guitar himself".

After the performance in Hartford, Young flies by jet to Miami to spend the best part of a day remixing vocals for the album. He tells Stills: "If we both go, neither of us will come back". What sounds like a joke on Young's part, turns out to be deadly accurate. Just over a week later, following their show in South Carolina, Young unexpectedly departs, following reports that he was not singing well at the show. Stills is already waiting forlornly at the next date in Atlanta when he receives a terse telegram from Young which reads: "Dear Stephen, Funny how some things that start spontaneously end that way. Eat a peach, Neil". Stills is so shocked that he tells the press "All I know is that Neil turned left at Greensboro", inexplicably forgetting that they did complete two further gigs in Charlotte and South Carolina after that date.

SAMPLE SET LIST (JULY 5): LOVE THE ONE YOU'RE WITH; THE LONER; LONG MAY YOU RUN; FOR WHAT IT'S WORTH; HELPLESS; BLACK QUEEN; SOUTHERN MAN; ON THE WAY HOME; CHANGE PARTNERS; HEART OF GOLD; 49 BYE BYES/CIRCLIN'; AFTER THE GOLDRUSH; 4+20; OHIO; BLACKBIRD; BUYIN' TIME; EVENING COCONUT; LET IT SHINE; MAKE LOVE TO YOU; COWGIRL IN THE SAND; THE TREASURE; SUITE: JUDY BLUE EYES.

2 JULY

Crosby & Nash's *Whistling Down The Wire* is released and, like Stills' recent effort, fails to match the quality of its predecessor. It eventually peaks at number 26 in the US charts, a far cry from the Top 10 success of their other two albums.

22 JULY

In preparation for the release of the Stills/Young collaboration, Stephen copyright registers 'Black Coral', 'Make Love To You', 'Guardian Angel' and '12/8 Blues'.

23-25 JULY

Stills plays the trouper by agreeing to play three dates in Florida, even though he has to follow Lynyrd Skynyrd performing in their home town. He soon contacts Chris Hillman and George Perry with a view to completing some of the postponed dates in August. While Stills attempts to help out the beleaguered promoters, Young's management announce that their star has been suffering throat problems and curtailed the tour on doctor's orders. The chirpiness of the "Eat A Peach" telegram suggests that Young's wilfulness may also have been a factor. Either way, it

seems amazing that the duo committed themselves to such a lengthy tour, which was due to play almost uninterrupted until as late as 18 September.

4 AUGUST

Stills copyright registers the still unreleased 'Walk Before You Run', composed with Barry Gibb. Stills vainly hopes to show his potential as a Bee Gee by getting the song included on the soundtrack of *Grease*.

10-13 AUGUST

Crosby & Nash play a short season at the Greek Theater, Los Angeles, which climaxes with a surprise appearance from Stephen Stills. Unannounced, he appears backstage, humble and contrite over their previous falling-out following the Miami sessions. Nash's instinctive reaction is endearingly positive. "I hugged him and it amazed me," he told *Rolling Stone*. "I realised in the middle of the hug that the last time we'd met he'd wiped some very valuable work of David's and mine... but it didn't matter. We're all incredibly changeable people, God knows, and Stephen had come with his hat in his hand."

A fine performance ensues, with Nash playing harmonica on 'Lady Of The Island' and Joel Bernstein adding acoustic guitar to

'Naked In The Rain'. One of the highlights of the evening is a riveting version of Crosby's unreleased 'King Of The Mountain', which is preceded by a lengthy piano solo from Craig Doerge. After closing the set with 'Wooden Ships', Crosby & Nash reappear with Stills for a rapturously received 'Teach Your Children'.

After the show, Nash invites Stills back to his house, where they proceed to get drunk and talk about the possibility of taking on the world as CS&N. "He was really the Stephen

that I had always hoped I'd see back again," Nash enthused. "I piled him back into his room at 4am."

SET LIST: PRE-ROAD DOWNS; IMMIGRATION MAN; PAGE 43; THE LEE SHORE; I USED TO BE A KING; NAKED IN THE RAIN; SPOTLIGHT; LOVE WORK OUT; LADY OF THE ISLAND; MARGUERITA; GUINNEVERE; KING OF THE MOUNTAIN; OUT OF THE DARKNESS; CARRY ME; TO THE LAST WHALE/WIND ON THE WATER; DÉJÀ VU; MILITARY MADNESS; WOODEN SHIPS; TEACH YOUR CHILDREN.

15 AUGUST

While Stills and Nash are still recovering from the previous night's revelries, Crosby is willing to explain the fascinating group dynamics between the three of them and the problems they face should they work together again. "It's a very difficult situation," Crosby admits. "We're all very strong people and we view things differently. We disagree. Stills and I, in particular, disagree very, very strongly... I've had arguments with Stephen Stills that would have gotten you out of the room – you'd have been frightened, OK... I will not play baseball stadiums; I think it's a rip off... There are many other problems, and I'm not going to lay them out to you because it's family and it's family dirty laundry. But, look, I sang with Stephen last night. Now there's a reason I did that and a reason that Graham and I asked him to come on and sing with us... The truth is I've faced too many people with him; I've made too much music with him; I've loved him for too long, and I'll never be able to shut him off. You don't care about somebody that much and then turn it off like a faucet. You can't. That's true of Neil Young and Stephen Stills. I can never truly shut him off and they've both done things to me I don't like... but there's always music there... and I would never bet against us making music at some point in the future. It's just that it's very difficult, man – we're all independently strong people and trying to get the four of us in one space is like juggling four jugs of nitro-glycerine... if you just drop one, they all go off. But I tell you that the door's never closed, man, not inside of me. It's never going to be closed to those guys, ever.'

24 AUGUST

Stills continues to fill in some of the cancelled dates on the Stills/Young tour, including a performance this evening at the LA Forum. The emotional upheavals of the last month are bad enough, but he faces further problems upon returning home to Boulder, where his marriage to Veronique Sanson is in severe trouble. "I was definitely on the roof," Stills recalled. "It was incredible. August of 1976 will go down in the history of my life as being the worst! The Neil Young tour fell apart and I went home and my old lady had left me. That can make you stop and look – maybe these people are trying to tell me something."

Stills subsequently resettles in LA, seeks help from a Santa Barbara doctor and learns more about his capacity for self-destruction. "I guess maybe I don't like myself," is his own

reading of his personality. He expresses a desire to take a few years off and again mentions his desire to write a book.

AUGUST
At the Santa Monica Civic Center, Young joins the reformed Spirit on-stage for a cover of Dylan's 'Like A Rolling Stone' and is ignominiously pushed off stage by Randy California. He re-emerges to join Firefall on 'Just Like Tom Thumb's Blues'.

PTEMBER
Having completed a summer tour of the USA, Crosby & Nash undertake a brief European tour later this month, taking in the Edinburgh Playhouse (September 16), Manchester Free Trade Hall (17), to be followed by dates in Germany, Holland and Scandinavia, concluding with an appearance at London's Hammersmith Odeon (27). Since several members of their backing group are touring with James Taylor, only the nucleus of keyboardist Craig Doerge and violinist/steel guitarist David Lindley (violin/pedal steel guitar) are available for the visit.

SEPTEMBER
Sounds prints the most acerbic interview ever uttered by Nash in which he denounces Stills and Young for callously wiping his and Crosby's vocals from the recent album. Reacting to Stills' plea that he didn't want to "put his feet in the meat grinder" by delaying the recording, Nash retorts: "I think it's his cock he keeps putting in the meat grinder... Stephen's fucking around with great music, and that's what both of them have been doing for three years. I'm a fool and I'll put my personal things aside and go. But

how many times can you keep going up and saying, 'OK, I'll stand here while you hit me again – just don't hit me as hard as you did last time'. I'll go for any break but, man, it was dirty. I will not work with them again."

Of course, by this time Nash has already forgiven Stills, who seems characteristically unfazed after reading this heated diatribe. "Graham asked me whether I'd seen some of the things he'd said about me," Stills concluded. "I said I had and that I thought it was some of the funniest stuff ever written. There was something about Graham wanting to punch me in the nose, but that's ridiculous. It's all so petty."

24 SEPTEMBER
Stills copyright registers 'Treetop Flyer', with additional words and music credited to James O Dacus (Donnie Dacus). The song remains unissued on album until as late as 1991 when it appears on *Stills Alone*. By that point, Dacus' writing credit has been inexplicably removed.

27 SEPTEMBER
The release of the eagerly awaited Stills/Young collaboration *Long May You Run* (officially scheduled September 10), proves severely anti-climactic. Far from reviving the spirit of The Buffalo Springfield, the set reveals the duo in strangely lacklustre form. Not for the first time, Young's weak songs are politely tolerated while Stills is left to suffer the brunt of the critical onslaught. The album founders at number 26, an appalling statistic for such a high profile record and, worse still, is outsold by Crosby & Nash's recent release. Stills at least recognises his problems as a lyricist in a characteristic mixture of humility and self-aggrandisement: "These last few years I've been concentrating on my guitar work. I want to be considered one of the masters."

While Stills/Young receive their brickbats, Crosby & Nash are appearing at London's Hammersmith Odeon and picking up some surprisingly effusive reviews. The following week, *Melody Maker* even argue the case for a full critical re-evaluation: "Old critical habits die hard. Most of us are so thoroughly grounded in the belief that Crosby and Nash constitute the weaker end of a defunct supergroup that we rarely attempt to stand back and look again with the barest smattering of objectivity. I have a suspicion, however, that last Monday's concert at London's Hammersmith Odeon will mark a breakthrough for the duo and bring about an overdue reassessment of the real essence of CSN&Y... Unsurprisingly, the concert was an intimate one, a low-decibel affair, but its intimacy transcended mere cosiness... It's true that neither Crosby nor Nash is any great shakes as an instrumentalist, but David's fondness for offbeat chord structures seemed to spur the more adept Lindley and Doerge to heights of creativity that they could not scale playing over more orthodox rock changes... So it went. And I assure you, a tape of the proceedings would have made a mockery of *Long May You Run*."

OCTOBER – NOVEMBER

In the wake of the Stills/Young débâcle, Stephen is in the midst of a short solo tour of US colleges and small clubs, including the Civic Auditorium, San Jose, CA (October 17), Palladium, NYC, NY (25), East Lansing, MI (31) and Tulane University, New Orleans, LA (November 7). As he tells *Melody Maker*'s Chris Charlesworth: "I did three shows, two in theatres and one at a college and after the college show I thought if they want to boogie, I can't stop them. So I'm getting a drummer and bass player for the bigger shows. They'll only do five or six songs at the end, so it'll basically be me." During his set, Stills pays tribute to Crosby & Nash by performing 'Taken At All', one of the songs CSN&Y had attempted during the ill-fated Miami sessions.

SET LIST (31 OCTOBER): CHANGE PARTNERS; HELPLESSLY HOPING; TAKEN AT ALL; EVERYBODY'S TALKING; KNOW YOU GOT TO RUN; BLACKBIRD; DO FOR THE OTHERS; 4+20; BUYING TIME; CROSSROADS/YOU CAN'T CATCH ME; CIRCLIN'; FOUR DAYS GONE; BLACK CORAL; MYTH OF SISYPHUS; MAKE LOVE TO YOU; 49 BYE BYES/FOR WHAT IT'S WORTH.

23 OCTOBER

Young performs a pre-tour warm-up gig with Crazy Horse at the Bodega, Campbell, CA.

NOVEMBER

Young commences a month's tour with Crazy Horse, during which he plays at the Dorothy Chandler Pavilion, Los Angeles, CA (November 1), Community Center, Berkeley, CA (2), Inglewood Forum, Los Angeles, CA (4), Balch Fieldhouse, Boulder, CO (7), Municipal Auditorium, Austin, TX (9), Tarrant County Convention Center, Fort Worth, TX (10), Summit, Houston, TX (11), Dane County Coliseum, Madison, WI (14), Arie Crown Theater, Chicago, IL (15), Palladium, NYC, NY (18–20), two shows at the Boston Music Hall, MA (22) and two shows at the Fox Theater, Atlanta, Georgia (24). He also appears at The Band's *The Last Waltz*, at the Winterland, San Francisco (25). There he performs 'Four Strong Winds' and 'Helpless', plays harmonica on Joni Mitchell's 'Furry Sings The Blues' and partakes in the all-star finale of 'I Shall Be Released'. As the film shows, Young is grinning maniacally, having gorged himself on cocaine.

SAMPLE SET LIST (NOVEMBER 22, LATE SHOW): TELL ME WHY; ROLL ANOTHER NUMBER; JOURNEY THROUGH THE PAST; THE NEEDLE AND THE DAMAGE DONE; HARVEST; CAMPAIGNER; POCAHONTAS; A MAN NEEDS A MAID; SUGAR MOUNTAIN; COUNTRY HOME; DON'T CRY NO TEARS; DRIVE BACK; COWGIRL IN THE SAND; BITE THE BULLET; LOTTA LOVE; LIKE A HURRICANE; AFTER THE GOLDRUSH; ARE YOU READY FOR THE COUNTRY?; CINNAMON GIRL; CORTEZ THE KILLER; HOMEGROWN; SOUTHERN MAN.

1 NOVEMBER

Elton John's *Blue Moves* is released, with Crosby & Nash adding vocals to 'Cage The Songbird' and 'Wide Eyed And Laughing'.

6 NOVEMBER

Melody Maker's ace US reporter Chris Charlesworth provides the latest news on the future of CSN&Y. "We're all too sensible to give up thoughts of getting together again," Stills claims. "We're like brothers and we have tiffs. It's always been like that with me and Graham and David and Neil. Sometimes we'll get mad at one or the other, but six months later we'll just meet and we'll say, 'Good to see you'. In any band a lot of the internal bickering is directly proportional to the pressure. We never competed with each other as much as people thought. We used that energy in an entirely different way. What we wanted to do was please the others and many times when we failed, we'd fight. It wasn't a rivalry so much as wanting to please each other, so everybody got super critical of themselves."

8 NOVEMBER

Jackson Browne's *The Pretender* is released, with Crosby & Nash providing harmonies to the title track.

19 NOVEMBER

Stills appears at Princeton University, and reflects on the merits of his current solo acoustic tour. "I've always known that I've been capable of it," he stresses, "but I've never done it. Right at the moment I'm between bands and it seemed like the thing to do. I think, though, that I'm going to get a bass player and drummer to come along with me too. We're doing a lot of colleges, so I'll need them. In theatres, I can carry this very, very easily but in basketball joints, they want to get up. I just get out there with six guitars, a banjo and a dobro, plus a 12-string and maybe one little electric guitar for the last number. I even have my music book with me at the piano in case I forget the words.. I'm not proud".

30 NOVEMBER

Joni Mitchell's *Hejira* is released with Neil Young playing harmonica on 'Furry Sings The Blues'.

13 DECEMBER

Nash copyright registers 'Just A Song Before I Go' and 'I Watched It All Go Down'. The latter remains unreleased. Meanwhile, Young completes 'Captain Kennedy', which will not appear until as late as *Hawks And Doves* in 1980

19 DECEMBER

CS&N convene at the Record Plant in LA to record some preliminary material for a possible new album, including Stills' 'See The Changes' and Nash's 'Just A Song Before I Go'.

20 DECEMBER

Still Stills: The Best Of Stephen Stills is released without fanfare and fails to sell.

ODEON HAMMERSMITH Tel. 01-748-4081
Manager: Philip Leivers

John Reid presentations present
An Evening with CROSBY & NASH
EVENING 7-30 p.m.
Monday, Sept. 27th, 1976

STALLS
£3·50
BLOCK
18   SEAT
      S52

NO TICKET EXCHANGED NOR MONEY REFUNDED
is portion to be retained   No re-admission

SELECTED BOOTLEGS : CONCERTS 1969-1976

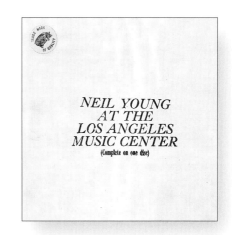

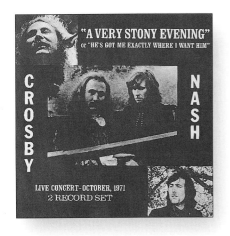

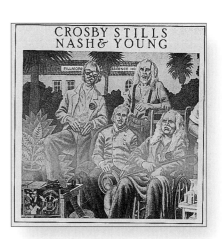

TOP: CROSBY BESIEGED BY FANS AT THE BYRDS' FAN
CLUB CONVENTION AT LONDON'S ROUNDHOUSE
BOTTOM: THE BYRDS, FEBRUARY 1967

THE BYRDS, 1965
MIDDLE LEFT: CHRIS HILLMAN/DAVID
CROSBY, STOCKHOLM, 1967

TOP LEFT: BUFFALO SPRINGFIELD, 1967
BOTTOM RIGHT: THE BYRDS, 1967
THE BYRDS/BUFFALO SPRINGFIELD, CAFF BENEFIT, 22 FEBRUARY 1967

OPPOSITE PAGE
COVER ARTWORK FOR THE UNRELEASED 'STAMPEDE'
STILLS AND YOUNG IN THE BUFFALO SPRINGFIELD

THIS PAGE
EARLY AND LATE PERIOD HOLLIES
GRAHAM NASH WITH HIS WIFE, ROSE ECCLES

GRAHAM NASH SHOT IN PSYCHEDELIC COLOUR, 1967

THE HOLLIES AT THEIR HIPPIE ZENITH

CROSBY, STILLS, NASH & YOUNG, 1969–1970

MANASSAS, 1972

TOP: NEIL YOUNG, 1975
BOTTOM: CROSBY & NASH, 1975

GRAHAM AND SUSAN NASH
DAVID AND JAN CROSBY
NEIL AND PEGI YOUNG
STEPHEN STILLS MARRIES
PAMELA ANN JORDAN,
DECEMBER 1987

PART IV
WASTED ON THE WAY
1977-1985

By 1977 CS&N realised that Young was as much a liability as a benefit. He had helped them achieve their greatest work and greatest fame, but robbed them of their original identity. For both record company and public, the initials CSN&Y had become a magical talisman, but for the performers it symbolised an impossible ideal. More worryingly, the thirst for a CSN&Y record posed problems for their still developing solo careers. Even the maverick Young, who had by now released nine solo albums, still suffered the unwanted suffix "of CSN&Y". It would be several more years before he broke that psychic connection and, even during the Eighties, interviewers would still quiz him about possible reunions.

CS&N desperately needed to re-establish themselves in the public imagination as a trio and succeeded thanks to some solid touring and Nash's penchant for writing hit singles. The strength in unity approach sustained their careers but also blighted the possibility of individual work. A paltry handful of solo efforts emerged over the next decade and all sold poorly. Even the new pairing of Stills & Nash found themselves greeted with apathy and indifference when they attempted to persuade Atlantic to sanction a release. The corporate attitude and public demand dictated "CS&N or nothing".

Unfortunately, CS&N were no longer working with the same passion and commitment that had characterised their first get together. Changes in musical fashions threatened their standing in the music industry and the lack of new product saw them increasingly resemble an act agonisingly attuned to the past. Worse still, Crosby's insidious decline into heroin addiction weakened their powers at a time when they needed to be at their strongest. With Stills also failing to produce the high quality songs that he wrote so effortlessly back in the early Seventies, it was small wonder that they foundered. After a brilliant new start in 1977, they issued only one new studio album over the next 10 years and even that was not a unified affair. As they struggled into the mid-Eighties, CS&N seemed a forced arrangement which would soon be irrevocably dismantled by the imprisonment and self-destruction of David Crosby.

1977

12-14 JANUARY

CS&N record Crosby's 'In My Dreams' (January 12) and his startling 'Shadow Captain' (14), a dream sequence which will provide the opening track on their forthcoming album. Crosby recalls the origins of the song: "I woke up at 4 o'clock in the morning in my bunk, 150 miles off the coast of California in my boat and I just wrote the whole thing, one verse after another. When I woke up I couldn't figure out what the music should be for a long time and when I came back I showed my friend Craig Doerge the words, and he flipped for it. So, he wrote the music. I like collaborative efforts every now and then. I'm into cooperative effort rather than competitive".

22 JANUARY

Nash's February 1974 acid trip at Winchester Cathedral provides the inspiration for the frantic 'Cathedral' which is recorded at Criteria Sound Studios in Miami.

25 JANUARY

Nash records 'Cold Rain', a song inspired by his recent return to Manchester on family business. While standing on the city streets, he found himself remembering days long past. "I realised everybody had seemed to change but me," he recalls. "Then I realised that maybe I had stayed the same also and I began to talk to myself about it, as writers do".

APRIL

"The best thing for me to think about Neil Young is: *later*", Crosby tells Cameron Crowe during recording sessions for the CSN album. "If he showed up right now he'd just weird it out. He can't do the painstaking work on vocals that we're doing right now. He doesn't believe in it. He can't even sit there while you do it. He'd rather clunk around with that garbanzo band of his..."

As if on cue, Young duly turns up, listens to some of their material and reportedly has a good time. "I love singing with those guys," he admits. "But CSN&Y tends to get too big. Too many people attach too much importance to them. I enjoy being able to visit but I want to avoid people thinking, 'Oh, there's Neil Young from CSN&Y'."

4 APRIL

Reprise Records' tape files indicate the receipt of completed tapes for Young's 'The Old Country Waltz', 'Saddle Up The Palomino', 'Hey Babe', 'Hold Back The Tears' and 'Bite The Bullet'.

8 APRIL

Nash's 'Carried Away' and 'Cold Rain' are registered for copyright purposes.

14 APRIL

Crosby registers 'Anything At All' and 'In My Dreams' for copyright purposes.

18 APRIL

Dave Mason's *Let It Flow* features Stills as guest vocalist.

2 MAY

In preparation for the release of the new CS&N album, Stills copyright registers 'Run From Tears', 'Fair Game', 'See The Changes', 'Dark Star' and 'I Give You Give Blind'.

3 MAY

Reprise Records' belatedly log the receipt of tapes for the unreleased 'It Might Have Been' and 'Dance Dance Dance'.

4 MAY

Nash marries Susan Sennett, for whom he will later compose 'Song For Susan'.

9 MAY

Crosby and Craig Doerge's 'Shadow Captain' is copyright registered one month before the release of the new CS&N album.

25/26 MAY

Young copyright registers the songs from the forthcoming *American Stars 'n Bars*. The composition 'Bite The Bullet' is jointly credited to Young and Mark Phillips but the latter's name is conspicuously absent from the record's credits.

JUNE

CS&N embark on their first ever tour as a trio, including dates this month at the Pine Knob Music Theater, Clarkston, MI (June 2), Capitol Center, Landover, MD (8), Pittsburgh Civic Center, Pittsburgh, PA (11), Providence, RI (13), Hartford Civic Center Arena, Hartford, CT (15), Nassau Coliseum, Long Island, NY (17), Madison Square Garden, NYC, NY (21), The Spectrum, Philadelphia, PA (23/24), The Forum, Inglewood, CA (28/29), San Diego Sports Arena, CA (30).

The opening show at the Pine Knob, Clarkston, Missouri, reveals their attempt to combine songs from their new album with the classics of yore. Revealingly, they still perform more songs from their celebrated début album than their latest effort. However, the song ratio per member is far more even than on the 1974 CSN&Y tour, with Stills singing 10 of his compositions (plus two covers), Nash performing eight, and Crosby seven (plus his co-write on 'Wooden Ships'). Although exciting, these shows are less intimate and celebratory than their 1974 equivalents. Crosby's criticisms of stadia rock sound a little more convincing when applied to this and later CS&N tours than the epochal mini-Woodstocks of three years before.

SET LIST (JUNE 2): PRE-ROAD DOWNS; LOVE THE ONE YOU'RE WITH; THE LEE SHORE; I USED TO BE A KING; DARK STAR; JUST A SONG BEFORE I GO; SHADOW CAPTAIN; TURN BACK THE PAGES; LONG TIME GONE; SUITE: JUDY BLUE EYES; YOU DON'T HAVE TO CRY; GUINNEVERE; OUR HOUSE; CATHEDRAL; CROSSROADS/YOU CAN'T CATCH ME; HELPLESSLY HOPING; BLACKBIRD; CARRY ME; CRITICAL MASS/WIND ON THE WATER; MILITARY MADNESS; I GIVE YOU GIVE BLIND; RUN FROM TEARS; DÉJÀ VU; CARRY ON; WOODEN SHIPS; TEACH YOUR CHILDREN; FIND THE COST OF FREEDOM.

20/27 JUNE

Young releases *American Stars 'n Bars*, a frustratingly inconsistent collection that fails to reach the US Top 20. Strangely enough, it provides his highest chart placing in the UK since *Harvest*, a testament perhaps to the enduring memory of his 1976 concerts.

This same week *CSN* is issued and eclipses Young's album commercially and artistically. The trio's primary strength at this point lies in a willingness to pool their best tunes, rather than holding back material for solo ventures. The immediate result is a formidable collection of songs that provide the consistency missing from recent individual efforts. Public response to the record is extremely positive, as it climbs to number 2 (US), narrowly failing to provide CS&N/CSN&Y with a fourth consecutive number 1 album. When asked how he thinks Young will respond to *CSN* Crosby says: "I hope it makes him think. He's not doing justice to his records – and it's bullshit... I hope he listens to this album and says, 'Oh, shit, I shouldn't settle for less'. That would be great... I've argued all these things with him, to his face."

> *"Neil's not doing justice to his records – and it's bullshit... I hope he listens to this album and says, 'Oh, shit, I shouldn't settle for less'. That would be great... I've argued all these things with him, to his face."*
>
> **DAVID CROSB**

2 JULY

CS&N's 'Just A Song Before I Go' enters the charts, eventually peaking at number 7, their biggest ever single. Nash recalls how the song was written: "I was in Hawaii once and I had about an hour to kill before I took the plane. I was at this friend of mine's house and being a smart arse, which he was at the time, he said: "You're so good, why don't you write a song before you go?" So I wrote 'Just A Song Before I Go'."

15 JULY - 2 SEPTEMBER

Young tours the bars of Santa Cruz with back-up group The Ducks, whose line-up features bassist Bob Mosley and guitarist Jeff Blackburn. The sample set list featured below is from the Catalyst, Santa Cruz (August 22) and includes a reading of Crazy Horse's 'Gone Dead Train', plus Young's 'Sail Away', 'Crying Eyes', 'Are You Ready For The Country?' 'Mr Soul' and 'Comes A Time', and a number of R&B-influenced numbers, none written by Young. The highlight though is the extraordinary Young instrumental 'Windward Passage', one of his most thrilling and alas unreleased songs from this period.

SET LIST: DEEPER MYSTERY; GYPSY WEDDING; SAIL AWAY; TAKE ME DOWN BEHIND THE SUN; ONLY LOVING YOU; CRYING EYES; BYE BYE JOHNNY; YOUR TIME WILL COME AROUND; DO ME RIGHT; ARE YOU READY FOR THE COUNTRY?; SILVER WINGS; TWO RIDERS; YOUR LOVE; GONE DEAD TRAIN; MR SOUL; HOLD ON BOYS; MY, MY, MY; I'M READY; COMES A TIME; WINDWARD PASSAGE; YOUNGER DAYS.

SUMMER

Jerry Aiello dies of a liver complaint, rumoured to have been drug-related. Stills performs alongside Bonnie Bramlett and Felix Pappalardi at a benefit for the pianist's family, staged at the Whisky.

"This is like an Irish wake," Stills jokes prior to the show. The group of musician friends, reinforced by George Perry (bass), Joe Vitale (drums), Mike Finnigan (keyboards) and Joe Lala (percussion), have only an afternoon to rehearse. As Stills promises: "The music will be loose and funky."

After a 40-minute set by Little Feat, Stills & Friends take the stage. They open with a tentative 'Amazing Grace', followed by 'Love The One You're With', 'Black Queen', 'Turn Back the Pages' and a cover of 'Midnight Rider'. Bramlett occasionally misses some lyrics while reading words scribbled on her hand, but shows her worth during a spirited version of

Sam and Dave's 'Hold On I'm Comin''. Pianist Mike Finnigan sings 'I Need Someone To Love' after which Stills returns for the upbeat 'Rocky Mountain Way'. In deference to the memory of the Springfield at the Whisky, he performs 'For What It's Worth' and quips, "I'm Neil Young!!"

12 AUGUST

Nash and Young join David Crosby on-stage at a benefit for the United Farmworkers' Union at the Civic Center, Santa Cruz. Crosby plays six of his compositions, before Nash arrives for 'Southbound Train'. After five songs as a duo, Young emerges for 'Human Highway', followed by another seven songs. A singalong 'Sugar Mountain' closes the show.

SET LIST: THE LEE SHORE; PAGE 43; TRIAD; HOMEWARD THROUGH THE HAZE; NAKED IN THE RAIN; LAUGHING; SOUTHBOUND TRAIN; GUINNEVERE; CATHEDRAL; CARRY ME; LOWDOWN PAYMENT; HUMAN HIGHWAY; NEW MAMA; DÉJÀ VU; ONLY LOVE CAN BREAK YOUR HEART; OUR HOUSE; WOODEN SHIPS; TEACH YOUR CHILDREN; SUGAR MOUNTAIN.

LATE SUMMER

CS&N are presented to President Jimmy Carter at the White House. The invitation has been prompted by Stills' work for the Democratic Party.

OCTOBER – NOVEMBER

CS&N continue their tour with performances at the Portland Coliseum, OR (October 18), PNE Coliseum, Vancouver, BC, Canada (19), Seattle Coliseum, WA (20), Oakland Coliseum, CA (23), Lincoln, NB (28), Civic Center Arena, St Paul, MN (31), Riverfront Coliseum, Cincinnati, OH (November 4), Athletics and Vocation Center, Notre Dame University, South Bend, IN (5), Rupp Arena, Lexington Center, Lexington, KY (6), Mid-South Coliseum, Memphis, TN (9), Greensboro, Coliseum, NC (12), The Omni, Atlanta, GA (14), Jefferson County Civic Center, Birmingham, AL (15), Civic Center, Lakeland, FL (19), The Sportatorium, Miami, FL (20), The Summit, Houston, TX (22), Tarrant County Convention Center, Fort Worth, TX (23), Myriad, Oklahoma City, OK (24). During these shows, keyboardist Craig Doerge is replaced by Kim Bullard. The Houston performance includes the versions of 'Shadow Captain' and 'For Free' later used for the live album, *Allies*.

SAMPLE SET LIST (TARRANT COUNTY CONVENTION CENTRE, NOVEMBER 23): PRE-ROAD DOWNS; LOVE THE ONE YOU'RE WITH; THE LEE SHORE; JUST A SONG BEFORE I GO; SHADOW CAPTAIN; WILD TALES; TURN BACK THE PAGES; SUITE: JUDY BLUE EYES; HELPLESSLY HOPING; BLACKBIRD; FOR FREE; OUR HOUSE; CATHEDRAL; TREETOP FLYER; CROSSROADS/YOU CAN'T CATCH ME; CRITICAL

MASS/WIND ON THE WATER; DÉJÀ VU; I GIVE YOU GIVE BLIND; MILITARY MADNESS; LONG TIME GONE; CARRY ON; WOODEN SHIPS; TEACH YOUR CHILDREN; FIND THE COST OF FREEDOM.

31 OCTOBER
Reprise Records log the acquisition of completed tapes for Young's 'Sail Away', 'Goin' Back' and 'Human Highway'.

7 NOVEMBER
Crosby-Nash Live seems a largely redundant attempt by ABC to cash in on CS&N's current success. An album already out of time.

14 NOVEMBER
Young's triple album *Decade* provides an impressive summation of his recording career, complete with a teasing handful of previously unreleased songs of varying quality.

On this same day, the soundtrack of *Saturday Night Fever* is issued, with Stills adding percussion to The Bee Gees' 'You Should Be Dancing'.

19 NOVEMBER
Young collaborates with the Gone With The Wind Orchestra for a concert at the Bicentennial Park, Miami. Among the songs featured is the unreleased 'Lady Wingshot' and an amusing medley of 'Albama' and the Lynyrd Skynyrd diatribe 'Sweet Home Alabama'.

SET LIST: ARE YOU READY FOR THE COUNTRY?; DANCE, DANCE, DANCE/LOVE IS A ROSE; OLD MAN; THE LOSING END; HEART OF GOLD; THE NEEDLE AND THE DAMAGE DONE; SUGAR MOUNTAIN; ALREADY ONE; LADY WINGSHOT; FOUR STRONG WINDS; DOWN BY THE RIVER; ALABAMA/SWEET HOME ALABAMA; ARE YOU READY FOR THE COUNTRY?

21/22 NOVEMBER
Young copyright registers 'Already One', 'Sail Away', 'Spud Blues' (aka 'Country Home') and the unreleased 'Lady Wingshot'. On this same day, Reprise Records' tape archive logs the unissued 'Daughters', 'Please Help Me I'm Falling' and 'We're Having Some Fun'.

5 DECEMBER
Lonnie Mack's *Lonnie Mack With Pismo* is released with Nash as guest vocalist.

6 DECEMBER
Crosby appears alongside former partners McGuinn and Clark at the Boarding House, San Francisco. Despite having problems remembering some of the lyrics, Crosby gamely joins in on 'Mr Tambourine Man', 'He Was A Friend Of Mine', 'You Ain't Going

Nowhere', 'So You Want To Be A Rock 'n' Roll Star' and 'Eight Miles High'.

Although everyone insists that this is most likely a one-off, Crosby later joins the duo when they play the Roxy. He is invited to take part in an extended version of 'Mr Tambourine Man' which, appropriately, features McGuinn and Clark trading verses, as if they were back at World Pacific Studios. 'You Ain't Going Nowhere' follows, but Crosby is gone by the time McGuinn announces 'Season Song' ('Bye Bye Baby') and remains off stage through 'Turn! Turn! Turn!' and 'Knocking On Heaven's Door'. Audience cheers midway through 'Feel A Whole Lot Better' suggest that Crosby is back and he sticks around for most of the remaining set: 'So You Want To Be A Rock 'n' Roll Star', 'Eight Miles High' and 'He Was A Friend Of Mine'.

The performance is tantalising in its precise re-enactment of the formation of The Byrds. "It was the best sound that I thought we ever got," Crosby enthuses. The historical analogies are also intriguing. Here we have McGuinn and Clark playing as a duo, bringing in Crosby on additional vocals and soon adding Chris Hillman once more. In the wake of these appearances, it is announced that Capitol are signing McGuinn, Clark & Hillman. Crosby later appears at the sessions for the trio's album, only to be shunned. "I flew to Miami on purpose to see them, and to go in and ask them if I could sing," David recalls. "And they didn't want me to. I did it. I came in there and asked if I could sing. I offered, and I even asked... I wasn't trying to shine my own light. The emotion that was foremost in my mind was affection for them and a feeling that I could both focus attention on them and help them to make a better record. It hurt me that they didn't want me to sing because I wanted to".

1978

JANUARY
CS&N reconvene at Criteria Studios with the intention of completing a new album. Fans are optimistic about the outcome having just read a major interview with Stills in *Crawdaddy*, during which he outlines the group dynamics of CS&N in a noticeably positive fashion. "We make up for each other's inadequacies," he explains. "We help each other through each other's stupidities. I play guitar and I try to help them get the best out of their songs and their music, and they try to help me... without taking over. Sometimes I'll get a flash on one of David's songs and I know exactly how it should be done, and I can be totally wrong. Then I'll get hung up and cut him a mind-blowing track. Or he'll say, 'No, man, that's not what I want to do, man'. It's *gestalt* mentality. Very interdependent – and we finally admitted that it is. Graham's the only one with the patience to go in there and take four or five partial vocals and make one good vocal out of all of them. David can put together really neat harmonies that sometimes are incredible and sometimes are not incredible. I set the feel. I get the band together. I make everybody play like there's no tomorrow. And I make double goddamn sure that David is satisfied with the performance of his song and Graham is satisfied with the performance of his song... even if I lay out."

This over-optimistic analysis ultimately ends in hubris, for the trio only succeed in part recording Crosby's 'Drive My Car', Stills/Kortchmar's 'Can't Get No Booty', Nash's 'Helicopter Song' and two yet to be released compositions, Crosby & Nash's 'Jigsaw' and Nash's 'Mirage'. The sessions then break down and the trio disperse, with Stills electing to pursue another solo album.

JANUARY
Art Garfunkel's *Watermark* is released with Crosby guesting on vocals.

FEBRUARY
Nash writes 'Magical Child' for his new born son, Jackson, whom he names in honour of Jackson Browne. Meanwhile, work nears completion on *The Graham Nash Collection*, a 71-page book of his photo archives, which is published later in the year by the Nash Press, to mark the exhibition of his collection at the University of Santa Clara, CA.

-28 MAY
Young plays five nights at the Boarding House, San Francisco, in what emerges as some of his most impressive concerts of the period. Among the songs featured are a strong selection from what will eventually emerge as *Rust Never Sleeps* , an excellent 'Shots' then still in acoustic form, and a surprise revival of 'Out Of My Mind'.

SET LIST (MAY 24): POCAHONTAS; HUMAN HIGHWAY; ALREADY ONE; COMES A TIME; BIRDS; MY MY, HEY HEY (OUT OF THE BLUE); SHOTS; COWGIRL IN THE SAND; AFTER THE GOLDRUSH; THRASHER; THE WAYS OF LOVE; I BELIEVE IN YOU; SUGAR MOUNTAIN; SAIL AWAY.

19 JUNE
Dave Mason's *Mariposa De Oro* features Stills and Nash as guest vocalists.

21 JUNE
Stills and Nash appear at the unveiling of a CS&N star to be placed on Hollywood Boulevard's Walk Of Fame. Crosby is conspicuous by his absence.

JULY – AUGUST
CS&N undertake a summer tour, including dates at the Market Square Arena, Indianapolis, IN (July 7), Freedom Hall, Louisville, KY (8), Pine Knob, Clarkston, MI (11 14), Masonic Temple, Detroit, MI (15), Memorial Auditorium, Buffalo, NY (16), The Forum, Montreal, Canada (18), Providence Civic Center, RI (20), Madison Square Garden, NYC,

CROSBY ON STAGE WITH McGUINN, CLARK & HILLMAN

NY (22), Pittsburgh Civic Center, PA (26), Nassau Coliseum, Long Island, NY (30/31), Boston Garden, MA (August 2), Robin Hood Theatre, Philadelphia, PA (4/5), Richfield Coliseum, Cleveland, OH (9).

The sample set list below from the Madison Square Garden show (July 22) features Joni Mitchell guesting on 'Teach Your Children'.

SET LIST: PRE- ROAD DOWNS; FOR WHAT IT'S WORTH; THE LEE SHORE; JUST A SONG BEFORE I GO; RUN FROM TEARS; SHADOW CAPTAIN; CATHEDRAL; TURN BACK THE PAGES; SUITE: JUDY BLUE EYES; YOU DON'T HAVE TO CRY; 4+20; BLACKBIRD; FOR FREE; GUINNEVERE; MAGICAL CHILD; LADY OF THE ISLAND; OUR HOUSE; MYTH OF SISYPHUS; CROSSROADS/YOU CAN'T CATCH ME; CRITICAL MASS/TO THE LAST WHALE; DÉJÀ VU; LONG TIME GONE; WOODEN SHIPS; CARRY ON; TEACH YOUR CHILDREN.

31 JULY
Stills copyright registers the recently completed 'We Will Go On', 'What's The Game?', 'Woman Lleva', 'Beaucoup Yumbo', 'Can't Get No Booty' and 'That's The Way It Was'. The latter remains unreleased, while the rest will appear on his next solo album.

14 AUGUST
A double celebration as Nash finally receives American citizenship on the occasion of Crosby's 37th birthday.

4 SEPTEMBER
Stills performs an acoustic set at the Bread and Roses Festival at the Greek Theater, Berkeley, San Francisco. His enthralling performance includes the blues influenced 'Take Me Back To The Ohio Valley' and 'Old Man Trouble', plus a reading of Rick Roberts' 'Colorado'. The undoubted highlight, however, is a new composition played on Spanish guitar: 'One Moment At A Time' (aka 'Love Becomes A Trial'). It remains unissued at the time of writing. The show ends with an elongated version of 'For What It's Worth' during which Stills is backed spectacularly by The Persuaders.

SET LIST: LOVE THE ONE YOU'RE WITH; NOT FADE AWAY; ONE MOMENT AT A TIME (AKA LOVE BECOMES A TRIAL); EVERYBODY'S TALKIN'; 4+20; COLORADO; TAKE ME BACK TO THE OHIO VALLEY; JESUS GAVE LOVE AWAY FOR FREE; FALLEN EAGLE; OLD MAN TROUBLE; THOROUGHFARE GAP; CROSSROADS/YOU CAN'T CATCH ME; 49 BYE BYES/FOR WHAT IT'S WORTH.

18 SEPTEMBER - 24 OCTOBER
Young tours with Crazy Horse, beginning at the Pine Knob Theater, Clarkston, MI and ending at the Inglewood Forum, LA. Their show at the

DAVID CROSBY

Cow Palace, San Francisco (October 22) is filmed for the forthcoming movie, *Rust Never Sleeps*. During the tour, they première the unissued 'Bright Sunny Day' (sometimes erroneously titled 'The Price You Pay'). The set list below, taken from the Chicago Stadium (October 15), is representative of an unusually static set list on a national Young tour.

SET LIST: SUGAR MOUNTAIN; I AM A CHILD; COMES A TIME; ALREADY ONE; AFTER THE GOLDRUSH; THRASHER; MY, MY, HEY HEY (OUT OF THE BLUE); WHEN YOU DANCE I CAN REALLY LOVE; THE LONER; WELFARE MOTHERS; COME ON BABY LET'S GO DOWNTOWN; THE NEEDLE AND THE DAMAGE DONE; LOTTA LOVE; SEDAN DELIVERY; POWDERFINGER; CORTEZ THE KILLER; CINNAMON GIRL; LIKE A HURRICANE; TONIGHT'S THE NIGHT.

OCTOBER

Young releases *Comes A Time* (officially scheduled for September 29), a commercial, yet thoroughly engaging and aesthetically impressive work that brings him back into the US Top 10 for the first time since *Harvest*.

5 OCTOBER

The Best Of David Crosby & Graham Nash seems little more than a pointless exercise in recycling from a disgruntled record company.

8 OCTOBER

While Young is on-stage with Crazy Horse at the Inglewood Forum, news filters through that his house on Zuma Beach has been razed by a brush fire.

OCTOBER

Stills' releases *Thoroughfare Gap*, his answer to the disco boom. Its failure to register a Top 40 entry, combined with almost universal critical antipathy, does severe damage to his future prospects as a solo recording artiste.

LATE OCTOBER – NOVEMBER

Stills auditions a new group, comprising Bonnie Bramlett, Mike Finnigan, George Perry, Carl Pickard, Gerry Tolman, Al Perkins, Dallas Taylor and Joe Lala. Among the songs they rehearse are two unissued Stills compositions: 'Streetwise' and 'Precious Love'.

NOVEMBER

An unwelcome ghost from the past returns in the form of former CSN&Y bassist Greg Reeves, who attempts to sue the quartet for $1 million of alleged unpaid royalties.

NOVEMBER

Crazy Horse release *Crazy Moon*, with Young guesting on 'She's Hot', 'Going Down Again', 'Downhill' and 'Thunder And Lightning'.

1979

JANUARY

Stills unveils his new group at the Roxy in Hollywood, with Bonnie Bramlett receiving surprise prominence on vocals. Meanwhile, Nash is playing sporadic solo dates in California.

8 JANUARY

Stills copyrights a batch of recently completed songs. These include 'Country', 'Shuffle' (a successor to 'Shuffle, Just As Bad'), '(Got To Keep) Open', 'I Am With You Girl', 'Ain't It Always?', 'Bitter Pill' (with Joe Vitale), 'Emperor Of Disco Dreams' and 'Feed The People'. All of these, with the exception of '(Got To Keep) Open' (issued on *Live It Up* in 1990, with additional lyrics from Nash) will remain unreleased.

26/27 & 29 JANUARY

Graham Nash and Jackson Browne share a bill, performing three nights in San Diego, LA and Oakland for the benefit of the Abalone Alliance, an anti-nuclear organisation. Nash plays a number of songs from his new album, including an unfinished version of 'Barrel Of Pain (Half Life)'. He also explains that 'I Used To Be A King' was written for The Hollies, with special reference to 'King Midas In Reverse'. Towards the end of his set, he pays tribute to his backing group, which comprises David Lindley, Joel Bernstein, Tim Drummond, Craig Doerge and Russ Kunkel. Later in the evening, he returns to the stage after Browne's set for encores of 'Love Work Out' and 'Teach Your Children'.

SET LIST: SOUTHBOUND TRAIN; IMMIGRATION MAN; WILD TALES; TAKE THE MONEY AND RUN; IT'S ALL RIGHT; JUST A SONG BEFORE I GO; OUT ON THE ISLAND; MAGICAL CHILD; BARREL OF PAIN (HALF LIFE); OUR HOUSE; WIND ON THE WATER; PRE-ROAD DOWNS; I USED TO BE A KING; CATHEDRAL; CHICAGO; LOVE WORK OUT; TEACH YOUR CHILDREN.

FEBRUARY

While drinking at the Holiday Inn in Columbus, Ohio, Elvis Costello makes the mistake of facetiously calling Ray Charles "a blind, ignorant nigger" in the presence of Stills' band and is floored by the indignant fist of Bonnie Bramlett.

7 FEBRUARY

Stills enters LA's Record Plant to try out their new 32-track system. Following a 15-hour workout, he records and produces four songs, including re-runs of 'Cherokee' and 'Make Love To You'. A rare audio demonstration record is later issued featuring two versions of 'Cherokee' on analog and two versions on digital. The "test run" recordings ensure that Stills is hailed in the music press as the first rock performer to use digital recording.

MID-FEBRUARY

Having switched labels from ABC to CBS, Crosby & Nash enter Britannia Studios in LA to record their latest album as a duo. Several

CROSBY, STILLS & McGUINN WITH OLIVIA NEWTON-JOHN

songs are recorded, including 'Drive My Car', 'Out On The Island', 'Barrel Of Pain (Half Life)' and 'Love Has Come', but the sessions prove frustrating. By this point, Crosby is severely addicted to cocaine and Nash feels he can no longer focus adequately on the music. A pivotal moment in their musical relationship occurs during a session when Crosby's freebase pipe shatters on the floor and he drops to his knees to retrieve the pieces. As Nash recalled: "David

and when I write about him being naked in the arms of another woman, it sounds like I'm talking about my wife being in the arms of another woman, so it becomes really strange."

4 APRIL
Nash's ecologically minded 'Barrel Of Pain (Half-Life)' is recorded at Britannia Studios, LA, with vocal assistance from Cleo Kennedy, Brenda Eager and Gloria Coleman.

> "We've been together about three days," Nash tells the audience. "We didn't have much time to rehearse but our spirits are strong and we're going to do the best show we can for you tonight."
> "You're the only reason we do this," Crosby enthuses. "Stand up and be counted. Let them know which side you're on. No Nukes!"
>
> MADISON SQUARE GARDEN, SEPTEMBER 1979

stopped everybody playing to pick up a pipe that was way beyond repair. I knew then that the drug was much more important to him than the music... We were getting to the point where we couldn't sing harmony any more." Disillusioned, Nash aborts the sessions and elects to pursue a solo record instead.

28 FEBRUARY
Nash copyrights 'Magical Child', a tribute to his recently born son Jackson, which later appears on the following year's *Earth And Sky*.

3 MARCH
Stills' group flies to Cuba to appear at the Karl Marx Theater for Havana Jam, the country's first major rock festival, which is sponsored by CBS Records. Among the artistes on the bill are Kris Kristofferson and Rita Coolidge. Stephen and Ti Stills write a new song in Spanish specially for the event: 'Cuba al fin', which is later featured on the Various Artistes' compilation *Havana Jam*. Immediately after the event, Stills returns to the US, augmented by the Cuban group Irakere, whom he takes on a brief East Coast tour.

5 MARCH
Gary Wright's *Headin' Home* is released, with Crosby & Nash adding vocals to 'Love's Awake Inside'. During this same period, Stills appears on Hoyt Axton's *A Rusty Old Halo*, playing guitar on 'Hotel Ritz' and 'Wild Bull Rider'; and Nash produces and sings on Steve Gillette's *A Little Warmth*.

20 MARCH
Nash copyrights a batch of recently completed songs: 'On The Other Side Of Town', 'Love Has Come', 'Barrel Of Pain (Half-Life)', 'Out On The Island' and 'Helicopter Song'. The last three later appear on *Earth And Sky*, but 'On The Other Side Of Town' remains unissued. "It was a song I wrote for my son, the first time that he ever went to a doctor," Nash explained. "It's a very strange song because I'm writing from his perspective

30 APRIL
James Taylor's *Flag* is released, with Nash singing on 'Company Man'.

9 JUNE
Stills appears at San Francisco's Warfield Theater with a revised line-up of his current group. Brooks Hunnicutt replaces the departing Bonnie Bramlett, while Lala, Vitale and Perry make way for drummer Bill Meeker, bassist Gerald Johnson and percussionists Pete and Sheila Escovedo.
That same night, Nash appears on a bill with Jackson Browne and John Sebastian at the Greek Theater, Berkeley.

14 JUNE
Stills and Nash appear at Survival Sunday, a benefit concert at the Hollywood Bowl for MUSE (Musicians United for Safe Energy). Other artistes performing include Bruce Springsteen, Bonnie Raitt and Gary US Bonds.

JULY
The Section's *Fork It Over* is released, with Crosby contributing vocals to 'Magnetic Lady'.

2 JULY
Having played in Buffalo, New York, the previous week, The Stephen Stills Band partakes in a Woodstock reunion in Central Park, with a performance that is the antithesis of CSN&Y. This is rough house blues with Stills reinventing himself in a fashion worthy of Neil Young. At the time, these band shows seemed further evidence of Stills' decline as a songwriter and performer in the wake of *Thoroughfare Gap*, but 16 years on, the tape of the gig sounds a lot more interesting than my memories of the performance. Indeed, rather like Young during his *Time Fades Away* period, it's possible to look back and see how much Stills may have been misjudged. Without question, he subverts his audience's response in a remarkable way that is unbelievably audacious. There's an exciting, lengthy

workout of 'Cherokee', that great brass-dominated track from his first album. The only problem is that there are no horns in his current group, but he does the song anyway. If that sounds weird, then just imagine Stills' 'Love The One You're With', his biggest hit and greatest crowd pleaser, sung by Brooks Hunnicutt. What other performer would allow his most famous song to be sung by someone else in the band? And it doesn't stop there. Pianist Mike Finnigan sings two of his own songs, 'Got To Find Love' and 'Part Time Love', and does most of the introductions too. It's as if Stills is deliberately deconstructing his rock star myth before a good-time crowd who fail to grasp the implications of his actions or see anything untoward.

When Stills does speak at length, it's to recall his recent trip to Cuba. Introducing 'Cuba al fin' he reveals: "This is a song I wrote especially for a tour that we made for the fine young people and everything down in Cuba about two months ago. Had a ball. Kind of way of saying from all of us to all of them, 'Howdy, it's OK – the governments can yell all they want but we be friends." The odd feature of this announcement is that Stills speaks it in the accent of a Cuban, and without a trace of irony.

Clearly immersed in his bluesman persona, Stills performs 'For What It's Worth' as a pure blues workout, prefaces 'Go Back Home' with Hendrix's 'Red House', and even sings Robert Johnson's 'Come On In My Kitchen', the same number that Crosby muttered before the beginning '49 Bye Byes' on the first CS&N album.

If Young had performed these gigs, they'd have been hailed as the work of an eccentric genius. In its own way, this show and others around this period were almost as radical, iconoclastic and downright confusing as Young's *Tonight's The Night* tour. Nobody was ready to reappraise Stills or to regard these performances as anything other than a seemingly inexplicable aberration. But there is a definite wilfulness here that characterised Stills' anarchic spirit as perhaps never before.

Stills sums up this blues excursion for the Central Park audience as "The most relaxing, fun tour I've been on in many years".

"Thanks for the money, Steve," retorts Mike Finnigan – and you feel he means it.

SET LIST: PRECIOUS LOVE; RED HOUSE/GO BACK HOME; GOT TO FIND LOVE; LOVE THE ONE YOU'RE WITH; CUBA AL FIN; PART TIME LOVE; FOR WHAT IT' WORTH; CHEROKEE; TURN BACK THE PAGES; THOROUGHFARE GAP; COME ON IN MY KITCHEN; WOODSTOCK.

9 JULY
Young releases *Rust Never Sleeps* (officially scheduled for June 22), one of the strongest and most accomplished albums of his career. Its timing could hardly have been better and prompts *Village Voice* to proclaim him "Artist Of The Decade".

0 JULY

Stills copyrights the Spanish language 'Cuba al fin' which he co-wrote with Ti Stills.

AUGUST

Nash performs three shows at Los Angeles' Universal Amphitheater, from which 'Wild Tales' is belatedly taken for inclusion on the 1991 CSN boxed set.

0 AUGUST

Chicago 13 features Stills playing guitar on his own composition, 'Closer To You'.

EPTEMBER

Crosby and writer Carl Gottlieb collaborate on *Push Play*, a screenplay for Warner Brothers whose theme centres on the unfinished recordings of a dead rock star. Given Crosby's plight, the work sounds dangerously prophetic.

SEPTEMBER

Crosby & Nash appear at the Schaeffer Music Festival in New York's Central Park.

SEPTEMBER

Nash reunites CS&N for the final night of a series of star-studded MUSE benefits at the Madison Square Garden. "We've been together about three days," Nash tells the audience. "We didn't have much time to rehearse but our spirits are strong and we're going to do the best show we can for you tonight."

"You're the only reason we do this," Crosby enthuses. "Stand up and be counted. Let them know which side you're on. No Nukes!"

While Crosby & Nash do the talking, Stills dominates the set, opening with five straight acoustic songs, including the lengthy 'Suite: Judy Blue Eye'. Nash just about has time to squeeze in a quick 'Our House' before they move on to the electric segment, backed by the familiar line-up of Craig Doerge, Joe Lala, Tim Drummond and Russ Kunkel. The highlight of the evening is Nash's 'Cathedral' which opens with the sound of a church organ and is the best arranged song in the set.

One noticeable statistic from the evening is the lack of Crosby material. Stills sings seven songs, Nash six and Crosby a mere one ('Long Time Gone'). Nor can this be explained away as resulting from the recent Stills/Nash collaboration, since all the material they play is pre-1978.

SET LIST: HELPLESSLY HOPING; CHANGE PARTNERS; YOU DON'T HAVE TO CRY; 4+20; SUITE: JUDY BLUE EYES; OUR HOUSE; PRE-ROAD DOWNS; LOVE THE ONE YOU'RE WITH; JUST A SONG BEFORE I GO; LONG TIME GONE; CATHEDRAL; WOODEN SHIPS; CARRY ON; CHICAGO; TEACH YOUR CHILDREN.

CTOBER

Crosby & Nash briefly reunite to appear on the final day of the Bread And Roses Festival at the Greek Theater, University of California at Berkeley. Selections from their set are later captured on an album, released by Fantasy Records. Crosby appears with Russ Kunkel on 'The Lee Shore', Nash and Joel Bernstein perform 'Just A Song Before I Go' and 'Military Madness' and Crosby, Bernstein & Nash sing John and Johanna Hall's 'Power'.

14 NOVEMBER

Young releases the double album *Live Rust*, a disappointing affair that features no new songs and seems conceived purely to promote the film *Rust Never Sleeps*. When asked to rationalise the release, Young can only offer a confused and contradictory message to his fans: "If they don't want to hear the old songs they don't have to buy it to hear the new ones."

9 DECEMBER

Stills plays the California State University, where Nash makes a surprise guest appearance.

10 DECEMBER

The triple album *No Nukes* features CS&N performing 'You Don't Have To Cry', 'Long Time Gone' and 'Teach Your Children'; Nash performing 'Cathedral' and joining Jackson Browne on 'Crow On The Cradle'; the combination of Nash, Carly Simon and James Taylor on 'Times They Are A-Changin', and Nash adding harmony to The Doobie Brothers' 'Power' and 'Takin' It To The Streets' and Jesse Colin Young's version of 'Get Together'.

14/15 DECEMBER

Crosby plays two benefit concerts at the Palace of Fine Arts, San Francisco. These acoustic shows reveal Crosby's undeniable presence as a solo performer, convincing his new manager David Scott to organise a series of shows in London early in the New Year. At this point, Crosby's drug problems have not succeeded in blighting his creativity, as he demonstrates by playing three excellent new songs: 'Distances', 'Drive My Car' and 'Delta'. This trilogy forms the basis of a powerful solo album but will not be built upon strongly enough to satisfy his record company. In concert, he still pulls a few surprises, most notably an ambitious attempt at 'Déjà Vu' characterised by some wonderful scat singing. He also performs the first song he ever wrote on piano, 'Bittersweet', plus its successor 'Homeward Through The Haze'. As ever with Crosby, on-stage banter ("Are you gonna ask me where Neil is? You gonna ask if I can boogie") adds a pleasant intimacy to the show and he even sings some lines from 'My Way' and 'Born Free' while tuning up for the closing 'Long Time Gone'. At the close of the second show, he bravely performs 'Blackbird', without the benefit of Stills & Nash.

SET LIST (14TH): CARRY ME; THE LEE SHORE; DÉJÀ VU; FOR FREE; DISTANCES; DRIVE MY CAR; BITTERSWEET; DELTA; PAGE 43; TRIAD; GUINNEVERE; LONG TIME GONE.
SET LIST (15TH): CARRY ME; THE LEE SHORE; GUINNEVERE; FOR FREE; DELTA; DISTANCES; DRIVE MY CAR; TRIAD; LONG TIME GONE; WOODEN SHIPS; BLACKBIRD.

1980

1 FEBRUARY

Nash copyrights 'T.V. Guide' and 'In The 80s' from his forthcoming album, which will be released by Capitol.

10 FEBRUARY

Nash copyrights 'It's All Right' (originally premièred on CSN&Y's 1974 tour) and the title track from his new album, 'Earth And Sky'.

15 FEBRUARY

Nash releases his third solo album *Earth And Sky*, which features Crosby & Stills prominently on 'Helicopter Song'; plus Crosby singing on 'Love Has Come' and adding guitar to 'Out On The Island'. Unfortunately, the album appears at a time when Nash is at his most unfashionable. Its commercial failure puts his solo career in jeopardy.

26-28 FEBRUARY

Crosby's dates at London's Venue are postponed when he suffers an extreme bout of flu and exhaustion.

MARCH – APRIL

Nash embarks on a two-month solo tour of the USA, employing Cass Elliot's sister Leah Kunkel as the opening act. The backing group comprises Joel Bernstein (guitar/harmony) and David Kessler (keyboards), the latter soon replaced by Dylan sideman William Smith. Playing small theatres, Nash provides an intimate show with a healthy selection of recent songs. Jackson Browne guests at the Pantages Theater, Hollywood (March 28), with Nash harmonising on 'Crow On The Cradle'. Even more intriguing is the set list below, which features five songs from Nash's last album, plus rare covers of Richard and Linda Thompson's 'Pavanne' and John and Johanna Hall's 'Power'.

SET LIST (PALLADIUM, NEW YORK CITY, APRIL 27): MILITARY MADNESS; SOUTHBOUND TRAIN; OUT ON THE ISLAND; JUST A SONG BEFORE I GO; SKYCHILD; BARREL OF PAIN (HALF-LIFE); RIGHT BETWEEN THE EYES; PAVANNE; CARRIED AWAY; MAGICAL CHILD; IN THE 80S; WIND ON THE WATER; CATHEDRAL; CHICAGO; TEACH YOUR CHILDREN; POWER; OUR HOUSE; SIMPLE MAN.

APRIL

Leah Kunkel's album *I Run With Trouble* features Nash as guest vocalist on 'Let's Begin' and 'Never Gonna Lose My Dream Of Love Again'.

21-23 APRIL

Crosby appears at the Venue in London for six shows spread over three nights. The performances are largely ignored by critics, with *The Guardian*'s Robin Denselow concluding: "Crosby's audience has quite correctly lost interest... He wandered on like a caricature of an ageing hippy, in shoulder-length hair, Woolworth's moustache and cowboy shirt. He had no band but accompanied

himself on acoustic guitar and piano for songs so unmemorable that it was a wonder how he remembered them. His voice was sweet and fine and was wasted on a series of self-satisfied musical doodlings."

The "musical doodlings" represent nothing less than the finest material Crosby has sung in years. Undoubtedly, the highlight of the set is a staggering trilogy of 'Delta', 'Distances' and 'Drive My Car' that confirm Crosby's continued strength as a writer and performer. Even during the soundcheck he attempts 'King Of The Mountain' and 'Samurai', proving that a strong album is ready if Capitol Records are willing.

The set list below is from the opening show of the first evening. On successive nights, he varies the song list slightly to feature 'Long Time Gone' and 'For Free'.

SET LIST: THE LEE SHORE; PAGE 43; CARRY ME; LOW DOWN PAYMENT; HOMEWARD THROUGH THE HAZE; DELTA; DISTANCES; DRIVE MY CAR; DÉJÀ VU; GUINNEVERE; WOODEN SHIPS; TRIAD.

22 APRIL

Crosby sits with me in a hotel room in Denbigh Street, Pimlico, spending the entire day freebasing cocaine. At the time, this seems as normal as smoking a packet of cigarettes. Despite the worrying scale of his addiction, he is lucid, alert, perceptive, entertaining and betrays that curious mixture of arrogance and pained humility. There are signs of a worrying fatalism in his attitude towards freebasing, but I've never encountered a musician with a greater self-awareness. At one point, anticipating doom, I ask him, "How long do you think you've got left?" He hardly pauses. "Five years or so," he says. I nod in resigned agreement. Later that evening he gives one hell of a performance, despite what *The Guardian* thinks.

25 MAY

CS&N reconvene at the Hollywood Bowl for Survival Sunday III, dedicated to the use of non-nuclear power. Nash performs a solo set, then introduces Crosby for a couple of songs, after which Stills arrives. Stills plays the rare 'Dangerous Woman On The Loose', co-written with George Perry, plus 'For What It's Worth'. CS&N also back Don Felder, Tim Schmit and Joe Walsh on The Eagles' 'I Can't Tell You Why'. The full ensemble, including Dr John, re-emerges for a lengthy jam on 'Hoochie Coochie Man'.

SET LIST: MILITARY MADNESS; IN THE 80S; OUT ON THE ISLAND; MAGICAL CHILD; BARREL OF PAIN (HALF-LIFE); CARRY ME; GUINNEVERE; WIND ON THE WATER; CATHEDRAL; JUST A SONG BEFORE I GO; DANGEROUS WOMAN ON THE LOOSE; FOR WHAT IT'S WORTH; WOODEN SHIPS; TEACH YOUR CHILDREN; I CAN'T TELL YOU WHY; CROSSROADS/ YOU CAN'T CATCH ME; HOOCHIE COOCHIE MAN.

MAY

Crosby records 'Delta' which he later erroneously claims is the final song he wrote before his imprisonment. It is this composition that will effectively transform *Daylight Again* from a Stills/Nash project into a CS&N recording. Even in the depths of freebase addiction Crosby can still write great songs but, as he admits, he had to be coaxed into completing this classic by the ever supportive Jackson Browne.

SPRING

The unlikely coupling of Stills & Nash team up for a gig in Hawaii, and their interaction is so stress-free that they decide to attempt a joint recording together later in the year. The decision is a crucial one for Stills, who has recently delivered an R&B-styled album to CBS which the record company rejects.

2 JULY

Reprise Records' tape archive logs the following Young recordings: 'Stayin' Power', 'Coastline', 'Union Man', 'Comin' Apart At Every Nail' and 'Hawks And Doves'.

CROSBY AT THE VENUE

15 JULY

Stills appears at the San Siro Stadium, Milan, playing a blues-dominated set. Mike Finnigan sings 'Going Down To Dallas', 'It's Just A Rumour' and 'Part Time Love'. Stills opens with the group's powerhouse 'Precious Love', one of several unreleased songs he has written during this period. Other surprises include 'Come On In My Kitchen' and the medley 'Hoochie Coochie Man'/'Rocky Mountain Way'.

SET LIST: PRECIOUS LOVE; LOVE THE ONE YOU'RE WITH; GOING DOWN TO DALLAS; MAKE LOVE TO YOU; CHEROKEE; IT'S JUST A RUMOUR; PART TIME LOVE; WOODEN SHIPS; CHANGE PARTNERS; COME ON IN MY KITCHEN; BLACKBIRD; HELPLESSLY HOPING; HOOCHIE COOCHIE MAN/ROCKY MOUNTAIN WAY.

26 JULY

Continuing their European trip, Stephen Stills' California Blues Band play Freilichtbuhne Loreley, St Goarshausen, Germany. Nash joins the entourage and contributes some familiar songs to the set. Back in America, Crosby can only dream of a CS&N/CSN&Y reunion, pointing out: "We're different cats. It would be a different band. It's a different chemistry every time we see each other. I think it'd be fantastic. I think we'd be better now than we were then. We're all older and smarter and we could stay out of each other's way a hell of a lot more. For instance, Stills and I don't butt heads any more. We still argue in the studio, but it's friendly. I think our work now is better than it was then."

SET LIST: PRE-ROAD DOWNS; LOVE THE ONE YOU'RE WITH; JUST A SONG BEFORE I GO; FOR WHAT IT'S WORTH; PART TIME LOVE; CHEROKEE; HELPLESSLY HOPING; CHANGE PARTNERS; OUR HOUSE; TURN BACK THE PAGES; WOODEN SHIPS; CARRY ON; TEACH YOUR CHILDREN.

10 AUGUST

Stills and Michael Stergis compose 'You've Got A Nice Way', which will be recorded by Ringo Starr for his next album, released in October 1981.

11-14 AUGUST

Stills is busy producing Ringo Starr's *Stop And Smell The Roses* at Devonshire Sound Studios, Hollywood, CA.

29 AUGUST

Stills, in the midst of a short tour, plays Central Park, NYC, after which he confirms his commitment to complete an album with Nash for release the following year.

6-9 OCTOBER

Reprise Records' tape archive logs Young's 'Get Back On It', 'Southern Pacific', 'Opera Star', 'Are There Any More Real Cowboys?', 'Turbine' and 'Motor City'.

29 OCTOBER

Young releases *Hawks & Doves*, a curious yet often underrated album, which uneasily mixes country-tinged songs and reflective ballads.

17 NOVEMBER

Stills and Nash record Traffic's 'Dear Mr Fantasy' an old favourite from the early CS&N days. This was originally intended for a Stills/Nash album but did not surface until the CSN boxed set in 1991.

This same day, Emmylou Harris' *Light Of The Stable* includes Young guesting on the title track.

8 DECEMBER

CS&N's *Replay*, compiled under protest by Stills & Nash, is an unremarkable and unnecessary product. Stills recuts 'Carry On', minus the 'Questions' segment, which serves little purpose other than to remove Young from the equation. Crosby is embarrassingly slighted in the song selection with only one track to his name, 'Shadow Captain'.

1981

JANUARY

Stills & Nash reconvene for recordings at Rudy's Records in Los Angeles. Among the tracks they cut is a re-recording of Stills' classic 'As I Come Of Age' and 'Turn Your Back On Love'. Crosby's exile from the duo continues, echoing a similar cold rejection from McGuinn, Clark & Hillman three years before.

JANUARY

Reprise Records' tape archive logs the unissued Young song 'Get Up Now', followed two days later by 'Rapid Transit'.

MARCH

In the early hours of this morning, Young plays an impromptu blues/rock 'n' roll set with the Danny Shea Band at the "Mike Bloomfield Tribute", taking place at the Ritz, New York.

RIL - MAY

Under pressure from Capitol Records, Crosby delivers what he hopes to be his second album, only to receive a cool response from the company who claim that the work is incomplete and anachronistic. The tape comprises: 'Melody', 'Drive My Car', 'Delta', 'Kids And Dogs', 'Flying Man', 'Might As Well Have A Good Time', 'Distances', 'King Of The Mountain' and 'Samurai'. Clearly, it is two songs short of an album, but the material is reasonably strong even by Crosby's standards and, indeed, the majority of its contents will later be featured on CS&N's next album and David's later A&M recording. The real problem for Crosby at this point is that he is an unfashionable artiste in need of a new approach. The dictates of the prevailing rock marketplace, combined with reservations about his obvious drug habit, persuade Capitol that he is a suspect investment. Following minimal revisions, his album is resubmitted, then rejected, after which he is dropped from the label.

In the meantime, Crosby survives by playing US clubs and college dates with his band, comprising Tony Saunders (bass), Slick Aguilar (guitar), Austin Delone (keyboards) and Jay David (drums). The set list below, taken from his performance at the Town Hall, NYC, indicates that he can still pull some surprises. Although stricken with a sore throat, he attempts a brave, unaccompanied 'Samurai' and a riveting acoustic version of 'Low Down Payment'. A wily heckler shouts for 'Mind Gardens', prompting Crosby to shrug "Give me a break!" before teasing us by strumming the intro to 'Mr Tambourine Man'. Despite his alarming drug habit, these shows are forceful and far more focused than expected. Indeed, it's difficult to credit how bad Crosby's drug intake was during this period when you hear performances as confident and attractive as these.

SET LIST (APRIL 24): DÉJÀ VU: THE LEE SHORE: PAGE 43: LOW DOWN PAYMENT; CARRY ME; FOR FREE: HOMEWARD THROUGH THE HAZE: DELTA: SAMURAI: GUINNEVERE: TRIAD: DRIVE MY CAR; WOODEN SHIPS.

MAY

While touring the East Coast, Crosby scores some bad cocaine and suffers his first seizure. The news shocks his friends sufficiently to take decisive action. On the day that he returns to his house on Greenwood Way, Mill Valley, Crosby is confronted by more than a dozen of his associates, including Jackson Browne, Paul Kantner, Grace Slick, a doctor and a psychiatric social worker. The "crisis intervention" is a last ditch attempt to convince him that he is killing himself and must seek treatment in a drug rehabilitation programme, which Nash has generously financed. Crosby tentatively agrees to enroll immediately at the Scripps Hospital in La Jolla, but while they think he is packing a suitcase, he is in the bathroom desperately freebasing. When Nash discovers this, they have a furious argument.

After much prevarication and pathetic excuses, Crosby and girlfriend Jan Dance are taken by Jackson Browne and Carl Gottlieb on a chartered plane to La Jolla later that evening. The following day Crosby checks out of the hospital, having irrevocably alienated his closest friends.

15 MAY

Joe Vitale's album *Plantation Harbor* includes 'Lady On The Rock', a song co-written with Bill Szymczyk and Stephen Stills. Nash and Stills also provide vocals to 'I'm Flying'.

LATE SPRING

Between working with Nash, Stills and his band play before the high rollers at Caesar's Palace in Lake Tahoe. Crosby, meanwhile, continues playing small gigs in Mill Valley and sporadic dates across the USA.

17 JUNE

Reprise Records' tape archive logs Young's 'Surfer Joe And Moe The Sleaze', 'Shots' and the unissued 'To Me, To Me'.

20 JULY 1981

Reprise Records' archives log Young's 'T-Bone'. "I didn't like that song, 'Mashed Potatoes'," admits Crazy Horse drummer Ralph Molina. "It was one I felt wasn't typical of Neil Young and Crazy Horse. At that time we weren't used to being in the studio at 10 in the morning and playing rock 'n' roll. We were going through

our little drug thing at the time. It was unheard of for me, Billy and Frank to go to bed at three and wake up early to go to the studio."

SEPTEMBER

'Holliedaze', a medley of Hollies' hits, charts in the UK, and both Eric Haydock and Nash accept an invitation to join the group for an appearance on *Top Of The Pops*. The reunion pleases Nash sufficiently to suggest a recording venture in the New Year.

12 OCTOBER

The Michael Schenker Group's *MSG* features Stills as guest vocalist.

23 OCTOBER

Stills publishes his lyrics to 'You've Got A Nice Way' (co-written with Michael Stergis), which appears on Ringo Starr's *Stop And Smell The Roses*, released this same week. Stills plays lead guitar and sings on the track.

28 OCTOBER

Young releases *Re-ac-tor*, an erratic R&B-influenced album, most notable for its fierce, impassioned closing track, 'Shots'.

14 NOVEMBER

Crosby plays J. B. Scott's in Albany, New York, knowing that his days as a solo troubadour playing small clubs and bars are about to be replaced by a reunion with his estranged colleagues. Nash swallows his pride sufficiently to telegram Crosby and invite him to contribute

> *"I didn't like that song, 'Mashed Potatoes'. It was one I felt wasn't typical of Neil Young and Crazy Horse. At that time we weren't used to being in the studio at 10 in the morning and playing rock 'n' roll. We were going through our little drug thing at the time. It was unheard of for me, Billy and Frank to go to bed at three and wake up early to go to the studio."*
>
> RALPH MOLINA

material to the completed Stills & Nash album. The reasons are less altruistic than expedient, as Nash is willing to admit. "Atlantic Records weren't interested in a Stills & Nash album," he reveals. "They wanted a Crosby, Stills & Nash album purely for economic reasons. That forced Stephen and I to rethink... because we'd paid for it ourselves, almost $400,000. So we were stuck with this album that we thought was good but Atlantic didn't want. We were committed by contract to Atlantic."

Nash's decision is a mixed blessing for Crosby, at once confirming that his musical contribution is valid while promoting the delusion that he can function indefinitely as a freebase addict.

7 DECEMBER

Stills appears at Cardi's nightclub, San Antonio, Texas, playing a standard set with his blues band. Michael Finnigan adds some humour to the proceedings with a cover of Warren Zevon's 'Werewolves Of London'.

SET LIST: LOVE THE ONE YOU'RE WITH; FOR WHAT IT'S WORTH; DARK STAR; MAKE LOVE TO YOU; WEREWOLVES OF LONDON; CHEROKEE; WOODEN SHIPS; TURN BACK THE PAGES; HOOCHIE COOCHIE MAN/ROCKY MOUNTAIN WAY; MIDNIGHT RIDER; DAYLIGHT AGAIN/FIND THE COST OF FREEDOM.

DECEMBER

One completely new song is recorded after Crosby's arrival at the studio, the Stills/Stergis composition, 'Since I Met You'. David adds harmony to the majority of songs on the album, but dares not interfere with Art Garfunkel's sterling work on 'Daylight Again'. In order to provide the façade that the album is a three-way effort, Crosby is allowed to contribute a couple of songs from his abandoned solo album, 'Delta' and the Craig Doerge/Judy Henske composition 'Might As Well Have A Good Time'. It speaks volumes about S&N's ambivalent attitude towards Crosby at this time that such quality songs as 'Distances', 'Drive My Car' and even 'Melody' are not deemed worthy of consideration.

1982

28 FEBRUARY

Nash belatedly celebrates his 40th birthday with a party at the Continental Senior Care Center on Cahuenga Boulevard. Guests are instructed to turn up looking "over 65" and, according to the invitations, food consists of creamed chipped beef, mashed potatoes, bread pudding and prunes, in deference to those who might have "left their false teeth at home". Nash's already greying hair is tinted for the occasion, while Stills appears in a bath chair, clad in a colonel's uniform. Other prematurely aged guests at the bash include Donovan, Terry Reid and various members of the Section.

1 MARCH

Dwight Twilley's *Scuba Divers* is released with Nash guesting on vocals. During this same period, Nash can be heard singing on Jimmy Webb's *Angel Heart*.

20 MARCH

Nash appears alongside Jackson Browne at the *Sing Out For Sight* concert in Santa Monica. He is also busy recording instrumental parts for The Hollies' reunion venture. The novelty of the latter is already wearing thin, however, as Nash observes, "Half-way through The Hollies' reunion album I began to remember why I'd left in the first place."

26 MARCH

Stills appears with Nash on the Easter Seals Telethon.

28 MARCH

Stills & Nash appear at an anti-nuclear rally in San Onofre, CA. Crosby is scheduled to join them but crashes his car into a divider fence on the San Diego Freeway, while travelling at 65 mph. When police search the wreck of Crosby's car they discover an array of freebase cocaine paraphernalia and a .45 pistol. Asked why he is carrying a gun, Crosby curtly replies: "John Lennon".

Following a court appearance, Crosby is fined $751, placed on three years' probation and ordered to join a drug rehabilitation programme.

2 APRIL

Crosby is appearing at Cardi's night-club in Dallas, Texas. Just before midnight, officers arrive on the scene, supposedly for a "routine investigation for liquor violations". They enter the club's dressing room where Crosby is desperately attempting to conceal his freebasing equipment. "Don't do this to me!" he moans in horror. A quick search of his bag reveals a gun, a bunsen burner and a quarter gram of cocaine. The singer is arrested, taken to Dallas City Hall and released on bail four hours later. After two arrests within a couple of weeks, Crosby is clearly a marked man.

3 APRIL

Business as usual for Crosby who, despite the previous night's bust, still manages to appear in Houston.

JUNE

CS&N appear for Peace Sunday at the Rose Bowl Pasadena, alongside Bob Dylan, Joan Baez, Stevie Wonder, Jackson Browne, Stevie Nicks, Dan Fogelberg, Tom Petty and others. Over 85,000 people attend the show and Crosby performs 'Long Time Gone' almost 14 years to the day since he wrote the song in reaction to the assassination of Bobby Kennedy. Stills invites Dave Mason to play on the medley 'Hoochie Coochie Man/Rocky Mountain Way' and the evening ends with the chant 'Give Peace A Chance'.

SET LIST: MILITARY MADNESS; LONG TIME GONE; CHICAGO; LOVE THE ONE YOU'RE WITH; FOR WHAT IT'S WORTH; DARK STAR; HOOCHIE COOCHIE MAN/ROCKY MOUNTAIN WAY; TEACH YOUR CHILDREN; GIVE PEACE A CHANCE.

JUNE

Stills copyrights 'Southern Cross' (previously titled 'Seven League Boots'), co-written with the Curtis Brothers. Recorded the previous year, it will prove one of the stand-out tracks on the new CS&N album.

/21 JUNE

Nash copyrights 'Wasted On The Way' (14), followed by 'Song For Susan' and 'Into The Darkness' (21).

JUNE

CS&N release *Daylight Again*, an album that is, in reality, a Stills/Nash package with Crosby belatedly added. Overall, the work is good but suffers from Crosby's lack of involvement and the parsimony of his partners in allowing him only one song, the stunning 'Delta'. This, despite the fact that Crosby for once had a wealth of new material left over from his rejected solo album, including the excellent 'Distances' and 'Drive My Car'. As a result of this imbalance Stills ends up with seven songs on the album.

JULY

CS&N's 'Wasted On The Way' enters the charts, eventually climbing to number 9, their second most successful US single.

9 JULY

Crosby and Carl Gottlieb copyright register *Push Play*, a 119-page screenplay that they began in 1979. It is dropped by Warner Brothers.

13 JULY

Young plays at the Catalyst, Santa Cruz as a warm-up for his forthcoming *Trans* tour. The group features Nils Lofgren, Bruce Palmer, Ben Keith, Joe Lala and Ralph Molina.

30 JULY

Nash's 'Love For A Reason' is featured on the soundtrack album *Fast Times At Ridgemont High*.

31 JULY – 6 SEPTEMBER

CS&N undertake an extensive US tour, the first leg of which includes dates at the Civic Center Arena, Hartford, CT (July 31), Cumberland County Civic Center, Portland, ME (August 1); Providence Civic Center, RI (2); Hersheypark Stadium, Hershey, PA (10); Spectrum, Philadelphia, PA (11); Nassau Coliseum, Hempstead, NY (14); Kemper Arena, Kansas City, MO (25); Red Rocks Amphitheater, Denver, CO (September 1/2); Greek Theater, Berkeley, CA (4); Irvine Meadows, CA (6).

Their backing group for the tour comprises Michael Hanna (keyboards/synths), Michael Finnigan (B3 organ), Michael Stergis (rhythm guitar), George Perry (bass), Joe Vitale (drums), and Efrain Toro (percussion). As the set list below reveals, the material is over-reliant on the past with only a handful of songs from the new album. Finnigan's work on 'Cathedral' and 'Delta' is impressive, however, while Stills performs 'Word Game' as a slow blues.

SAMPLE SET LIST (CHARLESTON CIVIC CENTER, CHARLESTON, WV, AUGUST 18): LOVE THE ONE YOU'RE WITH; TURN YOUR BACK ON LOVE; THE LEE SHORE; SOUTHERN CROSS; JUST A SONG BEFORE I GO; TOO MUCH LOVE TO HIDE; CRITICAL MASS/WIND ON THE WATER; CHICAGO; TURN BACK THE PAGES; LONG TIME GONE; SEE THE CHANGES; YOU DON'T HAVE TO CRY; BLACKBIRD; WASTED ON THE WAY; GUINNEVERE; SUITE: JUDY BLUE EYES; CATHEDRAL; DÉJÀ VU; DARK STAR; FOR WHAT IT'S WORTH; WOODEN SHIPS; CARRY ON; OUR HOUSE; TEACH YOUR CHILDREN; DAYLIGHT AGAIN/FIND THE COST OF FREEDOM.

AUGUST – OCTOBER

Young embarks on the *Trans* tour, armed with a vocoder and dark glasses. Former Duck bassist Bob Mosley temporarily replaces the ever troubled Bruce Palmer for two gigs at the Keystone Club, Palo Alto, California (August 2/4). Soon after, Palmer is invited to rejoin the group on condition he curbs his excessive drinking. They then move steadily onward to France, West Germany, Italy, Switzerland, Holland, England and Belgium, ending the tour with a show at the Deutschlandhalle, Berlin, part of which is subsequently issued on the video *Berlin Live*. During the tour, two still unreleased Young songs are featured: 'Soul Of A Woman' and 'Love Hotel'.

SAMPLE SET LIST (PARC DE SPORTS, ANNECY, FRANCE, 31 AUGUST): ON THE WAY HOME; DON'T CRY NO TEARS; EVERYBODY KNOWS THIS IS NOWHERE; CORTEZ THE KILLER; IF YOU GOT LOVE; SOUL OF A WOMAN; ARE YOU READY FOR THE COUNTRY?; SOUTHERN MAN; A LITTLE THING CALLED LOVE; OLD MAN; THE NEEDLE AND THE DAMAGE DONE; COMES A TIME; BIRDS; BEGGAR'S DAY (LOFGREN); LIKE AN INCA; HEY HEY, MY MY (INTO THE BLACK); CINNAMON GIRL; LIKE A HURRICANE; SAMPLE AND HOLD; MR SOUL.

2 AUGUST

Warren Zevon's *The Envoy* features Nash as guest vocalist on 'Looking For The Next Best Thing'.

6 SEPTEMBER

Crosby is arrested for a third time. The latest charge concerns an altercation with two women which supposedly took place in Culver City back in 1981. "I'm a gentleman," Crosby pleads. "I've never hit a girl in my life." The charge is subsequently dropped, but adds to the singer's feelings of harassment.

7 SEPTEMBER

Young copyright registers a sound cassette containing the unreleased songs 'Raining In Paradise', 'Silver & Gold', 'Big Pearl' and 'Island In The Sun'. Meanwhile, CSN&Y's live recording of 'Pushed It Over The End' from Chicago (August 1974) finally receives an official release on a Young boxed set, issued solely in Italy.

24 SEPTEMBER

Young copyright registers the unissued songs 'If You Got Love' and 'Hold On To Your Love'.

13 OCTOBER

Young copyright registers the still unreleased 'Soul Of A Woman'.

MID-OCTOBER – NOVEMBER 1982

CS&N resume their US tour, including performances at the Omni, Atlanta, GA (October 20); Greensboro Coliseum, Greensboro, NC (21); Charlotte Coliseum, NC (22); Stokely Athletic Center, University of Tennessee, Knoxville, TN (29); Mid-Tennessee State University, Murfreesboro, TN (30); Dome Center, Rochester, NY (November 5); Veterans' Memorial Coliseum, New Haven, CT (6); The Centrum, Worcester, MA (7); Dane County Coliseum, Madison, WI (10); La Crosse County Coliseum, WI (12), Cyclone Stadium, Ames, IA (14). The tour closes with three shows at the Universal Amphitheater, Studio City over Thanksgiving weekend which are taped for inclusion in the video *Daylight Again* and also provide the bulk of the material used on *Allies*.

SAMPLE SET LIST (NOVEMBER 14): TURN YOUR BACK ON LOVE; CHICAGO; THE LEE SHORE; JUST A SONG BEFORE I GO; DARK STAR; BARREL OF PAIN (HALF-LIFE); CRITICAL MASS/WIND ON THE WATER; LONG TIME GONE; LOVE THE ONE YOU'RE WITH; SEE THE CHANGES; YOU DON'T HAVE TO CRY; BLACKBIRD; WASTED ON THE WAY; DELTA; GUINNEVERE; SUITE: JUDY BLUE EYES; CATHEDRAL; SOUTHERN CROSS; FOR WHAT IT'S WORTH; WOODEN SHIPS; CARRY ON; TEACH YOUR CHILDREN; DAYLIGHT AGAIN/FIND THE COST OF FREEDOM.

13 DECEMBER

Young submits a sound cassette for copyright purposes containing the still unreleased 'Bad News Has Come To Town'. Additional notes indicate that the song was written in 1981.

1983

5 JANUARY

Young undertakes an impressive two-month solo tour of the USA which is terminated mid-way through his performance in Louisville, Kentucky (March 4) when he collapses from exhaustion, exacerbated by influenza. Angry spectators vent their wrath by flinging chairs at the stage.

SAMPLE SET LIST (ASSEMBLY HALL, UNIVERSITY OF ILLINOIS, 1 FEBRUARY): THE OLD LAUGHING LADY; MOTOR CITY; REVOLUTION BLUES; DON'T LET IT BRING YOU DOWN; SOUL OF A WOMAN; ARE THERE ANY MORE REAL COWBOYS?; OLD MAN; MY BOY; HELPLESS; DANCE, DANCE, DANCE; HEART OF GOLD; DON'T BE DENIED; POCAHONTAS; SAIL AWAY; POWDERFINGER; OHIO; HUMAN HIGHWAY; AFTER THE GOLDRUSH; TRANSFORMER MAN; MY MY, HEY HEY (OUT OF THE BLUE); MR SOUL; COMES A TIME; I AM A CHILD.

10 JANUARY

Young releases *Trans*, a Kraftwerk-inspired album of computerised music dominated by the sound of the vocoder. Strong in parts, but lacking cohesion, the work is novel, experimental and playful but guaranteed to alienate many among his audience.

14 FEBRUARY

The most unlikely coupling of Graham Nash and Frank Zappa copyright a song they have written together for George Bulterman (aka Jasper) titled 'Jasper's Tune'. As far as I know the song has not been released, but can be found in the songbook *The Complete Songs Of Jasper*.

28 FEBRUARY

Firefall's *Break Of Dawn* features Stills guesting on vocals, guitar and piano.

MARCH – MAY

Crosby is temporarily back on the road as a solo act playing such noted venues as the Wax Museum, Washington (March 15) and Bettie's Boathouse in Norfolk, VA (24). The tour continues sporadically throughout the spring, with Crosby risking his reputation in small clubs where the onus is on producing a good rocking set. Due partly to his need for cocaine, Crosby breaks up the set, allowing his backing group to indulge themselves in a harder electric workout. The standard routine is for Crosby to sing a solo acoustic set, take a break,

then return with his group, take another break, then complete the show. During a performance at the Stone Balloon (May 2) however, he short changes the audience with a 10-song set, cutting his acoustic segment to a mere four songs. Reviewer Jack Croft sympathises with Crosby's band: "They were left sitting at the bar, trying to explain to disappointed fans why they couldn't play any more, while Crosby locked himself in the bathroom of his bus and refused to come out for an encore." The fiasco ends with the promoter threatening to confiscate the group's equipment. By the following evening, at Ripley's, Philadelphia, PA, Crosby's set is back up to a dozen songs, including an electric version of 'Triad'.

SAMPLE SET LIST (MAY 3): THE LEE SHORE; FOR FREE; CARRY ME; DELTA; BITTERSWEET; SAMURAI; GUINNEVERE; DÉJÀ VU; LOW DOWN PAYMENT; ALMOST CUT MY HAIR; TRIAD; LONG TIME GONE.

16/17 APRIL

Stills guests with The Grateful Dead at the Brendan Byrne Arena, East Rutherford, New Jersey. On the first night, he sings 'Black Queen', plays guitar on 'One More Saturday Night' and 'Johnny B. Goode' and sings a verse on a cover of The Dixie Cups' 'Iko Iko'. The following night he performs 'Love The One You're With' and plays on 'Not Fade Away'.

MAY

While Nash is out on the road playing a handful of solo dates, The Hollies' reunion album *What Goes Round...* is issued, but does not include any Nash compositions. Among the cover versions featured is a reading of The Supremes' 'Stop In The Name Of Love' which provides an unexpected US Top 30 hit. Nash's solo dates include shows in California where he is backed by Joel Bernstein (guitar), Craig Doerge (keyboards), and Jim Messina (vocals). Among the surprises is a cover of The Beatles' 'Norwegian Wood'.

SET LIST (MAY 23): MILITARY MADNESS; JUST A SONG BEFORE I GO; COWBOY OF DREAMS; SOUTHBOUND TRAIN; I USED TO BE A KING; COLD RAIN; MAGICAL CHILD; BARREL OF PAIN (HALF-LIFE); MIGHT AS WELL HAVE A GOOD TIME; WIND ON THE WATER; RIGHT BETWEEN THE EYES; OH! CAMIL (THE WINTER SOLDIER); LOVE IS THE REASON; WASTED ON THE WAY; IMMIGRATION MAN; CATHEDRAL; OUR HOUSE; NORWEGIAN WOOD; TEACH YOUR CHILDREN.

STILLS IN PARIS

TRANS BAND

EASTER

Stills and Nash appear on The Easter Seals Telethon, a benefit for the handicapped. Nash, fresh from working with The Hollies, sings 'Bus Stop' while Stills performs the medley 'Hoochie Coochie Man'/'Rocky Mountain Way'.

26 MAY

Stills copyrights 'War Games', which will be the first track on the forthcoming live album, *Allies*.

3 JUNE

Crosby appears in a Dallas court before Judge Patrick McDowell and makes the impassioned plea: "Jail is no joke. Handcuffs are no joke. It's real serious stuff. It's been very lonely. I spent a lot of nights lying there thinking about it. Those bars are very real. It certainly frightened me. I don't want to do anything ever again that puts me in jeopardy. I want to feel proud of myself and stand for something again."

The Dallas Times Herald seems less impressed by Crosby's rhetoric than his tendency to doze off: "Several times he fell asleep and snored loudly, his head tilted back and his mouth open. When the snoring became too loud, one of his attorneys leaned and shook him awake."

At the close of the hearing, Crosby is found guilty of various drugs and weapons charges, but sentencing is postponed until 15 July and subsequently delayed until August.

JUNE–JULY

CS&N take advantage of Crosby's limited freedom by embarking on a tour of Europe, including appearances in Paris, Lyon, Hamburg, Berlin, Essen, Darmstadt, Augsburg, Milan, Birmingham and London. The set list below from the NEC, Birmingham, England (July 9) testifies to their reliance on older material buoyed by Nash's recent hit compositions.

SET LIST: LOVE THE ONE YOU'RE WITH; CHICAGO; JUST A SONG BEFORE I GO; TURN YOUR BACK ON LOVE; THE LEE SHORE; DARK STAR; CRITICAL MASS/WIND ON THE WATER; SOUTHERN CROSS; LONG TIME GONE; YOU DON'T HAVE TO CRY; BLACKBIRD; WASTED ON THE WAY; DELTA; SUITE: JUDY BLUE EYES; CATHEDRAL; WAR GAMES; MILITARY MADNESS; ALMOST CUT MY HAIR; BARREL OF PAIN (HALF-LIFE); FOR WHAT IT'S WORTH; WOODEN SHIPS; CARRY ON; TEACH YOUR CHILDREN.

14 JUNE

Young copyright registers 'Cry, Cry, Cry' on a sound cassette and lead sheet along with 'Old Ways' and others.

20 JUNE

CS&N release the live *Allies*, which includes two studio songs previously unavailable on album, 'Raise A Voice' and 'War Games'. Both are recorded by Stills & Nash, while Crosby is on the road.

1 JULY – 1 OCTOBER

Young embarks on an ambitious three-month tour of the USA with his retro project The Shocking Pinks, featuring the familiar line-up

of Tim Drummond, Ben Keith and Karl Himmel backed by The Redwood Boys (Anthony Crawford, Larry Byrom and Rick Palombi).

SAMPLE SET LIST (REUNION ARENA, DALLAS, TX, JULY 15): COMES A TIME: MOTOR CITY: DOWN BY THE RIVER; SOUL OF A WOMAN; OLD WAYS: OLD MAN; HELPLESS: DANCE, DANCE, DANCE; HEART OF GOLD; DON'T BE DENIED: SAIL AWAY; POWDERFINGER; OHIO; AFTER THE GOLDRUSH; TRANSFORMER MAN; MY MY, HEY HEY (OUT OF THE BLUE); MR SOUL; SUGAR MOUNTAIN; JELLYROLL MAN; BETTY LOU'S GOT A NEW PAIR OF SHOES: THAT'S ALL RIGHT (MAMA); KINDA FONDA WANDA; BRIGHT LIGHTS, BIG CITY; WONDERIN'; EVERYBODY'S ROCKIN'; DO YOU WANNA DANCE?

3 JULY

CS&N complete their European tour with an appearance at Wembley Arena. Given Crosby's imminent sentencing, speculation is rife that this may be the last ever show by the trio. The performance is professional but void of the passion, power and relevance that they once commanded.

LATE JULY

Upon his return to the USA, Nash prepares to turn back the pages of history by touring with The Hollies. Their itinerary includes performances at Rockford, IL, Chicago, IL, Vienna, VA, Baltimore, MD, Bottom Line, NYC, Worcester, MA, Passaic, NJ, Saratoga, NY, Cleveland, OH, Williamsburg, VA, Charlotte, NC, and Atlanta, GA. Nash mixes old Hollies' hits with several CS&N classics.

SAMPLE SET LIST: I CAN'T LET GO; JUST ONE LOOK; BUS STOP; CASUALTY; ON A CAROUSEL; SOMEONE ELSE'S EYES; LOOK THROUGH ANY WINDOW; KING MIDAS IN REVERSE; WASTED ON THE WAY; TEACH YOUR CHILDREN; SOLDIER'S SONG; STOP! STOP! STOP!; THE AIR THAT I BREATHE; CARRIE-ANNE; STOP! IN THE NAME OF LOVE; HE AIN'T HEAVY, HE'S MY BROTHER; LONG COOL WOMAN (IN A BLACK DRESS).

-24 JULY

Nash makes a guest appearance at Neil Young's two shows at Irvine Meadows, Laguna Hills, singing 'Ohio' both nights.

AUGUST

Back in Dallas, Crosby is sentenced to five years' imprisonment for illegal possession of cocaine. He is given a further three years to run concurrently for firearm offences. His lawyers immediately issue an appeal and he is released on an $8,000 bond. Nash assists his beleaguered partner by writing a letter to the judge, stating: "I truly believe that what David needs at this juncture of his life is help, guidance, and professional supervision. I believe that a confinement in prison would probably kill him." How wrong he was!

Outside the court room Crosby tells reporters: "I'm being treated like a murderer. They put manacles on my hands and put me in solitary. And I didn't do anything to anybody. I didn't. This is now. This is happening to me. They got me for a quarter of a gram pipe residue. For that I'm going to spend five years in the state penitentiary?"

8 AUGUST

Young's stylistic experiments falter with the appalling *Everybody's Rockin'*, an ill-fated attempt at rockabilly that also serves as a vindictive riposte to Geffen Records. At less than 25 minutes in length, it seems closer to a mini-album than a fully realised work.

14 AUGUST

Crosby celebrates his 42nd birthday by inviting *People* magazine into his home. His naïve attempt to elicit support from the sensationalist periodical backfires badly. Two weeks later, they feature him on the front page under the heading "How Cocaine Ruined The Life Of Rocker David Crosby". In the piece he is portrayed as a cocaine casualty who has squandered his life. It makes for painful, though accurate, reading.

7 SEPTEMBER

Stills & Nash appear on *Rock 'n' Roll Tonight*, playing alongside Willie Dixon in a Muddy Waters' Tribute. Among the songs performed are 'Love The One You're With, 'For What It's Worth', 'Dark Star', 'War Games', 'Military Madness', 'Change Partners', '4+20' and 'Crossroads/You Can't Catch Me'.

10 OCTOBER

Young appears on the radio show *Rockline* and informs listeners: "Everyone is concerned about David Crosby... He has a lot of problems that are unique to him, and he's having a rough time... I've told him that if he straightens up, I'll join the group again and we'll do something. And that's all I can do. The building is still standing, it didn't burn down or anything."

MID-OCTOBER

Crosby enrols in a drug rehabilitation programme at Ross General Hospital, Marin County, but walks out within days. He is later admitted to Marin General Hospital suffering from kidney stones, but mid-way through treatment he is caught attempting to smuggle

heroin into the hospital. After an argument with a doctor, he pulls an IV drip from his arm and exits the hospital, followed by a trail of blood. Meanwhile, the IRS hover in the background with various demands for unpaid taxes.

11 DECEMBER

Stills plays solo at the Palms Playhouse, Davis, near Sacramento in a benefit for the Democratic Party. The set includes a version of 'Right By You' with amended lyrics.

16 DECEMBER

Crosby, now at Gladman Memorial Hospital, Oakland, is placed in custody after claiming that he might commit suicide. He soon returns to an open ward, freebases once more, and leaves the institution. Increasingly, his life is dominated by the mysterious Jack Casanova, a fellow freebaser, who takes on the impossible role of managing the singer.

1984

JANUARY
Donovan's *Lady Of The Stars* is released with Nash contributing vocals to the title track, 'I Love You Baby' and 'Sunshine Superman'.

6/7 FEBRUARY
Young reunites with Crazy Horse for two nights at the Catalyst, Santa Cruz. As the below set list reveals, they perform three still unreleased songs: 'Rock, Rock, Rock', 'So Tired' and 'Your Love'. The shows are intended to kick-start a new album project but sessions break down soon afterward, precipitating Young's move away from working with Crazy Horse.

SET LIST (LATE SHOW, 6 FEBRUARY): ROCK, ROCK, ROCK; SO TIRED; VIOLENT SIDE; STAND BY ME; I GOT A PROBLEM; YOUR LOVE; POWDERFINGER; BARSTOOL BLUES; WELFARE MOTHERS; TOUCH THE NIGHT; TONIGHT'S THE NIGHT; CINNAMON GIRL; HOMEGROWN.

14 FEBRUARY
Nash publishes another unreleased song, 'Turn It Around (It's A Toyota)'.

23 MARCH
Crosby is in the midst of a two-month solo tour, playing small halls in St Louis, Chicago, Ohio, Denver, Cleveland, Torrington and New York. On this evening, he appears at the Beacon Theater, New York for a sterling acoustic performance that gives the lie to suggestions that he is a burned-out coke fiend. Despite his frightening addiction, he plays and sings excellently and his between-song observations are both amusing and eloquent. Referring to *Daylight Again*, he complains about Stills & Nash's reluctance to feature his material,

"We still have it. We still mean it. It's not for the money. It never was. It's for the music."

GRAHAM NASH

"They only gave me one damn song, it pissed me off; but it was a good one..." After playing 'Delta' he invites Roger McGuinn on-stage and they perform two marvellous acoustic versions of 'Mr Tambourine Man' and 'Eight Miles High'. When McGuinn regularly features these songs in his own shows, he invariably plays an electric Rickenbacker. To hear these classics played with a sparse acoustic backing, highlighting the vocal interaction between the two former Byrds is indeed a privilege. "I haven't done that in 10 years," Crosby enthuses at the close of 'Eight Miles High'. For

the second half of the show, Crosby brings on his band for workmanlike runs through the CS&N repertoire.

SET LIST: THE LEE SHORE: FOR FREE: CARRY ME; DELTA: MR TAMBOURINE MAN; EIGHT MILES HIGH: GUINNEVERE; DÉJÀ VU; LOW DOWN PAYMENT; TRIAD; ALMOST CUT MY HAIR; LONG TIME GONE.

APRIL

Crosby's freebasing is making him a fire hazard. His backing group have taken to arming themselves with fire extinguishers on their bus. Meanwhile, Crosby torches his suite at the Vista Hotel, New York and damages furnishings at the Yankee Pedlar in Torrington, Connecticut. Promoter Michael Gaiman observes: "People would say half-kiddingly that he's down from 7 grams to 2 grams a day, but he and his girlfriend Jan Dance were going to hell arm in arm".

15 MAY

The birth of his daughter inspires Young to write 'Amber Jean'.

6 JUNE

Young introduces his new group, The International Harvesters, at the Saddle Rock Club, San Jose. They will continue playing with him throughout June, reconvening in late August for a full-scale tour which lasts until the end of October. During their tour, they will play a number of still unreleased songs, including 'Razor Love', 'Amber Jean', 'Let Your Fingers Do The Walking' and 'Hillbilly Band'.

SAMPLE SET LIST (EMENS AUDITORIUM, BALL STATE UNIVERSITY, MUNCIE, IN, SEPTEMBER 16): ARE YOU READY FOR THE COUNTRY?: LOVE IS A ROSE; COMES A TIME; HAWKS & DOVES; LONG MAY YOU RUN; LET YOUR FINGERS DO THE WALKING; BOUND FOR GLORY; ARE THERE ANY MORE REAL COWBOYS?; AMBER JEAN; HEART OF GOLD; TOO FAR GONE; ROLL ANOTHER NUMBER; SOUTHERN PACIFIC; THE NEEDLE AND THE DAMAGE DONE; HELPLESS; CALIFORNIA SUNSET; IT MIGHT HAVE BEEN; FLYING ON THE GROUND IS WRONG; SOUL OF A WOMAN; FIELD OF OPPORTUNITY; OLD MAN; POWDERFINGER; GET BACK TO THE COUNTRY; BITE THE BULLET.

AUGUST

CS&N are back on the road for another summer tour, with a line-up featuring Kim Bullard (keyboards), Michael Finnigan (B-3 Organ), Joe Lala (percussion), Kenny Passarelli (bass) and Ian Wallace (drums). Dates this month include the Garden State Performing Arts Center, Holmdel, NJ (August 8); Orange County Fairgrounds, Middletown, NY (10); Spencer Fairgrounds, Spencer, MA (11) and Mt Cranmore, North Conway, NH (12). They also appear for the fifteenth anniversary of the Woodstock Festival at an open air concert in New York City. Nash includes a new song, 'Vote', and tells journalists: "We still have it. We still mean it. It's not for the money. It never was. It's for the music." *Time* magazine looks positively on the trio, suggesting: "They looked older certainly, and perhaps even a little wiser,

but CS&N had no trouble rekindling the spirit of the Sixties..."

SAMPLE SET LIST: (AUGUST 8): LOVE THE ONE YOU'RE WITH: CHICAGO; TURN YOUR BACK ON LOVE; THE LEE SHORE; VOTE; STRANGER; JUST A SONG BEFORE I GO; BLUEBIRD; CRITICAL MASS/TO THE LAST WHALE; SOUTHERN CROSS/CHANGE PARTNERS; LONG TIME GONE; YOU DON'T HAVE TO CRY; BLACKBIRD; WASTED ON THE WAY; DELTA; SUITE: JUDY BLUE EYES; CATHEDRAL; BARREL OF PAIN (HALF LIFE); FOR WHAT IT'S WORTH; WOODEN SHIPS; CARRY ON; TEACH YOUR CHILDREN.

6 AUGUST

Stills releases *Right By You*, a frustratingly below average album that needs to be far more substantial to warrant Atlantic's continued support of his solo work. Its commercial failure proves a serious setback.

SEPTEMBER

The CS&N tour is completed, with Crosby earning enough money to sustain his habit and pay his legal bills in preparation for the next round of court action.

17 OCTOBER

Stills appears at Rockefellers, Houston, Texas. "This will be a different type of show," he announces. "We've got all the swells here, so we have to be literate and stuff." He proceeds to play an immensely refreshing acoustic solo set, briskly moving from one song to another. 'Do For The Others' segues into 'The Blind Fiddler', a traditional composition that inspired 'Know You Got To Run' which follows as a medley. The songs flow quickly and efficiently, interspersed briefly with some political asides in favour of the Democratic Party. At one point, Stills reflects on his former partner's scathing comments on the state of CS&N, noting: "I understand my Canadian friend, Mr Neil Young, made some, shall we say, 'ill-considered remarks' to the press. Well, the funny part about it is that the press don't know when it's been had. You see they're so busy taking themselves seriously that they actually believe this small boy... He does that too, man. I've known him a long time. Look you right in the eye and lie to you... Lie! I don't believe that any more, man. Nuke 'em! Nuke the gay whales! I mean, can you dig it? He's just poking fun at me and Nash for doing all this shit. I appreciate it myself. My God, how else could we get any press?" As if in an act of solidarity, Stills closes the show with his own version of Nash's 'Teach Your Children'.

SET LIST: THOROUGHFARE GAP; DO FOR THE OTHERS/THE BLIND FIDDLER/KNOW YOU GOT TO RUN; TREETOP FLYER; NO HIDING PLACE; SOUTHERN CROSS; CHANGE PARTNERS; LOVE THE ONE YOU'RE WITH; RIGHT BY YOU; DAYLIGHT AGAIN/FIND THE COST OF FREEDOM; WORD GAME/CROSSROADS; TEACH YOUR CHILDREN.

20 OCTOBER

Crosby is stopped for a traffic violation in Ross, California, then arrested for possessing narcotics paraphernalia, illegal drugs, an uncovered dagger and driving with a revoked licence. After appearing at Marin County Municipal Court, he is freed on a $5,000 bond. This latest misdemeanour is less than ideal preparation for his other upcoming court hearings.

24 OCTOBER – 1 DECEMBER

Despite Crosby's problems the CS&N roadshow continues with scheduled gigs in Rochester, NY (October 24); Erie, PA (25); Dayton, OH (26); Louisville, KY (28); South Bend, IN (29); Columbus, OH (30); Kalamazoo, MI (November 1); Lancing, MI (2); Champaign, IL (3); Iowa City, IA (4); Omaha, NB (8); Tulsa, OK (9); Fayetteville, AR (10); Albuquerque, NM (12), Las Cruces, NM (13); Tucson, AZ (14); Tempe, AZ (15); San Bernardino, CA (17); Universal Amphitheater, LA, CA (19/20), Reno, NV (25); Caspar, WY (28); Salt Lake City, UT (29), Seattle, WA (December 1).

5 NOVEMBER

Young records the unreleased 'Someone Who Cares For Me' at New York's Power Station.

7 DECEMBER

Young records the unreleased 'Don't Make Me Wait' at New York's Shakedown Studio.

18 DECEMBER

Crosby's conviction for the incident at Cardi's on 12 April 1982 is overturned on the grounds that the search was illegal. Judge Patrick McDowell nevertheless subsequently revokes Crosby's $15,000 bond in view of his various other transgressions and rules that he must seek treatment in lieu of a jail sentence.

1985

JANUARY

Crosby enters Fair Oaks Hospital in New Jersey, where he is expected to remain for several months. He initially refuses to co-operate with their programme but, after several weeks of treatment, his condition improves. Hopes of rehabilitation are delusory, however, for Crosby is already hatching a daring escape plan.

28 JANUARY

Nash copyrights a batch of new compositions: 'I Got A Rock', 'Over The Wall', 'Sad Eyes', 'Before The Moon Is Full', 'Lonely Man', and 'Water From The Moon'. The first three will subsequently appear on his 1986 album *Innocent Eyes*, while the remainder are still unreleased.

10 FEBRUARY

Young attends a recording session as part of the star-studded Canadian ensemble Northern Lights. They record the single 'Tears Are Not Enough' in aid of famine relief in Ethiopia.

22 FEBRUARY – 22 MARCH

Young reunites with Crazy Horse for a one-month tour of Australia and New Zealand, including gigs in Auckland, Wellington, Christchurch, Perth, Adelaide, Melbourne, Sydney and Brisbane. Nash appears onstage at Auckland's Western Springs Stadium (February 22) in a benefit for Greenpeace. The set list below, taken from the Festival Hall,

Melbourne, Victoria (March 12), reveals a varied selection of material which continues to reveal his recent interest in country music.

SET LIST: ARE YOU READY FOR THE COUNTRY?: MOTOR CITY: COMES A TIME: LET YOUR FINGERS DO THE WALKING: TOO FAR GONE: ROLL ANOTHER NUMBER: SOUTHERN PACIFIC: THE NEEDLE AND THE DAMAGE DONE: HEART OF GOLD: TELL ME WHY: DON'T TAKE YOUR LOVE AWAY FROM ME: AFTER THE GOLDRUSH: MY MY, HEY HEY (OUT OF THE BLUE): HELPLESS: CALIFORNIA SUNSET: LOVE IS A ROSE: OLD MAN: GET BACK TO THE COUNTRY: CINNAMON GIRL: CORTEZ THE KILLER: VIOLENT SIDE: EVERYBODY KNOWS THIS IS NOWHERE: TOUCH THE NIGHT: MISFITS: HEY HEY, MY MY (INTO THE BLACK): TONIGHT'S THE NIGHT: LIKE A HURRICANE.

24 FEBRUARY

Crosby scales the walls of Fair Oaks Hospital and is whisked away in a car by an accomplice, after which he is taken to a hotel in Manhattan for a long overdue freebasing session. Less than 48 hours later, he is arrested in Greenwich Village for possession of cocaine and the usual tired litany of accompanying offences. This time there is no escaping jail. Unable to pay the $15,000 bond, he is sent to the Tombs and Riker's Island while awaiting a hearing. Meanwhile, two deputies arrive from Texas to bring him back for violating his bond. Although still in denial, Crosby provides a convincing summation of his crazed reasoning in leaving Fair Oaks: "I was desperate to play music, my sustaining force, my job on this earth. I was just about to turn the corner. I blew it, it was my mistake. But I missed the music and my friends and I was frustrated."

MARCH

Judge McDowell denies Crosby another bond and orders his incarceration in Dallas County Jail. He is given a job of trust, working in the cafeteria and infirmary, but has to suffer the indignity of guards playfully saying, "Hey, rock star, come here and mop up that floor".

5 MARCH

Crosby is caught stealing bacon from the cafeteria and reprimanded. After missing work for several days, he is stripped of his limited privileges and isolated from the other prisoners. During this period, he cries himself to sleep every night.

APRIL

USA For Africa's album includes Young as part of Northern Lights on 'Tears Are Not Enough'.

0/22/26 APRIL

Young records the unissued 'Silver & Gold', 'One More Sign', 'Try' and 'Your Love Again'.

MAY

The recent flurry of unissued recordings cut at The Castle, Nashville, is completed by Young's tribute to his daughter, 'Amber Jean'.

This same day, Crosby is released from jail, claiming: "I went through such a long period of time in jail kicking, getting clean. It's an immense psycho chemical readjustment." His words are partly for the benefit of Graham Nash, whom he hoodwinks into believing that he is straight. Within 24 hours of his release, Crosby is back in LA and freebasing once more.

MAY

Stills plays at his favourite warm-up venue, the Palms Playhouse, Davis, near Sacramento, CA. The short acoustic set proves a pleasant prelude to the forthcoming CS&N tour.

SET LIST: MIDNIGHT RIDER; THOROUGHFARE GAP; TREETOP FLYER; EVERYBODY'S TALKIN'; NO HIDING PLACE; SOUTHERN CROSS; RIGHT BY YOU; LOVE THE ONE YOU'RE WITH; FOR WHAT IT'S WORTH; WORD GAME; DAYLIGHT AGAIN/FIND THE COST OF FREEDOM.

NE-AUGUST

CS&N set out on an extensive US tour with scheduled dates at the Californian Expo, Sacramento, CA (June 28); Concord Pavilion, Concord, CA (29/30); Pacific Amphitheater, Costa Mesa, CA (July 2); Greek Theater, Los Angeles, CA (3/4); Thomas Mack Center, University of Nevada, Las Vegas, NV (5); Park West Resort, Park City, UT (7); Red Rocks, Morrison, Denver, CO (9/10); Zoo Amphitheater, Oklahoma City, OK (12); South Park Meadow, Austin, TX (13); Southern Star Amphitheater, Houston, TX (14); Reunion Arena, Dallas, TX (16); Fox Theater, St Louis, MS (18); Prairie Capitol Center, Springfield, MA (19); Coliseum, Fort Wayne, IN (20); Centennial Hall, Toledo, OH (23); Riverband Music Center, Cincinnati, OH (24); Alpine Valley Music Theater, East Troy, Alpine Valley,

WI (26); Pine Knob Theater, Clarkston, MI (27/28); Hoffman Estates, Poplar Creek, Chicago, IL (30); Blossom Music Center, Cuyahoga Falls, OH (August 1); Civic Arena, Pittsburgh, PA (2); Auditorium, Buffalo, NY (3); Merriweather Post Pavilion, Columbia, MD (6); The Scope, Norfolk, VA (7); Mann Music Center, Philadelphia, PA (9/10); West Side Pier, NY (12/13); Jones Beach Theatre, Wantagh, Long Island, NY (15/16); Hartford Civic Center Arena, CT (17); Garden State Performing Arts Center, Holmdel, NJ (19/20); Colt State Park, Bristol, RI (22); Lewiston Race Track, ME (25), New York State Fair, Syracuse, NY (27); Saratoga Performing Arts Center, Saratoga Springs, NY (28); Boston Common, Boston, MA (29), and Allentown Fair, PA (31).

Part of the appeal of these concerts is voyeuristic. It is assumed by many that Crosby will be either dead or in jail before long, so this could be the last chance to see the trio onstage.

endure the wrath of Nash who joins Stills in berating him for his unexpected exit. Later, a more diplomatic Nash admits: "David caught the stomach flu. It's tough to sing, vomit and shit at the same time."

Overall, the press looks unkindly on the summer tour, with the *LA Times'* Duncan Strauss perceptively noting CS&N's present limitations: "The trio trotted out an array of mouldy-but-goody pieces, underscoring its recent devolution into a nostalgia act masquerading as a fully active pop force. The often ecstatic crowd response during the nearly two-hour show demonstrated just how effective CS&N has become at generating second-hand emotions. The feeling their shows now elicit are ones you remember rather than new ones you experience directly."

SAMPLE SET LIST (JULY 14): LOVE THE ONE YOU'RE WITH; PRE-ROAD DOWNS; JUST A SONG BEFORE I GO; THE LEE SHORE; STRANGER; CAN'T LET GO;

Meadows, Austin, Texas. During the festivities Young collaborates with Jerry Jeff Walker on 'This Land Is Our Land'.

13 JULY
Live Aid unveils the first CSN&Y on-stage reunion for 11 years. Alas, production problems result in unmemorable performances of 'Only Love Can Break Your Heart', 'Daylight Again' and 'Find The Cost Of Freedom'. Despite his poor condition, Crosby agrees to be interviewed on MTV along with Stills & Nash. He looks terrible but, with eyes half closed, still manages to stir up false optimism: "I'm a happy man. I'm a very happy man. If I was put here on this planet to do anything, it was this. I'm just happier than I could possibly be, man. Things are looking great. You saw what we do, you saw how well we're doing, you see my friends are still my loyal friends. I'm just overjoyed to be back

As a result, they break the house attendance figure at Concord, where people wave banners proclaiming: "David, We Love You". *Rolling Stone* magazine is less sympathetic and describes the singer as resembling "an eighteenth century pirate sorely in need of vitamin C". Onstage, he seems impassive for much of the proceedings, but occasionally bursts into life for a song like the empowering 'Long Time Gone'.

It is noticeable from the above itinerary that CS&N play a considerable number of dates in Texas, where Crosby is clearly perceived as a rebel outlaw figure. At the Southern Star Amphitheater (July 14), he cries: "Hi Texas! I came back! I came back for you!" It is clear though that Crosby is uneasy about staying in the State and after the show a limousine takes him straight to the airport.

During a performance in Norfolk, Virginia, Crosby feels nauseous and walks off stage midway through the show. While he is resting on a couch in the hospitality room, Stills enters and pours a jug of water over him. He then has to

LONELY MAN; 50/50; YOU DON'T HAVE TO CRY; BLACKBIRD; WASTED ON THE WAY; DELTA; GUINNEVERE; SUITE: JUDY BLUE EYES; WIND ON THE WATER; SOUTHERN CROSS; LONG TIME GONE; CARRY ON; TEACH YOUR CHILDREN.

JUNE
The African famine aid single 'Here Is My Love, Pass It Along' is released by Texas –World Reunion, with Stills among a formidable cast of allegedly Texan-born stars, including Billy Preston, B.J. Thomas, Charley Pride and Mary Wilson.

30 JUNE
Young's unreleased 'Beautiful Bluebird', 'Nothing Is Perfect' and 'Leaving The Top 40 Behind' are recorded at the Castle, Nashville, with 'Time Off For Good Behaviour' completed the following day at Bennett House, Franklin, Nashville.

4 JULY
Young and the International Harvesters appear at Willie Nelson's 4th July Picnic at South Park

doing exactly what I'm supposed to be doing."

Unknown to Crosby, Nash has just granted an impromptu interview to *Spin* reporter Edward Kiersh, who is researching an investigative piece. For once, the mask slips and Nash exposes his true feelings about David's future. "I'm amazed that he's still alive," he stresses. "He'll eventually die – it's only a question of when. He won't want to hear that. He'll read that and despise me for a while. I've armoured myself, but it's heartbreaking."

Back in his trailer, Crosby is surrounded by heavies and kept away from potential drug pushers. His relationship with Stills and Nash remains cordial but cool. Despite being humiliated by Stills back in Norfolk, Virginia, the guitarist is one of the few people in Crosby' circle who still believes that he'll pull through. "Dave'll be fine," Stills tells *Rolling Stone*. "Pity the man who says another word about him. I'm sick of this Perils of Pauline attitude in the press. It really makes me ill. It's not like this is some rare disorder or something. You got ball players with the same problem."

It is interesting to see how each person reacts to Crosby's plight in different ways. Nash veers violently from an over-supportive role to sad disillusionment while Stills, perhaps considering his own excesses over the years, remains stiff-lipped and impatient with all the media hypocrisy.

9 JULY
Young delivers a sound cassette for copyright purposes containing the unreleased songs 'Beautiful Bluebird', 'Nothing Is Perfect (In God's Perfect Plan)', 'Time Off For Good Behaviour' and 'Leaving The Top 40 Behind'.

AUGUST
Young and the International Harvesters embark on a two-month US tour, culminating in Farm Aid at the Memorial Stadium, University of Illinois (September 22). The benefit raises almost $9 million for the beleaguered American farmers. During the tour, Young introduces several still unreleased songs, including 'Grey Riders' and 'Interstate'.

SAMPLE SET LIST (HAMPTON ROADS COLISEUM, HAMPTON, VA, SEPTEMBER 12): COUNTRY HOME; COMES A TIME; LOOKING FOR A LOVE; HEART OF GOLD; THIS OLD HOUSE; SOUTHERN PACIFIC; INTERSTATE; SUGAR MOUNTAIN; HELPLESS; CALIFORNIA SUNSET; NOTHING IS PERFECT; FIELD OF OPPORTUNITY; DOWN BY THE RIVER; OLD MAN; POWDERFINGER; GET BACK TO THE COUNTRY; GREY RIDERS.

AUGUST
Young releases *Old Ways*, amid rumours that he now intends to retire from rock and concentrate on country 'n' western. The album is predictably erratic but features some impressive work, most notably the brilliant and baffling 'Misfits'.

PTEMBER
CS&N tag on some extra dates to their summer tour, including the Irvine Meadows Amphitheater, CA (September 5/6); Chastain Park, Atlanta, GA (20/21); Tallahassee-Leon County Civic Center, Tallahassee, PL (25); James L. Knight Center, Miami, FL (28/29); Orange County Civic Center, Orlando, FL (30).

The conclusion of the tour coincides with the publication of an article in *Spin* magazine, sensationally titled "The Death Of David Crosby". It is accompanied by a description of Crosby that would not be out of place in a Hogarth painting: "His stomach is bloated, his thinning, frizzy hair leaps wildly in the air. A few of his front teeth are missing, his pants are tattered, and his red plaid shirt has a gaping hole. The most frightening thing is his pale, swollen face, riddled with thick, white scales, deep and encrusted blotches that aren't healing. Looking at him is painful. A 14-year addiction to heroin and cocaine has caused David to resemble a diseased Bowery bum. The spiritual leader of the Woodstock generation is now a vision of decay."

Crosby's reaction to the piece is suitably indignant: "Want to know the latest wrinkle? That I'm already dead! Not a dope addict any more, not even a vegetable, but already dead. Man, that hurts. Reading that shit."

What most hurts though is reading the premature obituaries from his former friends, including Nash's resigned conclusion that David will die. "He's my best friend," Crosby reminds reporter Mark Christensen. "He said I was going to *die*. How could he have said that? So cold. I would never have said something like that about Graham in a million years, man. It was so crude, so out of hand... Does Graham think that I'm so stupid he's going to shock me into some perception I haven't already attained. You think I haven't thought about this every moment of the day?" What's interesting about the above is the mixture of genuine and understandable hurt over Nash's despair combined with the classic denial syndrome of the long-term addict.

30 SEPTEMBER
Willie Nelson's *Half Nelson* features Young guesting on his own composition, 'Are There Any More Real Cowboys?'

9 OCTOBER
Young delivers a cache of two-page lyric sheets for copyright purposes featuring the still unreleased titles 'Your Love Again', 'Hillbilly Band', 'Amber Jean' and 'Daughters', plus a further page containing 'Let Your Fingers Do The Walking'.

16 OCTOBER
Nash copyrights 'Sad Eyes' which will feature on his next solo album.

17 OCTOBER
Young delivers a sound cassette for copyright purposes containing the unreleased songs, 'Interstate' and 'Grey Riders', plus 'This Ole House' which will later be recorded by CSN&Y under the amended title 'This Old House'.

23 OCTOBER
While driving his car, Crosby hits another fence in Mill Valley. After emerging from the wreckage, he flees from the scene but is soon found with the usual drugs paraphernalia, and a Colt .45. He is released after posting a $5,000 bond, but this latest transgression extinguishes any remaining hopes he may have harboured of avoiding a long-term jail sentence.

11 NOVEMBER
James Taylor's *That's Why I'm Here* is released with Nash singing on 'Mona' and 'The Man Who Shot Liberty Valance'.

23 NOVEMBER
With a court appearance imminent, Crosby realises the game is up, sells a grand piano for $5,000 and flees. He hires a private plane to take him to his beloved boat *The Mayan* in Florida. His latest plan is to sail to the Bahamas in a bizarre real life enactment of the 'Wooden Ships' fantasy.

25 NOVEMBER
Crosby's failure to appear for his appeal bond revocation hearing prompts Texas District Judge Patrick McDowell to issue a warrant for his arrest. Attorney David Vogelstein explains: "I talked to him over the weekend and he was concerned about Texas. He didn't know what to do. My impression was that his failure to appear may have been a last minute decision. I hope it doesn't end tragically... His only chance of doing a reduced amount of time in jail was to appear at the hearing and throw himself at the mercy of the court".

30 NOVEMBER
Not surprisingly, Crosby's appearance at the Golden Bear, Huntington Beach is cancelled. "I guess he doesn't feel safe playing, being a fugitive," the venue's manager remarks.

1-11 DECEMBER
Crosby is on the run, penniless and barefoot. He has shaved his moustache and taken to wearing cheap wigs in an attempt to disguise his identity. He is still consuming a quarter ounce of cocaine and half a gram of heroin per day, but supply lines are now running out. The IRS has seized his home and *The Mayan* has run aground. Even the drug-induced fantasies of escaping justice are now exposed as delusory. "The plan was ridiculous," he admits.

12 DECEMBER
Crosby finally admits to himself that running from the law is futile. At 3.45 pm, he walks into the FBI's office at West Palm Beach, Florida and surrenders. The following day he is jailed without bond while awaiting the arrival of the Texas authorities. "Wish me luck, huh," he tells reporters.

19 DECEMBER
Crosby is taken to Lew Sterrett Justice Center, then moved back to the Government Center where he is placed in solitary. He spends the remainder of the year suffering intense withdrawal symptoms, exacerbated by his poor physical condition. Dallas County's assistant District Attorney already speaks of him in the past tense: "They say he was a man with a great deal of talent. I guess the only word I can use to describe him now is 'ruined'. Ruined by drugs."

PART V
AFTER THE STORM
1986-1994

Crosby's incarceration during 1986 provided an unlikely means of salvation. Following his release, he embarked on a spree of creative activity, completing his autobiography, recording his second solo album, and playing with a variety of musical friends. The newly revitalised CS&N finally showed how accomplished they could be with a highly successful series of acoustic concerts. These performances were undoubtedly their best in nearly a decade. While the media seemed impressed, there remained the far larger spectacle of a full-blown CSN&Y reunion. Young fulfilled his promise by agreeing to record an album but, this time around, there would be no tour. This lack of effective promotion robbed the album of its full impact but it was gratefully received by those who had waited patiently for the past 18 years.

The CSN&Y reunion occurred at a fortuitous time for Young, who was just emerging from the creative wreck of a decade, hampered by family commitments, musical uncertainty, poor sales and litigious hostility from his own record company. Following American Dream, his solo career took another dramatic upswing, with a formidable run of commercially successful and critically acclaimed releases that re-established his reputation as rock's great auteur.

Surprisingly, CS&N failed to take advantage of their improved profile and instead issued their worst album to date, Live It Up, later admitting that it was not originally conceived as a three-way effort. Not for the first time, they could still look to the past for creative redemption and this was achieved with the highly praised CSN boxed set. It was a powerful

reminder of all that they had achieved during the past two-and-a-half decades. As the Nineties began they settled into their role as a rock institution, even re-enacting the glory days at Woodstock II. A new album, After The Storm, was reasonably received auguring well for the future.

One of the most notable features of CS&N over the past decade has been their willingness to become involved in countless causes, fund raising activities and benefits. As this chronology reveals, it is not simply high profile charities such as Live Aid that they have involved themselves with, but a startling number of more localised appeals. Despite all that has happened to them over the years, they have retained their belief in the importance of community – both social and musical.

CS&N have now reached the point where the expectancy that once surrounded their get togethers is no longer a pressure. They can function largely on the level of nostalgia if they wish and few will complain. Nobody expects groundbreaking work from CS&N and, as a result, they are now in the perfect position to make a record which will more likely be greeted with sympathy than derision. They have been through several rites of passage as both cult heroes and superstars, rock dinosaurs and near casualties. Finally, they seem to have reached a more even plateau where their best work may be reappraised and recognised for its influence and quality. It's difficult to imagine them capturing the minds of modern listeners in the way that Young has done in recent years but, whatever they do hereafter, represents much more than we could reasonably expect or deserve.

1986

JANUARY

Stills commences a US tour, playing many Southern dates backed by Mike Finnigan (keyboards), George Perry (bass) and Mark T. Williams (drums). During the same period, the original Buffalo Springfield reconvene at Stills' house to play some songs, including Young's 'Road Of Plenty' (a prototype version of 'Eldorado').

6 JANUARY

Crosby is denied bail and ordered to remain in jail until a State Appeals Court rules on his drug and weapons convictions. Judge Patrick McDowell agrees with the prosecution that if Crosby is released, he will commit further offences and not return to Texas. "I don't think incarceration is the answer," Crosby meekly suggests.

26 JANUARY

Stills appears on *The American Music Awards* in a presentation with Lou Rawls.

14 FEBRUARY

Crosby copyrights a sound cassette and lead sheets for 'Drive My Car', 'Distances' and 'Melody'. All three songs were composed around 1980 but will not be released until 1989.

23 FEBRUARY

Young is invited to induct The Everly Brothers into the Rock 'n' Roll Hall of Fame.

24 FEBRUARY

Young joins Nash on-stage at the Vietnam Veterans' Benefit in Inglewood, California, performing 'Ohio' and 'Teach Your Children'. "I found it very strange to be doing a benefit for Vietnam Veterans," Nash recalls. "Neil and I and David and Stephen have been so anti-war for so many years, then we began to realise that there were so many people that went and fought in Vietnam that did not agree, that were forced to go by their country... and they were treated so badly when they returned from the war. There was no heroes' welcome, no brass bands... there were people that hated them, who thought they were child killers."

6 MARCH

Crosby is transferred to Huntsville Prison, where he can earn parole and even play guitar. His health is improving but he refuses requests for interviews. Prison officials confirm: "He just wants to be left alone, fade into obscurity, do his time and get away. He doesn't feel like publicity would be beneficial to him." Nash admits that he is not in direct contact with Crosby at this time: "I can't bring myself to visit David again. It's a deadly serious place and justifiably has the reputation of being one of the toughest penitentiaries in the country. It's very tense. There isn't a lot of smiling going on and the people are some of the craziest I've ever seen. The other prisoners are treating David with respect. He hasn't been attacked and I think music saved his ass."

17 MARCH

Nash copyright registers 'Keep Away From Me' and 'Newday' (co-written with Craig Doerge).

5 APRIL

Nash, Young and Jackson Browne appear at the Greenpeace International Benefit in Auckland, New Zealand. Stills, meanwhile, is playing occasional low-key dates throughout the US.

7 APRIL

Nash attempts some Young-style experimentation with the Linn-drum dominated *Innocent Eyes*. Only half the songs on the album are written by Nash and the change of musical style fails to win over a new audience, resulting in a chart low of US 136.

30 APRIL

Stills, Finnigan, Perry and Williams continue their tour, this night playing at the Bayou, Washington, DC. The below set list reveals the low key nature of the enterprise, with Finnigan singing the blues 'Take Care Of Business, Baby' and Stills unexpectedly combining 'Bluebird' with a snatch of The Byrds' 'So You Want To Be A Rock 'n' Roll Star'.

SET LIST: LOVE THE ONE YOU'RE WITH: STRANGER: MAKE LOVE TO YOU: CAN'T LET GO: 50/50: TAKE CARE OF BUSINESS BABY: DARK STAR: BLUEBIRD/SO YOU WANT TO BE A ROCK 'N' ROLL STAR: FOR WHAT IT'S WORTH: TREETOP FLYER: DAYLIGHT AGAIN/ FIND THE COST OF FREEDOM: SOUTHERN CROSS.

JUNE

Stills tours throughout this month, co-headlining with America.

9 JUNE

Nash performs 'Wings To Fly' (written by Giorgio Moroder and Tom Whitlock) on the soundtrack album *American Anthem*.

14 JUNE

Stills continues his loose gigging schedule playing at Syria Mosque, Pittsburgh, PA.

17 JUNE

Crosby copyright registers the lyrics to a new song 'Compass', which will later feature on CSN&Y's *American Dream* in 1988.

JULY – AUGUST

Nash supports Joan Armatrading on a short US tour. He plays a neat mixture of familiar songs plus newer material from *Innocent Eyes*. He is backed by keyboardist Bill Boyston and guitarist Hugh Ferguson. Along the way, he provides some revealing song anecdotes, explaining that 'Right Between The Eyes' was written for John Sebastian while 'Keep Away From Me' was an angry response to being asked to appear in Sun City. The sample set list below from the Club Casino, Hampton Beach, New Hampshire indicates the range of songs performed, with 'Critical Mass' featured on tape.

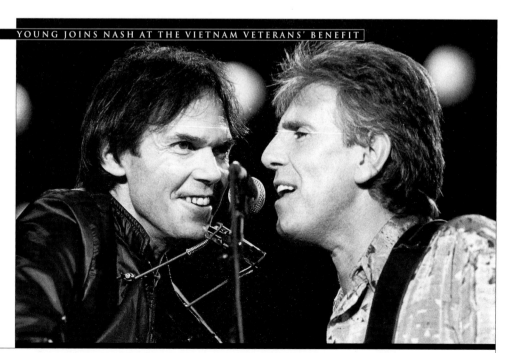

YOUNG JOINS NASH AT THE VIETNAM VETERANS' BENEFIT

"I found it very strange to be doing a benefit for Vietnam Veterans. Neil and I and David and Stephen have been so anti-war for so many years, then we began to realise that there were so many people that went and fought in Vietnam that did not agree, that were forced to go by their country..."

GRAHAM NASH

SET LIST (JULY 3): MILITARY MADNESS; PRE-ROAD DOWNS; CHICAGO; OVER THE WALL; CHIPPIN' AWAY; I USED TO BE A KING; SAD EYES; GLASS AND STEEL; MAGICAL CHILD; RIGHT BETWEEN THE EYES; SIMPLE MAN; CRITICAL MASS/WIND ON THE WATER; BARREL OF PAIN (HALF-LIFE); KEEP AWAY FROM ME; INNOCENT EYES; JUST A SONG BEFORE I GO; TEACH YOUR CHILDREN; OUR HOUSE.

JULY

Crosby's prison group performs a show for Independence Day, including music written by inmates and several CS&N classics. The singer is interviewed exclusively by the prison newspaper *Echo*: and reveals: "It's either drugs or my life. It had got to the point where if I continued with the drugs then that means no more music, no more of my daughter and no more of my life. I'm off the drugs."

Not far away, in Austin, Texas, Neil Young is busy with Farm Aid II, which this year has a considerably lower profile and profit margin.

JULY

The Texas Board of Pardons and Paroles agrees to Crosby's parole. Jack Corrie, spokesperson for the California Department of Correction, explains: "They'll be checking out the programme – where he's going to live, where he's going to work and whether he has family support. Crosby may be required to take urine tests to prove he is no longer addicted to drugs as one of the conditions of parole".

JULY

Still playing occasional gigs, Nash appears solo at the The Pier, NYC, New York.

AUGUST

Young's career arguably reaches an all-time nadir with *Landing On Water*, a sterile work, replete with synthesiser backing, a characterless production and a forced modernity. Even the sleeve artwork seems shoddy and uninspired.

AUGUST

Nash plays a benefit concert in Hiroshima, Japan to commemorate the 41st anniversary of the bombing.

AUGUST

Crosby is released from jail and emerges in dark glasses, clean shaven, short-haired and portly. He resembles nothing less than a Texan cop. Greeting reporters and a couple of dozen onlookers, he announces: "I'm extremely happy. I don't have too much to say, but I thank you all for coming. I'm off drugs and happy to be."

/21 AUGUST

Crosby celebrates his 45th birthday and release from jail by appearing with Nash at Rockefeller's, Houston. Security is tight at the gig and photo shoots are prohibited. Nash's solo set concludes with 'Glass And Steel', the song he wrote about Crosby's drug problem. The ex-convict then emerges from the wings, short-

haired with stubble replacing his familiar moustache. Amid welcoming cheers, he performs several C&N classics, plus the first airing of his song of redemption, 'Compass'.

SET LIST (AUGUST 21): MILITARY MADNESS; CHIPPIN' AWAY; OVER THE WALL; KEEP AWAY FROM ME; I USED TO BE A KING; GLASS AND STEEL; CRITICAL MASS/WIND ON THE WATER; JUST A SONG BEFORE I GO; CARRY ME; COMPASS; GUINNEVERE; OUR HOUSE; TEACH YOUR CHILDREN.

22 AUGUST

Exactly two weeks after Crosby's release, the Texas Board of Pardons and Paroles confirms that he is free to leave the Houston half-way house at which he has been staying and return to Los Angeles. He immediately flies out of Texas and moves in with his writer friend Carl Gottlieb. The singer is bankrupt and presently owes the IRS approximately $1 million.

15 SEPTEMBER – 21 NOVEMBER

Young and Crazy Horse embark on the arduous Rusted-Out Garage tour which continues through till the end of November. In common with the *Rust Never Sleeps* tour of 1978, Young uses an elaborate stage set to provide a suitable setting for this self-styled "third best garage band in the world".

SAMPLE SET LIST (THE PATRIOT CENTER, GEORGE MASON UNIVERSITY, FAIRFAX, VA, SEPTEMBER 26): MR SOUL; CINNAMON GIRL; WHEN YOU DANCE I CAN REALLY LOVE; TOUCH THE NIGHT; BAD NEWS BEAT; DOWN BY THE RIVER; HEART OF GOLD; INCA QUEEN; AFTER THE GOLDRUSH; TOO LONELY; OPERA STAR; ELDORADO; CORTEZ THE KILLER; SAMPLE AND HOLD; COMPUTER AGE; VIOLENT SIDE; MIDEAST VACATION; LONG WALK HOME; THE NEEDLE AND THE DAMAGE DONE; HIPPIE DREAM; POWDER-FINGER; LIKE A HURRICANE; HEY HEY, MY MY (INTO THE BLACK); PRISONERS OF ROCK 'N' ROLL.

27 SEPTEMBER

Crosby & Nash join Young onstage at the Brendan Byrne Arena, East Rutherford, New Jersey for 'Only Love Can Break Your Heart' and 'Ohio'. The following day, Young accompanies them at a Get Tough On Toxics benefit in the Long Beach Arena.

OCTOBER

Nash reveals that he is producing the soundtrack of *Eight Miles High*, a documentary on Crosby's illustrious life, featuring additional material from Young and Joni Mitchell. The project remains unrealised.

7 OCTOBER

Crosby & Nash again join Young onstage, this time at Madison Square Garden, New York. They reprise 'Only Love Can Break Your Heart' and 'Ohio'.

8 OCTOBER

Stills copyright registers a recently completed song, 'Bit About Love', which remains unreleased, plus 'Night Song'. At this time, the latter is credited solely to Stills, but Neil Young will later receive a co-writing credit prior to the CSN&Y reunion album *American Dream*.

13 OCTOBER

CSN&Y reunite on stage at the first Bridge School Benefit, a charity organised by Young and his wife for the handicapped. Young performs 'Comes A Time' and 'Heart Of Gold' solo, then joins Nils Lofgren and Bruce Springsteen for 'Helpless'. Following 'I Am A Child', Young is joined onstage by CS&N for 'Only Love Can Break Your Heart', 'Change Partners', 'Daylight Again/Find The Cost Of Freedom' and 'Ohio'. Springsteen is later augmented by CSN&Y for his 'Hungry Heart' and the full ensemble, including Tom Petty and Don Henley, re-emerge for an encore of 'Teach Your Children'.

27 OCTOBER

Crosby copyright registers the lyrics to 'Alexander Graham Bell', a song recently written in prison in praise of the telephone – his sole lifeline to the outside world. Despite his initial enthusiasm for the song, it is neither developed nor released. The same fate befalls his love song to Jan Dance 'You're Worth Waiting For'.

CROSBY & NASH AT THE 'CRACK DOWN' CONCERT, MADISON SQUARE GARDEN

Crosby: "I hadn't written any music for nearly three years. When the words started to come back I knew I was on the way back. I started to be able to think again, to be able not to have dreams about drugs all the time."

29 OCTOBER
Crosby appears at the Catalyst, Santa Cruz at the beginning of a short tour of the West Coast.

31 OCTOBER
CS&N appear at the Madison Square Garden for "Crack Down", a fund-raiser to fight the alarming spread of crack cocaine. Their all-acoustic set includes a riveting version of 'Long Time Gone' which now has fresh significance for the impassioned Crosby. The evening ends with an all-star jam featuring CS&N, Carlos Santana, Mick Taylor, Gregg Allman and Felix Cavaliere.

2 NOVEMBER
CS&N prepare for their forthcoming all-acoustic tour, with a warm-up show in Troy, New York.

11 NOVEMBER
Crosby and Stills appear at a Vietnam Veterans' Benefit in Lawrence, Kansas City. Following a couple of numbers from associate Mike Finnigan, Crosby performs two songs solo: 'Wooden Ships' and 'Almost Cut My Hair'. Stills then takes the stage for 'For What It's Worth', 'Treetop Flyer' and 'Change Partners'. Crosby then reappears for 'Long Time Gone', followed by a strong version of 'Southern Cross'. David is still performing occasional solo dates, including an appearance at the Kona Auditorium (November 13).

NOVEMBER – DECEMBER
Crosby & Nash with Craig Doerge undertake a brief acoustic tour of the USA. Their set is unapologetically dominated by songs from the early Seventies, while the on-stage raps sound over-familiar. Only three songs written after 1977 are featured: 'Delta', 'Compass' and 'Try To Find Me'. The set list below from the Front Row Theater, Cleveland, Ohio, underlines the immersion in nostalgia.

SET LIST (DECEMBER 6): MILITARY MADNESS; WASTED ON THE WAY; THE LEE SHORE; SOUTHBOUND TRAIN; ALMOST CUT MY HAIR; I USED TO BE A KING; CARRY ME; CRITICAL MASS/WIND ON THE WATER; RIGHT BETWEEN THE EYES; TRY TO FIND ME; DELTA; KING OF THE MOUNTAIN; COMPASS; GUINNEVERE; JUST A SONG BEFORE I GO; WOODEN SHIPS; OUR HOUSE; LONG TIME GONE; TEACH YOUR CHILDREN.

1 DECEMBER
Young delivers a sound cassette for copyright purposes containing the still unreleased songs 'Born To Rock' and 'Around The World'.

10 DECEMBER
Crosby plays The Coach House, San Juan Capistrano, CA. He is also preparing material for his second solo album, updating 'Samurai' which he later holds back for a projected but ultimately unrealised Crosby/Nash album.

31 DECEMBER
Crosby closes the year with a solo appearance at the Kaiser Convention Center, Oakland, CA, opening for The Grateful Dead. During the show, he keeps the audience entertained with tales of sewing mattresses in jail and being humiliated by redneck prison guards who nickname him "rock star". Throughout this evening, he is very talkative but his voice sounds unusually high-pitched and hoarse.

SET LIST: THE LEE SHORE; TRIAD; ALMOST CUT MY HAIR; DRIVE MY CAR; COMPASS; GUINNEVERE; WOODEN SHIPS; LONG TIME GONE.

1987

JANUARY

CS&N embark on their first ever acoustic tour. This is the type of show they might have undertaken in 1969 if Young had not been recruited. The arrangements are impressive and the vocals even stronger than expected. Stills provides a long overdue reminder of his excellence as a guitar player, while Crosby wows the crowd with amusing raps about life in jail: "I have some advice. If you're going to get busted, don't get busted in Texas."

The set list below from the DAR Constitution Hall, Washington DC, (January 23) may look familiar but the crucial difference lies in the acoustic arrangements which are fresh, invigorating and display the enormity of the trio's talent. They should have done this acoustic tour a decade ago.

SET LIST: WASTED ON THE WAY; CHANGE PARTNERS; YOU DON'T HAVE TO CRY; BLACKBIRD; ALMOST CUT MY HAIR; JUST A SONG BEFORE I GO; SOUTHERN CROSS; CRITICAL MASS/WIND ON THE WATER; GLASS AND STEEL; TRY TO FIND ME; DELTA; COMPASS; GUINNEVERE; WORD GAME; LOVE THE ONE YOU'RE WITH; LONG TIME GONE; OUR HOUSE; SUITE: JUDY BLUE EYES; TEACH YOUR CHILDREN; DAYLIGHT AGAIN/FIND THE COST OF FREEDOM.

FEBRUARY

CSN&Y reunite for two acoustic shows at the Arlington Theater, Santa Barbara in aid of Greenpeace. Crosby arrives at the show on his Harley Davidson, as if living out old fantasies in his home town. The show itself is a revelation and a massive shock to those who assumed this partnership had nothing left to offer. Unlike their previous anti-climactic get togethers, they take time out to rehearse, and instead of churning out the expected old favourites, they slot in several new songs. At its best, the concert provides memories of how uplifting the foursome can be when they are focused and committed.

Proceedings open with an exuberant 'Wasted On The Way', a stark reminder of the many reunions thrown away over the years. Stills is in fine form on guitar, as he will be throughout the evening.

"We've been doing this for years," Nash tells us as they move into 'Change Partners' which features some memorable harmony work and a harmonica accompaniment. Young continues these reflections of the life and times of CSN&Y by introducing 'Long May You Run'. Its opening lines ("We've been through some things together/With trunks of memories still to come") neatly echo Nash's comments and, for a moment, transform the song into a nostalgic reflection on his relationship with his present colleagues, rather than a tribute to some lost car. Crosby performs the same trick with 'Long Time Gone', which takes on an additionally poignant aspect in view of his dark nights of drug addiction. Young can be heard clearly harmonising in the background for probably the first time on any performance of

this classic. The clever, dextrous harmony work reflects the seriousness with which they are taking this concert, as well as indicating their obvious willingness to rehearse.

Clearly, the most noticeable aspect of the gig is Crosby's rehabilitation. He speaks with a slightly hoarse voice, but his singing is smoother, more controlled, and he actually sounds younger. Revelling in his return home, he amuses the audience with sober variations on his former stoned persona. Now, he is the reformed drug addict with a sardonic smile. "This is not a preach to you about drugs," he warns, "because, quite frankly, I think you've got to figure it out for yourself. If, however, you think of my life, it'll take you three seconds to figure out."

He goes on to explain his writer's block and the eerie feeling of finding his creative instincts reawakening in prison. 'Compass' follows – the first of a series of new songs that make this gig so memorable. "We talked about this concert when we were getting together," Crosby explains, "and we said, 'We're going to do all the new stuff'... and if you bear with us, we are going to. This is the first time I've played this in front of people..."

'He's An American' follows – a song that will soon join that exclusive list of unreleased Crosby compositions. It's a pleasant melody with strong nationalist overtones which sound odd coming from the anti-establishment figure that protested against the war and flouted WASP values so blatantly. The lines "You better watch out for him, he's an American and he's not afraid of you" sound like military propaganda until you realise that the song's primary message is to celebrate the power of the ordinary working American in righting wrongs through the democratic process ("He's an American... and he can see right through your games"). The song makes more sense when seen in the context of 'My Country 'Tis Of Thee' and 'Lady Of The Harbor' where he unambiguously states his love of America, rather than attacking the system as he does on 'Long Time Gone', 'Almost Cut My Hair' and 'Nighttime For The Generals'.

One of the more interesting features of this concert is the ingenious way in which the songs are programmed. Perhaps it is subliminal, but you cannot help noticing that clusters of songs reflect similar themes – the resurrection of CSN&Y after years of wasted opportunities; reflections on the present state of America seen through older, less radical eyes. Young takes up the latter theme in 'Nothing Is Perfect (In God's Perfect Plan)', a *Harvest*-like song that appeals

to traditional American values – the very kind that both Crosby and Young spent much of their careers rebelling against. Young reiterates this theme in 'This Old House' with its strong pull towards kinship and "apple pie" imagery. Coincidentally, both singers deliberately move away from the introspective style of their early songwriting to present a more mature, if less arresting, view of societal values.

Nash also looks outwards in his new song of the evening, 'Try To Find Me'. The song was written after a benefit concert in aid of cerebral palsy sufferers. As Nash explained: "We tried to raise money to utilise the equipment and the high-tech stuff that we have today to communicate with these beings that live inside their bodies. It was brought home very emotionally to me one night when this little seven-year-old girl in her wheelchair started to cry. She'd had enough, she wanted out of there, and this little boy next to her, also in his wheelchair, took 10 agonising minutes to put his hand slowly but surely on hers and stopped her crying. I realised at that moment it's a terrible prison to have a mind that works inside a body that doesn't and I wrote this song..." Those critics who attack Nash for his overt sentimentality will find fresh ammunition with 'Try To Find Me'. The tone is mawkish, even though the sentiments are sincere enough.

Stills next takes the stage to remind us of the golden days of CSN&Y with 'As I Come Of Age', a song that first featured in their sets way back in the summer of 1970. He also displays

> "I have a message that I'd like to impart to a bunch of trash in Forsyth County, Georgia. This sort of behaviour and attitude is not acceptable in society..."
> STEPHEN STILLS ON STAGE AT THE ARLINGTON THEATER, SANTA BARBARA

some of his old anger, prefacing 'Word Game' with the announcement: "I have a message that I'd like to impart to a bunch of trash in Forsyth County, Georgia. This sort of behaviour and attitude is not acceptable in society..." The song is taken at a faster pace than usual but works surprisingly well, over 15 years on. Not for the first time, Stills censors the final line, this time singing, "They might turn on you". He concludes his segment with 'Daylight Again' – the album version rather than the extended narrative familiar from Manassas days.

Following 'Find The Cost Of Freedom', Young emerges for a couple of reflections on the effects of war: 'Mideast Vacation' and 'Long Walk Home'. Thereafter, the set reverts to that of a standard CS&N show, replete with their most celebrated moments. Inevitably, the virtuoso 'Suite: Judy Blue Eyes' is a highlight and prompts rapturous applause, after which they return for 'Ohio'. It sounds less powerful acoustically, although there are some interesting touches, including a fiddle in the background. "Here's a song that sums it all up,"

says Nash, as they chirp 'Teach Your Children'. Then Young adds one final surprise to the evening with 'Southern Man', again returning to an era when the foursome were regarded as genuinely innovative. Tonight, they prove that it is possible to recapture the magic not through playing old songs but by mixing the new with the familiar, just as they did in 1969–1970 and 1974.

SET LIST: WASTED ON THE WAY: CHANGE PARTNERS: LONG MAY YOU RUN; LONG TIME GONE: COMPASS: HE'S AN AMERICAN: NOTHING IS PERFECT (IN GOD'S PERFECT PLAN): TRY TO FIND ME: AS I COME OF AGE: THIS OLD HOUSE: WORD GAME/ CROSSROADS: DAYLIGHT AGAIN/FIND THE COST OF FREEDOM: MIDEAST VACATION: LONG WALK HOME: CRITICAL MASS/WIND ON THE WATER: SOUTHERN CROSS: SUITE: JUDY BLUE EYES: OHIO: TEACH YOUR CHILDREN; SOUTHERN MAN.

8 FEBRUARY

The King Biscuit Flower Hour broadcast this evening features CS&N on three acoustic tracks: 'Wasted On The Way', 'Guinnevere' and 'You Don't Have To Cry'.

MID-FEBRUARY

CSN&Y enter the studio to record their first studio album since *Déjà Vu* in 1970. Fears abound that David Geffen will not allow them to release the completed work unless it's on his label. "I don't know how that's going to work out," Young says with a touch of diplomacy. "But I'm sure the record companies, in their wisdom, will figure out a way for Crosby, Stills, Nash & Young to make a record. It's not my problem. We're going to make a record anyway."

23 MARCH

Crosby and girlfriend Jan Dance accompany Neil and Pegi Young on a sailing trip to the Caribbean aboard the Canadian's boat the *WN Ragland*.

26 MARCH

Crosby, Stills, Nash and Joe Vitale provide lead sheets and a sound cassette for a new song, 'Chuck's Lament (A Child's Dream)', which is subsequently issued as the B-side to 'Live It Up'.

8 APRIL

Crosby and Stills jam with Al Kooper at the Roxy, LA. Dave Mason and Jackson Browne also appear on the same bill.

24 APRIL–6 JUNE

Young and Crazy Horse travel to Europe for a lengthy tour, taking in Spain, Italy, West Germany, Luxembourg, Austria, Switzerland, France, Holland, Belgium, England and Eire.

SAMPLE SET LIST: (STADTHALLE, VIENNA, AUSTRIA, MAY 17): MR SOUL: CINNAMON GIRL; THE LONER: DOWN BY THE RIVER: HEART OF GOLD: SEE THE SKY ABOUT TO RAIN: AFTER THE GOLDRUSH: WHEN YOUR LONELY HEART BREAKS: DRIVE BACK: OPERA STAR: CORTEZ THE KILLER: SUGAR MOUNTAIN: COMES A TIME: MIDEAST VACATION: LONG WALK HOME: POWDERFINGER: LIKE A HURRICANE: HEY HEY, MY MY (INTO THE BLACK).

27 APRIL

Crosby is back in *People* magazine, this time for a positive profile, credited to himself. Headlined "The Happy Lazarus", the tone of the piece is salutary, with Crosby announcing: "I have a Ph.D. in drugs. Fool with them and you'll get strung out. Then there are about four ways it can go: you can go crazy; you can go to prison; you can die; or you can kick.

"At the peak of my consumption I was doing anywhere from an eighth of an ounce to a quarter of an ounce of cocaine ($500) a day and at least a half gram of heroin ($200) a day. When you're as well known a junkie as I was, it's easy to get drugs. Dealers come right over. They're faster than a pizza delivery."

He concludes on an optimistic note, stressing:

"I learned a great deal from all this. I learned that instead of instant gratification, I needed to learn patience and humility. I learned that music, love and friends are more important than getting high. But the biggest surprise was that I could quit drugs, that I had a choice. I thought I was going to die on drugs. When you've been as severely addicted as I was, you're real surprised to be alive."

30 APRIL

Stills and drummer Ian Wallace despatch a sound cassette of their joint composition 'Heart Of The Hearth', which remains unreleased.

9 MAY

Crosby and Stills appear on-stage together at Manor Downs, Austin, Texas, with guest David

Lindley in "Cowboys For Indians", a benefit concert promoted by the perennial hippie jester, Wavy Gravy. Stills plays a solo set, then invites Lindley on-stage, announcing: "Here's a song (it's a couple of hundred years old) that turned into something else that I wrote in the Sixties". A medley of 'The Blind Fiddler'/'Know You Got To Run' follows, with Lindley in sparkling form. After an impressive acoustic run through 'Love The One You're With', Stills leaves the stage to Crosby who is clearly enjoying himself. Consciously or otherwise, he uses a Texan accent throughout the entire show without a trace of irony. It's either brilliant acting or proof of the enduring effects of incarceration in Texas. Prior to 'For Free', he comes across as a sexist redneck when describing his love life with Joni Mitchell: "It's like falling into a cement mixer. She's a very turbulent girl. She wrote this song. She writes pretty good for a girl." The role play continues uninterrupted, even through the courtly love atmosphere of 'Guinnevere'. Crosby then brings Lindley on for an impressive arrangement of 'The Lee Shore', after which Stills joins them both for 'Long Time Gone'. The show ends with a grand finale of 'Teach Your Children' with former Seatrain guitarist Peter Rowan joining Crosby, Stills & Lindley.

SET LIST: MIDNIGHT RIDER; THOROUGHFARE GAP; TREETOP FLYER; THE BLIND FIDDLER/KNOW YOU GOT TO RUN; LOVE THE ONE YOU'RE WITH; ALMOST CUT MY HAIR; IN MY DREAMS; FOR FREE; CARRY ME; DELTA: COMPASS; GUINNEVERE; THE LEE SHORE; LONG TIME GONE; TEACH YOUR CHILDREN.

10 MAY

Crosby & Nash play a 50-minute set for "COMPADRES' (Committee of Mothers and Relatives Of Political Prisoners, Disappeared and Assassinated of El Salvador). The event is held on Mother's Day at the Fox International Theater, Venice, LA.

16 MAY

David Crosby and Jan Dance are married at a double wedding ceremony in which Graham and Susan renew their vows on their tenth anniversary. The happy event is attended by a fulsome guest list, which includes Stephen Stills, Roger McGuinn, Chris Hillman, Paul Kantner, Jackson Browne and Warren Zevon.

CROSBY MARRIES JAN DANCE AT A DOUBLE WEDDING CEREMONY WITH GRAHAM AND SUSAN NASH, 16 MAY.

On walks Jackson Browne who joins the trio for, of all things, 'Wooden Ships'. This was the song that prompted Browne's humane reply 'For Everyman'. He remains on-stage to perform the familiar 'Jamaica Say You Will', a song The Byrds once covered and which now benefits from the harmonies of CS&N. The show continues until after midnight, with Nash's own children surrounding their father for a finale of 'Teach Your Children'.

10 AUGUST

Nash copyrights the sound cassette and lead sheets for 'Soldiers Of Peace' (co-written with Joe Vitale and Craig Doerge). Around this same period, he can be heard on Marc Jordan's *Talking Through Pictures*.

13 AUGUST – 4 SEPTEMBER

Young tours with Crazy Horse on a series of shows that herald the arrival of his next project: The Blue Notes. Unreleased songs premièred during the tour include: 'Big Room', 'Farmer's Song', and 'Last Of A Dying Breed'.

SAMPLE SET LIST (SARATOGA SPRINGS PERFORMING ARTS CENTER, NY, AUGUST 24): MY MY, HEY HEY (OUT OF THE BLUE); HEART OF GOLD; THIS NOTE'S FOR YOU; COMES A TIME; FARMER'S SONG; FOR THE TURNSTILES; SOMEDAY; THE NEEDLE AND THE DAMAGE DONE; SUGAR MOUNTAIN; DON'T TAKE YOUR LOVE AWAY FROM ME; THIS NOTE'S FOR YOU; MR SOUL; CINNAMON GIRL; PRISONERS OF ROCK 'N' ROLL; DOWN BY THE

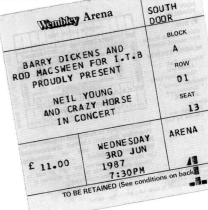

5 JUNE

Warren Zevon's *Sentimental Hygiene* features Young's blistering guitar work on the title track.

7 JUNE

Prompted by the exemplary research of teacher turned writer John Einarson, Young reunites with The Squires for a short set at the Blue Note Café, Winnipeg. It is the first time the group have played together in over 20 years. The fun continues the following day when Young attends the Convention Center, appearing with Chad Allan on a cover of The Guess Who's 'American Woman' and 'Albert Fisher', Dylan's 'Just Like Tom Thumb's Blues', his own 'Down By The River' and Bachman-Turner Overdrive's 'Takin' Care Of Business'.

JULY – AUGUST

CS&N undertake their traditional summer tour, this time with Crosby in full health. The scheduled itinerary includes shows in Binghampton, NY (July 2); Hershey, PA (3); Washington, DC (4); Columbia, MD (6); New York City, NY (7/8); Richmond, VA (10); Charlotte, NC (11); Atlanta, GA (13); Nashville, TN (14); Birmingham, AL (15); Houston, TX (17); Dallas, TX (18); Norman, OK (19); Memphis, TN (21); Louisville, KY (23); St Louis, MO (24); Bonner Springs, KS (25); Denver, CO (27); Seattle, WA (30); Portland, OR (August 1); Sacramento, CA (3); Concord, CA (4); Paso Robles, CA (5); Mountain View, CA (7); Laguna Hills, CA (8); Clarkston, MI (14); Hoffman Estates, IL (15); Milwaukee, WI (16); Cuyahoga Falls, OH (18); Columbus, OH (19).

Among the above shows is an Independence Day benefit for Vietnam Veterans at the RFK Stadium, Washington. As Crosby explains:

"We went down to that Vietnam wall... There's a reason why it's such a powerful memorial. It's very simple. There's too damn many names on it."

Both Mike Finnigan (July 19) and Crosby (August 14) celebrate birthdays onstage during the tour and the sell-out crowds respond well to the party atmosphere. Nash is buoyant throughout, having fun introducing "the dapper, handsome, remarkable David Crosby". The trio present a more vital and varied set than in recent years and indicate that they are capable of moving on and perhaps even escaping the legacy of their own history.

SAMPLE SET LIST (RADIO CITY MUSIC HALL, JULY 8): CHANGE PARTNERS: WASTED ON THE WAY; YOU DON'T HAVE TO CRY; BLACKBIRD: ALMOST CUT MY HAIR; COMPASS; TRY TO FIND ME; THE BALLAD OF HOLLIS BROWN; GUINNEVERE; SUITE: JUDY BLUE EYES; LOVE THE ONE YOU'RE WITH; JUST A SONG BEFORE I GO; NIGHTTIME FOR THE GENERALS; SHADOWLAND; 50/50; CRITICAL MASS/WIND ON THE WATER; SOLDIERS OF PEACE; FOR WHAT IT'S WORTH; LONG TIME GONE; SOUTHERN CROSS; WOODEN SHIPS; TEACH YOUR CHILDREN; OUR HOUSE; DAYLIGHT AGAIN/FIND THE COST OF FREEDOM.

13 JULY

Young releases *Life*, a decidedly below average album by his best standards, but blessed relief to some when compared to its predecessor and a welcome reunion with Crazy Horse.

19 JULY

CS&N appear on Johnny Carson's *Tonight Show* performing 'Southern Cross' and 'Teach Your Children'.

8 AUGUST

CS&N end their show at the Irvine Meadows Amphitheater by announcing a surprise guest.

RIVER; EVERYBODY KNOWS THIS IS NOWHERE; NAME OF LOVE; MIDEAST VACATION; LONG WALK HOME; POWDERFINGER; LIKE A HURRICANE; HEY HEY, MY MY (INTO THE BLACK).

19 AUGUST

Young delivers a sound cassette for copyright purposes containing the still unreleased songs 'For The Love Of Man' and 'Razor Love'.

SEPTEMBER

CS&N extend their summer tour with a series of autumn shows. Their repertoire features new songs such as Nash's 'Try To Find Me' and 'Soldiers Of Peace', plus Crosby's 'Compass' and 'Nighttime For The Generals', but Stills is increasingly and uncharacteristically reliant on older songs.

11 SEPTEMBER

Young delivers a sound cassette for copyright purposes containing 'Don't Take Your Love Away From Me' and the still unissued songs 'Farmer's Song' and 'Big Room'.

19 SEPTEMBER

Young appears at Farm Aid III at the Memorial Stadium, Lincoln, Nebraska.

3 OCTOBER

CS&N appear on the television show *West 57th*, with Stills clearly the worse for wear. During rehearsals, Nash complains about his drunken state, revealing signs of a new rift in the partnership.

2–13 NOVEMBER

Young launches The Blue Notes, astonishing audiences with a wealth of new material. The sample set list below, taken from The Omni, Oakland, CA (11 November), features seven songs that still remain unissued: 'Big Room', 'Find Another Shoulder', 'High Heels', 'Hello Lonely Woman', 'Soul Of A Woman', 'Bad News Has Come To Town' and 'Your Love'.

SAMPLE SET LIST: BIG ROOM; FIND ANOTHER SHOULDER; HIGH HEELS; HELLO LONELY WOMAN; AIN'T IT THE TRUTH; ONE THING; BAD NEWS HAS COME TO TOWN; YOUR LOVE; SUNNY INSIDE; LIFE IN THE CITY; SOUL OF A WOMAN; THIS NOTE'S FOR YOU; DON'T TAKE YOUR LOVE AWAY FROM ME.

9 NOVEMBER

Young delivers a sound cassette for copyright purposes containing the still unreleased songs 'Your Love', 'Soul Of A Woman' and 'Just One Thing'.

20 NOVEMBER

Crosby and Nash attend a party for U2 organised by Jane Fonda at her Santa Monica home.

21 NOVEMBER

Nash organises the UNICEF benefit concert "Children Of The Americas" explaining: "40,000 kids die every single day from diseases we could easily immunise them against. What we want to do is raise as much money as possible to help these children to live and to help the hungry of America to eat."

The satellite broadcast features artistes playing at the United Nations Building in New York and LA's Roxy Music Theater. By the end of the evening over $100,000 is raised, with CS&N throwing in an additional $11,000 donation during their set.

5 DECEMBER

Stills marries model Pamela Ann Jordan at a church wedding in Georgetown, Washington. Crosby & Nash are among the guests. At the reception, Stills jams with Joe Walsh and Buddy Guy.

7 DECEMBER

Young delivers a sound cassette for copyright purposes containing the still unreleased songs 'Find Another Shoulder', 'Hello Lonely Woman' and 'High Heels.'

14 DECEMBER

Crosby copyrights 'Nighttime For The Generals', 'Lady Of The Harbor' and 'Monkey And The Underdog'.

DECEMBER

Murray Hill Records issue *Never Before*, a collection of Byrds' rarities, including Crosby's 'Triad', a part re-recorded 'Lady Friend' and his previously unreleased composition 'It Happens Each Day'. The CD version of the record subsequently adds another Crosby composition, 'Psychodrama City'.

CROSBY & NASH AT JANE FONDA'S SANTA MONICA HOME.

1988

20 JANUARY
Young is back at the Rock 'n' Roll Hall of Fame, this time inducting Woody Guthrie.

25 JANUARY
Nash copyrights his recently written political admonition, 'Vote'. The song remains unreleased on album.

29 FEBRUARY
Young delivers a sound cassette containing the unreleased song 'One Thing'.

MARCH
Stealin' Horses' *Harriet Tubman* is released, with Young guesting on guitar.

3/14/17/19, 21-23 APRIL
Young resumes touring with The Blue Notes, taking in Los Angeles, New York and Cleveland, Ohio.

6 APRIL
Crosby and Nash play a SEVA benefit concert at the John Sexton Auditorium, Pasadena City College. The bill also features Jackson Browne, Bonnie Raitt, Bob Weir and Brent Myland.

8 APRIL
Back on Reprise Records, Young releases *This Note's For You*, another genre experiment – this time a blues album. Against the odds, it emerges as his best album of the decade thus far, with strong songs, impressive arrangements and a discernible focus lacking in its recent predecessors.

1-22 APRIL
Stills plays five acoustic shows in Cleveland in support of Democrat candidate Dennis Kucinich.

MAY
Stills plays a short set at the Palms Playhouse in Davis, near Sacramento, California.

4 MAY
Crosby, Stills & Nash appear at Atlantic Records' 40th anniversary concert in New York. Neil Young is conspicuous by his absence.

8 MAY
Young issues the otherwise unavailable 'I'm Goin'' as the B-side of his single 'Ten Men Workin''.

JUNE
Crosby performs a short set for the American Booksellers' Association Convention.

JUNE
CS&N appear in Montreal at a benefit for the International Physicians For The Prevention of Nuclear War. After their performance, the trio return to the stage to add harmonies to Bruce Cockburn's 'Rocket Launcher'.

7/10-11 JUNE
Young appears as guest guitarist on three Bob Dylan dates in California: Concord Pavilion (June 7); Greek Theater, Berkeley (10); Shoreline Amphitheater, Mountain View (11). None of Young's songs is featured.

16 JUNE
Crosby teams up with former Byrds Roger McGuinn and Chris Hillman at the Wiltern Theater to celebrate the reopening of the Ash Grove folk club. The trio are joined by John Jorgenson and Steve Duncan of The Desert Rose Band for a selection of Byrds hits including 'Mr Tambourine Man', 'Turn! Turn! Turn!', 'Eight Miles High' and 'So You Want To Be A Rock 'n' Roll Star'.

JULY - SEPTEMBER
CS&N embark on another summer tour, including gigs at the Oxford Plains Speedway, Portland, OR (July 31); Great Woods Performing Arts Center, Mansfield, MA (August 1/2); Saratoga Performing Arts Center, Saratoga Springs, NY (4); Civic Center Arena,

CROSBY IN LA, MARCH 1988

Hartford, CT (5); Jones Beach Theater, NY (6); Brendan Byrne Arena, Meadowlands, East Rutherford, NJ (8); Mann Music Center, Philadelphia, PA (10/11); Merriweather Post Pavilion, Columbia, MD (12/13); Riverbend Music Theater, Cincinnati, OH (15); Blossom Music Center, Cleveland, OH (16); Palace, Detroit, MI (18); Sports Center, IN (19); Alpine Valley Arts Music Center, East Troy, WI (20); Civic Center, Lacrosse, WI (22); Poplar Creek Music Center, Chicago, IL (24); Fox Theater, St

Louis, MO (25/26); Colorado State Fair, Pueblo, CO (28); Fiddlers Green, Englewood, CO (29); Park West, Salt Lake City, UT (30).

During September they visit PNE Coliseum, Vancouver, BC (1); Tacoma Dome, Seattle, WA (2); Coliseum, Portland, OR (3); Shoreline Amphitheater, Mountain View, CA (5); Compton Terrace, Phoenix, AZ (8); Pacific Amphitheater, Costa Mesa, CA (10); Caesar's Palace, Las Vegas, NV(11); Anchorage, AK (13) Fairbanks, AK (14); Waikiki Shell, Honolulu, HI, (17); Lahaina Civic Center, Maui, HI (18).

Nash covers Simon & Garfunkel's 'America' during this generally well-received tour. During the performance in Costa Mesa (10 September) a model of a Stonehenge ruin is lowered from the rafters during Nash's rendition of 'Cathedral'. He collapses in laughter, then crawls under his piano stool in mock embarrassment. Stills' boyish skip across the stage suggests that he was a party to the jape. The press enjoy the good humour and praise Crosby for his renewed vocal power. Clearly, Stills is the new fall guy in CS&N with one journalist wryly noting: "When he tried to stretch his range or embellish a phrasing, he sounded like a victim of strangulation... By omitting 'Suite: Judy Blue Eyes' CS&N spared considerable embarrassment for Stills, whose singing has gotten to the point where it's no fun any more."

SAMPLE SET LIST (SHORELINE AMPHITHEATER, SEPTEMBER 5): LOVE THE ONE YOU'RE WITH; PRE-ROAD DOWNS; CHANGE PARTNERS; JUST A SONG BEFORE I GO; THE LEE SHORE; NIGHTTIME FOR THE GENERALS; CRITICAL MASS/WIND ON THE WATER; WOODEN SHIPS; WASTED ON THE WAY; TRY TO FIND ME; AMERICA; COMPASS; ALMOST CUT MY HAIR; OLD MAN TROUBLE; DAYLIGHT AGAIN/FIND THE COST OF FREEDOM; GUINNEVERE; SUITE: JUDY BLUE EYES; MONKEY AND THE UNDERDOG; DARK STAR; SOLDIERS OF PEACE; FOR WHAT IT'S WORTH; LONG TIME GONE; SOUTHERN CROSS; CATHEDRAL; CARRY ON; TEACH YOUR CHILDREN.

12 AUGUST - 8 SEPTEMBER
Young and The Blue Notes undertake a one-month tour during which they play a number of still unissued songs, including 'Crime Of The Heart', 'Walking After Midnight', Doghouse', 'Fool For Your Love', 'Boxcar' and the extraordinary 12-minute 'Ordinary People'. He also features the full 20-minute version of 'Sixty To Zero' in what is undoubtedly one of the greatest Young tours.

SAMPLE SET LIST (GREAT WOODS CENTER, MANSFIELD, MA, AUGUST 31): TEN MEN WORKIN'; HELLO LONELY WOMAN; I'M GOIN'; MARRIED MAN; CRIME OF THE HEART; YOUR LOVE; COUPE DE VILLE; ORDINARY PEOPLE; DAYS THAT USED TO BE; AFTER THE GOLDRUSH; FOOL FOR YOUR LOVE; SUNNY INSIDE; BAD NEWS; AIN'T IT THE TRUTH; HEY HEY; THIS NOTE'S FOR YOU; DOGHOUSE; TONIGHT'S THE NIGHT.

4 OCTOBER
Crosby's harrowing autobiography *Long Time Gone* is published by Doubleday, New York, and sells spectacularly well, backed by heavy media promotion from the rehabilitated singer.

25 OCTOBER

Under legal threat from Harold Melvin, Young jettisons The Blue Notes name in favour of Ten Men Working, who play a handful of dates through the last week of October.

NOVEMBER

Kenny Rankin's *Hiding In Myself* is released, with Crosby contributing vocals to 'Down The Road'.

The Hollies' newly issued compilation *Rarities* includes three compositions co-written by Nash but previously unreleased in the UK: 'Relax', 'Tomorrow When It Comes and 'Like Every Time Before'.

6 NOVEMBER

Crosby & Nash are the support act on the current Jackson Browne West Coast tour. This date is a benefit concert at the Palace Theater, LA for the La Penca Lawsuit, the Christie Institute's Contragate Project.

done we're going to be gone a lot sooner than our kids are. We're going to leave this planet to them. I hope it can sustain them. I hope it will make them flourish instead of being blown apart in a nuclear holocaust. I hope that AIDS doesn't totally screw up the planet... I hope for a lot of things, but I know that I'll be gone and they'll still be here. They are our future and I can't put my energy any better place than this."

SET LIST: THIS OLD HOUSE; LOVE THE ONE YOU'RE WITH; IN THE NAME OF LOVE; TRACKS IN THE DUST; DON'T SAY GOODBYE; SOUTHERN CROSS; LONG TIME GONE; TEACH YOUR CHILDREN; MY COUNTRY 'TIS OF THEE.

11–13 NOVEMBER

Crosby travels to Glendale for the Love Five Bike Ride, a benefit ride for the Muscular Dystrophy Association. He also guests at the Anson Ford Theater, Universal City, LA (November 13), performing 'Long Time Gone', 'The Monkey And The Underdog' and 'Wooden Ships'.

jarring note is the decision to allocate Crosby a mere two songs, which seems odd when you consider that the work was partly conceived as a tribute to his redemption from drug addiction and near death. He seemed stoical about the apparent imbalance: "It's just how it happened. There was some resistance there from somebody, but I didn't worry about it. I had two very good songs and was more concerned with the quality rather than the quantity. I'm not worried about the pie-slicing." Overall, the album proved far better than anyone could reasonably have expected but required a full-scale tour to realise its full commercial potential and this was not forthcoming.

26 NOVEMBER

Crosby & Nash join Paul Simon, Laurie Anderson and Allen Ginsberg for a benefit for the homeless at the Cathedral of St John The Divine, New York. David and Graham close the show performing 'Wasted On The Way', 'The Lee Shore', 'Critical

NASH ON STAGE WITH CARLY SIMON, NOVEMBER 1988

12 NOVEMBER

CSN&Y reunite on-stage at the Palace Theater, LA, for "Graham Nash's Children Of The Americas Radiothon", a UNICEF benefit for the young underprivileged. After performances by Randy Newman and Midnight Oil, Crosby & Nash provide backing harmonies for Jackson Browne. Finally, there is the long-awaited main event: CSN&Y mixing selections from their new album with the expected classics. The audience even acknowledges the date by singing "Happy Birthday" to the 43-year-old Young. The set ends with Crosby's patriotic 'My Country 'Tis Of Thee' featuring John David Souther. As Nash concludes, as if paraphrasing 'Teach Your Children': "When all's said and

14 NOVEMBER

The magic of radio reunites CSN&Y on *Rockline*, with Stills & Young answering listeners in San Francisco, connected to Crosby & Nash in LA.

21 NOVEMBER

CSN&Y release *American Dream* (officially scheduled for November 3), their first studio album since 1970's *Déjà Vu*. Despite mixed reviews, the album fully demonstrates the strength of the quartet, as well as reminding the world of all that had been lost as a result of their failure to record together over the past two decades. With 14 tracks, stretching over one hour in length, the album proves exceptionally good value. The only

Mass/Wind On The Water', 'Tracks In The Dust', 'Don't Say Goodbye', 'Samurai', 'Guinnevere', 'Our House' and a collaboration with Carly Simon on 'Teach Your Children'. A resounding encore brings Paul Simon and C&N together on 'This Land Is Your Land'.

4 DECEMBER

The second Bridge Benefit, at the Oakland Coliseum features another short on-stage reunion of CSN&Y.

SET LIST: AMERICAN DREAM; HELPLESSLY HOPING; LOVE THE ONE YOU'RE WITH; THIS OLD HOUSE; SOUTHERN MAN; DON'T SAY GOODBYE; COMPASS; LONG TIME GONE; SOUTHERN CROSS; TEACH YOUR CHILDREN (WITH NILS LOFGREN AND TRACY CHAPMAN).

1989

JANUARY

Crosby again reunites with McGuinn and Hillman for three "Byrds Reunion" shows in the Coach House, San Juan Capistrano (January 4), the Bacchanal, San Diego (5) and Ventura Theater, Ventura (6). Among the hits, Crosby includes a surprise and much appreciated reading of 'Everybody's Been Burned'. As he enthused to me: "We got up there, man, and tore it up! We hit 'Chimes Of Freedom' and I got chills going up my back. And the audience went: 'Whoop! Up for grabs! Totally nuts!' I'm being very immodest but I'm telling you the truth. We got reviews from people that normally wouldn't give you the sweat off their brow, and they were raves. It was really exciting and, more importantly, it was a hell of a lot of fun."

SAMPLE SET LIST (JANUARY 6): CHIMES OF FREEDOM: IT WON'T BE WRONG; FEEL A WHOLE LOT BETTER; EVERYBODY'S BEEN BURNED; MY BACK PAGES; MR SPACEMAN; THE BELLS OF RHYMNEY; YOU AIN'T GOING NOWHERE; MR TAMBOURINE MAN; TURN! TURN! TURN!; EIGHT MILES HIGH; SO YOU WANT TO BE A ROCK 'N' ROLL STAR.

JANUARY

Young commences a short US tour with Blue Notes offshoot The Restless. His set mixes acoustic material with some of his hardest electric playing, including on occasion a 20-minute version of 'Tonight's The Night'.

SAMPLE SET LIST (CIVIC AUDITORIUM, PORTLAND, OR, FEBRUARY 20): COMES A TIME; SUGAR MOUNTAIN; THE NEEDLE AND THE DAMAGE DONE; AFTER THE GOLDRUSH; FOR THE TURNSTILES; SILVER & GOLD; THE WAYS OF LOVE; DAYS THAT USED TO BE; HEART OF GOLD; HEAVY LOVE; DON'T CRY; COCAINE EYES; ELDORADO; BOX CAR; MR SOUL; CINNAMON GIRL; BAD FOG OF LONELINESS; DOWN BY THE RIVER; HEY HEY, MY MY (INTO THE BLACK); ON BROADWAY; TONIGHT'S THE NIGHT.

JANUARY

Crosby & Nash appear at the Anti-war Christie Institute Benefit, DC, alongside Kris Kristofferson and Michelle Shocked.

FEBRUARY

Crosby & Nash record 'After The Dolphin' one of Nash's most memorable songs of recent times. The track will later be held over for the CS&N album *Live It Up*.

FEBRUARY

Stills, temporarily estranged from Crosby & Nash because of his penchant for drink and cocaine, plays some solo dates this month, backed by Lenny McDaniel (bass) and Ian Wallace (drums). This evening's short set at the Starry Night, Portland, OR, presents a range of material from throughout his career, but nothing too startling for the connoisseur.

SET LIST: LOVE THE ONE YOU'RE WITH; MAKE LOVE TO YOU; GOT IT MADE; THAT GIRL; BLUEBIRD; OLD MAN TROUBLE; CHANGE PARTNERS; SOUTHERN CROSS; DARK STAR; FOR WHAT IT'S WORTH; TREETOP FLYER.

6 FEBRUARY

Stills appears at the Coach House, San Juan Capistrano, CA, still suffering from the after effects of root canal dental treatment. He retains his engaging sense of humour though, informing the audience: "Reports of my obesity have been greatly exaggerated."

On this same day, Crosby releases *Oh Yes I Can* (officially scheduled for January 23), his first album since 1971's *If I Could Only Remember My Name*. Although far less radical or important than his first album, it is rightly hailed as a welcome and pleasing return from the creative stasis of the last decade.

21 FEBRUARY

Crosby reveals that he is presently working on a Crosby/Nash album. "I'm finding ways to be more prolific," Crosby tells me. "I've got a new song with Craig Doerge called 'Yours And Mine' that I've just finished. I've got a new one with Michael Hedges called 'Arrows'. I've got 'King Of The Mountain' and 'Samurai and all those are going on this new Crosby/Nash album". In the event, the intended album is scrapped and ultimately replaced by the CS&N project *Live It Up*. Alas, 'King Of The Mountain' and the stunning 'Samurai' remain unissued. "I wanted to save it until Nash and I could do it," Crosby protested to me. "We have such a rapport, man. Nobody else has ever had that rapport with me. The way 'Samurai' has to be done requires almost telepathic timing because there's no beat to it. You have to breathe in hard and let it go! Nash is the only one I could do that with. I think we'll do really well with 'Samurai'. I'm looking forward to it."

22 FEBRUARY

Crosby appears at a London reception for his autobiography *Long Time Gone*, published by Heineman. After a short speech, he happily

"I wanted to save it until Nash and I could do it," Crosby protested to me. "We have such a rapport, man. Nobody else has ever had that rapport with me."

DAVID CROSBY ON THE NON-RELEASE OF 'SAMURAI'

answers questions and as the evening draws to a close seems willing to be grilled about obscure forgotten recordings and suffer the odd gauche inquiry from the assembled music critics and publishing worthies.

18 MARCH

Stills' season of touring continues with a show at the Fillmore, San Francisco.

27 MARCH

CSN&Y are reunited for radio listeners on *In The Studio*, a programme dealing with the classic recording *Déjà Vu*.

APRIL

Young's group The Restless change into The Lost Dogs for a one-month tour of Australia and Japan (from April 5 – May 5), including performances in Perth, Adelaide, Darwin, Melbourne, Brisbane, Sydney, Launceston, Hobart, Auckland, Yokohama, Tokyo, Osaka and Nagoya.

SAMPLE SET LIST (BUNKA TAIIKUKAN, YOKOHAMA, APRIL 27): MY MY, HEY HEY (OUT OF THE BLUE); DAYS THAT USED TO BE; POCAHONTAS; SAIL AWAY; HELPLESS; FOR THE TURNSTILES; THIS OLD HOUSE; AFTER THE GOLDRUSH; HEART OF GOLD; ELDORADO; MR SOUL; CINNAMON GIRL; NO MORE; POWDERFINGER; ROCKIN' IN THE FREE WORLD; ON BROADWAY; HEY HEY, MY MY (INTO THE BLACK).

NEIL YOUNG IN JAPAN, APRIL 1989

APRIL/MAY

Both Stills and Crosby are touring solo in bars, hotel conference centres and small theatres throughout the USA. Highlights from Crosby's appearance at the Tower Theater, Philadelphia, are later captured on the radio show *King Biscuit Flower Hour*, including 'Tracks In The Dust', 'Guinnevere', 'Drive My Car', 'The Monkey And The Underdog', 'Déjà Vu', 'Wooden Ships', 'Almost Cut My Hair' and 'Long Time Gone'.

Stills, meanwhile, is enjoying his low-key appearances, playing a full set of acoustic music. The set list below from the Salt Palace, Salt Lake City (April 8) reveals the range of material, including his version of Nash's 'Teach Your Children'.

SET LIST: LOVE THE ONE YOU'RE WITH; CHANGE PARTNERS; MAKE LOVE TO YOU; THAT GIRL; GOT IT MADE; TEACH YOUR CHILDREN; MIDNIGHT RIDER; JOHNNY'S GARDEN; BLUEBIRD; OLD MAN TROUBLE; DARK STAR; FOR WHAT IT'S WORTH; DAYLIGHT AGAIN/FIND THE COST OF FREEDOM.

3 APRIL

Bonnie Raitt's *Nick Of Time* is released, with Crosby & Nash providing backing vocals to 'Cry On My Shoulder'.

10 APRIL

Crosby, McGuinn and Hillman (aka The Byrds) file a lawsuit in federal court suing Michael Clarke and his management for their appropriation of The Byrds' name, alleging false advertising, unfair competition and deceptive trade practices. Clarke's manager Steve Green tells me: "We tried to make them understand that we're not trying to misrepresent them, but their egos are so big that they think we're making money out of them. They don't want parity. I'll go with them being The Byrds if Michael can be The Byrds. I'll go with them saluting The Byrds if Michael can salute The Byrds. Anything they want to do is all right with me."

MAY

The CD version of The Byrds' *Never Before* is released with Crosby's previously unheard 'Psychodrama City' and co-arrangement of 'I Know You Rider'.

15 MAY

Stephen Stills and Michael Mileham copyright register a five-page screenplay titled 'Panama; or, The Canal Zone', which they had originally written back in 1985.

18 MAY

District Judge William J. Castagna finds in favour of the defendant Michael Clarke in The Byrds' brand name dispute. "We won a monumental decision," the drummer cries. Crosby's manager Bill Siddons is stoical in defeat: "It just cost too much money to force Michael to stop abusing The Byrds' name." The entire argument is subsequently made redundant by the sad death of Clarke in December 1993.

3 MAY

Crosby appears at the Piazza del Popolo, Roma, Italy, during a short Continental tour. Those who claim that CS&N are over-reliant on an old repertoire would do well to consider their solo sets, which are never short of interest. Here, Crosby sings a half-dozen selections from his second solo album and elects to omit most of the expected songs from his acoustic repertoire. Mike Finnigan is introduced by David as "one of the greatest singers in the world" and is even allowed to sing two songs: 'Judgement Day' and 'Part Time Love'. His blues/soul workouts sound jarringly out of place at a Crosby show, while his backing harmonies frequently threaten to drown the lead singer. The one point where his vocals genuinely are needed is during 'Almost Cut My Hair' but throughout this number he remains locked to the keyboards. With Crosby sounding disconcertingly hoarse, Finnigan thankfully finds a suitable role during the encore 'Long Time Gone', where his blues styling is at last appropriate.

SET LIST: DRIVE MY CAR; LADY OF THE HARBOR; OH YES I CAN; JUDGEMENT DAY; THE MONKEY AND THE UNDERDOG; DELTA; DÉJÀ VU; DROP DOWN MAMA; PART TIME LOVE; IN THE WIDE RUIN; NIGHTTIME FOR THE GENERALS; WOODEN SHIPS; ALMOST CUT MY HAIR; LONG TIME GONE.

JUNE–AUGUST

Young's sporadic touring continues with a series of US dates. Bruce Springsteen makes a guest appearance on 'Down By The River' in Wantagh, New York (June 14) and part of this same show is featured on the video *Freedom*.

SAMPLE SET LIST (KINGSWOOD MUSIC THEATER, MAPLE, ON, AUGUST 26): MY MY, HEY HEY (OUT OF THE BLUE); ROCKIN' IN THE FREE WORLD; SUGAR MOUNTAIN; SOMEDAY; HELPLESS; POCAHONTAS; CRIME IN THE CITY (SIXTY TO ZERO PART 1); FOUR STRONG WINDS; TOO FAR GONE; ROLL ANOTHER NUMBER; THIS NOTE'S FOR YOU; THE NEEDLE AND THE DAMAGE DONE; NO MORE; AFTER THE GOLDRUSH; HEART OF GOLD; OHIO; ROCKIN' IN THE FREE WORLD; POWDERFINGER.

JUNE

Crosby appears as backing vocalist on 'The Word Justice' from Jackson Browne's *World In Motion*.

AUGUST

Crosby & Nash join Young on-stage at the Greek Theater, LA for the encore 'Ohio'.

AUGUST

Stills joins Crosby & Nash onstage at Bally's Grandstand, Atlantic City, NJ. Having curbed his excesses over recent months, Stills puts in a fine performance. A strong set is punctuated by humorous asides, including jokes about Crosby and Boy George. One of the surprises of the evening is the inclusion of 'Woodstock', a full 20 years after the event.

SET LIST: WASTED ON THE WAY; CHANGE PARTNERS; BLACKBIRD; YOU DON'T HAVE TO CRY; JUST A SONG BEFORE I GO; CRITICAL MASS/WIND ON THE WATER; SUITE: JUDY BLUE EYES; ALMOST CUT MY HAIR; TRACKS IN THE DUST; AMERICA; DON'T SAY GOODBYE; TREETOP FLYER; OLD MAN TROUBLE; GUINNEVERE; LONG TIME GONE; LOVE THE ONE YOU'RE WITH; OUR HOUSE; SOUTHERN CROSS; WOODSTOCK; TEACH YOUR CHILDREN.

31 AUGUST

Crosby & Nash continue their late summer tour with a stirring show at the South Shore Music Circus, Cohasset, MA. The set list reveals a fresh variety in their repertoire which bodes well for later tours.

SET LIST: WASTED ON THE WAY; MILITARY MADNESS; THE LEE SHORE; JUST A SONG BEFORE I GO; CRITICAL MASS/WIND ON THE WATER; I USED TO BE A KING; CARRY ME; COMPASS; ALMOST CUT MY HAIR; TRACKS IN THE DUST; AMERICA; HOUSE OF BROKEN DREAMS; TRY TO FIND ME; GUINNEVERE; OUR HOUSE; WOODEN SHIPS; TEACH YOUR CHILDREN.

SEPTEMBER

CS&N continue their recent get togethers with a series of autumn shows, including dates at Darien Lake, NY (September 2); the Shoreline Amphitheater, Mountain View, CA (5/9), Holiday Star Theater, Mersiville (11); Symphony Hall, Springfield, MA (15) and the Hilton Hall, Albany, NY (17).

8 OCTOBER

Crosby & Nash appear at the Bread and Roses Festival, Greek Theater, San Francisco, on a bill that includes Bonnie Raitt, Kris Kristofferson, Joan Baez, Mickey Newbury, Boz Scaggs and Jennifer Warnes. The duo's set concludes with a moving version of Crosby's 'My Country 'Tis Of Thee' which the *San Francisco Chronicle* describes as "truly inspirational".

9 OCTOBER

Young's return to rock godhead is heralded with the release of *Freedom*, his most accomplished album since *Rust Never Sleeps*. From this point on, his reputation as a writer/performer is understandably unassailable.

On this same day, Tracy Chapman's *Crossroads* is issued with Young featured on 'All That You Have Is Your Soul'.

28 OCTOBER

The third Bridge Benefit takes place at the Shoreline Amphitheater, Mountain View, California, featuring sets by Young, CS&N and a finale of CSN&Y featuring 'Helplessly Hoping', 'Human Highway', 'Got It Made', 'Silver & Gold', 'Southern Cross', 'Ohio' and 'Teach Your Children'.

9 NOVEMBER

CS&N remain on the road, playing two shows at the Santa Cruz Civic Center.

14 NOVEMBER

Stills copyrights the recently completed 'Hard Ball', which remains unreleased.

18 NOVEMBER

CS&N appear at New York's United Nations General Assembly Hall for the third "Children Of The Americas" benefit. Their reading of Stills' 'Got It Made' that night is later issued on the 1991 boxed set.

20 NOVEMBER

Phil Collins' *...But Seriously* is released, with Crosby contributing vocals to 'That's Just The Way It Is' and 'Another Day In Paradise'. "He asked me to sing on my two favourite songs on the record," Crosby points out.

21/22 NOVEMBER

CS&N perform at the Berlin Wall, near the Brandenburg Gate. "We just showed up yesterday and said, 'Hi, we're here; we want to sing'," Stills tells the audience. With the assistance of the West German police, the trio slot in a 20-minute set, which includes Nash's reggae influenced version of Tom Fedora's 'Chippin' Away', a most appropriate song in the circumstances. In the dusk, Stills introduces Crosby's 'Long Time Gone', inviting the spectators to sing along and invest the song with a new meaning. Following this performance, CS&N issue a studio version of 'Chippin' Away' as a single, with James Taylor as guest vocalist.

26 NOVEMBER

CS&N appear at the Cow Palace, San Francisco, to raise money for victims of the earthquake. Young also plays a set, but does not join them onstage. However, Paul Kantner does make a guest appearance on 'Wooden Ships'.

SET LIST: WASTED ON THE WAY; CHANGE PARTNERS; THE LEE SHORE; WOODEN SHIPS; SUITE: JUDY BLUE EYES; TEACH YOUR CHILDREN.

EARLY DECEMBER

Crosby appears on the *Arsenio Hall Show* singing alongside Phil Collins on 'Another Day In Paradise'.

5–13 DECEMBER

Young begins a European tour, taking in Italy, West Germany, Holland, France and London. His acoustic sets are among the most dramatic and exciting of his entire career. Prowling the stage like a cross between Richard III and Hamlet, he enlivens his back catalogue, excels on his new extended narrative material and proves beyond doubt that he is one of the most important artistes of his era.

SAMPLE SET LIST (AHOY SPORTPALAIS, ROTTERDAM, HOLLAND, DECEMBER 13): MY MY, HEY HEY (OUT OF THE BLUE); COCAINE EYES; RAZOR LOVE; COMES A TIME; DON'T LET IT BRING YOU DOWN; SOMEDAY; CRIME IN THE CITY (SIXTY TO ZERO PART 1); ELDORADO; ROLL ANOTHER NUMBER; TOO FAR GONE; THIS NOTE'S FOR YOU; THE NEEDLE AND THE DAMAGE DONE; NO MORE; DREAMIN' MAN; F*!#IN' UP; WINTERLONG; HEART OF GOLD; ROCKIN' IN THE FREE WORLD; POWDERFINGER

14 DECEMBER
Fresh from Europe, Young makes a surprise appearance at the New York Ritz performing 'Rockin' In The Free World' with The Alarm.

23 DECEMBER
Nash hosts the television programme *The Ring* appearing alongside Grace Slick on a version of 'Panda'. Crosby joins the duo for 'Wooden Ships'.

26 DECEMBER
Nash copyrights 'House Of Broken Dreams', which will appear on the next CS&N album. The title was inspired by Pink Floyd's Dave Gilmour who, when phoned at home, answered, "Hello... house of broken dreams".

27 DECEMBER
Nash copyrights his recently completed collaboration with Craig Doerge, 'Better World', which remains unreleased.

1990

JANUARY
Warren Zevon's *Transverse City* is released with Young playing guitar on 'Splendid Isolation' and 'Gridlock'.

17 JANUARY
Nash inducts The Kinks into the Rock 'n' Roll Hall of Fame at the Waldorf-Astoria Hotel, New York.

2 FEBRUARY
'Yours And Mine', a Crosby/Nash/Doerge collaboration, is recorded for CS&N's *Live It Up*.

24 FEBRUARY
Crosby joins fellow ex-Byrds McGuinn and Hillman for the Roy Orbison Tribute Show at the Universal Amphitheater, Los Angeles. The group perform 'Mr Tambourine Man' and 'Turn! Turn! Turn!', the former featuring Bob Dylan on-stage with three Byrds for the first time since Ciro's back in 1965.

MARCH
The film *Love At Large* is premièred with Young cast as an ageing gangster. Meanwhile, Crosby is cast in the television drama, *Shannon's Deal*, playing a plagiarist country singer with a penchant for firing guns.

2 MARCH
Stills adds music to Joe Vitale's composition 'School Days'.

31 MARCH
CSN&Y reunite at the Santa Monica Civic Auditorium in a benefit concert to help raise money for drug education and assist their former drummer Dallas Taylor, who is awaiting a liver transplant. The Desert Rose Band and Don Henley are also on the bill. The concert serves as a reconciliation of sorts between Taylor and Young, who was responsible for the drummer's dismissal from CSN&Y many years before. After the usual individual spots, CSN&Y take the stage for 'Human Highway', 'Silver & Gold', 'Southern

Cross', with Taylor emerging for 'Wooden Ships' and 'Teach Your Children'.

SET LIST: ROCKIN' IN THE FREE WORLD; ELDORADO; SOMEDAY; MOTHER EARTH (NATURAL ANTHEM); WASTED ON THE WAY; CHANGE PARTNERS; BLACKBIRD; THE LEE SHORE; CRITICAL MASS/WIND ON THE WATER; HOUSE OF BROKEN DREAMS; ALMOST CUT MY HAIR; FOR WHAT IT'S WORTH; SUITE: JUDY BLUE EYES; HUMAN HIGHWAY; SILVER & GOLD; SOUTHERN CROSS; WOODEN SHIPS; TEACH YOUR CHILDREN.

APRIL

CSN&Y appear together for a second night at the Santa Monica Civic Auditorium to help raise funds for the California Environmental Protection Initiative. Young joins CS&N for 'For What It's Worth', then repeats the short set from last night, with the exception of 'Southern Cross', which is replaced by 'Ohio'. As Crosby notes: "We do a lot of benefits. All the way from UNICEF to getting our friend Dallas a new liver... We really like to make a contribution. It's my feeling that if you don't put some effort into a community and contribute to a community, then you don't have a community. The community is big now. It's world-wide, but it's still the human race. It's still a community and it needs a lot of help."

APRIL

CS&N record 'Haven't We Lost Enough', a collaboration between Stephen Stills and his neighbour Kevin Cronin.

APRIL

CS&N appear at Farm Aid IV on a bill that includes Neil Young. Following their performance of 'Suite: Judy Blue Eyes' he joins them for one song, 'This Old House', after which he plays 'Rockin' In The Free World' and 'Mother Earth (Natural Anthem)'. Despite the recent benefit reunions, it is clear that the CSN&Y dream is presently out of favour with Young. Although he avoids the temptation of saying he will never again record with them, he offers little hope for a future reunion. Looking back at the *American Dream* sessions, he is critical after the event. "It only lasted for a while," he muses. "Then it was over. We made a record, but I've gone so far, I've gone all over the place and they're still doing what they've always done. Coming back together wasn't as easy as I thought it would be."

APRIL

Twenty-four hours after Farm Aid IV, Young flies to London to participate in the Nelson Mandela International Tribute.

APRIL

450 photos from Nash's collection are auctioned at Sotheby's, New York, raising $2.38 million, the highest amount ever paid for a single owner collection. Part of the proceeds are donated to the LA County Museum of Art. This same day, Nash opens an exhibition of his own photographs at the Simon Lowinsky Gallery on Broadway, New York.

20 MAY

CS&N are featured on the television broadcast *Earth '90: Children And The Environment*, alongside Lisa Lisa And Cult Jam and Melba Moore.

26 MAY

Crosby attends Bernie Taupin's 40th birthday party at the Roxbury Restaurant, Beverly Hills.

11 JUNE

CS&N hit an unexpected nadir with the release of *Live It Up*, the first bad record they have made as a trio. Tasteless artwork, ill-advised covers and an unnerving lack of direction all contribute to the poorly conceived package. With Stills having only recently suppressed his hedonism sufficiently to be allowed back into the camp, the work betrays a lack of team effort. As Nash admitted: "It started out as a Crosby/Nash record and David and I cut nine things. Then we decided that we would wait for Stephen to see if he could add three to four things of his own and we could turn it into a CS&N record."

JUNE - SEPTEMBER

CS&N undertake an extensive tour of the USA and Canada accompanied by Kim Bullard (keyboards), Michael Finnigan (B-3 organ), Michito Sanchez (percussion), Jorge Calderon (bass) and Joe Vitale (drums). The scheduled cities covered include Richmond, VA (June 12); Knoxville, TN (14); Nashville, TN (15); Charlotte, NC (16); Norfolk, VA (18); Wilmington, NC (19); Atlanta, GA (22); Huntsville, AL (23); Louisville, KY (24); Bonner Springs, KS (26); Milwaukee, WI (28); Ames, IA (30).

During July they visit Pittsburgh, PA (8); East Rutherford, NJ (10); Bristol, CT (11); Wantagh, NY (13/14); Buffalo, NY (16); Mansfield, MA (17); Old Orchard Beach, ME (21); Binghamton, NY (25); Richfield, OH (26); Clarkston, MI (28); Toronto, ON (30), and in August the tour stops off at Columbia, MD (10/11); Toledo, OH (13); Cincinnati, OH (15); Columbus, OH (16); Deer Creek, IN (17); Peoria, IL (19); Tinley Park, IL (20); St Louis, MO (21); Cedar Rapids, IA (23); St Paul, MN (24); Omaha, NE (25); Sioux City, IA (27); Red Rocks, Denver, CO (28); Park City, UT (29).

September dates include Saskatoon, SK (1); Edmonton, AB (2); Calgary, AB (3); Kelowne, BC (5); Vancouver, BC (7); George, WA (8); Salam, OR (9); Reno, NV (11); Concord, CA (12); MountainView, CA (14); Sacramento, CA (15); Laguna Hills, CA (16); Tempe, AZ (18), Griffith Park, Los Angeles, CA (21), San Diego, CA (27).

The show at the Concord Pavilion features Nash's still unreleased 'Song For Barbara'.

Overall, the tour is notable for CS&N's belated incorporation of modern stage settings with a backdrop depicting various motifs such as stained glass windows, ship portholes and a New York skyline. The set list below emphasises their inclusion of material from *Live It Up*, but its aesthetic shortcomings backfire on them in reviews, with one noting: "Like The Beach Boys and far too many other performers that the VH-1 generation clings to, CS&N has become an institution, resistant to change or risk. And network slogans or no, as their frighteningly vital pal Young continually demonstrates in his work, just because we may have been alive in the legendary Sixties, we haven't yet seen it all by a long shot." It might have been a different story had they had a stronger album to promote.

SAMPLE SET LIST (GREAT WOODS PERFORMING ARTS CENTER, MANSFIELD, MA, JULY 17): LOVE THE ONE YOU'RE WITH; CHANGE PARTNERS; DRIVE MY CAR; CHICAGO; GOT IT MADE; IF ANYBODY HAD A HEART; JUST A SONG BEFORE I GO; TOMBOY; LIVE IT UP; FOR WHAT IT'S WORTH; WASTED ON THE WAY; TRY TO FIND ME; OUR HOUSE; GUINNEVERE; MY COUNTRY 'TIS OF THEE; HELPLESSLY HOPING; 4+20; MIDNIGHT RIDER; DÉJÀ VU; DAYLIGHT AGAIN/FIND THE COST OF FREEDOM; NIGHTTIME FOR THE GENERALS; YOURS AND MINE; CATHEDRAL; (GOT TO KEEP) OPEN; WOODSTOCK; THE LEE SHORE; CRITICAL MASS/WIND ON THE WATER; WOODEN SHIPS; SOUTHERN CROSS; TEACH YOUR CHILDREN.

AUGUST

Emmylou Harris' *Duets* includes Young guesting on his composition 'Star Of Bethlehem'.

YOUNG IN THE MOVIE 'LOVE AT LARGE'

> "It only lasted for a while. Then it was over. We made a record, but I've gone so far, I've gone all over the place and they're still doing what they've always done. Coming back together wasn't as easy as I thought it would be."
>
> NEIL YOUNG, 1990

DAVID AND JAN CROSBY AT THE
HARLEY DAVIDSON LOVE RIDE 7

6–8 AUGUST

Crosby teams up with McGuinn and Hillman
again, this time to add some songs to the
forthcoming Byrds boxed set. At Treasure Isle
Recorders, Nashville, they complete 'He Was A
Friend Of Mine', 'Paths Of Victory', 'From A
Distance' and 'Love That Never Dies'.

10 SEPTEMBER

Dan Fogelberg's *The Wild Places* is released,
with Crosby guesting on 'Song Of The Sea'.

17 SEPTEMBER

Bob Dylan's *Under A Red Sky* is released, with
Crosby providing backing vocals on 'Born In
Time' and '2X2'. This same day, Young releases
Ragged Glory, his acclaimed reunion with
Crazy Horse.

30 SEPTEMBER

CS&N are featured on MTV's *Unplugged*.
Although their set is impressive, the televised
version inappropriately contains nothing but
Stills songs, with a running order of 'Helplessly
Hoping', '4+20', 'Daylight Again'/'Find The Cost
Of Freedom' and 'Suite: Judy Blue Eyes'.

During this same period, their video *Long
Time Comin'* is issued. This 60-minute
retrospection includes the previously unissued
'Marrakesh Express' from *Woodstock*; the
appearance with Joni Mitchell on *The Dick
Cavett Show* in which Stills plays '4+20';
various Byrds, Hollies and Buffalo Springfield
television footage and 'You Don't Have To Cry'
from *The Tom Jones Show*. Alas, the highly
memorable clip of Jones singing 'Long Time
Gone' is not featured.

2 OCTOBER

CS&N appear on the *Arsenio Hall Show*
playing 'Woodstock' and '(Got To Keep) Open'.
Their host regales them with such familiar topics
as "What was Woodstock like?" and "Where's
Neil?", then tops it all by asking, without apparent
irony, why *Live It Up* sounds so modern.

12 OCTOBER

Nash begins hosting *The Inside Track*, a talk
and music show on the Arts and Entertainment
Network. His first guest is Crosby, who

discusses drug addiction, gun abuse and
prison, aided by fellow recovering addict Drew
Barrymore. Crosby plays 'Oh Yes I Can' and
'Tracks In The Dust' before Nash joins him on
'Critical Mass/Wind On The Water'. Speaking
of his new role as a television presenter, Nash
remarks, "It's not much different from the role I
play with the band… What I enjoy about it is the
forum it gives to artistes to be able to speak in
greater depth about issues that are close to
their hearts, rather than just have the five
minutes before they get on the tour bus."

19 OCTOBER

The second show of *The Inside Track* features
Nash interviewing Stills and Judy Collins. The
writer and subject of 'Suite: Judy Blue Eyes' perform together for the first time in over 20 years.

Around this same period, Nash guests on
Terrell's *On The Wings Of Dirty Angels*, adding
vocals to 'Bitter'.

23 OCTOBER

Stills appears at a benefit for Senator John
Kerry at the Wang Center for Performing Arts,
Boston. Appearances are also made by Peter,
Paul And Mary and Robin Williams.

26 OCTOBER

The fourth Bridge Benefit brings together
Young, Jackson Browne, Elvis Costello and
Edie Brickell, but no Crosby, Stills or Nash.

13 NOVEMBER

Young's traditional tour warm-up gig with
Crazy Horse takes place at The Catalyst,
Santa Cruz.

17 NOVEMBER

While riding his Harley Davidson along White
Oak Avenue in the Encino hills, Crosby loses
control of the bike and is dragged sideways
across a pavement for over 40 feet. He breaks
his left leg, ankle and shoulder and is
hospitalised at Cedars Sinai Medical Center.
Crosby insists that he was riding within the
25mph speed limit and blames the accident on
a "stuck throttle" as he sped around a curve.

21 NOVEMBER

Nash appears at the Club Quatro, Tokyo,
having previously played in Japan at the
Hiroshima Anniversary in the summer of 1986.
As the set list below reveals, he gives the
audience a pleasing and varied selection of his
most famous songs.

SET LIST: WIND ON THE WATER; JUST A SONG
BEFORE I GO; DON'T SAY GOODBYE; MARRAKESH
EXPRESS; SIMPLE MAN; LADY OF THE ISLAND;
WASTED ON THE WAY; AMERICA; COWBOY OF
DREAMS; HOUSE OF BROKEN DREAMS; I USED TO BE
A KING; MILITARY MADNESS; CATHEDRAL; OUR
HOUSE; TEACH YOUR CHILDREN.

31 DECEMBER

Crosby reactivates the publishing of his first
known composition, 'Cross The Plains', which
was originally published on 27 December 1962.
At the time of writing the song has never been
mentioned in print before and the chances of
its release seem remote.

MCGUINN, CROSBY & HILLMAN TEAM UP TO ADD
TRACKS TO THE BYRDS' BOX SET

1991

4 JANUARY

Roger McGuinn's *Back To Rio* is released with Crosby appearing on 'Suddenly Blue', 'Without Your Love' and 'Back From Rio Interlude'.

6 JANUARY

At the Waldorf Hotel, New York, The Byrds are inducted into Rock 'n' Roll Hall Of Fame. Crosby, still recovering from his recent motorcycle accident, pays tribute to his colleagues. "I feel a lot of gratitude," he acknowledges. "I have a lot of gratitude to these men who made it possible for me to make some of the best music of my life... and I am incredibly grateful after all the chances I've taken and all the trouble I've been through to be here tonight to do this, and still be able to play music. I thank you all." With the speeches completed, The Byrds re-group on stage for the first time since 1966 to perform 'Turn! Turn! Turn!', 'Mr Tambourine Man' and 'Feel A Whole Lot Better'. This will be the last ever performance by the original Byrds.

FEBRUARY

The Ragged Glory Tour commences in Minneapolis, with adventurous support from Sonic Youth and Social Distortion. The itinerary proves one of Young's most exhausting to date, criss-crossing America for three months.

SAMPLE SET LIST (EISENHOWER HALL THEATER, WEST POINT MILITARY ACADEMY, NY, FEBRUARY 23): HEY HEY. MY MY (INTO THE BLACK); CRIME IN THE CITY (SIXTY TO ZERO PART 1); BLOWIN' IN THE WIND; LOVE TO BURN; CINNAMON GIRL; MANSION ON THE HILL; F*!#KIN' UP; CORTEZ THE KILLER; POWDERFINGER; LOVE AND ONLY LOVE; ROCKIN' IN THE FREE WORLD; FARMER JOHN; LIKE A HURRICANE.

MARCH

Crosby & Nash appear at the Raymond Theater, Pasadena, where they are joined by Jackson Browne and David Lindley. During the same period, Crosby is featured playing a hippie in the movie *Backdraft* and Nash contributes vocals to 'Marianne' on the Modern Folk Quartet's *Wolfgang*.

APRIL

An exhibit of Graham Nash's artwork is on display at the G. Ray Hawkins Gallery, Santa Monica.

MARCH–APRIL

CS&N undertake a tour of Australia and Japan, appearing at the Concert Hall, Brisbane (March 30/31); Concert Hall, Melbourne (April 2–4); State Theatre, Sydney (6/7, 9/10); Festival Theatre, Adelaide (11), Concert Hall, Perth (13). These are followed by appearances at the Nagoyashi Kokaido Hall, Nagoya (20); NHK Hall, Tokyo (22 & 25); Koseinenkin Hall, Osaka (23); and Kanagawa Kemnin Hall, Yokohama (24). The Japanese tour brings back memories for Crosby/Nash who toured there during December 1975. Playing an enticing acoustic-

dominated set, the trio breathe life into their old repertoire and sound as though they have discovered fresh meaning in their songs. They have seldom performed better than this.

SET LIST: (APRIL 23): WASTED ON THE WAY; MILITARY MADNESS; BLACKBIRD; THE LEE SHORE; YOU DON'T HAVE TO CRY; JUST A SONG BEFORE I GO; HELPLESSLY HOPING; MARRAKESH EXPRESS; LONG TIME GONE; CRITICAL MASS/WIND ON THE WATER; BETTER DAYS; COLD RAIN; DELTA; ALMOST CUT MY HAIR; GUINNEVERE; LOVE THE ONE YOU'RE WITH; FOR WHAT IT'S WORTH; SOUTHERN CROSS; WOODEN SHIPS; OUR HOUSE; SUITE: JUDY BLUE EYES; TEACH YOUR CHILDREN.

MAY – JUNE

CS&N return home for a US tour, including appearances at Lakewood Amphitheater, Atlanta, GA (May 3); Ruth E. Hall, Clearwater, FL (4); two shows at the Sunfest, West Palm Beach, FL (5); Bally's Casino, Atlantic City, NJ

THE BYRDS, JANUARY 1991

(16/17); Victoria, Canada (June 2); Arlene Schnitzer Concert Hall, Portland, OR (3); Seattle Opera House, Seattle, WA (4); John F. Carlson Community Center, Fairbanks, Alaska (7); Santa Cruz, CA (24); Saratoga, CA (25/26). During the tour, Stills premières the still unreleased and provisionally titled, 'As Much As I Understand'.

SAMPLE SET LIST (MAY 3): WASTED ON THE WAY; MILITARY MADNESS; BLACKBIRD; THE LEE SHORE; YOU DON'T HAVE TO CRY; JUST A SONG BEFORE I GO; HELPLESSLY HOPING; MARRAKESH EXPRESS; LONG TIME GONE; CRITICAL MASS/WIND ON THE WATER; HOUSE OF BROKEN DREAMS; COLD RAIN; THOUSAND ROADS; DELTA; GUINNEVERE; LOVE THE ONE YOU'RE WITH; AS MUCH AS I UNDERSTAND; 4+20; FOR WHAT IT'S WORTH; SOUTHERN CROSS; WOODEN SHIPS; OUR HOUSE; SUITE: JUDY BLUE EYES; TEACH YOUR CHILDREN.

18 MAY

Crosby & Nash play the Westbury Music Fair, New York, where they are joined on-stage by Art Garfunkel, who had previously provided the harmony vocals on 'Daylight Again'.

7 JUNE

Nash copyrights the recently composed 'The Shell', which has still not been released.

He also adds 'These Empty Days' (co-written with Crosby).

5 JULY

Stills copyright registers 'Just Isn't Like You', 'The Right Girl' and 'Amazonia' for his forthcoming album.

15 AUGUST

Nash and Joe Vitale copyright their latest composition, the still unreleased 'Flying Fast'.

26 AUGUST

Stills releases *Stills Alone* on his own label, but the work lacks direction, mixing covers with ill-advised reworkings of songs from 20 years before. Although it's great to hear Stills playing acoustic, this skeletal album requires more striking new material to do itself full justice.

As Stills casually notes: "I was bored. I'd just finished a tour, and my voice was in good shape, my chops were up and I just said, 'I've got to get something on tape here, or else I'm going to go nuts!' So I went into the studio and sang for a week... and then I said, 'Let's put this out and see what happens!'"

16 SEPTEMBER

Crosby copyright registers 'Thousand Roads' which will be the title track of his next solo album.

OCTOBER

CS&N issue their long-awaited Boxed Set, *CSN*, a sterling collection of 77 tracks, including five previously unissued titles and a wealth of alternate takes, demos and different mixes. Nash had hoped to include the 1974 version of Young's 'Pushed It Over The End' but failed to secure clearance from the Canadian's lawyers. Young appears on 19 of the tracks, which feature poignant reminders of the various near reunions over the years. The closing shot of the *Human Highway* sleeve is a fitting epitaph to all that had been lost amid this treasure trove of music.

7 OCTOBER
Robbie Robertson's *The Story Of Storyville* features Young on 'Soap Box Preacher'.

27 OCTOBER
Young releases the sonic-booming *Weld*, a souvenir of his recent "Smell The Horse" tour which, disappointingly for such a prolific performer of unreleased compositions, features nothing new, except his cover of Dylan's 'Blowin' In The Wind'. The accompanying extra CD *Arc* offers 35 minutes of sonic experimentation which Young dubs "new age metal".

2 NOVEMBER
The Fifth Bridge Benefit features Young, but there is no sign of CS&N. Instead, Young's new friends Sonic Youth appear, but rapidly abandon their acoustic set due to sound problems and barracking from the audience.

3 NOVEMBER
The Bill Graham Tribute Concert at San Francisco's Golden Gate Park features an on-stage reunion of CSN&Y before 300,000 people. They perform 'Teach Your Children', 'Love The One You're With', 'Long May You Run', 'Long Time Gone', 'Southern Cross', 'Only Love Can Break Your Heart', 'Wooden Ships' and 'Ohio'. Young also provides his own tribute to the promoter, stating: "Bill Graham made us all look good. He gave us a chance to show you that we could do something beyond our own careers. He kept pushing us to do things for other people and making a place for us to do it, so there was no way out."

NOVEMBER
CS&N are briefly back on the road playing the Warfield Theater, San Francisco, CA (November 10) and the Shippensburg, Heiges Fieldhouse, PA (16). Four days later, they appear on *The David Letterman Show* singing 'As I Come Of Age'. Part of the Warfield Theater show was later used for the video *The Acoustic Concert*. As the set list below reveals, this concert also features a still unreleased Nash song, 'Sailor', dedicated to Crosby.

SET LIST (NOVEMBER 10): WASTED ON THE WAY; MILITARY MADNESS; BLACKBIRD; THE LEE SHORE; TAKEN AT ALL; AS I COME OF AGE; DÉJÀ VU; HELPLESSLY HOPING; AMAZONIA; MARRAKESH EXPRESS; LONG TIME GONE; CRITICAL MASS/WIND ON THE WATER; MAGICAL CHILD; SAILOR; THOUSAND ROADS; GUINNEVERE; LOVE THE ONE YOU'RE WITH; SOUTHERN CROSS; WOODEN SHIPS; SUITE: JUDY BLUE EYES; TEACH YOUR CHILDREN.

25 NOVEMBER
Graham and Susan Nash donate 280 *camera lucida* drawings by Sir John F.W. Herschel to the J. Paul Getty Museum in Los Angeles.

1992

JANUARY
The various artistes compilation *Nintendo – White Knuckle Scorin'* includes CS&N's cover of John Sebastian's 'How Have You Been?', a song they first recorded during the *Déjà Vu* sessions.

15 JANUARY
Young inducts Jimi Hendrix into the Rock 'n' Roll Hall of Fame. The following night he jams with Keith Richard, Jimmy Page, Johnny Cash and U2's The Edge at New York's Lone Star Roadhouse.

21 JANUARY
Young reopens his acoustic tour in Seattle, after which he plays sporadic gigs across the USA over the next five months, including Portland, OR (January 23); Spokane, WN (25); New York City, NY (February 13–15/17–19); Fort Worth, TX (March 14); Boston, MA (18–20); Philadelphia, PA (22–24); Detroit, MI; Walden Woods, LA, CA (April 1); Cleveland, OH (May 17–18); Detroit, MI (20–22); Lenox, MA (June 23); Holmdel, NJ (25); Columbia, MD (26); Pittsburgh, PA (28); Saratoga Springs, NY (29). Only one new song is premièred during this period: 'Hitchhiker'.

SAMPLE SET LIST (OPERA HOUSE, SPOKANE, WA, JANUARY 25): LONG MAY YOU RUN: FROM HANK TO HENDRIX; SILVER & GOLD; UNKNOWN LEGEND; YOU AND ME; WAR OF MAN; OLD KING; SUCH A WOMAN; HARVEST MOON; HEART OF GOLD; DREAMIN' MAN; NATURAL BEAUTY; DON'T LET IT BRING YOU DOWN; SUGAR MOUNTAIN; AFTER THE GOLDRUSH; OLD MAN.

25 JANUARY
Crosby & Nash appear at the DAR Constitution Hall, DC.

FEBRUARY
Bachman's *Any Road* is released, with Young guesting on 'Prairie Town'.

14 FEBRUARY
Crosby hosts ABC's *In Concert*, on which his special guest is Phil Collins. By this point, Crosby is reviving his youthful acting career with cameo appearances in the movies *Thunderheart*, *Hook* and the television series *Roseanne*. In the latter he performs 'Thousand Roads' with Bonnie Bramlett.

6 MARCH
CS&N's *The Acoustic Concert*, taken from the Warfield Theater, San Francisco (November 1991), is broadcast on American television. It includes Nash's otherwise unissued 'Try To Find Me'.

MARCH – APRIL
CS&N undertake a short European tour, including appearances in London (March 28–29), Paris (31), Milan (April 2) and Rome (?). Their predominantly acoustic set is stronger than ever and elicits some excellent reviews.

CROSBY AT THE BILL GRAHAM TRIBUTE

Writing of their London performance at the Hammersmith Odeon, *Melody Maker*'s Steve Sutherland enthuses: "Overdue, overweight and over here for the first time in 20 years, CS&N's whistle-stop return to these shores turned out to be a most unexpectedly triumphant occasion... More majestic than we had any right to expect, CS&N were simply marvellous."

His comments are reiterated by the very same critic who had mercilessly savaged Crosby's Venue shows back in 1980. Now, Robin Denselow of *The Guardian* can only marvel: "Well, who'd have thought it? A trio of old hippies breeze into town to promote their four-CD retrospective, and turn in an epic three hour set that was joyous, immaculate, rousing and adventurous."

In The Band', 'I Like To Live On The Bayou', 'Married Man', 'In The Backroom', 'Goin' Down To Louisiana' and 'Future Song'.

The Indigo Girls' *Rites Of Passage* features Crosby as guest vocalist on 'Galileo' and 'Let It Be Me'; and Stills can be heard singing 'Change Partners' on *Partners*, an album by accordion player, Flaco Jimenez.

JUNE – AUGUST

CS&N take their acoustic tour across America appearing at the Wolftrap, Vienna, VA (June 1–2); Classic Amphitheater, Richmond, VA (3); Mann Music Center, Philadelphia, PA (5/6); Performing Arts Center, Saratoga Springs, NY (7); Garden State Arts Center, Holmdel, NJ (9); Meadowlands Amphitheater, East Rutherford, NJ (10); Jones Beach Music Center, Wantagh,

(29); Shoreline Amphitheater, Mountain View, CA (31).

August dates include Cal Expo, Sacramento, CA (1); County Bowl, Santa Barbara, CA (2); Universal Amphitheater, LA, CA (4/5); Pacific Amphitheater, Costa Mesa, CA (7); Desert Sky, Phoenix, AZ (9); Starplex, Dallas, TX (15); Woodlands, Houston, TX (16); Sunken Garden Amphitheater, San Antonio, TX (18); Brady Theater, Tulsa, OK (19); Mud Island Amphitheater, Memphis, TN (21); Oak Mountain Amphitheater, Birmingham, AL (22); Starwood Amphitheater, Nashville, TN (23); Ocean Center, Daytona Beach, FL (25); Sunrise Musical Theater, Fort Lauderdale, FL (26).

Playing acoustic has tightened up CS&N musically over the past year, as Crosby reflects: "There's no rhythm section – just us. When it's

SAMPLE SET LIST (MARCH 28): DÉJÀ VU; MILITARY MADNESS; THE LEE SHORE; HELPLESSLY HOPING; BLACKBIRD; TAKEN AT ALL; JUST A SONG BEFORE I GO; MARRAKESH EXPRESS; LONG TIME GONE; SUITE: JUDY BLUE EYES; CRITICAL MASS/WIND ON THE WATER; TRY TO FIND ME; HOUSE OF BROKEN DREAMS; THOUSAND ROADS; ALMOST CUT MY HAIR; GUINNEVERE; LOVE THE ONE YOU'RE WITH; FOR WHAT IT'S WORTH; SOUTHERN CROSS; WOODEN SHIPS; OUR HOUSE; DAYLIGHT AGAIN/FIND THE COST OF FREEDOM; TEACH YOUR CHILDREN.

APRIL

Crosby copyright registers 'Yvette In English' (co-written with Joni Mitchell). As he explains: "I showed Joni the set of lyrics I had written; she liked it and went with it. She changed the lyrics and then wrote a melody. I changed the melody a little bit and we wound up with a song."

\AY

Rusty Kershaw's *Now And Then* is issued, with Young appearing on 'New Orleans Rag', 'Boys

NY (12/13); Mt Mansfield Performing Arts Center, Stowe, VT (14); Harvey's Lake Amphitheater, Wilkes Barre, PA (16); Star Lake Amphitheater, Pittsburgh, PA (17); Great Woods Music Center, Mansfield, MA (19/20); Tanglewood Music Center, Lenox, MA (21); Volvo Tennis Park, New Haven, CT (23); Finger Lakes, Rochester, NY (24); Meadowbrook Music Festival, Rochester, MI (26/27); Summerfest, Milwaukee, WI (28); Riverband, Cincinnati, OH (30)

During July they visit Blossom Music Center, Cleveland, OH (1); Blockbuster, Charlotte, NC (3); Walnut Creek Amphitheater, Raleigh, NC (4); Lakewood Amphitheater, Atlanta, GA (5); Riverport Amphitheater, St Louis, MO (18); Starlight Amphitheater, Kansas City, KS (19); Red Rocks Amphitheater, Denver, CO (22); Park West, Salt Lake City, UT (23); Champs de Brionne/Sumer Music Theater, George, Washington, DC (25); LB Day Amphitheater, Salem, OR (26); Selland Arena, Fresno, CA (28); Concord Pavilion, CA

just the three of us on-stage, we really have to put it out. As a result, Stephen's been playing the best guitar ever. You hate to tell him that, but it's true."

Among the highlights is an acoustic version of 'It Won't Go Away', the surprise harmonica accompaniment on 'Guinnevere' and Crosby's extraordinary new composition, provisionally titled 'The Fisher King Song'. Like 'I'd Swear There Was Somebody Here', it deals with the aftermath of Christine Hinton's death. "When I was watching the movie (*The Fisher King*) I realised that I'd never dealt with it," Crosby admits. "I'd never accepted that she'd died and it kind of overpowered me."

SAMPLE SET LIST (JUNE 23): WASTED ON THE WAY; HELPLESSLY HOPING; THE LEE SHORE; MILITARY MADNESS; AMAZONIA; IN MY DREAMS; MARRAKESH EXPRESS; IN MY LIFE; DÉJÀ VU; TAKEN AT ALL; LONG TIME GONE; CRITICAL MASS/WIND ON THE WATER; SOUTHERN CROSS; TRY TO FIND ME; CATHEDRAL; THE FISHER KING SONG (SOMEHOW SHE KNEW); GUINNEVERE; IT WON'T GO AWAY; FOR WHAT IT'S WORTH; SUITE: JUDY BLUE EYES; WOODEN SHIPS; TEACH YOUR CHILDREN.

JULY

Atlantic reissue CSN&Y's *Four Way Street* on CD with the extra tracks 'King Midas In Reverse', 'Laughing', 'Black Queen' and the medley: 'The Loner/Cinnamon Girl/Down By The River'.

This same month, Nils Lofgren's *Crooked Line* is released, with Young guesting on 'Someday' and 'Drunken Driver'. Crosby & Nash are also in action, appearing on the Various Artistes' album *Barcelona Gold*, where they can be heard harmonising with Marc Cohn on 'Old Soldier'.

30 JULY

Crosby & Nash are enlisted to add backing vocals to Young's 'Silver & Gold', which remains unissued at the time of writing.

4 AUGUST

Stills copyrights 'It Won't Go Away', which will be held over until the next CS&N album in 1994. During this same period, Stills' 'Livin' On Rock 'n' Roll' (co-written with Dallas Taylor and Thomas Jefferson Kaye) appears on the latter's *Not Alone*.

11 SEPTEMBER

The Young acoustic season reopens in Dayton, Ohio and he will play numerous dates across America for the remainder of the year, including Deer Creek, IN (September 12); St Louis, MI (13); Denver, CO (15); Park City, UT (16); Salem, OR (18); George, Washington, DC (19); Los Angeles, CA (21/22); San Diego, CA (23); Costa Mesa, CA (25); Las Vegas, NV (26); Phoenix, AZ (27); Milwaukee, WI (14/15 November); Chicago, IL (18/19); Minneapolis, MN (21).

SAMPLE SET LIST (SUMMER POPS BOWL, EMBARCADERO MARINA PARK, SAN DIEGO, CA, SEPTEMBER 23): LONG MAY YOU RUN: COMES A TIME: EVERYBODY KNOWS THIS IS NOWHERE: FROM HANK TO HENDRIX: YOU AND ME: OLD MAN: LIKE A HURRICANE: HOMEGROWN: ROLL ANOTHER NUMBER: THE NEEDLE AND THE DAMAGE DONE: TONIGHT'S THE NIGHT: POCAHONTAS: HEART OF GOLD: SUCH A WOMAN: HARVEST MOON: POWDERFINGER: DON'T LET IT BRING YOU DOWN: SUGAR MOUNTAIN: MR SOUL: DREAMIN' MAN: NATURAL BEAUTY: AFTER THE GOLDRUSH.

OCTOBER

CS&N return to Europe for another short tour, playing The Point, Dublin (October 3), Apollo, Manchester (4), Playhouse, Edinburgh (6), Royal Albert Hall (8), Music Hall, Hamburg (9), Alte Oper, Frankfurt (10), Muzikcentrum Viadenburg, Utrecht, Holland (12), Philipshalle, Dusseldorf (13), Falkoner, Copenhagen (14). Dylan's 'Every Grain Of Sand' is a surprise addition to the set, along with Nash's startling 'Liar's Nightmare'. During the Manchester show, Nash reveals that he has not played at the Apollo since performing with Allan Clarke as a duo back in 1959. At the Royal Albert Hall, Crosby nostalgically recalls that when they were there in January 1970, he smoked dope with Donovan on the roof of the building.

SAMPLE SET LIST (OCTOBER 6): WASTED ON THE WAY: HELPLESSLY HOPING: THE LEE SHORE: MILITARY MADNESS: IN MY DREAMS: MARRAKESH EXPRESS: IN MY LIFE: DÉJÀ VU: TAKEN AT ALL: LONG TIME GONE: SOUTHERN CROSS: CRITICAL MASS/WIND ON THE WATER: AFTER THE STORM: LIAR'S NIGHTMARE: THE FISHER KING SONG (SOMEHOW SHE KNEW): ALMOST CUT MY HAIR: IT WON'T GO AWAY: FOR WHAT IT'S WORTH: OUR HOUSE: SUITE: JUDY BLUE EYES: WOODEN SHIPS: TEACH YOUR CHILDREN.

16 OCTOBER

Young appears at Bob Dylan's 30th anniversary concert in Madison Square Garden, performing rough versions of 'Just Like Tom Thumb's Blues' and 'All Along The Watchtower'.

2 NOVEMBER

Young releases *Harvest Moon*, a return to homespun acoustic music after the recent sonic experiments and hard rocking with Crazy Horse.

6 NOVEMBER

Nash copyrights the recently composed 'Liar's Nightmare', one of the best songs he has written in years. Inspired by images he saw while under anaesthetic, the song has a distinct mid-Sixties' Dylan feel. Amazingly, the composition fails to appear on the next batch of CSN-related releases.

ROYAL ALBERT HALL

ARENA A
DOOR   2   ASGARD PRESENTS
ROW   8   AN ACOUSTIC EVENING WITH
SEAT   11   CROSBY STILLS & NASH
140792   THURSDAY   OCT. 08/92 AT 8:00 PM
PRICE   EVENING
19.50   DOORS OPEN 45 MINUTES BEFORE PERFORMAN
6-
22-480308   CA
SEE REVERSE FOR CONDITIONS OF SALE

1993

4 JANUARY

Young's *Lucky Thirteen* compilation of the Geffen years is issued, featuring four previously unavailable songs.

? JANUARY

Crosby performs at a benefit concert at the Lobero Theater, Santa Barbara for former 3rd District Supervisor Bill Wallace, who has just lost the local election by an agonising five votes. Assisted by Craig Doerge and Dean Parks, David plays a varied set, including 'Samurai', 'Old Soldier', 'Naked In The Rain' and 'Yvette In English'.

FEBRUARY

Young records a contribution to MTV's *Unplugged*, which will subsequently be issued as an album.

MARCH

Young performs alongside Simon & Garfunkel for the Children's Health Fund at the Dorothy Chandler Pavilion, LA.

APRIL

Both Crosby and Young appear at the Park By The River, Portland, Oregon for a concert in aid of Old Growth Forests. Meanwhile, Crosby makes a surprise appearance alongside George Harrison as a cartoon character in *The Simpsons*. He is also a guest on a Turner Broadcasting Company programme on the history of Harley Davidson motorbikes.

? APRIL

Crosby releases *Thousand Roads*, a predominantly covers album most notable for his collaboration with Joni Mitchell, 'Yvette In English'.

? APRIL

Farm Aid VI reveals Young's new found grunge credibility with the addition of The Jayhawks and Alice In Chains.

? AY

Marc Cohn's *The Rainy Season* is released, with Crosby & Nash as guest vocalists on 'From The Station' and 'She's Becoming Gold'. This same month, Crosby appears on Willie Nelson's *Across The Borderline*, singing on 'If I Were The Man You Wanted'.

MAY

Crosby plays a solo date at the Great American Music Hall, San Francisco. With sparse backing from guitarist Jeff Pavar, he plays a selection of songs from down the years but virtually ignores material from his recent album, *Thousand Roads*. The highlight of the evening is 'The Fisher King Song', a true account of Crosby's emotional breakdown after suffering a flashback of Christine Hinton's death. Other surprises in this set include 'Dancer'

(dedicated to his wife Jan Dance), the funky 'Motherless Children' and a cover of Albert King's 'Born Under A Bad Sign'. Towards the end of the evening, Crosby invites Nash on-stage for 'In My Dreams', 'Déjà Vu', 'Long Time Gone' and 'Wooden Ships' before returning solo for a finale of 'Almost Cut My Hair'.

JUNE

Young releases *Unplugged*, an album of his MTV appearance.

26 JUNE – 23 JULY

Having played a handful of warm-up gigs in California early in the month, Young embarks on a European festival tour backed by Booker T

& The MGs. The itinerary covers Germany, Sweden, Finland, Denmark, Belgium, Holland, France, Spain, Eire, England, Scotland, Italy and Switzerland. Unreleased Young songs premièred include 'Live To Ride' and 'Separate Ways'.

SAMPLE SET LIST (FORUM ASSAGO, MILAN, ITALY, JULY 15): MR SOUL; THE LONER; SOUTHERN MAN; HELPLESS; LIKE A HURRICANE; MOTORCYCLE MAMA; LOVE TO BURN; SEPARATE WAYS; CHANGE YOUR MIND; POWDERFINGER; ONLY LOVE CAN BREAK YOUR HEART; HARVEST MOON; THE NEEDLE AND THE DAMAGE DONE; LIVE TO RIDE; DOWN BY THE RIVER; ROCKIN' IN THE FREE WORLD; ALL ALONG THE WATCHTOWER.

27 JUNE

Crosby shares a bill with Chris Hillman's Desert Rose Band at an environmental benefit show at the Ventura Theater, California. David opens with 'Where Will I Be?'/'Page 43', followed by 'Tracks In The Dust' and 'The Fisher King Song' (aka 'Somehow She Knew').

He then invites guitarist Bernie Leadon on stage for 'Drop Down Mama' and a sparse 'Thousand Roads', after which Hillman emerges to duet on 'For Free' and 'Mr Tambourine Man'. With Kenny Loggins adding vocal weight to 'Long Time Gone', Crosby underlines his continuing strength as a soloist.

SET LIST: WHERE WILL I BE?/PAGE 43: TRACKS IN THE DUST: SOMEHOW SHE KNEW (THE FISHER KING SONG): DROP DOWN MAMA: THOUSAND ROADS: FOR FREE: MR TAMBOURINE MAN: LONG TIME GONE.

JULY

The Hollies' *30th Anniversary Collection* features Nash's 'Like Every Time Before' (previously only issued in Germany in 1968), plus his co-written 'She Gives Me Everything I Want', 'I Can't Get Nowhere With You' and 'Kill Me Quick' (previously only available in Italy)

1 JULY

David Crosby (Stay Straight Music) assigns his copyrights to Warner Tamerlane Publishing Corporation.

AUGUST

Jimmy Webb's *Suspended Disbelief* features Crosby as guest vocalist on 'Too Young To Die'. David also covered the song on his last solo album.

AUGUST – SEPTEMBER

Rather than their usual summer get together, CS&N split into two factions, with Stills and Crosby & Nash touring separately. Stills supports Chicago on a nationwide tour, playing a short set which usually features 'Love The One You're With', 'Change Partners',

'Amazonia', 'It Won't Go Away', Albert King's 'Born Under A Bad Sign', 'Dark Star' and 'Woodstock'.

Meanwhile, Crosby & Nash attempt to prove that they are not bound by a strict set list by offering audiences the opportunity to request any song they wish. Eager patrons are encouraged to raise their hands and request their favourite song. In what is undoubtedly their most spontaneous approach in aeons, the duo (backed by guitarist Jeff Pavar) rekindle some of the spirit that characterised their golden era back in 1971. Among the dates played are the Poplar Creek Music Theater, Hoffman Estates, IL (August 3); Merriweather Post Pavilion, DC (7); Westhampton China Club, NY (8); Syracuse, NY (14); South Music Circus, Cohasset, MA (17), Latham, NY (18), Red Rocks Amphitheater, Denver, CO. At the Denver date, they are backed by the Colorado Symphony Orchestra.

During September, the tour reaches a high point with a prestigious appearance at Carnegie Hall, NY (13), followed by dates in Jacksonville, FL (17); Orlando, FL (18); Sunrise, FL (19); Baltimore, MD (22). The set list below indicates a refreshing range of material, including the still unreleased 'Samurai', 'Liar's Nightmare' and 'Somehow She Knew (The Fisher King Song)'. There is the usual spread of material but, during the tour, they also feature memorable readings of 'Lady Of The Island', 'Marrakesh Express', 'Where Will I Be?', 'Page 43', 'Déjà Vu', 'Cold Rain', 'Cathedral' and 'Pre-Road Downs'.

SAMPLE SET LIST (SEPTEMBER 13): MILITARY MADNESS: WASTED ON THE WAY: THE LEE SHORE: JUST A SONG BEFORE I GO: DÉJÀ VU: TAKEN AT ALL: I USED TO BE A KING: MARRAKESH EXPRESS: LONG TIME GONE: CRITICAL MASS/WIND ON THE WATER: IN MY DREAMS: DELTA: AFTER THE STORM: LIAR'S NIGHTMARE: SAMURAI: SOMEHOW SHE KNEW (THE FISHER KING SONG): THOUSAND ROADS: GUINNEVERE: WOODEN SHIPS: OUR HOUSE: TEACH YOUR CHILDREN.

31 AUGUST

Young delivers a sound cassette for copyright purposes containing the still unissued 'Live To Ride'.

AUGUST - SEPTEMBER

Having played Europe, Young's latest tour with Booker T & The MG's traverses the USA and Canada. Among the areas played are Rapid City, SD (August 11); Milwaukee, WI (14); Chicago, IL (15); Detroit, MI (16); Toronto, ON (18); Wantagh, NY (20); Holmdel, NJ (22); Mansfield, MA (23); Pittsburgh, PA (26); Raleigh, NC (28); Atlanta, GA (29); Denver, CO (September 1); Vancouver, BC (4); George, Washington, DC (5); Portland, OR (6); Mountain View, CA (8); Costa Mesa, CA (9); Los Angeles, CA (11); San Diego, CA (12); Phoenix, AZ (14); Houston, TX (16); Austin, TX (17); Dallas, TX (18).

SAMPLE SET LIST (WALNUT CREEK AMPHITHEATER, RALEIGH, NC; AUGUST 28): MR SOUL: THE LONER: SOUTHERN MAN: HELPLESS: LIKE A HURRICANE: MOTORCYCLE MAMA: SEPARATE WAYS: LOVE TO BURN: ONLY LOVE CAN BREAK YOUR HEART: HARVEST MOON: UNKNOWN LEGEND: THE NEEDLE AND THE DAMAGE DONE: POWDERFINGER: LIVE TO RIDE: DOWN BY THE RIVER: DOCK OF THE BAY: ALL ALONG THE WATCHTOWER.

3 - 4 SEPTEMBER

Stills' tour continues with an appearance at the Coach House, San Juan Capistrano. Reflecting on CS&N and the current rock scene, he tells the *LA Times*: "Rock 'n' roll has become like Bosnia – eight different tribes that all hate each other."

OCTOBER

Crosby appears irregularly on *The John Laroquette Show*, appropriately playing an Alcoholics Anonymous counsellor. He also appears as guest vocalist on 'All Good Things' on Jackson Browne's newly released *I'm Alive*.

9 OCTOBER

Young again joins Bob Dylan, this time for an encore of 'Leopard Skin Pillbox Hat' at the Shoreline Amphitheater in Mountain View, California.

11 OCTOBER

Jack Tempchin And The Seclusion's *After The Rain* is released, with Crosby as guest vocalist.

6 NOVEMBER

At the seventh Bridge School Benefit, Young allows Simon & Garfunkel to headline. However, he still provides his audience with a few surprises, including a duet with Warren Zevon on 'Splendid Isolation' and a bizarre rendition of the standard 'Stranger In Paradise'.

24 NOVEMBER

A sound cassette of the collection 'Chain The Critics (Galileo's Sin)' is registered for copyright by Joseph Matthew Giegerich and Joseph Hand, with additional lyrics by Neil Young.

DECEMBER

Young appears with Pearl Jam on the MTV Awards performing 'Rockin' In The Free World'. This same month Crosby is recorded at the Whisky A Go Go for a live album that will be delayed until 1995. During his set, Crosby is joined on-stage by Graham Nash for 'Déjà Vu', 'Long Time Gone' and 'Wooden Ships' and by The Black Crowes' Chris Robinson for 'Almost Cut My Hair'. Two song are omitted from the album: 'Naked In The Rain' and 'Motherless Children'.

SET LIST: IN MY DREAMS: NAKED IN THE RAIN: RUSTY AND BLUE: HERO: TILL IT SHINES ON YOU: THOUSAND ROADS: COWBOY MOVIE: MOTHERLESS CHILDREN: ALMOST CUT MY HAIR: DÉJÀ VU: LONG TIME GONE: WOODEN SHIPS.

1994

24 JANUARY

Nash copyrights a batch of new songs: 'Penguin In The Palm Tree', 'I Can See The Dream', 'Love Lies Tonight (Somewhere, Somehow)', 'Watched It All Come Down', 'Magic', 'Game Of Hearts', 'Seas Like These', 'The Chelsea Hotel', 'Try To Find Me' (originally written in 1986), 'After The Storm' and 'These Empty Days'. The latter two will appear on the next CS&N album, but the other nine remain unissued at the time of writing.

27 JANUARY

Nash's 'Unequal Love' is recorded at Groove Masters, Santa Monica, CA. This is the first completed track from the forthcoming CS&N album *After The Storm*. James 'Hutch' Hutchinson (bass) and Ethan Johns (drums) will be used frequently on these sessions.

FEBRUARY

Rob Wasserman's *Trios* is released with Young guesting on 'Easy Answers'.

1 FEBRUARY

Crosby's 'Till It Shines' is recorded at Groove Masters, Santa Monica, CA. Michael Finnigan (Hammond B-3) replaces Benmont Tench from the previous week's session.

2 FEBRUARY

Nash's 'These Empty Days' (with additional music by Crosby) is recorded at Groove Masters, Santa Monica, CA. Stephen Stills' son Christopher plays piano on the track.

13 FEBRUARY

Crosby & Nash, plus Paul Kantner, Jorma Kaukonen, Jack Casady, Bob Weir, Phil Lesh, Arlo Guthrie and Country Joe McDonald are featured in "A Musical Reunion Of Old Friends", a benefit for Wavy Gravy's charitable SEVA Foundation, which takes place at the Masonic Auditorium, San Francisco. Among the songs featured are 'Déjà Vu', 'I Used To Be A King', 'Rusty And Blue', 'Cowboy Movie', 'Laughing', 'Box Of Rain' (Grateful Dead) and 'Military Madness'. Crosby also guests with Kantner on 'Have You Seen The Stars Tonite?' The show concludes with all the musicians joining in on Woody Guthrie's 'This Land Is Your Land'.

16 FEBRUARY

Crosby's 'Street To Lean On' is recorded at Ocean Way Studios, Hollywood. Michael Hedges joins the session on acoustic guitar.

17 FEBRUARY

Nash's 'Find A Dream' is recorded at Ocean Way Studios, Hollywood. CS&N each contribute acoustic guitar work as well as vocals.

28 FEBRUARY

Crosby despatches a sound cassette of a new

song he has written, 'Rusty And Blue'. The track eventually appears on his 1995 live album.

MARCH

The IRS demand $1 million in back taxes from Crosby, which results in the seizure of his house in San Fernando Valley, after which he and his wife Jan move into rented accommodation in Santa Barbara.

Meanwhile, Crosby's latest guest appearance is on Hootie And The Blowfish's *Cracked View Mirror* adding vocal harmony to 'Hold My Hand'.

MARCH

CS&N appear at Stephen's Theater, Ames, IA, previewing many of the songs that will later be included on their new album. It's interesting to see 'Marrakesh Express' elevated to a catchy opening number in place of the perennial favourite 'Wasted On The Way', which has now been dropped from the set.

SET LIST: MARRAKESH EXPRESS; HELPLESSLY HOPING; SEE THE CHANGES; IN MY DREAMS; IN MY LIFE; TAKEN AT ALL; DÉJÀ VU; MILITARY MADNESS; SO BEGINS THE TASK; LONG TIME GONE; CRITICAL MASS/WIND ON THE WATER; UNEQUAL LOVE; FIND A DREAM; RUSTY AND BLUE; CAMERA; IT WON'T GO AWAY; SOUTHERN CROSS; WOODEN SHIPS; SUITE: JUDY BLUE EYES; TEACH YOUR CHILDREN.

APRIL

Bonnie Raitt's *Longing In Their Hearts* is released with Crosby providing backing vocals to 'Circle Dance'. During this same period, he can also be heard on the title track to Stevie Nicks' *Street Angel*.

APRIL

'In My Life' is recorded at O'Henry Sound Studios, Burbank, CA. Stills had previously tackled this Beatles song on his last solo album, *Stills Alone*.

APRIL

Nash's 'After The Storm', the title track of CS&N's next album, is recorded at O'Henry Sound Studios, Burbank, CA.

APRIL

Crosby despatches a complete sound cassette recording of 'The Fisher King Song', a composition already familiar to those who have attended recent CS&N concerts. The song is generally regarded as one of Crosby's best in recent years. Amazingly, it will not only fail to appear on the forthcoming CS&N album, but will also be omitted from Crosby's next solo album. At the time of writing, it remains unissued.

APRIL

Stills' 'Bad Boyz' is recorded at O'Henry Sound Studio, Burbank, CA. The rhythm section comprises Alexis Sklarevski (bass), Rick Marotta (drums), and Ethan Johns (percussion).

21 APRIL

Stills' 'It Won't Go Away' is recorded at O'Henry Sound Studios, Burbank, CA. Stephen plays both bass and electric guitar on the song.

25 APRIL

Crosby's 'Camera' (with additional music by Stills) is recorded at O'Henry Sound Studios, Burbank, CA. Additional musicians include Alexis Sklarevski (bass), Tristan Imboden (drums) and Rafael Padilla (percussion).

26 APRIL

Stills' 'Panama' is recorded at O'Henry Sound Studios, Burbank, CA. The previous day's rhythm section is retained, along with Joe

Rotondi (keyboards) and Christopher Stills (Spanish guitar).

29 APRIL

Stills makes a surprise appearance at the New Orleans Jazz and Heritage Festival.

1 MAY

Young's 'Barefoot Floors' appears on Nicolette Larson's CD *Sleep, Baby Sleep*. He has yet to release his own version of the song.

16 MAY

Nash performs at Sonoma Valley High School, California, for a SNACK Benefit. His associates Craig Doerge and Russ Kunkel also appear as

well as Nicolette Larson, Paul Barrere and
Kenny Gradney.

2 JUNE

CS&N preview their 25th anniversary tour with
an impromptu club appearance before a
standing-room only audience at LA's House Of
Blues. Mixing familiar songs with selections
from their new album, they receive an
enthusiastic critical response with *The LA
Times* concluding, "This was a spirited,
nostalgia transcending return to relevance.
Welcome back, guys."

6 JUNE – 21 AUGUST

CS&N embark on a tour of North America,
including scheduled dates at TCC Music Hall,
Tucson, AZ (June 6); Desert Sky Pavilion,
Phoenix, AZ (7); Starplex Amphitheater, Dallas,
TX (11); Woodlands Pavilion, Houston, TX (12);
Saenger Theater, New Orleans, LA (13); Mud
Island, Memphis, TN (15); Starwood
Amphitheater, Nashville, TN (17); Chattanooga
Festival, TN (18); Sundome, Tampa, FL (20);
Knight Center, Miami, FL (21/22); Lakewood
Amphitheater, Atlanta, GA (24); Blockbuster
Pavilion, Charlotte, NC (26); Queen Elizabeth
Theater, Vancouver, BC (July 7); Labor Day
Amphitheater, Salem, OR (8); The Gorge,
George, WA (9); Park West, Salt Lake City, UT
(11); Red Rocks Amphitheater, Denver, CO
(12); Riverport Amphitheater, St Louis, MO
(14); Poplar Creek Music Center, Chicago, IL
(15); Brown Arena, Green Bay, WI (16); Des

Moines Civic Center, IO (18); Bradley Center,
Milwaukee, WI (19); Blossom Music Center,
Cleveland, OH (21); Pine Knob Music Center,
Clarkston, OH (28); Palace Theater, Louisville,
KY (29); Civic Arena, Pittsburgh, PA (31);
Wolf Trap, Vienna, VA (August 2/3); Montage
Mountain, Scranton, PA (5); Darian Lake
Amphitheater, Buffalo, NY (6); SC Arts Center,
Saratoga Springs, NY (7); Hershey Park,
Hershey, PA (9); Stowe Mountain Pac, VT (10);
Great Woods Music Center, Mansfield, MA
(15/16); Jones Beach Amphitheater, Wantagh,
NY (17); Garden State Arts Center, Holmdel,
NY (19); Mann Music Center, Philadelphia,
PA (20/21).

SAMPLE SET LIST (JUNE 11): LOVE THE ONE YOU'RE
WITH: MARRAKESH EXPRESS: HELPLESSLY HOPING:
DÉJÀ VU: IT WON'T GO AWAY: TILL IT SHINES ON
YOU: UNEQUAL LOVE: IN MY LIFE: LONG TIME GONE:
FIND A DREAM: CAMERA: BAD BOYZ: WOODEN
SHIPS: SOUTHERN CROSS: WOODSTOCK.

1 JULY

Stills' 'Only Waiting For You' is recorded at
O'Henry's Sound Studios, Burbank. Jody Cortez
(drums) and Lenny Castro (percussion) are the
latest session musicians to join the crew.

11 JULY

Crosby is suffering severe abdominal pains and
cancels CSN's show at Park West, Salt Lake
City. The following week he is driven to John
Hopkins Hospital in Baltimore where doctors
inform him that he has liver disease. Against
their advice he continues the CS&N tour.

AUGUST

Crosby's live album *It's All Coming Back To Me*,
originally scheduled for release this month is
placed on hold and will not be issued until
February 1995.

Meanwhile, Young's *Sleeps With Angels* is
released to critical acclaim. The work is
another milestone in a career already blessed
with probably more creative resurgences than
any other artiste of his generation.

12 AUGUST

CS&N promote their upcoming return to
Woodstock by appearing on *The Tonight Show*
with Jay Leno.

13-14 AUGUST

CS&N appear at Woodstock II, Saugerites, NY,
minus Young, who has been designing
Woodstock hats with a vulture on the guitar
neck as his own comment on the festival. As his
manager Elliot Roberts euphemistically points
out: "The whole affair is something that Neil
doesn't believe in."

Clearly, CS&N have no such ideological
quibbles and regard the festival as a positive
reaffirmation of all they once stood for. Nash
peels away the years by telling the audience:
"The last time we played this concert, the
country was divided by the Vietnam War.
Wars are still going on. How much longer?
Military Madness!"

One of the highlights of the set is a dramatic
'Déjà Vu' during which the trio are joined by

John Sebastian on harmonica, re-enacting his contribution to the studio version. We are reminded how Sebastian was once considered as the most likely fourth member long before the recruitment of Young. After 'Wooden Ships', Nash announces in jubilation: "This is your festival. This is yours". But it is also CS&N's festival, once and always, as they demonstrate by featuring a strong selection of new songs and asserting their determination to improve as a creative force.

For Crosby, the festival is eventful as his 53rd birthday is only hours away. Towards the end of the set he is presented with a birthday cake and kissed by his wife, Jan. The festivities continue with an encore of 'Woodstock', providing the most appropriate conclusion of all.

SET LIST: LOVE THE ONE YOU'RE WITH; MILITARY MADNESS; HELPLESSLY HOPING; DÉJÀ VU; ONLY WAITING FOR YOU; MARRAKESH EXPRESS; IT WON'T GO AWAY; UNEQUAL LOVE; BLACKBIRD; LONG TIME GONE; STREET TO LEAN ON; FOR WHAT IT'S WORTH; PRE-ROAD DOWNS; SOUTHERN CROSS; WOODEN SHIPS; CARRY ON; WOODSTOCK.

AUGUST

CS&N release *After The Storm* which wins them several very favourable reviews. Although the album sounds a little self-consciously slick in parts, it comes across as a welcome team effort from three strong songwriters. What they lack in radicalism is compensated for by the flashes of social commentary which, if presented in a more riveting musical context, auger well for future releases.

In the meantime, the Woodstock concert prompts Atlantic to celebrate the original event with the release of *Best Of Woodstock*; *Woodstock: 25th Anniversary Box Set* (including a previously unissued version of 'Find The Cost Of Freedom') and *Woodstock Diary* (which features CS&N's 'Blackbird').

LATE AUGUST

Crosby's condition curtails the current CS&N tour. Earlier in the month, he'd been experiencing cramps in his legs, a side-effect of the medication used to ameliorate his troubled liver. Now he is suffering "diminished mental capacity due to hepatic encephalopathy" as toxic substances in his blood enter his brain. Stills and Nash query his inability to provide his usual harmonies on key and he bursts into tears, admitting that the liver disease is even more advanced than they'd suspected.

SEPTEMBER

Crosby is examined by specialists at Cedars-Sinai Hospital and UCLA, after which he is told that he will die unless a successful liver transplant operation is completed in the near future. Meanwhile, Jan Crosby, now 43, confirms that she is pregnant, a cosmic irony that is not lost on her husband. "I was dying, and unless I got a liver transplant it would happen soon," he explained. "I'd faced death before. God knows, I could and probably should have died at least a dozen times from overdoses and motorcycle wrecks. I never thought I'd live long enough to give a damn. But I'd been clean for nine years, and I only had to look at Jan to know there was every reason to cherish life. After years of seeing specialists and fertility treatments, we'd found out she was pregnant. Anybody who doesn't think God has a sense of humour isn't watching."

Fortunately, the pregnancy proceeds without complications and the baby, Django Dance, is delivered safely on 10 May 1995.

14 SEPTEMBER

CS&N's 'Teach Your Children' is featured on *Red Hot & Country*, a compilation released to promote AIDS awareness. Despite the billing, this sounds suspiciously like a Nash solo recording.

18 SEPTEMBER

Farm Aid VII features Young and Crazy Horse.

1/2 OCTOBER

Young appears at the annual Bridge School Benefit staged at the Shoreline Amphitheater.

5 OCTOBER

CS&N appear at the closing of the Tou Can Du restaurant in New Orleans, LA, an establishment that Stills had opened the previous January.

20 OCTOBER

Young joins Bob Dylan and Bruce Springsteen on-stage at the Roseland Ballroom, New York, performing 'Rainy Day Women # s 12 & 35' and 'All Along The Watchtower'.

22 OCTOBER

Young appears at the Hamilton Warren Amphitheater on the campus of the Verde Valley School, Oak Creek, Arizona, in a benefit concert for the Native American Scholarship Fund.

25 OCTOBER

Ben Keith's *Seven Gates* features a guest appearance by Young on 'The Little Drummer Boy', 'Les Trois Cloches', 'Away In A Manger' and 'Greensleeves'.

OCTOBER

Young is nominated for the Rock 'n' Roll Hall Of Fame. He is subsequently inducted on 12 January 1995 and during the evening appears alongside Pearl Jam. They later record an album together, *Mirror Ball*, which is released in June 1995.

5 NOVEMBER

Crosby suffers liver failure and is rushed to UCLA Medical Center. An appeal is immediately launched for blood donors and it is anticipated that the singer will require 100 units for his operation.

20 NOVEMBER

Doctors confirm that a suitable liver has been found for Crosby, who has been in intense pain over recent weeks, with a stomach swollen by excessive fluids.

22 NOVEMBER

Bobby Charles' *Wish You Were Here* is released in Japan with Young playing guitar on 'I Want To Be The One', 'I Remember When', 'Ambushin' Bastard' and 'I Don't See Me'.

26 NOVEMBER

The liver prepared for transplant is discovered to be cancerous, but another is immediately found. The donor is revealed as a 31-year old car crash victim.

28 NOVEMBER

Crosby is taken to the operating theatre, singing 'Amazing Grace' as he is wheeled down the corridor. He undergoes a seven-hour liver transplant after which his condition is described as "critical but stable". Some of the more sensationalist tabloids headline with the alarming "CROSBY CRITICAL" but, as a doctor points out, "Who wouldn't be after such a serious operation?" The singer's condition continues to improve but slight complications ensure that he will not be allowed to return home immediately.

14 DECEMBER

Crosby is declared well enough to leave hospital and return home. Ironically, the former drug addict now has to consume a veritable bathroom cabinet of pills daily simply to survive. His condition effectively closes the book on CS&N in 1995.

"I'm basically taking the next year off to get healthy," Crosby confirms. "I plan to diet and exercise and to help Jan have our miracle baby... All in all, this has been an exalting experience. I've discovered a depth of compassion and feeling I didn't know existed. The mail I get still brings me to tears – strangers offering support, people waiting for transplants asking for advice, people fighting the same fight. Some of us will make it, some won't, but I've been given every reason to believe in starting over."

DAVID CROSBY, 1994

ALBUMS DISCOGRAPHY

The discography below covers official and archive albums recordings. Greatest hits compilations and soundtrack recordings featuring already issued material are excluded. The year of release is in parentheses.

CROSBY, STILLS & NASH

Crosby, Stills & Nash (1969)
CSN (1977)
Daylight Again (1982)
Allies (1983)
CSN [Boxed Set] (1991)
After The Storm (1994)

The boxed set includes material from the various CS&N/CSN&Y permutations. Otherwise unavailable CS&N material is also featured on *Woodstock, Woodstock II, Woodstock Diary, Replay* (Stills' re-recording of 'Carry On', minus Young), *No Nukes, Red Hot And Country* and *Nintendo: White Knuckle Scorin'*, plus the single B-side 'Chuck's Lament (A Child's Dream)' – the latter written by Crosby, Stills, Nash and Joe Vitale – and the single 'Chippin' Away'.

CROSBY, STILLS, NASH & YOUNG

Déjà Vu (1970)
4 Way Street (1971)
American Dream (1988)

Otherwise unavailable CSN&Y tracks are also featured on *Woodstock, Woodstock II, Woodstock: 25th Anniversary Boxed Set*, plus Young's *Journey Through The Past, Zuma* and *Decade* and the compilation *So Far* (featuring the single, 'Ohio'/'Find The Cost Of Freedom'). A live version of 'Pushed It Over The End' from the 1974 CSN&Y tour was released in Italy in 1982 on a 12-inch single, accompanying a boxed set. It has often been rumoured, but never confirmed, that CSN&Y all played on Joni Mitchell's 'The Circle Game', from *Ladies Of The Canyon*.

DAVID CROSBY

WITH THE LES BAXTER BALLADEERS:
Jack Linkletter Presents A Folk Festival (1963)

WITH THE BYRDS:
Mr Tambourine Man (1965)
Turn! Turn! Turn! (1965)
Fifth Dimension (1966)
Younger Than Yesterday (1967)
The Notorious Byrd Brothers (1968)
Byrds (1973)

Selections from the World Pacific recordings can be found on the archive albums *Early LA, Preflyte* and *In The Beginning*. The former features two songs from The Jet Set, plus two solo cuts from Crosby. Additional unreleased material from the CBS period can be found on *Never Before* and the box set *The Byrds*, plus The Beefeaters' single 'Please Let Me Love You'/'Don't Be Long'. The Byrds' *The Original Singles, Vols I & II* feature some alternate takes.

AS DAVID CROSBY:
If I Could Only Remember My Name (1971)
Oh Yes I Can (1989)
Thousand Roads (1993)

The B-side of the single 'Hero' features the otherwise unavailable, 'Fare Thee Well' (composed by The Indigo Girls' Emily Saliers). Crosby's live album *It's All Coming Back To Me Now...* was postponed until January 1995.

AS CROSBY & NASH:
Graham Nash/David Crosby (1972)
Wind On The Water (1975)
Whistling Down The Wire (1976)

Crosby & Nash Live (1977)
C&N are also featured on *The Bread And Roses Festival Of Music*.

Guest Appearances/Productions/Additional Songwriting Collaborations: See main text for details of Crosby's work with the following: Travis Edmonson (1962); Joni Mitchell (1968; 1969; 1974; 1975); Things To Come (1968); Jefferson Airplane (1968); Flying Burrito Brothers (1968); John Sebastian (1970); Paul Kantner/Jefferson Starship (1970); Bob Gibson (1971); Paul Kantner/Grace Slick (1971); Cyrus Faryar (1971); Hot Tuna (1972); Jackson Browne (1972; 1973; 1976; 1989; 1993); Everly Brothers (1972); Rick Roberts (1972); Gene Clark (1973); Kantner, Slick & Freiberg (1973); Dan Peterson (1973); Roger McGuinn (1973; 1991); Grace Slick (1974); Art Garfunkel (1975; 1977); James Taylor (1975; 1976); Phil Lesh & Ned Lagin (1975); Dave Mason (1975); Carole King (1976); John David Souther (1976); Elton John (1976); The Section (1977); Gary Wright (1979); Kenny Rankin (1988); Bonnie Raitt (1989; 1994); Phil Collins (1989; 1994); Bob Dylan (1990); Michael Hedges (1990); Marc Cohn (1992; 1993); Indigo Girls (1992); Jimmy Webb (1993); Willie Nelson (1993); Jack Tempchin And The Seclusion (1994); Stevie Nicks (1994); Hootie And The Blowfish (1994). Crosby also appears on Cate School's student production *Cuttin' Capers* (1957/58), released as a limited edition private pressing. He also participated in the spoken word record, *The Astrology Album* (1967). Crosby has obviously also guested on solo and related albums by Stills, Nash and Young.

STEPHEN STILLS

WITH THE AU GO-GO SINGERS:
They Call Us Au Go-Go Singers (1964)

WITH THE BUFFALO SPRINGFIELD:
Buffalo Springfield (1967)
Buffalo Springfield Again (1967)
Last Time Around (1968)

Early versions of the début album feature Stills' 'Baby Don't Scold Me'. The 1973 compilation *Buffalo Springfield* features an elongated, unissued version of 'Bluebird'; the single version of 'Uno Mundo' is an alternate take

AS MIKE BLOOMFIELD - AL KOOPER - STEVE STILLS
Supersession (1968)

AS STEPHEN STILLS:
Stephen Stills (1970)
Stephen Stills 2 (1971)
Stills (1975)
Stephen Stills Live (1975)
Illegal Stills (1976)
Thoroughfare Gap (1978)
Right By You (1984)
Stills Alone (1991)

Stills' otherwise unreleased 'Cuba al fin' can be heard on the Various Artists' *Havana Jam* (1979).

AS MANASSAS:
Manassas (1972)
Down The Road (1973)

AS THE STILLS/YOUNG BAND:
Long May You Run (1976)

Guest Appearances/Productions/Additional Songwriting Collaborations: See main text for details of Stills' work with the following: Fred Neil (1967)

Judy Collins (1968); Monkees (1968); Mama Cass (1968); Joan Baez (1969); Richie Havens (1969); Joni Mitchell (1969; 1971); Jefferson Airplane (1969); John Sebastian (1970); Ringo Starr (1970; 1971; 1994); Timothy Leary (1970); Eric Clapton (1970); Doris Troy (1970); Lois Griffiths (1970); Rita Coolidge (1971); Jimi Hendrix (1971); Bill Withers (1971); Delaney & Bonnie (1971); Humble Pie (1972); Loggins & Messina (1972); Merryweather (1972); Mickey Hart (1972); REO Speedwagon (1973); Elvin Bishop (1974; 1975); Veronique Sanson (1974); Dave Mason (1977; 1978); Bee Gees (1977); Chicago (1979); Hoyt Axton (1979); Joe Vitale (1980); Michael Schenker Group (1989); Firefall (1982); Texas World Reunion (1985); Flaco Jimenez (1992); Thomas Jefferson Kaye (1992). Stills has obviously also guested on solo and related albums by Crosby, Nash and Young.

RAHAM NASH

ITH THE HOLLIES:

Stay With The Hollies (1964)
In The Hollies Style (1964)
The Hollies (1965)
Would You Believe (1966)
For Certain Because (1966)
Evolution (1967)
Butterfly (1967)
What Goes Round... (1983)

Some rare Nash compositions can also be found on The Hollies' archive albums, *The 30th Anniversary Collection* and *Rarities*, while *The Other Side Of The Hollies* features various B-sides.

GRAHAM NASH:

Songs For Beginners (1971)
Wild Tales (1974)
Earth And Sky (1980)
Innocent Eyes (1986)

Nash's otherwise unavailable 'Love For A Reason' is featured on the soundtrack album, *Fast Times At Ridgmont High*. His co-written 'Wings To Fly' can be found on the soundtrack album *American Anthem*.

CROSBY & NASH:

Graham Nash/David Crosby (1972)
Wind On The Water (1975)
Whistling Down The Wire (1976)
Crosby & Nash Live (1977)
C&N are also featured on *The Bread And Roses Festival Of Music*.

Guest Appearances/Productions/Additional Songwriting Collaborations: See main text for details of Nash's work with the following: Rolling Stones (1964); Mirage (1966); Everly Brothers (1966; 1972); Beatles (1967); John Walker (1967); Lee Kings (1968); Piccadilly Line (1968); Mama Cass (1968); McGough & McGear (1968); Scaffold (1968); The Fool (1969); Donovan (1969; 1983) John Sebastian (1970); Paul Kantner/Jefferson Starship (1970); Rita Coolidge (1971); Paul Kantner/Grace Slick (1971); Charles John Quarto (1971); Grin (1972); Seemon & Marijke (1972); Judee Sill (1972); Jackson Browne (1972; 1976); Dave Mason (1972; 1973; 1975; 1978); Joni Mitchell (1972; 1974; 1975); David Blue (1973); Dave Mason (1973); Ned Doheny (1973); Michael D'Abo (1974); Dan Fogelberg (1974); James Taylor (1975; 1976; 1979; 1985); Art Garfunkel (1975); Carole King (1976); Terry Reid (1976); Waylon Jennings (1976); Elton John (1976); Lonnie Mack (1977); Steve Gillette (1979); Gary Wright (1979); Joel Bernstein (1979); Leah Kunkel (1980); Joe Vitale (1981); Warren Zevon (1982); Dwight Twilley (1982); Jimmy Webb (1982); Marc Jordan (1988); Bonnie Raitt (1989); Terrell (1990); Modern Folk Quartet (1991); Marc Cohn (1992; 1993). Nash has obviously also guested on several of his partners' albums, and receives a co-billing credit on Young's 1972 single, 'War Song'.

NEIL YOUNG

WITH THE BUFFALO SPRINGFIELD:

Buffalo Springfield (1967)
Buffalo Springfield Again (1967)
Last Time Around (1968)

The single version of Buffalo Springfield's 'Mr Soul' is an alternate take.

AS NEIL YOUNG/NEIL YOUNG WITH CRAZY HORSE:

Neil Young (1968)
Everybody Knows This Is Nowhere (1969)
After The Goldrush (1970)
Harvest (1972)
Journey Through The Past (1972)
Time Fades Away (1973)
On The Beach (1974)
Tonight's The Night (1975)
Zuma (1975)
American Stars 'N Bars (1977)
Comes A Time (1978)
Rust Never Sleeps (1979)
Live Rust (1979)
Hawks & Doves (1980)
Re-ac-tor (1981)
Trans (1983)
Everybody's Rockin' (1983)
Old Ways (1985)
Landing On Water (1986)
Life (1987)
This Note's For You (1988)
Freedom (1989)
Ragged Glory (1990)
Arc/Weld (1991)
Harvest Moon (1992)
Unplugged (1993)
Sleeps With Angels (1994)

The compilations *Decade* and *Lucky Thirteen* feature unissued material, as does the film soundtrack *Where The Buffalo Roam* and the Japanese mini-album *Eldorado*. The otherwise unavailable single 'War Song' is credited to Neil Young & Graham Nash; a fascinating alternate take of 'Everybody Knows This Is Nowhere' is available on promotional single; the B-side single 'Birds' is an alternate take; a live version of 'Sugar Mountain' is featured on various Young B-sides; an extended version of 'Oh Lonesome Me' is issued on single; a live version of 'Last Trip To Tulsa' is on the B-side of 'Time Fades Away'; an elongated 'Campaigner' is on a test pressing of *Decade* an extended disco-style 'Sample And Hold'/'Mr Soul' is on a 12-inch single; an alternate take of 'When You Dance I Can Really Love' is on CD; the otherwise unavailable 'I'm Goin'' (B-side of 'Ten Men Workin'') and 'Don't Spook The Horse' (B-side of 'Mansion On The Hill') are on single; 'Philadelphia' is included on single and featured in the film soundtrack of the same name. A handful of other songs have been remixed or edited but these do not appear to be alternate takes or different versions. In 1995, Young collaborated with Pearl Jam on *Mirror Ball*.

AS THE STILLS/YOUNG BAND:

Long May You Run (1976)

Guest Appearances/Productions/ Additional Songwriting Collaborations: See main text for details of Young's work with the following: Squires (1963); Mynah Birds (1966); Cascades (1967); Love (1967); Monkees (1968; 1969); Buffy Saint-Marie (1971); Grin (1972); Joni Mitchell (1976); Crazy Horse (1978); Emmylou Harris (1980; 1990); Northern Lights (1985); Willie Nelson (1985); Warren Zevon (1987; 1989); Stealin' Horses (1988); Tracy Chapman (1989); Emmylou Harris (1990); Robbie Robertson (1991); Bachman (1992); Rusty Kershaw (1992); Nils Lofgren (1992); Joseph Matthew Giegerich/Joseph Hand (1993); Rob Wasserman (1994); Ben Keith (1994); Bobby Charles (1994). Young has also guested on solo recordings by Nash and Crosby.

UNRELEASED COMPOSITIONS

Crosby, Stills, Nash and Young have each written or co-written a substantial number of songs that they have never released.
A very small number of the songs below were written for, or recorded and released by, other artists, but the vast majority of these compositions
remain unissued in any form. The year in parentheses indicates the approximate or rough date of creation, based on either copyright
registration details, interview comments or public performance, whichever is the earlier.

DAVID CROSBY

Cross The Plains (1962)
Brotherhood Of The Blues (1963)
Jack Of Diamonds (trad. with add. lyrics by
    Crosby) (1963)
Flower Bomb Song (1965)
Stranger In A Strange Land (1965)
Draft Morning (solo version with alternate
    lyrics) (1967)
Is It Really Monday? (1968)
You Sit There (1968)
Naiomi (co-written with Terrance O. Callier)
    (1969)
Kids And Dogs (1970)
Gothic Blues (1970)
Coast Road (1970)
Dirt Poor (co-written with Dan Peterson)
    (1973)
Your Life Is What You Fill Your Day With (1973)
King Of The Mountain (originally titled:
    Winning) (1974)
Little Blind Fish (co-written with Stills, Nash &
    Young) (1974)
Last 100 Yards Of Freedom (co-written with
    Nash) (1976)
Paper Glider (1976/79)
Stand And Be Counted (1976/79)
Jigsaw (co-written with Nash) (1978)
Samurai (1979)
Alexander Graham Bell (1986)
You're Worth Waiting For (1986)
He's An American (1987)
I'm Flying (co-written with Michael Hedges)
    (1988)
Somehow She Knew (aka The Fisher King
    Song) (1993)

Crosby also recorded a number of songs with
Jerry Garcia/Paul Kantner in 1971 which may
deserve classification as co-writing
collaborations: Leather Bat, Electric Bat, Dope
Rap, Walking In The Mountains, Under
Anaesthesia, Over Jordan and Planet
Earth/Rock 'n' Roll Orchestra.

STEPHEN STILLS

Don't You Feel Rained On? (1965)
Hello I've Returned (co-written with Van Dyke
    Parks) (1965)
Neighbour Don't You Worry (1966)
We'll See (1966)
Raga No. 1 (co-written with Young, Furay,
    Martin and Kunkel) (1967)
Raga No. 2 (co-written with Young, Furay,
    Martin and Kunkel) (1967)
So You Got A Lover (1967)
Come On (Here) (1967)

Kahuna Sunset (co-written with Neil Young)
    (1967)
All I Know Is What You Tell Me (1969)
Right On Rock And Roll (1969)
Dreaming Of Snakes (1969)
The Need Of The Giving (1969)
Visiting Hours (1969)
Rocky Mountain Rhyming (1969)
White Nigger (1970)
Just For This One Moment (co-written with
    Lois Griffiths) (1970)
Gonna Get My Baby Back (co-written with
    Doris Troy, George Harrison and Richard
    Starkey) (1970)
You Give Me Joy Joy (co-written with Doris
    Troy, George Harrison and Richard
    Starkey) (1970)
Witching Hour (1972)
Music Song (1972)
High And Dry (1972)
City Boy (co-written with Merryweather)
    (1972)
Pretty Roses (1972)
Willy's Tune (1973)
Open Up (1973)
Black Sheep (1973)
Little Miss Bright Eyes (1973)
Little Blind Fish (co-written with Crosby, Nash
    & Young) (1974)
Open Up America (1974)
Start Over Again (1974)
Walk Before You Run (co-written with Barry
    Gibb) (1976)
One Way Ride (One Way Ticket) (1976)
Precious Love (1978)
That's The Way It Was (1978)
One Moment At A Time (aka Love Becomes A
    Trial) (1978)
Streetwise (1978)
Dangerous Woman On The Loose (co-written
    with George Perry) (1978)
Country (1979)
I Am With You Girl (1979)
Shuffle (1979)
Ain't It Always? (1979)
Susie Jane (1979)
Bitter Pill (co-written with Joe Vitale) (1979)
Emperor Of Disco Dreams (1979)
Feed The People (1979)
You've Got A Nice Way (co-written with
    Michael Stergis) (1980)
Lady On The Rock (co-written with Joe Vitale
    and Bill Szymczyk) (1981)
Feel Your Love (1982)
Bit About Love (1986)
Heart Of The Hearth (co-written with Ian
    Wallace) (1987)

Hard Ball (1989)
Hungry (1990)
As Much As I Understand (1991)
School Days (co-written with Joe Vitale) (1990)
Livin' On Rock 'n' Roll (co-written with Dallas
    Taylor and Thomas Jefferson Kaye) (1992)

During the Buffalo Springfield period, the
Atlantic archives listed four songs, No Sun
Today, Who's The Next Fool?, Can't Keep Me
Down and Ash On The Floor which do not
feature in Stills or Young's copyright listings.
The Stills/Young Band sessions also produced
a number of songs listed in the Atlantic
archives (some no doubt mistitled) that are not
copyrighted to either Stills or Young. They
include: Western Witches, Talk Too Much, 10
90, Let Me Down, Can't Handle This, Sleep,
Secrets and After Hours.

GRAHAM NASH

Party Line (co-written with Clarke/Hicks)
    (1964)
It's Raining Teardrops (co-written with
    Clarke/Hicks) (1964)
She Said Yeah (co-written with
    Clarke/Hicks)(1964)
Cry Now (co-written with Clarke/Hicks) (1964)
You Must Believe Me (co-written with
    Clarke/Hicks) (1964)
Listen Here To Me (co-written with
    Clarke/Hicks) (1965)
Bring Back Your Love To Me (co-written with
    Clarke/Hicks) (1965)
You In My Arms (co-written with Clarke/Hicks)
    (1965)
Schoolgirl (co-written with Clarke/Hicks)
    (1967)
Ashes To Ashes (co-written with Clarke/Hicks)
    (1967)
Go Away (co-written with Clarke/Hicks) (1967)
Without You (co-written with Clarke/Hicks)
    (1967)
Survival Of The Fittest (co-written with
    Clarke/Hicks) (1968)
Man Of No Expression (co-written with
    Clarke/Hicks) (1968)
Cologne (Why Baby Why) (1969)
Be Patient (1970)
Can Any Man (1970)
Song For My Father (1970)
Isle Of Dew (1970)
Who Can Teach A Songbird How To Fly? (co-
    written with Scott English) (1970)
Agree With Me (co-written with Kirk Duncan
    and Nicky James) (1971)
I'll Follow You (co-written with Kirk Duncan

and Nicky James) (1971)

If You'd Only Come Back (co-written with Kirk
Duncan and Nicky James) (1971)

Jake The Fake (co-written with Kirk Duncan
and Nicky James) (1971)

Miss You (co-written with Kirk Duncan and
Nicky James) (1971)

Yellow Ribbon (co-written with Kirk Duncan
and Nicky James) (1971)

Little Blind Fish (co-written with Crosby, Stills
& Young) (1974)

Last 100 Yards Of Freedom (co-written with
Crosby) (1976)

I Watched It All Come Down (1976)

Taxi Ride (1976)

Mirage (1978)

Jigsaw (co-written with Crosby) (1978)

Turn It Around (It's A Toyota) (1984)

Before The Moon Is Full (1985)

Lonely Man (1985)

Water From The Moon (1985)

Vote (1988)

On The Other Side Of Town (1989)

Jasper's Tune (co-written with Frank Zappa)
(1989)

Better World (co-written with Craig Doerge)
(1989)

Song For Barbara (1990)

The Shell (1991)

Flying Fast (co-written with Joe Vitale) (1991)

Try To Find Me (1991)

Sailor (1991)

Liar's Nightmare (1993)

Penguin In The Palm Tree (1994)

I Can See The Dream (1994)

Love Lies Tonight (Somewhere, Somehow)
(1994)

Magic (1994)

Game Of Hearts (1994)

Seas Like These (1994)

The Chelsea Hotel (1994)

The Moment I Saw You (1994)

Half Their Angels (1995)

During rehearsals at Moscow Road in late
1969, CS&N played a song titled Black Wing,
the composer of which remains uncertain.

EIL YOUNG

Image In Blue (1962)

I Wonder (1964)

White Flower (1964)

Hello Lonely Woman (1964/87)

Find Another Shoulder (1964)

I'll Love You Forever (1964)

Together Alone (1964)

I'm A Man And I Can't Cry (1964)

A Thing Called Snow (1965)

Casting Me Away From You (1965)

Girl In The Mirror (1965)

Extra Extra (aka When It Falls, It Falls All Over
You) (1965)

Runaround Babe (1965)

Don't Pity Me Babe (1965)

The Rent Is Always Due (1965)

I Ain't Got The Blues (1965)

Baby Go (co-written with Craig Allen) (1965)

Our Time (1965)

I'll Wait Forever (co-written with Ricky James
Matthews) (1966)

It's My Time (co-written with Ricky James
Matthews) (1966)

High School Graduation (1966)

One More Sign (1966)

There Goes My Babe (1966)

Slowly Burning (1967)

Whatever Happened To Saturday Night (1967)

Sell Out (1967)

Raga No. 1 (co-written with Stills, Furay,
Martin & Kunkel) (1967)

Raga No. 2 (co-written with Stills, Furay,
Martin & Kunkel) (1967)

Kahuna Sunset (co-written with Stephen Stills)
(1967)

Falcon Lake (1968)

Everybody's Alone (1969)

It Might Have Been (adaptation, co-written by
John Greenleaf Whittier) (1970)

Big Waves (1970)

I Need Your Love To Get By (1970)

Bad Fog Of Loneliness (aka
Singlemindedness) (1970)

Dance, Dance, Dance (1970)

In The Wild (aka In The Wind) (1971)

Gator Rag (1971)

Gator Rag 2 (1971)

Gator Stomp (1971)

Come Along And Say You Will (aka Lonely
Weekend) (1973)

Sweet Joni (1973)

Vacancy (1974)

Little Blind Fish (co-written with Crosby, Stills
& Nash) (1974)

Traces (1974)

Goodbye Dick (1974)

Hawaiian Sunrise (1974)

Love Art Blues (1974)

Four Walls (1974)

Separate Ways (1974)

Try (1974)

Homefires (1974)

Frozen Man (1974)

Mexico (1974)

Florida (1974)

Kansas (1974)

Barefoot Floors (1974)

Daughters (1974)

Mediterranean (1974)

Hitchhiker (1975/92)

We Don't Smoke It No More (1974)

The Tie Plate Yodel No. 3 (1975)

No One Seems To Know (1976)

Sad Movies (1976)

Give Me Strength (1976)

Evening Coconut (1976)

Changing Highways (1976)

Lady Wingshot (1976)

Windward Passage (1977)

Please Help Me I'm Falling (1977)

We're Having Some Fun (1977)

Bright Sunny Day (1978)

Turbine (Winter Winds) (1980)

To Me, To Me (1980)

Get Up Now (1981)

Bad News Has Come To Town (1981)

Island In The Sun (1982)

Raining In Paradise (1982)

If You Got Love (1982)

Hold On To Your Love (1982)

Big Pearl (1982)

Love Hotel (1982)

Silver & Gold (1982)

Soul Of A Woman (1983)

Johnny (1983)

Rock, Rock, Rock (1984)

So Tired (1984)

Your Love (1984)

Overnight (1984)

Higher Than Anyone Can Count (1984)

Up Jump Love (1984)

Mystery Man (1984)

Hillbilly Band (1984)

Someone Who Cares For Me (1984)

Don't Make Me Wait (1984)

Let Your Fingers Do The Walking (1985)

Amber Jean (1985)

Your Love Again (1985)

Leaving The Top 40 Behind (1985)

Beautiful Bluebird (1985)

Nothing Is Perfect (1985)

Time Off For Good Behaviour (1985)

Grey Riders (1985)

Interstate (1985)

Born To Run (1986)

Born To Rock (1986)

For The Love Of Man (1987)

Big Room (1987)

Razor Love (1987)

Farmer's Song (aka Last Of A Dying Breed)
(1987)

Hello Lonely Woman (1987)

High Heels (1987)

Just One Thing (1987)

One Thing (1988)

Crime Of The Heart (1988)

Walking After Midnight (1988)

Ordinary People (1988)

Doghouse (1988)

Fool For Your Love (1988)

Boxcar (1988)

Live To Ride (1993)

During the 1969-70 CSNY sessions, a number
of songs appeared in the Atlantic archive
listings that are not copyright registered to any
individual member. Most of these are
probably erroneously titled. The list includes:
30 Dollar Fine, Master My Fear, She Can't
Handle It, Whole People, Boat Song, Far On,
Everyday We Live, You Can Dance Real Good,
Beginning, You're Wrong Baby and Everybody
We Love You.